'*Learning from Other Religions* reveals the analytical strengths of a leading scholar who has reflected over decades on the nature of religion. It shows the characteristics of a serious thinker whose engagement with religiosity and belief has changed with the times. Here the transformations of the modern world are recognised in a changed context where practitioners of other faiths are often one's immediate neighbours. The book marks a new level of inter-religious understanding and is motivated by a positive sense of hospitality towards the religious other in its many different forms. It is rare to find such a detailed, broad-based account of the principal religions. It is also encouraging to find a genuine openness towards these other religions and a preparedness to take them seriously on their own terms.'

Oliver Davies, Emeritus Professor of Christian Doctrine, King's College London

'While this masterful survey evidences an extraordinarily wide knowledge of the world's religious traditions, Brown's imaginative readings – marked by both rigour and generosity – move us ineluctably beyond mere pluralism towards a richly textured, complex and reverential re-envisioning of the very meaning of revelation. Anybody engaged in interfaith encounter will find their insight deepened and their sympathy enlarged through his always careful, yet often surprising, reflections.'

Michael Ipgrave OBE, Bishop of Lichfield

'*Learning from Other Religions* brings new impetus to the debate about relations between other religions and one's own. Written by a leading Christian theologian, it contests the conventional classifications of exclusivism, inclusivism and pluralism and raises the challenging prospect that God's activities can be seen in all religions. It urges followers of each religion to appreciate the insights achieved in others and to discover the massive wealth and variety within them. The book takes this well-worn discussion in an appealing, if demanding, new direction.'

David Thomas, FBA, Emeritus Professor of Christianity and Islam, University of Birmingham

'This good and interesting book has a definite and clear aim – to improve understanding of religions by greater knowledge of their origins, histories and inner diversity. It has great merit, focussed on a well-argued advocacy of a particular view of revelation and religious understanding.'

Keith Ward FBA, Regius Professor of Divinity Emeritus, University of Oxford

LEARNING FROM OTHER RELIGIONS

One common argument against taking the notion of divine revelation seriously is the extraordinary diversity which exists between the world's major religions. How can God be thought to have spoken to humanity when the conclusions drawn are so very different? David Brown authoritatively and persuasively tackles this issue head-on. He refutes the idea that all faiths necessarily culminate in Christianity, or that they can be reduced to some facile lowest common denominator, arguing instead that ideas may emerge more naturally in one context than another. Sometimes, because of its own singular situation, another religion has proved to be more perceptive on a particular issue than Christianity. At other times, no religion will hold the ultimate answer because what can be asserted is heavily dependent on what is viable both scientifically and philosophically. Although complete reconciliation is impossible, a richer notion of revelation – so the author suggests – can be the result.

DAVID BROWN, FBA, is Emeritus Wardlaw Professor of Theology, Aesthetics and Culture at the University of St Andrews. He was previously Fellow and Chaplain at Oriel College, Oxford, and Van Mildert Professor of Divinity at Durham University. An Anglo-Catholic of wide and sympathetic interests, he has also served as President of the Society for the Study of Theology (SST) and Deputy Chair of the Church of England's Doctrine Commission. His many substantial publications on theology, aspects of biblical revelation, and art and culture have garnered much critical acclaim.

LEARNING FROM OTHER RELIGIONS

DAVID BROWN
University of St Andrews

Shaftesbury Road, Cambridge CB2 8EA, United Kingdom

One Liberty Plaza, 20th Floor, New York, NY 10006, USA

477 Williamstown Road, Port Melbourne, VIC 3207, Australia

314–321, 3rd Floor, Plot 3, Splendor Forum, Jasola District Centre, New Delhi – 110025, India

103 Penang Road, #05-06/07, Visioncrest Commercial, Singapore 238467

Cambridge University Press is part of Cambridge University Press & Assessment, a department of the University of Cambridge.

We share the University's mission to contribute to society through the pursuit of education, learning and research at the highest international levels of excellence.

www.cambridge.org
Information on this title: www.cambridge.org/9781009367707

DOI: 10.1017/9781009367677

© David Brown 2024

This publication is in copyright. Subject to statutory exception and to the provisions of relevant collective licensing agreements, no reproduction of any part may take place without the written permission of Cambridge University Press & Assessment.

First published 2024

Printed in the United Kingdom by TJ Books Limited, Padstow, Cornwall, 2024

A catalogue record for this publication is available from the British Library

A Cataloging-in-Publication data record for this book is available from the Library of Congress

ISBN 978-1-009-36770-7 Hardback

Cambridge University Press & Assessment has no responsibility for the persistence or accuracy of URLs for external or third-party internet websites referred to in this publication and does not guarantee that any content on such websites is, or will remain, accurate or appropriate.

*To **Ann Loades** (1938–2022)*

*Whose support, enthusiasm and critique proved invaluable.
A model for how religious dialogue might be conducted.
A formidable, ebullient character: 'larger than life'.
As ready to learn from others as to impart understanding.
Passionate in innovation and in righting wrongs.*

CONTENTS

Preface	*page xi*
Acknowledgements	*xiii*
Note on the Text	*xiv*
1 Complementary Shards	1
2 Ancient Paganism and the Biblical God	30
3 Different Eyes: Hinduism	78
4 The Religions of India	115
5 The Religions of China	168
6 The Religions of Japan	212
7 Islam: Warning or Hope	260
8 Revelation's Enrichment	310
9 Beyond Inclusivism and Pluralism	355
Suggestions for Further Reading	*369*
Index	*385*

PREFACE

Unlike much work written in the field of comparative religion, this book adopts an explicitly Christian perspective. This is done not out of any feeling of superiority but because such an approach can, I believe, secure a more penetrating analysis of what my fellow Christians might learn from other faiths. Instead of a strained effort to stand above or outside (which was likely in any case to prove too demanding in so short a work), I have sought to achieve two main aims. The first, essentially factual, is a brief but effective characterisation of each of the world's major religions in both their historical and contemporary context (with their salient differences from Christianity also highlighted). Secondly, there is a theological purpose, an attempt to answer the difficult question of what might have been happening across those religions, if the existence of the Christian God were to be assumed. In other words, is it possible to make sense not just of the human aspirations and searchings involved but also of a divine reality in turn reaching out to humanity in revelation – a revelation nonetheless constrained by the specifics of cultural conditioning? One novel feature in what follows is in consequence the suggestion of various insights in those alternative traditions where that revelation has penetrated more deeply than seems to be the case within Christianity.

After indicating some reasons for the topic's contemporary importance, Chapter 1 fleshes out this particular

Preface

understanding of revelation as resulting in what I call 'complementary shards', overlapping but imperfect constructions, rather like beautiful but broken pots. Chapter 2 then challenges any notion of Christianity's own self-containment. Instead, its forms and ideas as developed in both the Jewish and classical worlds can be seen to have been heavily indebted to surrounding pagan religions. Then, while Chapters 3 and 7 are devoted to a single religion each, to what are perhaps the oldest and newest world religions (Hinduism and Islam), Chapters 4, 5 and 6 turn instead to examine the several interacting religions that are to be found in India (Jainism, Theravada Buddhism and Sikhism), China (Daoism, Confucianism and Mahayana Buddhism) and Japan (Shinto, Zen and Pure Land Buddhism), respectively. Chapter 8 then contends that, far from all this leading to the diminishment of revelation, such an approach can actually provide an enrichment of its understanding. Finally, Chapter 9 briefly concludes with an examination of how my own work relates to earlier existing dichotomies within the field.

ACKNOWLEDGEMENTS

Although such a book as this was a long-standing intention on my part, only the COVID crisis provided the necessary restrictions on other activities to make the endeavour possible. In this I was helped throughout by my friend, Gregor Duncan, former Anglican Bishop of Glasgow, who read each successive draft with care and provided helpful and perceptive comments. I was fortunate to have Alex Wright, Head of Humanities and Senior Executive Publisher at Cambridge University Press, as the person to whom I became ultimately responsible, for he proved consistently encouraging and helpful, as did the two anonymous academic reviewers of the manuscript. It is at the suggestion of one of them that I have added the final chapter.

Last but not least, mention needs to be made of the various friends and acquaintances from other faiths I have had over the years. Not only has there been much to learn from so many of them but usually also a quality of life that had drawn me to them in the first place, and which I wished in some sense to share.

NOTE ON THE TEXT

There is no concluding bibliography. Instead, full bibliographical details are provided in the footnotes at the first occurrence in each chapter of any particular reference. The NRSV (New Revised Standard Version, 1989) is used for biblical quotations.

I
Complementary Shards

In this discussion of what should be seen as an appropriate Christian approach to other religions, my plan is to adopt a rather different strategy, either from patterns that used to prevail in the more distant past or from what tends to be most common today. I shall begin by identifying three features of the contemporary situation which have motivated me in this direction. Thereafter, the resultant strategy will be sketched in a way which makes plain why the following chapters take the structure that they do. Although I make generous use of modern studies in comparative religion and Christian theology, where I differ from most practitioners of the former is by insisting on going beyond objectivity into sympathetic identification with the religion concerned; from the latter, I go beyond generalities into recognition of specific areas where I believe God may have spoken through that religion. Accordingly, in each case one or more topic of this kind is identified, though without any suggestion that this is all that might be discovered. The second half of this chapter will address my chosen image of complementary shards to define the relationship but first we need to note some reasons for a change of approach.

Reasons for a Change in Approach

Below I briefly discuss three of the reasons which have led me to rethink how one might best interpret the extraordinary variety of perspectives in the world's major faiths.

From Distant to Near Neighbour

The first, and perhaps most obvious reason, is the way in which the other has ceased to be remote from ourselves in some distant land but, quite frequently, is our own near neighbour. Post–war immigration resulted in significant religious minorities in most European nations, while Australia and the United States have opened up their borders as never before.[1] In France there are large numbers of Muslims whose roots lie in the country's former colonies in North Africa. In Germany a labour shortage after the Second World War resulted in the large-scale immigration of *Gastarbeiter* (foreign or migrant workers) from Turkey and more recently the admission in a single year of over a million refugees fleeing the Syrian crisis.[2] Meanwhile in Britain, the country's close relationship with its former imperial territories in the Indian subcontinent resulted in a situation in which, to evoke a familiar contrast, there are now more practising Muslims in the United Kingdom than there are Methodists.[3] While in respect of such movements Islam is generally the most numerous, figures for other religions are by no means insignificant. In the United States, for

---

[1] Australia's white-only immigration policy was gradually dismantled between 1949 and 1973.
[2] In 2015. *Gastarbeiter* or 'guest workers' was a term and policy adopted between 1955 and 1973. Since then some have returned home but most became either permanent residents or citizens.
[3] According to the 2011 census there were 2.8 million Muslims living in Britain, with roughly one and a half million adherents of Hinduism, Sikhism or Buddhism. In the 2021 census the number of Muslims had increased to 3.9 million (6.5 per cent of the population). The number of Muslims living in the European Union (according to 2007 figures) was 16 million.

instance, Buddhism and Hinduism can each claim about a million adherents, with Islam currently at 3.45 million. Architecturally significant places of worship have been slower to appear but there are now prominent buildings in quite a number of European and American cities.[4]

Such immigration is of course by no means entirely new. One need only recall Christendom's long shameful relationship with Jews living in its midst.[5] There has also been a long history of sporadic attempts at interfaith dialogue,[6] sometimes complemented even today at the practical level in the use of each other's shrines.[7] However, two features in the modern world are different.

---

[4] Two prominent examples in London are the Central London Mosque on the edge of Regent's Park and the Hindu temple, Shri Swaminarayan Mandir, in Neasden. For a rather unusual example, note the creation of a Kagyu monastery of Tibetan Buddhism on Holy Isle in the Firth of Clyde, gifted by a devout Catholic, Kay Morris. She was responding to a vison of the Virgin Mary instructing her to do so.

[5] Dislike of difference was intensified by the effect of usury laws which allowed Jews to lend but not Christians. There were also various legends of the Jewish ritual murder of Christian children, the most famous being William of Norwich in 1144. All Jews were expelled from England in 1290 and not readmitted until under Cromwell in 1655. England was not alone in this. In Germany the People's Crusade of 1096 resulted in the mass murder of Jews in Mainz, Speyer and Worms, a pattern that was to repeat itself over subsequent centuries.

[6] On Islam, see David Thomas, *Christian-Muslim Relations: A Bibliographical History* (Leiden: Brill, 5 vols., 2009–13), and his selected extracts, David Thomas ed., *The Bloomsbury Reader in Christian-Muslim Relations, 600–1500* (London: Bloomsbury, 2022). For a book that concentrates mainly on modern developments, T. A. Howard, *The Faith of Others: A History of Interreligious Dialogue* (New Haven, CT: Yale University Press, 2021).

[7] Peter Gottschalk, *Beyond Hindu & Muslim: Multiple Identity in Narratives from Village India* (Oxford: Oxford University Press, 2000); Angie Heo, *The Political Lives of Saints: Christian-Muslim Mediation in Egypt* (Berkeley: University of California Press, 2018).

The first is that, while some minority ghettoes still exist, on the whole there is much more integration. Schools are mixed and some attempt is made to provide understanding of the faiths which others practise. So the issue is more 'alive' than it would have been in the past where various forms of separate development were practised.[8] Although a movement like Black Lives Matter indicates that integration still has a long way to go, it is nevertheless the case that those of other faiths have now become prominent in public life and other major positions of influence, as with Rishi Sunak, Chancellor of the Exchequer from 2020 and then Prime Minster from 2022 (a practising Hindu), or Sadiq Khan, Mayor of London since 2016 (a Muslim).[9] Secondly, it is a world in which 'Christian' countries are no longer self-evidently culturally and economically superior. Oil has helped to advance various Arab nations, while China and Japan have already overtaken Britain in wealth, with India projected to do likewise in due course.[10] So even at the pragmatic level there is good

---

[8] Although the Ottoman Empire was considerably more tolerant of Jews than Christian Europe, even major centres of population had little interaction. Prior to the First World War, Baghdad had 80,000 Jews out of a total population of 200,000. Salonika was even a predominantly Jewish city.

[9] There are also some examples in continental Europe, among them Ahmed Aboutaleb, who became Mayor of Rotterdam in 2009, Cem Özdemir, a prominent member of the Green Party in Germany and now Minister of Food and Agriculture, and Rachida Dati, who served as the French Justice Minister from 2007 to 2009. In Ireland, the Hindu Leo Varadkar was Taoiseach (Prime Minister) from 2017–20, while in the Netherlands Kauthar Bouchallikht was the first Dutch MP to wear a hijab. In 2021, in the United States House of Representatives there were three Muslims, two Hindus and one Buddhist, all Democrats.

[10] Current estimates suggest that China will have become the world's most powerful economy by 2028.

reason for advocating a deeper understanding of the alternative cultures with which Christians must now engage.

Even where separation through distance continues, a different pattern now exists from what once did in the past. Tourism ensures that, even if there is no immediate interaction with other faiths in one's home environment, these are to be seen in organised visits, for example, to prominent mosques or temples in other lands. It is also the case that the literature of some of these nations has become part of a general cosmopolitan culture. This is especially true of writers from the Indian subcontinent and from the island of Japan.[11] Contemporary popular and classical music exhibits a similar range of influences. As examples of the former, think of Leonard Cohen's debt to Buddhism, George Harrison to Hinduism or Cat Stevens to Islam,[12] or again in classical music the fundamental change of view found in the later John Taverner's approach to, and use of, other religions.[13]

Accordingly, just like the mixed character of modern communities, so a shrinking world also argues for greater respect between the religions and a more sustained attempt to understand each other. Such greater awareness

---

[11] Among contemporary Japanese writers, apart from Kazuo Ishiguro, who became a British citizen as a child and who won the Nobel Prize for Literature in 2017, one might mention novelists I happen to have read in translation in recent years: Takashi Hiraide, Toshikazu Kawaguchi, Yasunari Kawabata, Hiromi Kawakami, Haruki Murakami, Sayaka Murata, Yōko Ogawa and Yōko Tawada.

[12] George Harrison practised Hinduism from 1966 until his death in 2001; in 1977 Cat Stevens converted to Islam, thereafter, giving up his singing career; Leonard Cohen lived in a Zen monastery for five years from 1996.

[13] See further my comments in D. Brown and G. Hopps, *The Extravagance of Music* (London: Palgrave MacMillan, 2018), 114–16.

has also brought another consequence more directly relevant to this project: the need for greater humility in approaching what others believe. Most readers will have had encounters in which the religious perceptions of someone of another faith proved no less profound than what was available from within their own faith, or something illuminated which had only been dimly grasped in their own religious practice.

Changing Perceptions of the Origins of the Major Faiths

A second reason for a different approach is change in the understanding of how the major faiths evolved. Historically, each of them had to various degrees settled into acceptance of a rather simplistic view of their own origins. The divine was understood to have addressed lead figures in an uncomplicated way which allowed revelation to be seen as a straightforward gift from heaven that, once delivered, remained easy in appropriation and unchanging in meaning. Modern academic research has decisively undermined any such story. Whatever specific religion one considers, there is a complicated story of development that needs to be told. Think, for instance, of the battles in the early Christian centuries over alternative accounts of Christ's significance, or of Muslim debates in their early centuries about how one Qur'anic text might supersede another or the oral tradition of hadith be used to qualify possible applications.[14] Any notion of

---

[14] For further discussion of the principle of *naskh* or abrogation in the Qur'an and the clarification of *isnad* or chain of transmission in the oral tradition, see my *Tradition and Imagination: Revelation and Change*

immediate and uncontextualised exchange between God and humanity has gone. In its place has come the necessity for acknowledging that all 'knowledge' of the divine is heavily shaped by the particular settings in which it is received or advanced.

This is an important change because it radically undermines the once common practice of offering the best interpretation of one's own revelatory texts and practice and the worst for those of other faiths. All now prove to be a mixture, sometimes with the human contribution seen to be most evident in one's own religion. By contrast, elements in another religion are sometimes better able to be interpreted positively, precisely through now being able to be set within their proper context. For example, although attempts are still made to defend the *herem* or 'sacred ban' which involved the extermination of other peoples within Israelite territory or the blood-curdling sentiments with which Psalm 137 concludes, the most obvious explanation almost certainly lies in the resentments of a defeated people and a consequent lust for revenge.[15] As such, while the texts might still be used to reflect on how such sentiments can be overcome, it needs to be declared quite unequivocally that their expression has nothing to do with what God desired to communicate and everything to do with human limitations. Markedly different is what has now become possible in interpretating charges of idolatry against Hindu worship. Not only does such an objection ignore

---

(Oxford: Oxford University Press, 1999), 155–67. There is also a brief discussion in Chapter 7 of this work.

[15] Deut. 20. 16–20, Ps. 137. 8–9. Both texts probably originate from the period after the collapse of the southern kingdom of Judah.

the various ways in which the imagery seeks to point beyond itself, it also needs to be conceded that there is no less danger of idolatry within Judaism and Christianity. Thus, on the former point so many images are provided and with such variety that it is impossible to absolutise any single one. Again, on the other side 'respect' for the biblical word can all too easily collapse into a veneration that prevents the text from escaping such limited perspectives.[16] In short, it is necessary to see both divine and human at work not only in one's own faith but also more widely. Such changes in understanding bring with them two important consequences

First, it means that all claims to religious truth need to be properly set in context. In other words, such comparisons need to always be adjusted to take account of relationships with the wider cultural context. While major differences may still remain, even against such deeper settings, this is not always so. Sometimes as a consequence of such contextual analysis greater harmony between apparently competing revelations may well be the result. In an earlier book I took advantage of this possibility to suggest that the varying treatments of the story of the sacrifice of Isaac in the three Western monotheisms are not in fact as opposed as initially might appear (Islam even focuses on a different son, Ishmael).[17] This is because their surface differences reflect different embedded traditions which nonetheless can each be seen to move

---

[16] The question of images is discussed further in Chapter 3 on Hinduism.
[17] Strictly speaking, the Qur'an does not name the boy, but subsequent tradition moved overwhelmingly in favour of Ishmael as ancestor of the Arabs.

eventually towards the same basic principle: that the most profound form of sacrifice is self-sacrifice.[18] That is where the implication of the story is finally taken to point in all three cases, even if in its earliest written form in Genesis 22 the dilemma had been made to centre round the father rather than the son. Islam's focus primarily on the elder son is matched by later Judaism's re-orientation towards an older Isaac,[19] while Christians of the patristic world saw in the victim a 'type' or anticipation of Jesus' own sacrifice. Although Hinduism offers no direct parallels, there is a similar emphasis on the value of self-sacrifice.[20]

It might well be possible to extend this kind of conciliatory move more widely, even in the case of what seem apparently intractable divergences. The Christian doctrine of the Trinity, the Hindu assumption that an impersonal Braham is ultimate and Islam's strong stress on Allah as a single person certainly sound sharply divergent. But, as we shall see later, by reflecting on internal discussion and practice within the three faiths some limited degree of reconciliation could become possible. Even so, such partial conciliation hardly amounts to exactly the same affirmation. Likewise, at first sight the Hindu doctrine of avatars might be thought to offer some appropriate parallels to the Christian doctrine of the incarnation.[21]

---

[18] Discussed at length in my *Tradition and Imagination*, 237–60.
[19] In one text (Genesis Rabbah) it is even inferred from the timing of Sarah's death that Isaac was in fact 37 years old at the time of the incident.
[20] As in the various stories associated with Prajapati's creation of the world: Rig Veda 10.21 & 10.90.
[21] Krishna, for instance, is reputed to have been the eighth avatar or 'incarnation' of the god Vishnu. The two major differences from the Christian doctrine are the lack of historical foundation (though this

But, while accommodation might appear possible for Hinduism as it has in its treatment of Buddhism,[22] Christianity presents two seemingly insuperable obstacles: its strong stress on both historicity and uniqueness. No doubt there are comparable sticking points across the various religions. As I shall explain in the second part of this chapter, I do not think that in such circumstances reduction to the lowest common denominator is the right answer. Instead, adherents of the different faiths (including Christians) should remain committed to their own perspective but at the same time more open than they were in the past to the possibility of learning how revelation may have operated elsewhere.

Secondly, although from a purely human perspective such an analysis could (as in the Isaac example) be wholly positive in offering additional possibilities for reconciliation, it actually adds to the difficulties of making coherent sense of the workings of the divine. Of course, at one level we may speak of divine respect for the human condition. God does not wish to overthrow the ordinary processes of human cognition. Instead, individuals are allowed to discover divine reality at their own pace and that of their culture rather than according to any absolute standard. Yet, although such a way of proceeding may be taken to demonstrate deep respect for the integrity of human beings as they are, such a proposed perspective would still raise some difficult questions. Not least is the issue of what advantage there might be in allowing such

---

would be challenged by many Hindus) and the insistence that none of the god's powers remained in abeyance.

[22] Buddha is treated as yet another avatar of Vishnu.

apparently diverse conclusions to have been reached. Might the easiest response to such evidence not be to acknowledge either that no such pattern of communication has ever occurred, or else that the variety has only been overcome to a very small degree, with human and divine still remaining at an enormous distance from one another?[23] No major religion would want to reach that conclusion. So the question is posed in its most acute form: how are we to conceive of God as still active amidst such astonishingly diverse, perceived variety? It is part of the purpose of this book to work towards a partial answer.

Escaping Over-Simple Explanations

In a book such as this, one can scarcely avoid mention of the modern rise of fundamentalism in all the world's major faiths. How modern, indeed recent such dogmatism is, it is salutary to recall.[24] Not implausibly, much can be viewed from the outside as a rather cowardly retreat in response to the challenges presented by questions of the compatibility of scripture with science and historical research. But it can also be seen in part as a response to the levelling of all religions by secularist assumptions. An equal right to be heard can so easily turn into an

---

[23] The latter is in effect the solution offered by John Hick in *God and the Universe of Faiths* (London: Macmillan, 1973) and subsequent publications.
[24] Although the movement was growing throughout the later nineteenth century, within Christianity it particularly associated with the Princeton theologian Charles Hodge and the five Princeton 'fundamentals' of 1910.

equally curt dismissal.[25] Yet the best way to deal with the secular challenge is surely not to run before it but rather to face squarely the objections. Of course, in order to achieve some degree of plausibility a more complex story of the development of the world's religions will need to be told but there is surely no harm in that. On the contrary, it may be countered that it is often the secularist as much as the fundamentalist who is plagued by the search for over-simple explanations. To see how applicable such an observation is, just consider for a moment some of the accounts of the origin of religion which have been offered.

As each new discipline in the social sciences has emerged, they have produced advocates for the view that their own discipline would now provide a full 'explanation' of religious belief. This is well illustrated by successive attempts in sociology, psychology and anthropology. Yet it is not difficult to detect in the process how particular elements of truth were implausibly universalised. For example, while it is indubitably true that there is a strong social component to religion, the famous reduction proposed by the sociologist Émile Durkheim (1858–1917) ignored the fact that this is by no means all that religion amounts to. Nor is it even always the major component in any religious belief system.[26] Indeed, there is no

---

[25] A good example of this is attitudes towards religious education in schools, where a demand that all religions be represented equally is often quickly turned into the rejection of their presence altogether.

[26] In *The Elementary Forms of Religious Life* (Oxford: Oxford University Press, 2008; original French edition, 1912) Durkheim argued that the role of religion was to form a social undergirding to communal life.

consistency regarding the period during which a strongly socially structured pattern to belief is likely to emerge. Whereas with Christianity this was a prominent feature in the middle ages which has subsequently declined, some other religions have moved in the opposite direction. Even some major religions like Hinduism or Shintoism have only become consciously self-reflecting as a social phenomenon in modern times.[27] In other words, there is considerable complexity which is being ignored.

Much the same criticism can be applied to the more recent phenomenon of the 'cognitive science of religion'. The term was first coined by J. L. Barrett in 2000 and since that time its literature has become extensive, not least through its International Association (founded in 2006). Barrett argues that human beings are hardwired to believe in the supernatural because of the evolutionary advantage postulating agency gives human beings even when no such agent is present (for example, in response to a sound precisely because of the warning thereby normally given of potential predators).[28] While Barrett's advocacy of the explanation is quite moderate, other researchers who have adopted the same sort of approach have shown much less caution. Even if contributing an

---

[27] Shintoism only really became self-consciously a distinct religion as a result of imperial policy in nineteenth-century Japan. Even Hinduism only gradually differentiated itself from others in reaction to the religion of successive invaders of the Indian subcontinent, notably Muslim and Christian.

[28] In *Why Would Anyone Believe in God?* (Lanham, MD: AltaMira Press, 2004) Barrett gives a formal name to the process: HADD or 'Hyperactive Agency Detection Device'. That is, the action of an agent tends to be presupposed even where a natural explanation is readily available, such as the rustle of the wind.

element of truth, a partial cause can scarcely be used to account for numerous other aspects of religion with which it bears little or no relation.[29]

No doubt belief in the supernatural among 'primitive' peoples was in part motivated by aetiology or a search for causal explanation. While the origin of the world is an obvious case in point, it is not hard to identify similar reflections at work with respect to specific emotions, such as powerful sexual passion which can sometimes feel like an invasion from outside the person.[30] But again to concede that much is scarcely to suggest that universalising the explanation carries with it any inherent plausibility. Not all religious belief appears motivated by such a search for explanation. Even where it was at the start, it by no means follows that this will account for its continuation. Consider the earliest known religious practice, which was in all likelihood veneration for the dead.[31] To suggest as an explanation purely apotropaic purposes (to ward off possible harm through damage to present projects) would be to make our ancestors' behaviour less subtly complex than our own. While no doubt a factor, it is surely dangerous to discount love and respect for the dead, and so a desire that they share positively in the next generation's projects. Similarly, sacrifice (another early practice) was sometimes certainly motivated by the desire to prevent a capricious deity from doing harm to one's crops. But,

---

[29] For some more criticisms of this position, see my comments in D. Brown and G Hopps, *The Extravagance of Music*, 42–3.
[30] A likely origin for deities such as Aphrodite and Venus.
[31] Even Neanderthals seem to have shown respect for their dead, while many ancient civilisations buried their dead beneath their houses: see *Extravagance*, 44–5.

equally, could not the motive also have been at other times simply to express gratitude for the flourishing of those same crops? Sacrifice would then be less about appeasement and more about maintaining a proper balance between our world and that of the gods. The offering during a Roman or Greek meal of part of the animal to be eaten and of some accompanying wine poured out as a libation surely suggests not just caution (the gods as a rule did not even get the best bits!).[32] Rather, it conceded their role in making such feasting possible, and so gratitude to them for allowing human beings to share in it.

In other words, what I am protesting against are somewhat naïve, unduly simple explanations. This observation holds equally to how the life of the gods was first envisaged. It is all too easy to contrast a religion like Christianity and an allegedly naïve anthropomorphism with which religion may have begun. While a spatial location in the heavens and features of character that resemble those of human beings appear dominant in earlier times, there are plenty of indications that these assumptions were not taken entirely literally. The way in which Egyptian gods were all given animal features at one time or another surely suggests rejection of any straightforward understanding of them as merely larger versions of ourselves. Indeed, what may well be the earliest representation of a god so far found nicely illustrates this point:

---

[32] Similarly, at Jewish as well as much pagan sacrifice, while the blood of the sacrificial animal was poured over the altar, only the inedible parts were burnt as an offering to the gods. The edible parts were consumed by the celebrants.

the so-called Lion Man of Ulm, believed to have been carved from mammoth ivory over 40,000 years ago.[33] Recent research indicates that the place where the object was discovered functioned as a kind of ritual sanctuary. This would be compatible with thinking of the Lion Man as used in worship to indicate an imaginative leap to another world, where there was to be found something much greater than the two already impressive creatures used in the carving (mammoth and lion).[34] So even at the distant birth of religion there was a subtlety that many a modern scholar lacks.

Not that such lack of refinement is always present. A recent encouraging example of willingness from an evolutionary scientist to acknowledge greater complexity in the origins and development of religion comes from Robin Dunbar in his recently published book, *How Religion Evolved*.[35] Although without religious belief himself, he acknowledges that at its heart even primitive religion sought subtle kinds of connection with an alternative world.[36] Their evolutionary importance lay in the way in which such moves secured the stability of society, though not always in the same way.[37]

---

[33] See further the discussion in Neil MacGregor, *Living with the Gods* (London: Allen Lane, 2018), 1–13, esp. 6 (illustration) and 12–13.
[34] The original is in Museum Ulm in Germany. It was called the Lion Man because the figure was given human legs with which to stand upright.
[35] Robin Dunbar, *How Religion Evolved and Why It Endures* (London: Pelican, 2022). He is Professor of Evolutionary Psychology at Oxford.
[36] Ibid., 149–75.   [37] Ibid., 177–212, esp. 194–8.

A Distinctive Approach: Complementary Shards

Having thus outlined these three considerations for adopting a different approach, let me turn now to first outlining my own proposed alternative model and then explaining why what follows seeks to go well beyond either of the two most common conventional understandings of the relation between the religions (inclusivism and pluralism).

An Alternative Model

For most of its past, Christianity has been quite dismissive of other religions. The 'compliment' was usually returned but Christianity had the advantage, at least until modern times, of being part of the ideology of the dominant, colonial powers and so looked more 'progressive'. Apart from one major exception,[38] more recently within Christian theology a respectful attitude has prevailed for the most part, with some version or other of inclusivism becoming the norm: the view that other religions may be seen as at most partial and imperfect anticipations of Christianity. Such attitudes are increasingly common, even among more conservative groups such as Pentecostalism. One of its major theologians has used features such as the witness of pagans in scripture and potential parallels in other religions to their own

---

[38] Karl Barth insisted that other religions were constituted by a human search for God rather than any reaching out of God towards them. His position was given classical expression by the Dutch theologian, Hendrik Kraemer, *The Christian Message in a Non-Christian World* (New York: Harper, 1938).

charismatic experience to argue for the activity of the Holy Spirit in all religions.[39] Characteristically, such inclusivism has taken one of two main forms. Either the focus has been at a high level of generality in which case gradations of truth (in favour of Christianity) have been postulated,[40] or else a very specific type of practical ecumenism is recommended, with joint ventures in acting or listening but with no expectation of real change on either side.[41] Both approaches are to my mind quite defective. What they ignore is the complexity I have briefly indicated above: complexity both in how the divine might be seen to communicate in general with humanity and complexity with regard to the story of that development within any particular religious tradition.

That is to say, what is ignored is the way in which conditioning by cultural context might allow different insights to reach prominence at different times within the perspective of the various faith communities. So there is no reason in principle why Christianity might not be more profound than, say Hinduism or Islam, in one area, but yet further behind in another. Indeed, that is precisely what I shall suggest in the examples chosen for

---

[39] Amos Yong, *Beyond the Impasse: Toward a Pneumatological Theology of Religions* (Carlisle: Paternoster Press, 2003), esp. 75–6, 113–14.

[40] The views of Karl Rahner are usually quoted in this context, in particular his notion of 'anonymous Christians'. Adherents of other faiths are seen as on the way towards more explicitly Christian perceptions: *Theological Investigations* (London: Darton, Longman & Todd, 1960), 6.390–8.

[41] The best-known contemporary approach of this kind is probably the practice known as Scriptural Reasoning, initiated by the Jewish scholar, Peter Ochs in 1995. It involves different faiths observing how others study their own sacred texts. Rose Castle in Cumbria is currently the headquarters of the movement in England.

subsequent chapters. An analogy might help at this point. The most complete divine disclosure possible would be rather like a beautiful inlaid pattern on a collection of ancient vases, alluring and fascinating in detail yet currently only detectable in part on a number of shards or broken parts. Sometimes aspects of the pattern are replicated on more than one shard. Sometimes the pattern is only discoverable by fitting together different pieces from different broken aspects. And sometimes (and more difficult to resolve) the same corresponding piece seems quite different, almost suggesting no recognizable common identity.[42] In other words, each and every religion falls short of the ideal or totality. They are more like these shards or broken potsherds, full of promise yet incomplete in themselves. The fullest pattern is only recoverable by noting complementary elements, different bits of the jigsaw, as it were: fuzzy parallels that need to be worked at, in order to provide a more complete picture of the whole.

Perhaps some will take offense at the analogy and suggest that it offers too low a view of revelation, but, as even as orthodox a theologian as St John Henry Newman concludes, 'no revelation can be complete and systematic, from the weakness of the human intellect ... A Revelation is religious doctrine viewed on its illuminated side; a mystery is the selfsame doctrine viewed on the side unilluminated. Thus, religious truth is neither light nor darkness, but both together; it is like the dim view of a country seen in the twilight, which forms half extricated from the

---

[42] How that particularly challenging issue might be best resolved is pursued in most detail in Chapter 8.

darkness, with broken lines and isolated masses. Revelation, in this way of considering, is not a revealed system, but consists of a number of detached and incomplete truths, belonging to a vast system unrevealed'.[43] So, elsewhere even of the Trinity Newman observes: 'Break a ray of light into its constituent colours; each is beautiful, each may be enjoyed; attempt to unite them, and perhaps you produce only a dirty white. The pure and indivisible Light is seen only by the blessed inhabitants of heaven; here we have but faint reflections of it as its diffraction supplies ... Attempt to combine them into one, and you gain nothing but a mystery which you can describe as a notion, but cannot depict as an imagination'.[44] In other words, however strong an image we are able to form of the individual members of the Trinity, it will defy our powers of imagination to make complete sense of the notion.

Beyond Inclusivism and Pluralism to Contextualism and Discovery

A quite different sort of objection will come from those who argue for a pluralist approach, with all religions seen as equally distant from ultimate Reality. Sometimes this operates as a maximising strategy, but usually at a price as critics often claim that in the process real differences are insufficiently acknowledged. It is an objection that has been raised, for instance, against Keith Ward's claim that

---

[43] J. H. Newman, *Essays Critical and Historical* (London: Longmans, 1887), vol. I, 41–2 (Essay 2.4).
[44] J. H. Newman, *Grammar of Assent* (New York: Doubleday, 1955), ch.5, sec. 2, 116–17.

the philosophical conception of God in the Western monotheisms exhibits 'strong similarities with Vedanta' and even with the 'atheistic religion of Buddhism',[45] in 'a picture of the religious life as one which turns from the concern of the world to find eternal bliss in a source beyond the finite and temporal, which yet manifests in personal form, possessing supreme bliss and knowledge'.[46] More typical is a thoroughly minimalist strategy. For example, John Hick reduced much of Christian orthodoxy to myth,[47] and in this he has been followed by the most recent significant utilisation of such an approach in Perry Schmidt-Leukel's impressive 2015 Gifford Lectures.[48] In effect both offer a reconstruction of the Christian religion rather than any essential continuity. This was recognised by Hick himself, when towards the end of his life he abandoned the confessional church he had espoused for most of his life (Presbyterianism) for the

---

[45] Keith Ward, *Images of Eternity* (Oxford: Oneworld, 1987), 181.
[46] Ibid., 29. The differences between the two contrasting Hindu approaches of Shankara and Ramanuja are, it is alleged, minimized. Again, on Buddhism it is suggested that the doctrine of no-self could be 'taken as teaching that beyond the relatively illusory self, there is an underlying Mind ... with which one can be united' (73), certainly a controversial, if not necessarily false, claim.
[47] Notoriously in the book which he edited, entitled *The Myth of God Incarnate* (London: SCM Press, 1977).
[48] *Religious Pluralism & Interreligious Theology* (Maryknoll: Orbis Books, 2017). Although fully comprehensive in its range of reference, the book strikes me as too concerned to achieve a common mind without regard to how beliefs have functioned in the history of the traditions concerned. So, for example, the author thinks it enough to note that Jesus never claimed to be God, whereas the gospels (and John in particular) are already shaping Christianity in this direction. For the method in action applied to relations with Islam, see 146–63, esp. 151–54.

non-dogmatic Society of Friends. Alan Rice, the person who invented the commonly used categories of exclusivism, inclusivism and pluralism, was himself a postgraduate research student of Hick's. Judging by his latest book,[49] he would probably regard my own proposals as merely yet another version of inclusivism, and of course in one important sense he is exactly right. I do think it important that in religious practice preferential judgements are made. An open agenda actually avoids any real commitment. Yet there is another sense in which what I am offering in this chapter and those that follow is something fundamentally different. There is, I would contend, a willingness to acknowledge a much more complex reality in which one's own religion does not always 'win'. In short, pluralism is emphatically not the only option in expressing openness to others.

Similar endorsements of pluralism are also occasionally to be found in those of other faiths. Perhaps no one has done more to popularise mindfulness in the West than the Vietnamese Buddhist monk, Thich Nhat Hanh (1926–2022). But it is arguable that in his desire to draw parallels between Christianity and Buddhism he actually substantially rewrote the basic contents of each.[50] A hint in that direction is suggested by the way in which the

[49] Alan Race, *My Journey as a Religious Pluralist: A Christian Theology of Religion Reclaimed* (Eugene, OR: Wipf & Stock, 2021).

[50] Controversially, he argued for an alternative translation for the short Zen treatise, The Heart Sutra. Instead, of emptiness being seen as the ultimate aim, it becomes compassion, with inter-dependence now seen as its fundamental assertion. The result is that '"emptiness" is an expression we could say is equivalent to "God"': *The Other Shore* (Berkeley, CA: Parallax Press, 2017), 58.

patristics scholar Elaine Pagels in her introduction to his *Living Buddha, Living Christ* opts for ancient Christian Gnosticism as the nearest analogue to what he wants to say.[51] Yet, even if at times he does take implausible shortcuts,[52] Nhat Hanh's reflections may be seen as those of a deeply holy man, seeking somewhat too enthusiastically to mediate the ideas of the east where he originated and the Christian West where he eventually settled.[53] A more accurate eastern estimate of the difference might, therefore, be the work of another holy Buddhist monk, the current fourteenth Dalai Lama (b. 1935) who exhibits much more caution in drawing parallels.[54]

Apart from the question of whether sufficient identity is maintained and thus the engagement of existing adherents, two further fundamental challenges need to be set against pluralist approaches. First, there is the problem of why unqualified equality should be deemed of such supreme worth; secondly, why everything is analysed from a human perspective and never from the divine. Presumably, lurking in the background of the former is an assumption that any other attitude would denigrate the faith of others. But surely this would only be so if a

---

[51] Thich Nhat Hanhn, *Living Buddha, Living Christ* (New York: Rider, 1996), xix-xxvii.
[52] Ibid. 'Jesus pointed to the same reality of no-birth, no-death. He called it the Kingdom of God'. (143).
[53] Plum Village monastery was founded in the Dordogne in 1982. There are three daughter monasteries in the United States, as well as others elsewhere in the world.
[54] See further his book *The Good Heart: A Buddhist Perspective on the Teaching of Jesus* (Boston, MA: Wisdom Publications, 1996). For example, he observes that 'the conception of God and creation are a point of departure between Buddhists and Christians' (55).

position of arrogant exclusivism were adopted and not what is being advocated here: a willingness to listen and learn that will sometimes at least result in recognition of better insight on the part of one's interlocutors than within one's own community. Another element in play, though, may be the thought that, since we are dealing with a purely human search, none can be placed more highly than any other. But why accept such reductionism? The failure of simple models for proposing a divine initiative in revelation need not entail that no more satisfactory, complex account can be given. Chapter 8 will in fact offer some more formal proposals precisely along these lines. In the meantime, as our discussion proceeds, some hints will emerge, not least because it is that very complexity which earlier chapters will be seeking to address. Chapter 9 will then return to this issue of pluralism versus inclusivism by examining more closely some major figures in that dialogue but this time with our project largely behind us.

In an ideal world, no matter what the topic, a full dialogue between different perspectives would involve alternating contributions with each interlocutor doing as much listening as talking. But for such interaction to flourish it is necessary that some common presuppositions and values are shared. Otherwise, frequent misunderstanding will be the result. Unfortunately, the various world religions are not yet at such a point. At most, what we can hope for is a sympathetic exploration of other religions that endeavours to take with maximum seriousness those alternative presuppositions. This is what I shall seek to do, as I attempt in what follows two main aims: both to set the religions concerned in their various appropriate cultural contexts and to identify some prominent features from which I believe Christianity could learn. So each chapter begins by setting the origins and present practice of the religions concerned in their specific contexts before going on to identify some contribution which might be appropriated. Contextualisation is usually assumed to be reductionist, with belief and practice in effect equated with cultural constraints. But because different contexts generate different forms of limitation, another way of viewing the situation is as potentially liberating; enabling the possibility of seeing issues from some new perspective.

Although I write as a believing Christian, this is not the place to say something about what Christianity might itself be able to contribute. This is not because I suppose my own religion to have less to offer but precisely because there is a need to reverse the traditional Christian evangelistic approach which has supposed that the benefits would run exclusively in one direction, from itself to others. In other words, there is now a real need for much greater humility, a willingness to pursue the learning process in reverse. Accordingly, what follows is not treated as simply an intellectual exercise. There is also a deliberate focus on actual practice in the religions concerned. By deliberate intent the discipline of religious studies usually focuses upon an 'objective' presentation, viewing any particular religion from the outside, as it were. It is also a policy pursued by most biblical scholars who see their task as an historical one, essentially no different from that of any other historian investigating secular history. While there is undoubtedly a place for such objectivity, it does come in both cases at a considerable price: putting it somewhat crudely, the failure to take into account what makes a particular religion 'tick', what might enable a sympathetic observer to enter into its spirit. So, for example, while Christianity is at root an historical faith, this by no means entails that its only interest is in the historical value of its texts. Rather, of far greater importance is the potential meaning which they might convey, in engaging a new perspective and affective commitment.[55] Equally, such 'objectivity' can lead to the treatment of Buddhism as more philosophy than religion.[56] While such an analysis might better capture aspects of its general perspective, it also undoubtedly side-lines much of what actually goes on in the practice of its various forms. Cultic behaviour at Buddhist shrines suggests a very different account.[57] That is why, in order to avoid such potential misunderstandings, in preparing to write this book I deliberately sought out encounters with believers in the world's other major religions, especially in countries where that particular religion constitutes the majority faith and so would prove especially easy to observe in practice. As well as focused visits to China, India and Japan, I took the opportunity to visit a number of Muslim countries, as well as some other Buddhist

---

[55] I have sought to argue for this sort of approach in *Gospel as Work of Art: Imaginative Truth and Open Text* (Grand Rapids, MI: Eerdmans, 2024).

[56] No one could deny a strong philosophical element in Buddhism but treating it exclusively in this way is probably primarily motivated by the current widespread negative cultural response to 'religion'.

[57] I recall a memorable afternoon in Yangon (the principal city of Myanmar) observing a range of practices from individual adults adding gold leaf to statues to a group of young children singing chants. Clearly evident was the joy and devotion on the faces of most of them.

nations.[58] That practical dimension has meant that, although more conceptual issues eventually take centre stage, I have not infrequently initiated discussion with a focus on devotional issues.[59] Perhaps in terms of an appropriate precedent one might mention the current creation of the House of One in Berlin.[60] With a church, mosque and synagogue sharing the same building, it is hoped that frequency of encounter at a practical level may well induce some more tolerant and sympathetic attitudes.

So my hope is that this book demonstrates greater humility than Christian theologians have commonly shown in the past. A sympathetic reading demands that one see the divine at work elsewhere as well as in one's own religion, and this I have sought to do. One way of helping towards such a perception is to take careful note of the kind of interactions between religions which have already occurred in some cases, as for instance, between Hinduism and the various other religions practised on the Indian subcontinent, or between Buddhism and Shintoism in Japan. That is one reason why three of the chapters address religion in specific nations (India, China and Japan) precisely because, even if seldom fully admitted, there has been a long history of such interaction.[61] However, I shall begin in Chapter 2 with something that

---

[58] Muslim countries included Albania, Iran, Kosovo, Morocco, Turkey and Uzbekistan; Buddhist countries included Cambodia, Myanmar and Vietnam.
[59] As in Chapter 3 on Hinduism.
[60] The foundation stone was laid on 14 April 2020 in Fischerinsel, where apparently Berlin's first church once stood.
[61] As we shall see, China will prove the most complicated to analyse with Buddhism, Confucianism and Daoism all having major impacts on the other two.

is even less widely recognised. Indeed, it is only becoming fully apparent in the light of more recent historical research, and that is the extent to which both Judaism and Christianity were indebted to pagan religion. Judaism and Christianity were also constrained by specific contexts.

Chapters 3 and 7, devoted exclusively to Hinduism and Islam, respectively, frame the central chapters on religions in the three nations (China, India and Japan) and may initially seem exceptions to that pattern. Yet even here a more complicated dynamic needs to be admitted. Hinduism only came to see itself as a single entity in modern times. It was thus interaction between originally semi-independent strands which produced its present greater internal coherence. Equally, it cannot be denied that there were some changes in overall emphasis in response to the challenges set by the dominant religions of the colonial powers.[62] Again, with respect to Islam, as will be noted in due course, the Qur'an cannot be properly or fully understood without additional awareness of some of the major narratives of Judaism and Christianity.[63] Finally, towards the book's end I return to the question of how revelation may be understood across the religions and in particular how the most intractable differences might be, if not resolved, at least ameliorated

---

[62] It is not implausible to claim that it was competing pressure from Christianity and Islam which led to a much stronger emphasis in more recent times on a central place for monotheism.

[63] Muhammad alludes to the stories in a way that presupposes knowledge of relevant details in the other two religions.

Perhaps in a relatively short book I have tried to achieve too much. As it is, there are some obvious omissions. Not all religions are included. Modern Judaism in particular receives no mention. However, of all contemporary faiths, this is the one with which modern Christian theology has most often sought to engage, so readers may confidently be left to the many reflections on the matter in other writers. We begin, though, with Judaism in its most ancient form. Here, the natural superiority it once assumed along with Christianity in supposing a self-contained development needs to be challenged, and the great debt both religions owe to surrounding pagan culture duly acknowledged. It is to such questions that we now turn.

2
Ancient Paganism and the Biblical God

In Chapter 2 I want to consider what lessons might be learnt from the way in which modern scholarship has transformed our understanding of the origins of both Judaism and Christianity. The saddest aspect of this new situation is how little attention is paid at present to the conclusions which could be drawn for a proper understanding of the nature of faith. On the whole, following the narrow historical bias set by the Enlightenment, both scholars of ancient religion and contemporary theologians alike see their role as lying in recording what has happened instead of making any sustained effort to deduce what might be said about the hand of God in such events. Yet in the case of Judaism we are now acutely aware of the high degree to which the forms it later took were influenced by the surrounding culture. In the case of Christianity the key role of an already existing major religion (Judaism) must be noted,[1] though its impact was not as straightforward as was once supposed. But also, when Christianity moved out into the classical world, it likewise took on some forms derived from the pagan religion of the time. In analysing this new understanding,

---

[1] In Chapter 2, in order to avoid unnecessarily complex explanations, I use terms like Judaism and Israel rather loosely. Strictly speaking, Judaism properly refers only to the post-exilic form of the religion and Israel only to the northern kingdom and not to Judah, its main rival in the south.

Chapter 2 is divided into two main parts. First, an exploration is offered of the role played by ancient Mesopotamian and Egyptian religion in the shaping of Judaism; second, the contribution made to Christianity through ancient religious philosophy and the mystical religions of paganism is examined. By the end of Chapter 2 I hope to have indicated a number of ways in which it might be appropriate for Christianity to acknowledge elements of dependence on paganism (indirectly through Judaism as well as directly). It is, therefore, necessary to admit the need to learn from others as never before.

The Origins of Judaism in Its Near-Eastern Context

Here I want to explore the debt of Judaism to the wider pagan culture in two stages: first, by examining the present historical consensus; second, more controversially, by exploring the degree to which it might be appropriate to speak of the divine as also active in that wider culture.

Archaeology, Borrowing and Transformation

I shall begin this section by exploring what archaeology can tell us about the history of the region and potential borrowings before examining in more detail some of the myths that were adapted for use in scripture. A huge amount of material has in fact been discovered both inside and outside Israel but with the most significant material usually originating from beyond its borders. The major exception is the discovery of numerous *astarte* which may well imply a once extensive goddess cult within Israel.[2] There are also quite a number of temple complexes in the country besides that in Jerusalem.[3] Although Israel's geographical position might have led to the conclusion that greater influence would have been exercised by its nearer neighbour Egypt than the more distant successive states in Mesopotamia (the fertile area between the two rivers of the Euphrates and Tigris), this seems not to have been so. This is partly because of the more aggressive policy of these latter states, partly because of an eventually shared language (Akkadian and Aramaean are both Semitic languages. unlike Egyptian or, for that matter, the earlier Sumerian) and partly because climatic conditions were closer. Although weather patterns were quite uncertain in Israel, the same was true in Mesopotamia. While there was no doubt about the land's fertility, the two rivers could be quite unpredictable in the amount of water they produced. By contrast, despite the description of a famous exception in the story of Joseph,[4] the Nile's annual flooding was almost guaranteed and so could be read as a sure sign of the Pharaoh adequately performing the appropriate rituals.

Our knowledge of interaction with Egypt is in any case somewhat limited. Even the famous deposit of official

---

[2] Sometimes these took the form of obelisks, as can be seen at the temple of Baal in Byblos: cf. 2 Kings. 17.9–10. While the small *astarte* forms of the goddess are usually found in people's homes, these more abstract poles or pillars (known as *asherim*) could possibly (and confusingly) admit to other, unrelated interpretations. *Astarte* is the Greek form of the name of Asherah, the wife of Baal.

[3] Archaeology confirms that the *bamah* or 'high place' did not disappear. Tell Arad is a good example.

[4] Genesis 41.1–45.

correspondence found at Amarna, about 300 kilometres south of Cairo, tells us more about those who sent the letters (from Mesopotamia and Canaan) than their recipient, Pharaoh Akhenaten (c. 1352–1336), or interactions between them. Although some scholars argue that Akhenaten's exaltation of Aten or the sun as sole god should be seen as the source of Hebrew monotheism,[5] this suggestion has been largely rejected, not least because the latter's emergence appears to stem from a very much later date. Commitment to monotheism only becomes clear in Second Isaiah.[6] Even potential parallels between Akhenaten's Hymn to the Sun and Psalm 104 need to be handled with care,[7] both because any such influence could have happened centuries later and because in any case the precise nature of Akhenaten's monotheism remains to a large degree a mystery.[8]

So it is wise to focus instead on the main sites in Mesopotamia, beginning with the famous Sumerian city of Ur, usually identified with Abraham's original home

---

[5] The German archaeologist Jan Assmann is especially associated with this claim in books such as *Moses the Egyptian: The Memory of Egypt in Western Monotheism* (1998) and *From Akhenaten to Moses: Ancient Egypt and Religious Change* (2016). For consideration of Akhenaten's views in their own right (traced to nostalgia for a simpler past), see James K. Hoffmeier, *Akhenaten and the Origins of Monotheism* (Oxford, Oxford University Press, 2015).

[6] For example, 43.10–11. Moses may have only been committed to one god while not denying the existence of others (a position known as henotheism and common in earlier Hebrew scriptures e.g. Ps. 82.1).

[7] Called 'The Great Hymn to the Orb' in Toby Wilkinson ed., *Writings from Ancient Egypt* (London: Penguin, 2016), 101–6.

[8] For two opposed accounts of his motivation, Cyril Alred, *Akhenaten: King of Egypt* (London: Thames & Hudson, 1988), esp. 237–48 and Nicholas Reeves, *Akhenaten: Egypt's False Prophet* (London: Thames & Hudson, 2005), esp. 133–52.

(Ur of the Chaldees),[9] near the mouth of the two rivers. Although archaeological work on its ziggurat began in 1854, the main excavations were not carried out until under Sir Edward Woolley in 1922–34. His main discovery was large royal tombs in which the kings were buried, not only with some attendants but also numerous pieces of fine artwork and seals. Although Woolley was sometimes too quick in drawing biblical parallels,[10] he was undoubtedly right in seeing Ur as a remarkably advanced civilisation of high calibre. There was even trade with the ancient Harappan culture in the Indus valley, a culture whose very existence had been forgotten until modern times.[11] Nearby was another Sumerian city, Uruk, the subject of extensive German excavation and original home to the hero Gilgamesh (although the only complete version of the story we possess comes from the Neo-Babylonian period). Rightly acknowledged as a world classic, it is a fascinating tale of a contest between nature and nurture that includes an unsuccessful search for immortality, as well as an early version of the story of the flood.[12]

The Babylonians had in fact two periods of significant power: first, when they overcame the Sumerians and introduced Akkadian, a Semitic language, as the *lingua*

---

[9] Gen. 15.7.
[10] As with the famous Ram in the Thicket which he identified with the story of Abraham and Isaac. More probably, the creature is a goat and the sculpture intended to adorn the foot of a table or chair. The original is now in the Penn Museum in Philadelphia.
[11] Discussed in Chapter 3.
[12] The text is widely available in translation: *Myths from Mesopotamia*, trans. Stephanie Dalley (Oxford World's Classics rev. 2008); *Epic of Gilgamesh*, trans. Andrew R. George (Penguin Classics, 1999).

franca (bridge language) of the people. It was during this time that the famous code of Hammurabi (1792–50) was produced. Second, the later Neo-Babylonian period associated especially with Nebuchadnezzar (602–562 BCE). Although complicated by Saddam Hussein's reconstructions, Babylon is undoubtedly still the most impressive of ancient near-eastern sites. A more tasteful reconstruction of the Ishtar Gate is on offer in Berlin. This was the gate through which the annual procession passed from the Temple of Marduk to the main site of the annual New Year festival or *akitu*.[13] In the interval between these two periods of dominance, power had passed to the Assyrian Empire, with its capital at Nineveh, much further north on the east bank of the Tigris and opposite modern Mosul. The city yielded roughly 24,000 cuneiform tablets from the state archive of Ashurbanipal (668–27). As a reflection of the natural conservatism of religion, it may be noted that at Babylon and Nineveh the Sumerian language continued to be used for religious ritual long after Sumerian power had declined,[14] just as rough woollen vestments were worn by clergy long after they had gone out of fashion.[15]

But perhaps most important of all from a biblical perspective were excavations at the village of Ras Shamra, ten kilometres north of Lattakia on the Syrian

---

[13] Lasting twelve days, not only did it celebrate the spring barley harvest but also a mythical story of creation and the re-enthronement of the king.
[14] Sumerian seems to have died out as an ordinary spoken language by c.1650 BCE but its religious use continued as late as the first century BCE, with scribes at Babylon still copying out poems in Sumerian.
[15] Evident from artefacts such as stelae.

coast.[16] Here was the ancient city of Ugarit which yielded numerous finds in both Akkadian and in Ugaritic, the local Canaanite language. Its myths reflected the fact that its principal temples were dedicated to Baal and Dagan.[17] Eventually, Jerusalem was to fall to the Babylonians in 587 BCE, with its leading citizens carried off into exile. But not long after, Babylon met a similar fate, yielding place to the Persians who, under Cyrus the Great, proclaimed an edict of toleration for all religions,[18] and so some of the Jews at least were allowed to return. As a result the prophet Second Isaiah even declared Cyrus 'God's anointed'.[19] The experience of exile was probably sufficient in itself to generate his new belief in absolute monotheism: God was experienced as still present with his people, even in exile. The prophet's reflections cannot but have been helped, though, by Cyrus' own religion of Zoroastrianism, and the concern for all indicated in that famous edict.[20]

The wealth of comparative material available has led some to speak of a shared pattern of myth. However, what such generalisations ignore is the way in which similar ideas are sometimes independently generated and at other

---

[16] Present–day Syria's fourth largest city, situated to the north of Lebanon and south of Turkey.
[17] For some of these myths in an easily accessible form, Michael D. Coogan & Mark S. Smith eds., *Stories from Ancient Canaan* (Louisville, KY: Westminster John Knox, 2nd ed., 2012).
[18] Seen in the so-called Cyrus Cylinder, discovered in the ruins of Babylon in 1879, and now in the British Museum.
[19] Isaiah 42.1. Chapters 40–66 are usually ascribed in whole or in part to this later prophet.
[20] Not without influence even in today's Iran where Zoroastrianism and Christianity continue to enjoy limited freedom of worship.

times significant modifications made, as borrowings are adapted to suit the specific needs and already existing perspectives of different communities.[21] The latter form of influence can be found reflected (though inevitably occurring to differing degrees) within Israelite religion. Take, for instance, the creation story with which the Bible now opens. When read against the backdrop of its Babylonian equivalent *Enuma Elish*, it reads more like a critique than any simple adaptation.[22] Gone are any self-interested motives on the part of the gods for the creation of humans, and in its place comes a world repeatedly declared unqualifiedly good. While the battle with counterforces survives in some of the psalms and in legends of tamed sea-monsters,[23] in the opening verses of Genesis the god who has first to be defeated in the earlier version (Tiamat) is reduced to the vague, impersonal 'deep' (*tehom*). Although the Babylonian version also renders Tiamat powerless, the defeat is commonly rendered as less complete. So, for instance, a seal illustration depicts her as a petulant but now impotent dragon as she lies at Marduk's side more in the manner of a modern pet dog

---

[21] For an erudite but flawed attempt to reduce the various myths to a few salient themes, see David Leeming, *Jealous Gods, Chosen People: The Mythology of the Middle East* (Oxford: Oxford University Press, 2004). The often very subtle but important differences between common ideas are ignored.

[22] Found in 1849 by the British archaeologist, A. H. Layard, in the ruins of the library of Ashurbanipal at Nineveh, it takes its title from its first two words 'When on high...' It is sometimes given the alternative title 'The Seven Tablets of Creation.'

[23] Particularly in relation to the sea monster, Leviathan, for example, Ps. 74.12–14; Is. 27.1; Job 3.8; 41.1–34.

than the great goddess she once was.[24] Nonetheless, the Genesis version effectively went one stage further: she is assumed never to have had such power, which is why she is replaced in the story by a mere thing.

Again, in borrowing the story of the flood from the *Epic of Gilgamesh*, more honourable reasons for divine action are postulated than was true in the original tale. Instead of sin, the gods had taken exception to a very noisy humanity. More of the details, though, are retained in this case compared with the creation myth, including specific birds and the length of the flood.[25] Clearly the biblical authors assume some historical content, and in this they are probably correct (though the flood would have been on a much more limited scale). By contrast, the story of the Tower of Babel looks like pure invention, although its likely inspiration is to be found in the multi-layered Mesopotamian ziggurats stretching up to heaven which modern archaeology has revealed. However, on this occasion there is some reason for thinking the biblical narrative not only historically false but also theologically inaccurate. The building of such ziggurats is presented as a sign of human arrogance in attempting to rival the divine, whereas this was almost certainly not the original

---

[24] A line dividing the waters is used to indicate that Tiamat has already been carved up. The ninth century BCE cylindrical seal dedication by the Babylonian king, Marduk-zakir-sumi, is illustrated in James B. Prichard ed., *The Ancient Near East: An Anthology of Texts and Pictures* (Princeton, NJ: Princeton University Press, 2nd ed., 2011), 141.

[25] Gen. 6.5–8.22. The main narrative from J assumes a length of forty days but E's continued use of the original seven days can be seen in the treatment of the birds: Gen. 8.6–12.

intention.[26] More likely, it expressed the desire for the gods to come down and give humanity their aid. Certainly, this notion seems to be suggested by the fact that only a small temple was placed at their summit, with a much larger one reserved for the base.[27] Even within Genesis itself an alternative account to Babel is canvassed when the story of Jacob's vision is told. Traditionally referred to as 'Jacob's ladder' and often so translated in our English bibles,[28] the Hebrew actually refers to steps or a stairway. What precisely was meant can be seen if one examines the nature of the surviving structure at Ur. The small temple at the top was actually known as 'the gate of heaven' with the larger one at its base described as 'the house of God'. A partly reconstructed series of steps rises up through the various layers directly to the top.

The story of Moses may equally be seen as a mixture of fact and borrowed fiction. While there is no doubt that Semites were to be found as prisoners in Egypt (recognisable from their different hairstyles and short beards), there is still no evidence to suggest a specific Jewish presence in Egypt at the relevant time. In current thinking, the likelihood seems to be that at most the subsequent invasion of Canaan involved a minority, although this group did eventually succeed in integrating their story and ideas into those of the majority population. Moses' story even begins in a way that has earlier precedent. It was originally told of King Sargon I that he had

---

[26] Gen. 11.1–9, esp. 4–6.
[27] The occasional use of such architecture for minarets in the Islamic world (as at Samarra) would appear to support this interpretation.
[28] Gen. 28.10–17. Even the NRSV uses 'ladder' in the main text (v.12), though a footnote is added: 'or *stairway* or *ramp*'.

been abandoned in a basket on the Euphrates and rescued from there to become the founder of the dynasty of Akkad.[29] It would seem too much of a coincidence that the same fate had befallen Moses. While some of these historical elements are of no great importance either way, there are other apparent borrowings where the question of the religious significance of what is happening now required some sort of qualification.

To take a small example first, consider the effect the divine presence had on Moses' countenance. Modern translations speak of rays of light emanating from Moses' brow after his encounter with God on Sinai. Yet it turns out that Jerome's Vulgate 'mistranslation' may be right after all (where he speaks of horns). These duly (if puzzlingly) appeared in much subsequent Christian art, including Michelangelo's famous depiction.[30] The reason for now evaluating Jerome's work differently is because archaeology reveals that it was once common for ancient pagan priests to wear a bull's mask with horns before meeting with a divinity in its temple. While that is not

---

[29] His mother had been a priestess and he was initially raised by a gardener before eventually becoming king (2340–2284 BC). He should not be confused with the later kings of Assyria of the same name. Akkad was the first serious rival to Sumer. For text and commentary, Christopher B. Hays ed., *Hidden Riches: A Sourcebook for the Comparative Study of the Hebrew Bible and Ancient Near East* (Louisville, KY: Westminster John Knox Press, 2014), 113–19. Hays rightly observes that not only are the aims in telling the story rather different, but also that the mythic element does nothing to undermine the historicity of either figure.

[30] Ex.34.33–5. The Hebrew text can be read either way. Michelangelo's image is to be found in the church of San Pietro in Vincoli in Rome. It was originally intended as part of a tomb for Pope Julius II, commissioned in 1505. A greatly simplified version was finished in 1545.

enough evidence in itself to force a change of perspective, the bull does seem to have functioned as a symbol of divine power throughout the Middle East, including in Palestine. Already at Ur the divine is found represented by a bull's head adorned with a golden human beard and, perhaps not surprisingly, identified with the moon god given the curves of its horns.[31] Effectively, the bull was being used as a symbol of the life-giving, fruitful power of the deity. As such the image was also adopted for the Canaanite Baal, as can be seen at Ugarit. The survival of the image can be detected at various places in the Hebrew scriptures, among them in the story of the golden calf.[32] Bulls' horns on altars have also been found within Israel's borders, as at Megiddo. The point of the story would then still be that the glory of God was reflected upon Moses' face. But, instead of being mediated through light, it would now be indicated by those horns that had once characterised so many pagan deities. Even so, a major difference would remain: those horns are now presented as a miraculous gift rather than something intentionally worn.

Given that the Ten Commandments are the best-known section of the Pentateuch, quite naturally much has been made of parallels with the Code of Hammurabi found on a stele at Babylon. Above the cuneiform inscription the king is found represented as receiving these

---

[31] Originally made from gold and lapis lazuli, now in the Penn Museum, Philadelphia.
[32] For the story of the Golden Calf, Exodus 32. The text of Gen. 49.24 has been corrupted. However, it may contain a reference to 'Bull of Jacob', which would then constitute a powerful, contemporary metaphor for Yahweh as 'the Mighty One of Jacob'.

instructions symbolically through the gift of a ring and sceptre from the sun god Shamash (here understood as the god who brings illumination). An intriguing detail is the way in which the god's throne is set on a series of very small symbolic hills, presumably, as with Sinai, to indicate divine otherness or exaltation. Such a presupposed form of transmission explains the apodeictic or unconditional character of both pieces of legislation. The emphasis placed in both on the principle of the *lex talionis* or 'an eye for an eye' is often misunderstood. The intention was not vengeful but rather to limit the amount of equivalence or reparation allowed, so that subsequent blood feuds could be avoided: in other words, the avoidance of tit-for-tat where each exchange slightly ups the game. It is also worth noting that the earlier Code is vitiated throughout by class distinctions which is not so with the Law of Moses, apart, that is, from its treatment of slaves.[33] So the Mosaic legislation does represent a real advance, though it is worth adding that concern for the widow and orphan (which is such a marked feature of scripture)[34] is already anticipated as required of a ruler in a number of ancient codes.[35]

---

[33] For the complete text with scriptural parallels, Prichard, *The Ancient Near East*, 155–79. As one example of the difference, note edicts 197–8 and contrast Lev. 24.22: 'You shall have one law for the alien and for the citizen'.

[34] For example, Ex. 22.22; Deut. 10 18. The theme is also taken up in the New Testament, though qualified in important ways, in I Tim. 5.3–8.

[35] Parallels can be adduced from throughout the ancient Near-East and also from Egypt, long antedating biblical legislation. In the Ugaritic *Tale of Aqhat*, dating from c. 1350, the judge Danel is praised for his concern for the widow and orphan. In another Ugaritic work, *The Legend of King Kirta*, his son Yassib justifies rebellion against him on the grounds that he has failed to protect the poor, widow and orphan.

While it might in principle be possible to argue that, in cases such as those mentioned above, it is only the background frame that is borrowed, such a sharp distinction is hard to maintain, given that elements of imagery, morality and even explicitly religious content pass over from one to the other. Although sometimes exclusively hostile,[36] the more common pattern is one of interaction, with some shared assumptions nonetheless significantly modified in one direction or another. Even *tehom* in Genesis 1 must have developed out of more nuanced borrowings, given references elsewhere in the Hebrew canon to battles with forces hostile to creation. Such, for instance, is the usual explanation given for the huge water basin that stood outside the first temple.[37]

Indeed, the ritual and theology associated with the Jerusalem Temple is surely the most obvious indicator of considerable influence from the surrounding pagan culture. The temple was treated as a locus for divine presence in Israel no less than with temples in the wider pagan world. The same traditions of sacrifice were also adopted, and in both instances performed outside the building. Jewish legislation is extraordinarily detailed and includes holocaust or whole-burnt offerings. The more usual practice in both cases, however, was for 'communion' or shared offerings, in which most of the animal was eaten by priests and people but with the fat (and

---

[36] As in the interpretation noted above of the ziggurat given in the story of the Tower of Babel. Yet, as also noted earlier, such unqualified hostility was countered by the account of Jacob's Ladder.

[37] Called the 'brazen sea', it was thirty cubits in circumference: I Kings 7.23–6; 2 Chron. 4. 2–5. It appears to have celebrated a divine conquest over the waters which threatened to engulf creation.

sometimes also the bones) reserved for the divine.[38] Although myths were sometimes produced to explain why the gods were not given the best parts of the meat,[39] more interesting is the light the practice throws on how literally or otherwise the materiality of the gods was taken, for in effect they were only offered a good smell, the 'ambrosia' of the classical tradition.

While numerous theories have been put forward to explain the ubiquity of sacrificial practice, the simplest is surely also the most plausible: not that it was in general a form of appeasement (otherwise, why not always the best on offer?) but rather a way of seeking divine sanction for what was seen as in any case a questionable act of destruction. First, there was the appearance of usurping divine rights since, in killing the animal, a life-force was removed which it was universally acknowledged really belonged to the gods. Second, there may also have been a sense of betraying the familiar, an attack on creatures for whom the herders may well have become fond. Admittedly, the ancient practice of human sacrifice (such as at Ur and sometimes also within Israel) needs to be put on the other side. But not only are numbers rather difficult to determine, its outrageous character does need to be weighed alongside the often callous disregard for human life in the modern world. Thus, while there is no modern parallel to the ancient practice of the burial of servants along with

---

[38] The bones were included in pagan sacrifice, whereas in Israelite practice only the fat was offered. The justification given was that, like blood, fat was life-giving. See Lev. 3.16–17; 7.22–4. Probably, though, this was a later adaption of Jewish attitudes to blood.

[39] Usually with an element of trick involved, as in the classical story of Prometheus.

their masters (as at Ur), despite being wrongly motivated, sacrifice to prevent drought or floods does at one level make better moral sense than the millions sent to their deaths during the twentieth century for the political advancement of their rulers. Again, still contested is the extent of the influence of the Babylonian New Year or *akitu* festival on an annual re-enthronement ceremony within Israel for the king as the god's son. From a modern perspective one of its most interesting aspects of the rite was the way in which, at least within the Babylonian tradition, this involved the annual humiliation of the king, so that he would remember due humility before the gods.[40] There is surely a moral sensitivity there about the proper limits to the power of rulers that the modern world seems to have lost. To be clear, I am not defending human sacrifice in any way, only reminding readers that it would be quite wrong to suggest that the modern world is incontrovertibly better, given the absurdity of some of its ideas or the wickedness of some of its moral practices.

Concluding this brief survey, we may observe that the most important conclusion to draw is that the traditional picture of Judaism arising and developing in a self-contained manner is no longer tenable. There were real debts to the surrounding pagan world. At the same time,

---

[40] Similar practices seem to have been observed among the Aztecs. This is particularly revealing since it is certain that there could have been no cross-fertilisation of ideas (given the great distance between the two cultures in both time and space). For an attempt at a sympathetic analysis of Aztec religion, see my 'Human Sacrifice and Two Imaginative Worlds. Aztec and Christian: Finding God in Evil' in Julia Meszaros & Johannes Zachhuber eds., *Sacrifice and Modern Thought* (Oxford: Oxford University Press, 2013), 163–79.

this is not to deny the persistence of some continuing distinctive features.

Recognising an Experiential Dimension

But, in attempting a more sympathetic interpretation of ancient near-east religion, can we go further and speak of such religion as somehow also in contact with God? This is an important issue as the same question applies to other polytheistic systems still practised in today's world, most obviously Hinduism but also Aboriginal and Native American. I want to attempt an answer to this question in two stages; first, by considering whether any defensive strategies for polytheism can be offered by an unqualified monotheist like myself, and, second, by attending to the question of whether any experiential evidence can be found in support of a more sympathetic account.

Perhaps the first thing to note about ancient polytheistic systems is their fluidity in at least three directions. Except for within the shrine itself, in prayer and other such activity, a degree of caution is usually expressed regarding whether the appropriate deity has been identified. This emerges in the initial address where not only are various titles of that particular deity duly noted but a phrase is also usually added extending the address more widely, such as 'or by whatever other name it is lawful to name you'.[41] The second thing is that, over time, the role and extent of the authority of particular gods can

---

[41] Similar expressions are also found in Greco-Roman religion: for example, Aeschylus, *Agamemnon* 160; Apuleius, *Metamorphoses* 11.2; Macrobius, *Saturnalia* 3.9.10–11.

sometimes change. It is almost as though a decision had been taken to retire an older deity as a more appropriate, younger one is allowed to take its place. This is what happened in relations between El and Baal within the Canaanite pantheon. Once more like an executive officer to El as king of gods, eventually Baal became the Canaanite principal deity. El retreated even to the extent of simply becoming a general word for god.[42] Finally, there was a long tradition of cross-cultural comparison under which the gods of one society were matched against those of another, sometimes leading to modifications in one society or the other. The most extreme example of this phenomenon was the Roman pantheon where an almost perfect fit out of something quite different was eventually created by matching Latin deities with the Greek Olympian twelve. Not that the Greeks did not envisage doing much the same. In his *Histories*, the Greek historian Herodotus (484–25 BCE) makes several equations between Egyptian deities and the Greek gods. He even goes as far as to suggest that the Greek names were only invented as late as the poets Homer and Hesiod (wrongly, as it turns out).[43]

---

[42] As in the Hebrew Bible, or indeed in the Muslim religion where Allah is a term etymologically related to El.

[43] For expression of the general principle: *Histories* 2.50; for identification of Dionysus with the Egyptian Osiris, 2.144 (cf. 1.131). The decipherment of Linear B (the language of Mycenaean culture) by Michael Ventris and John Chadwick in 1952, led to the discovery that the Greek pantheon was very much older than had been previously thought. Even Dionysus was proved not to have been a later, foreign import, as classical Athens had claimed. For the general principle in a Latin writer: Pliny the Elder, *Natural History* II, 15: *nomina alia aliis gentibus* ('different names for different peoples').

That very fluidity means that seeing such gods operating at times as mediators of a single God becomes much easier. It would then turn out to be just one more variant on the already existing adaptability described above: in this case not just moving between two polytheistic deities but between them all and one unique being. Some readers may be horrified by the very suggestion and see in it a rather dangerous endorsement of idolatrous practice. But my proposal is not that such polytheistic beings should once again be worshipped, or that their separate existence be acknowledged. Rather, it is that it is possible to conceive of the single, unique God acting through the forms and symbolism deployed by polytheistic worshippers for a specific, more limited deity. One might compare the way in which, during the patristic period, the Jewish God was provided with elements of characterisation drawn from the Christian Trinitarian reality: for example, in the interpolation of a plural reality operating at the initial creation, or again in some specific member of the Trinity postulated as operating at some specific points in salvation history.[44]

One possible reason for continuing hesitation over such a partial endorsement is the often immoral character of such gods, but to acknowledge *some* mediation is scarcely to commit to the value of any particular cult as a whole. In addition, we need to be clear why such moral complexity existed. It was not just a matter of the gods being created in human likeness. There seems to have

---

[44] As with the use of the plural in Gen. 1.26 taken to refer to the Trinity, or the Lord God walking in the garden at 3.8 assumed to be the act of God the Son.

been a real attempt to reflect the totality of human experience. Such a complex metaphysical reality was used to provide some explanation for evil, in the purposes of the various gods understood to be at times in deep conflict with one another. Polytheism may thus be conceived as an alternative way of envisaging the relation between the divine and evil to what prevailed in later monotheistic thought,[45] where evil is seen either as organised by an alternative supernatural but inferior force or else as originating entirely from within the material and human world and thus most commonly as human sin.

Even so, can any experiential evidence be offered for such a mediating role? In a moment I would like to provide some plausible textual examples but first something needs to be said about complexity in symbolic representation. The shunting of such divinities into narrowly defined compartments is a common feature of much modern discussion. What is thereby ignored is the subtlety of polytheism, in its imaginative exploration of a range of options. So, for instance, modern pagans often write in defence of the notion of a Mother or Earth Goddess as though an immanent reality may be neatly contrasted with transcendent monotheism but this is altogether too simple an opposition. So too is the suggestion that male deities are characteristic of hunter gatherers and female of later agricultural settlements. As evidence against the latter division one may note that images of an earth goddess may date from as early as a hundred thousand years ago, that is, long before

---

[45] Individual gods were thus made more complex rather than setting a wholly good supernatural force against a wholly evil one.

agriculture. Again, the way in which such beings are commonly portrayed grasping their breasts need not necessarily be interpreted as representing concern for the harvest. Instead, it could be a sign of nurturing care for the family.[46] Equally, despite these roles, it is not uncommon to find some goddesses associated primarily with war, as with Anat, the sister and wife of Baal, or Athene, the principal goddess at Athens.

Similarly, art historians often write as though Christian borrowing of pagan images amounted to no more than a propaganda move, whereas in fact much more subtlety was involved. Admittedly, there is no doubt that Christian artists did borrow from images of Isis with her child Horus to portray the Christian Virgin and Child, just as Zeus provided a model for God the Father and Dionysus for the adult Jesus. But the Church Fathers detected something rather more than just an opportunity for propaganda from merely accidental parallels. For some at least certain features of Christianity had been anticipated by paganism.[47] So, although Christian theologians preferred to stress formal parallels, there seems little doubt that Egyptian worshippers did sometimes actually feel the care of Isis for them through such imagery. As one commentator observes, 'a person with a headache became Horus the Child, cared for by his mother, who herself became Isis'.[48] Again, rather than just describing as quaint

---

[46] Which would explain their presence primarily in the home.
[47] In a strategy known as *praeparatio evangelica*.
[48] Gary J. Shaw, *The Egyptian Myths* (London: Thames & Hudson, 2014), 9. Shaw observes a similar practice in death, as he continues: 'in death, the deceased transformed into various gods whilst transversing the after realm'.

the use of animal imagery in representations of Egyptian gods, we need to take some account of their likely underlying rationale. Animals which had once been seen as exclusively threatening and a source of anxiety now became images for the divine, partly because the otherness of divinity could be stressed in this way but partly also (and perhaps no less importantly) because it seemed to make their this-world equivalents more amenable to human concerns.[49] At Karnak, for example, one can find Amun represented as a mixture of ram and lion, while a contemporary hymn speaks of him as a snake and goose. Meanwhile Sobek was given the form of a crocodile. Although most pervasive in Egypt, the phenomenon was in fact common throughout the Middle East. Baal's identification with the bull has already been mentioned.

Of all ancient religions, ancient Egyptian can often appear the most bewildering. Sometimes such perplexity is not at all helped by specialists, where accuracy of detail is allowed to take precedence over overall coherence.[50] It is, therefore, a great relief to discover a different attitude emerging in some more recent writing. A good example is the work of Emily Teeter. Basing her argument on a wealth of supporting evidence, she detects a lively and active religion under which 'the gods were always there for the petitioners, and they were a constant comfort to their flock'.[51] The vast labour expended on

---

[49] In Egypt such creatures included the lion, snake, crocodile, bull, ram, jackal and falcon.
[50] As in attempts to differentiate between different versions belonging to different cities, for example Memphis or Heliopolis.
[51] Emily Teeter, *Religion and Ritual in Ancient Egypt* (Cambridge: Cambridge University Press, 2011), 76.

building the pyramids or the exclusion of ordinary folk from the everyday rituals of the temples should, therefore, not blind us to the way in which the common people nonetheless fully participated in shared myths and their implications. During their lives other ways of accessing the divinities were on offer.[52] In death not only were cheaper methods of mummification available for accessing the very literal Egyptian understanding of survival but also the same standards of judgement were applied to rich and poor alike.[53] Indeed, one reason why Akhenaten's introduction of monotheism never caught on and polytheism was quickly restored under his son Tutankhamun was because it produced too impersonal a religion. Every aspect was now mediated through the actions of the Pharaoh but not directly available to other worshippers.[54]

At this distance in time it is not possible to identify definitively where, if at all, God might be said to have been experienced, or in some sense legitimately be taken to have addressed members of some particular society. All we can say is that it does look as though this is sometimes a realistic possibility, whether we take the implicit acknowledgement made by the Hebrew scriptures in their occasional borrowing,[55] or the discovery made by modern

---

[52] Special side-chapels for ordinary folk were provided. The god could also be accessed during processions and even dedicatory tablets created in the open air. For types of response given by the god, 107–9; for stelae with hearing ears on them, 84.

[53] Drawing images of food or even reciting a list was deemed an acceptable substitute: Teeter, 130–1. Worshippers were even allowed to submit a corn mummy of Osiris.

[54] Teeter, *Religion and Ritual*, 182–96, esp. 184–87.

[55] The closest parallel is between *The Instruction of Amen-em-Opet* and Proverbs 22.17–24.22. For the text of the former, James B. Pritchard

believers of sentiments that seem very effectively to echo their own. Take, for instance, the following hymn in praise of Amun which might well have been written today: For humanity 'He created plants and cattle, fowl and fish to sustain them... For their sake he creates the daylight... and when they weep, he hearkens... It is He who watches over them by night and by day'. Indeed, his care even extends to the smallest of creatures. 'It is he who makes it possible for the mosquitoes to live together with the worms and fleas, who takes care of the mice in their holes, and keeps alive the beetles (?) in every tree'.[56] At the same time as making such comparisons we need to be on our guard against those who want to use them to indulge in reductionist strategies. So, for instance, despite repeated claims to the contrary, the resurrection of Christ cannot be subsumed as part of a more general Osiris myth. Apart from little signs of interest in the myth in the Palestine of Jesus' own day, Osiris was helped to return only for a day,[57] thereafter being left behind to rule the underworld.[58] A more important objective is surely to attempt to penetrate behind the ancient Egyptians' very different mythological way of thinking. A straining towards some deeper reality can perhaps thereby be detected.

---

ed., *The Ancient Near East: An Anthology of Texts and Pictures* (Princeton, NJ: Princeton University Press, 2011), 346–52.

[56] From *The Teaching for King Merikare* (Pharaoh who died in 2040 BCE); quoted in Shaw, *The Egyptian Myths*, 36.

[57] With the object of impregnating his sister Isis, and thus fathering Horus.

[58] Strictly speaking, not an underworld since it was situated at the other end of the sun's course.

Taking the rest of the Middle East more widely, I think that a similar point can be made. In their desire to present themselves as purely objective historians, biblical scholars have been reluctant to draw any conclusion about the status of Mesopotamian experience of the divine. A rare exception is the Assyriologist, H. W. F. Saggs.[59] He did not hesitate to conclude a very careful analysis with the observation that 'Mesopotamian religion may also ... have been one vehicle by which came knowledge of a finite part of the infinity of the divine'.[60] At the same time, he identified various distinctive contributions from Israel.[61] That of course needs to be recognised but so too do comparable movements elsewhere. Although intense devotion to divinity does not guarantee that divinity's existence, there is no shortage of examples of individuals entering into such deep commitments. The staring eyes of the priest with bull's horns whom we mentioned earlier does suggest (at least to me) intense, longing devotion. Again, just as there are Egyptian cases of people giving up everything in pursuit of one god,[62] so Babylonia offers us an extraordinary example in the case of King Nabonidus (556–39 BCE). He seems to have had a special devotion to the moon god, Sin. For his sake he left Babylonia for ten years in order to perform the god's

---

[59] In his obituary (*Independent* 26 Dec 2005) Saggs (1920–2005) was described as 'one of the outstanding Assyriologists of his generation'.

[60] H. W. F. Saggs, *The Encounter with the Divine in Mesopotamia and Israel* (London: Athlone Press, 1978), 188. For another scholar supporting him on the basis of Babylonian penitential hymns, 172.

[61] Mainly in terms of an eventually stronger transcendence and universality, though he notes that, ironically, the former put Israel at a further distance from Christianity:187–8.

[62] Simut in relation to the goddess Mut: Teeter, 102.

rites more effectively at places such as Harran and Ur, and even in Arabia.

Mention has already been made of influences upon the early traditions of Israel and on the way in which the story of Moses is told. This could be augmented by parallels in the way prophecy was practised and in the reflections of wisdom literature.[63] But one new factor that more recent scholarship has introduced is the possibility that the very idea of Yahweh was itself initially borrowed from local pagan tradition, and thereafter developed from this base. What is suggested is that Moses' notion of Yahweh probably originated in an encounter with a polytheist deity who was a storm god, with this happening perhaps somewhere to the south of Edom.[64] As such, it indicates a marked change in perspective from half a century or so ago when it looked as though archaeology was offering progressive confirmation of the early history of Israel almost as the Bible records it.[65] There is now much more doubt given the lack of any decisive evidence of the nation's sojourn in Egypt. A much more likely scenario, it is suggested, is that at most a minority was involved and

---

[63] Saggs, *Encounter with the Divine*, for prophetic parallels, 384–402; for wisdom literature, 343–83.
[64] Thomas Römer, *The Invention of God* (Cambridge: Mass.: Harvard University Press, 2015). 24–85. The title of the book is unfortunate but Römer merely intends 'a progressive construction arising out of a particular tradition' (4). For an Conservative Jew willing to contemplate similar possibilities, see Benjamin D. Somner, *Revelation and Authority: Sinai in Jewish Scripture and Tradition* (New Haven, CT: Yale University Press, 2015).
[65] As, for example, in John Bright's classic work, *History of Israel*, first published in 1959 and currently in its fourth edition (2000).

that it is this group that eventually persuaded the people as a whole to accept Yahweh as their god.

For quite a number of generations some degree of interchangeability with El, Baal and some foreign gods such as Chemosh probably existed.[66] What made the difference was the defeat of Judah and the exiling of its leading citizens. While imperial expansion led other nations to a position more like henotheism,[67] the Jewish response was to see Yahweh as Lord whatever the situation, and so as Lord over all space and time. This is the position one finds reflected in the writings of Second Isaiah. Unfortunately, in the process he speaks contemptuously of typical near-east patterns of ritual behaviour.[68] Not only is his account unfair but the form of argument he deploys could have been applied equally well in reverse 'without any distortion'. After all, Yahweh had been traditionally presupposed to live 'inside, or at the least in close association with, a decorated chest made of acacia wood'.[69] Yet, as noted earlier, it is not impossible that the prophet's depiction of Cyrus as 'anointed' for his role by God represents some sort of implicit acknowledgement of influence from Persian Zoroastrianism, the

---

[66] The case is argued at length in Mark S. Smith, *God in Translation: Deities in Cross Cultural Discourse in the Biblical World* (Grand Rapids, MI: Eerdmans, 2008), 91–130. Chapter 1 had already established the pattern for the Middle East more generally (37–90).

[67] As an empire expanded, only its god was seen to count, as with Marduk and Babylonia. Usually called 'henotheism' after a term coined by Max Müller, Smith proposes substituting 'summotheism' since subordinate deities were not wholly discounted: 163–69.

[68] For example, Isaiah 44.9–20. Not entirely fair since the ancient view was only that the deity assumed temporary habitation of the image, not that it was ever wholly confined within it.

[69] Saggs, *The Encounter with the Divine*, 15.

nearest thing to monotheism that the Middle East had hitherto seen.[70] So even here, as monotheism at last emerges, one might speak of debt as well as hostility and critique, and so of a more complicated dynamic. In all events, it is a pattern that continues with such indirect mediation or 'translatability' still acknowledged centuries later at Alexandria.[71] In short, I would seem by no means alone in recognising such divine action more widely. Even so, these exceptions are few and far between.[72] So it cannot be denied that I am advocating the necessity for a fundamentally different approach in the light of what we now know both about the history of Judaism and that of the surrounding cultures. That stressed, I want to now turn to the second part of this chapter and consider the impact on Christianity of paganism in the classical world.

Mystery Religions and Classical Philosophy in Relation to Christianity

In considering the origins of Christianity it was once fashionable to identify non-Jewish factors such as Gnosticism.[73] Although for most scholars it is now seen as sufficient to appeal to the internal complexity of Judaism, such conclusions apply only to its original biblical context. There is still

---

[70] Apart, that is, from the exceptional case of Akhenaten in Egypt. If so, Israeli's God could then be seen as acting through Ahura mazda, the Zoroastrian deity.
[71] For a couple of examples, see *The Letter of Aristeas* (16) and Aristobolus, Smith, 300–6.
[72] Less to do with the implausibility or otherwise of the claim and more about the reluctance of scholars of the Bible and ancient world to penetrate beyond conventional historical questions.
[73] As in Rudolph Bultmann's interpretation of John's Gospel.

the question of what happened once Christianity moved out into the wider classical world, where it did indeed undergo various transformations. Two of these will now be considered in some detail. First, and of lesser significance, there is the influence of mystery cults. Second, there is the impact of pagan philosophy. In both cases, recent scholarship has delivered some important insights.

The Impact of Greek Religion and Mystery Cults

Before exploring the impact of mystery cults on the shaping of Christian mission and practice, it will be useful first to place classical paganism in the wider context of its own distinctive history, which runs parallel with what has already been discussed in respect to the Middle East. Classical deities and the various roles assigned to them are for the most part better known. However, their remarkable effectiveness at maintaining prominence in subsequent centuries and even today, despite the more general marked decline in classical learning,[74] has its undoubted disadvantages: the widespread assumption that only purely human values are represented. To some degree this has been reflected in the history of scholarly study across the twentieth century. At the century's beginning Greek religion was located at the margins of culture, in the fertility rites detected by the so-called Cambridge Ritualists.[75] From the 1960s onwards,

---

[74] While knowledge of the original literature has declined, its place has been maintained through more modern media such as film or comic.

[75] Most obviously in the work of Jane Ellen Harrison but also in that of Cornford and Murray: J. E. Harrison, *Prolegomena to the Study of Greek Religion* (1903); F. M. Cornford, *The Origin of Attic Comedy* (1914);

however, change was evident in recognition of the key role played by religion in the functioning of the Greek city.[76] But it was only really from the 1990s onwards that this perspective too was acknowledged to be inadequate and religion seen to ground every aspect of life.[77] Even the move from the earlier semi-abstract *xoana* to more human representations of the gods does not necessarily represent retreat from a more religious perspective. They could simply constitute different ways of acknowledging divine difference, the former through utilising abstraction, the latter through an impossible beauty or perfection of form.[78] As one major survey of ancient Athens observes, 'myth and religion are pervasive, inescapable, all-shaping ... Religion was so close to the Athenians that it was easy to live with, like a comfortable old coat'.[79] The challenge to analyse this pervasiveness has resulted in a veritable explosion of writing on the subject.

While it is true that Roman religion continues to receive less attention, it does also raise some distinctive

---

G. Murray, *Four Stages of Greek Religion* (1912), increased to *Five* in 1925.

[76] Well represented by Walter Burkert, *Greek Religion* (1985) but for an early anticipation V. Ehrenberg, *The Greek State* (1960).

[77] For two helpful general surveys: Emily Kearns, *Ancient Greek Religion: A Sourcebook* (Oxford: Wiley-Blackwell, 2010); Esther Eidinow & Julia Kindt eds., *The Oxford Handbook of Ancient Greek Religion* (Oxford: Oxford University Press, 2015).

[78] The use of *xoana* continued into the later period. The surpassing beauty of Praxiteles' statue of Aphrodite at Cnidus might be read, as it was at the time, as indicating unattainable perfection: Julia Kindt, *Rethinking Greek Religion* (Cambridge: Cambridge University Press, 2012),155–89. For a discussion of *xoana*, A. A. Donohue, *Xoana and the Origins of Greek Sculpture* (Atlanta, GA: Scholars Press, 1988).

[79] Robert Parker, *Polytheism and Society at Athens* (Oxford: Oxford University Press, 2015), 452, 453.

issues of its own; for example, decline in the use of auguries, major reform movements such as those of Augustus, the impact of foreign cults and the role of emperor worship.[80] It is often observed how fortunate Christianity was to be promulgated at the time it was, with a large part of the world at peace under an empire which enjoyed easy communication and travel. It is also possible to point to other deeper features, among which may be observed a deep longing among many for a more personal kind of religion, something which one finds reflected in both a new prominence for mystery cults and a new type of philosophy which bears close analogues with religion. It is the mystery cults which must first engage our attention.

Mystery cults have a long history in the religious phenomena of the classical world. From the fifth century BCE, Euripides *Bacchae* offers an extraordinarily powerful tragic drama of the results of King Pentheus' attempts to spy upon the secret Dionysian countryside rituals of his mother and other followers. Best known, however, in the ancient world were undoubtedly the annual Eleusinian rites in honour of Demeter and her daughter Persephone that took place about twenty kilometres from Athens and to which all Greek speakers were invited.[81] That inclusive aspect, as well as the lively processions from Athens, undoubtedly implies a very corporate activity. Yet it should also be noted that, although many

---

[80] For a helpful general survey, J. H. W. G. Leibeschuetz, *Continuity and Change in Roman Religion* (Oxford: Clarendon Press, 1979).
[81] Even slaves could be initiated. A degree of revolt against hierarchy was encouraged and Lycurgus even attempted to legislate that all alike should go on foot (Parker, *Polytheism and Society*, 349–50).

aspects of the liturgy were indeed social, the culminating experience appears to have been much more personal: probably some heightened awareness of the possibility of surviving death. Given the number and range of initiates, it is astonishing that no precise information about the key ritual moments survives.[82] Perhaps even doubters retained respect for what they had experienced. Plutarch has been taken to imply that various forms of disorientation were created before an individual was then provided with some more positive vision. One modern commentator describes this in terms of the initiate having 'met the goddess and experienced her grace and power at first hand'.[83] Another more cautiously proposes that 'it worked by making familiar myth more vivid and immediate to the worshippers than did any other Greek cult'.[84] Certainly, in the third main ancient form of mystery cult, Orphic rites, even less is known, despite a profusion of reference to individual initiation in gold tablets discovered at various burial sites.[85]

What changes with the post-Alexandrian Hellenistic world is not then the first appearance of mystic cults as such but rather their greater number and popularity.

---

[82] Some have suggested something as simple as the vision of a new blade of corn, others some form of dramatic performance.
[83] Hugh Bowden, *Mystery Cults in the Ancient World* (London: Thames & Hudson, 2010), 48. The details are deduced by Burkert from Plutarch, fr. 168, although Plutarch, like Pausanias, does not offer a direct description anywhere.
[84] Parker, *Polytheism and Society*, 360.
[85] There is a not altogether complimentary reference in Plato's *Republic* (364 BCE). Most of the texts come from Italy and are in hexameter verse, offering advice on the journey through death. For further discussion, Bowden, *Mystery Cults*, 137–55.

Although Rome initially tried to impose some form of control on new introductions from the east,[86] eventually they were to prove as strong in the capital as elsewhere, with Cybele or the Great Mother and Mithras among the best known.[87] In attempting to explain their new prominence, some point to a world that felt itself more under the absolute control of fate and so desirous of release. But I doubt whether there is a need to look any further than the change in the political scene, with major decisions now removed and far from local control.[88] While emperor worship was popular,[89] at the same time its prevalence did underline how distant the forces determining the individual's life often were.

---

[86] In 186 BCE the Senate banned the Bacchanalia (the Roman name for the Dionysian mysteries), and the historian Livy also attacked them in the following century.

[87] The Magna Mater was welcomed because, according to a Sibylline oracle of 205 BCE, her arrival would help in the defeat of the Carthaginians. Attitudes became more complicated when she came to be associated with a consort Attis and the rituals now included castration of her priests. For further details, Mary Beard, John North & Simon Price eds., *Religions of Rome* (Cambridge: Cambridge University Press, 1998), II, 43–49. Mithras did not arrive until the first century AD and eventually became especially popular among the military. At the beginning of the twentieth century the French scholar, Franz Cumont, proposed a Persian origin and strong parallels with Christianity but both notions are now widely challenged.

[88] In his book *Hellenistic Religions: An Introduction* (New York: Oxford University Press, 1987), Luther H. Martin makes central to his analysis a distant Ptolemaic structure to the universe, coupled with the attempt, by way of compensation, to revive ancient female chthonic deities: 6–10.

[89] The cult expressed gratitude for a more peaceful and safer world. So it is not surprising that the initiative for new temples in honour of Rome or one of its emperors frequently came from the locality itself rather than as an imperial imposition from outside.

It would be quite wrong to think of earlier Greek religion as devoid of personal piety. Exceptions to the more common formulaic prayers were by no means unknown. Examples would include some of the so-called Homeric Hymns.[90] Likewise, it is not just to philosophers such as Xenophanes (d. 475 BCE) or Plato (427–347 BCE) that one must appeal to find critiques of myth. Moral reservations are also used to justify modification of myth in some of the poetry of Pindar (d. 438 BCE).[91] Yet Pindar and the Homeric Hymns cannot be entirely separated from their social context,[92] whereas by the time of the Hellenistic age more unqualifiedly personal forms of address were undoubtedly becoming quite common. A famous example is the *Hymn to Zeus* from the Stoic philosopher Cleanthes (331–232 BCE).[93] A recent phenomenon is the way in which contemporary scholars of Roman religion also now more readily admit the existence

---

[90] The *Homeric Hymn to Demeter* ends on a more personal note (lines 471–95) which may well imply that the author had been inducted into the mystery. One modern editor of the text does not hesitate to draw parallels with Christianity, not only in the poem's reference to wheat but also in the way in which a more intimate relation to the divine is substituted for earlier approaches: Helene P. Foley ed., *The Homeric Hymn to Demeter* (Princeton, NJ: Princeton University Press, 1993), 150–51.

[91] The subtlety of Pindar can be seen in his various modifications: for example, in *Olympians* 1 and 9.29–39.

[92] As in the Hymns' association with cultic centres, and Pindar's writing connecting with the great athletic festivals.

[93] Available in Mark Kiley ed. *Prayer from Alexander to Constantine: A Critical Anthology* (London: Routledge, 1997), 133–38. The whole section on pagan prayer is invaluable, not least in highlighting some of its complexities: 121–204, esp. 123–27. The original, together with a translation, is also available in Constantine A. Trypanis ed., *The Penguin Book of Greek Verse* (Harmondsworth: Penguin, 1971), 283–85.

of similar personal expressions across the same period.[94] But perhaps most pertinent here is a work which takes us back to the Greek world, the novel of Apuleius (c. 124–170 CE) commonly known as *The Golden Ass*. Superficially an engaging story of metamorphosis, it is also intended to recommend the mystery cult of Isis, in which the author was himself inducted. The author's own experience is reflected in the account of the hero's final initiation. The goddess speaks to him in a dream:

"Here I am, Lucius, roused by your prayers. I am the mother of the world of nature, mistress of all the elements, first-born in this realm of time. I am the loftiest of deities, queen of departed spirits, foremost of heavenly dwellers, the single embodiment of all gods and goddesses. I order with my nod the luminous heights of heaven, the healthy sea breezes, the sad silences of the infernal dwellers. The whole world worships this single godhead under a variety of shapes and liturgies and titles... I am here out of pity for your misfortunes. I am here to lend you kindly support. End now your weeping, abandon your lamentation, set aside your grief, for through my providence your day of salvation is now dawning ..." When she had reached the close of her sacred prophecy, that invincible deity retired to keep her own company. Without delay I was at once released from sleep. With mingled emotions of fear and joy I arose, bathed in sweat, utterly bemused by so vivid an epiphany of the powerful goddess... At that moment the clouds of dark night were dispersed, and a golden sun arose. My personal

---

[94] Jörg Rüpke opens his work *Religion of the Romans* (Cambridge: Polity, 2007) by considering how an ode of Horace might reflect genuine religious expression (1.30). A few pages later he draws attention to the way in which in the late third century BCE Scipio Africanus was alleged to have spent all night praying to Jupiter in his Temple: 3–5, 13–14.

sense of well-being seemed to be compounded by a general atmosphere of joy... For a sunny, windless day had suddenly succeeded the previous day's frost, so that even the birds were enticed by the spring warmth to burst tunefully into sweet harmonies, as with their charming address they soothed the mother of the stars, the parent of the seasons, the mistress of the entire world.[95]

It has been suggested that such rituals resembled some forms of modern charismatic worship.[96] While perhaps true in some cases, a more interesting question here is whether it is possible to detect early Christianity adapting some patterns of approach from the mystery cults in order to make its own mission more effective in the wider classical world. I would suggest that this was indeed so. While in the New Testament the baptism offered in Jesus' name and the teaching associated with it were treated as offered openly to all, notable is the degree to which in subsequent patristic literature baptism is presented as initiation into something which cannot otherwise be fully known and experienced. So, not only was a long period of preparation required but also casual unbaptised observers were forbidden access to observe the eucharist.[97] Little wonder, then, that Pliny the Younger, as governor of Bithynia, found himself investigating claims of strange, secretive practices among the

---

[95] Apuleius, *The Golden Ass*, XI. 5-7. trans & ed. P. G. Walsh (Oxford: Oxford University Press, 1994). 220-2.
[96] Bowden, *Mystery Cults*, 212–21.
[97] For a general history, Everett Ferguson, *Baptism in the Early Church: History, Theology and Liturgy in the First Five Centuries* (2009); for the kind of language used in the fourth century, Edward Yarnold, *The Awe-Inspiring Rites of Initiation* (1994).

Christians.[98] That being so, it requires little stretch of the imagination to see Gnosticism as a challenge to Christianity precisely because it too was engaging in a similar, though as it turned out, less successful exercise. Although not strictly a mystery religion, it did offer a secret way but mostly through knowledge rather than experience.[99] Christianity combined the two more effectively. Even so, it was often as a substitute for some earlier mystery cult that it was first recognised. This is particularly true of the large number of sites in which we find a church built on top of what had originally been a mithraeum, most notably in the famous church of San Clemente in Rome. Built c. 200 CE, the mithraeum was eventually blocked up when a church was built over it in the fifth century, which in its turn became a crypt for the present twelfth century church. All three edifices can now be viewed.

Of course, this is only one relatively small aspect of Christian practice. I have allowed my examination here to extend more widely to changing estimates of the impact of classical paganism, precisely because newer approaches better explain why Christian conversions moved relatively slowly in the ancient world. Missionaries can now be seen to have encountered real religious belief and experience in the pagan world. So it was only as greater stress was placed on mystical experience that it too could be seen as a real competitor. However, even more important and certainly far deeper in its influence was classical philosophy.

---

[98] But he found no evidence: *Epistle* 10.96.
[99] Some writers on Gnosticism do find some strong parallels, for example Kurt Rudolph, *Gnosis* (Edinburgh: T & T Clark, 1983), 214–20; 285–94.

Philosophy as Religious; Theurgy as Sacramental

In reaching out to the wider classical world, Christianity also faced one obvious difficulty: its lack of philosophical sophistication. So, it is scarcely surprising that its advocates needed to engage seriously with pagan philosophy in order to determine how the imaginative language of scripture might be translated into more abstract intellectual categories. Fortunately, the dominant thinking of the time in Stoicism and in Middle- and later Neo-Platonism was fundamentally sympathetic to religious belief.[100] The founder of Neo-Platonism, Plotinus (204–70 CE) in particular combined suggestions he found in a number of Plato's dialogues (especially the *Republic*, *Parmenides* and *Timaeus*) into the notion of divinity flowing hierarchically through three graded aspects of the One, Mind and World Soul that offered some obvious parallels to the Christian doctrine of the Trinity: with the Father as One or Source, the Son as Mind and the Holy Spirit as the immanent World Soul. Not that the relationship was an entirely straightforward one. Most Christian writers were loath to acknowledge their debt. Instead, they commonly spoke of the material they borrowed as itself having been borrowed earlier by pagans from

---

[100] Stoicism began in the early third century BCE with Zeno. It is best known for its stress on morality and its immanent notion of the divine Logos. In the period known as Middle Platonism (dating from the first century BCE to the third CE), followers of Plato were often happy to combine ideas from Plato and from Stoicism. Representatives include Antiochus of Ascalon, Philo, Plutarch and Numenius of Apamea. Although Plotinus was the originator of Neo-Platonism, other figures are relevant to the discussion which follows, among them Porphyry, Iamblichus and Proclus.

Judaism; similarly, with apparent parallels in pagan myth.[101] The *Praeparatio Evangelica* of Eusebius of Caesarea (d. 339 CE) is an obvious case in point.[102]

Nonetheless, the debt did indeed run deep. While there was reluctance to introduce a non-biblical philosophical term at the Council of Nicaea in 325 CE as a way of resolving internal disagreements,[103] in the second century the Apostolic Fathers had already developed their apologia for faith in part by deploying philosophical ideas.[104] In the third the two great teachers at Alexandria, Clement and Origen, were so deeply imbued with the ideas of pagan philosophy that they are commonly referred to as the so-called 'Christian Platonists of Alexandria'.[105] Nor was the pattern to change later. Ambrose used Cicero and Stoicism to develop his account

---

[101] The difference can be seen in attitudes to the Virgin Birth. Whereas a modern defender might stress difference from pagan myth, a patristic writer is more likely to see such myth as anticipatory, intended to undergird the doctrine's plausibility.

[102] For claims of Greek theft, see, for example, X.13.14–15.52. Over 70 per cent of the work consisted of quotations from pagan writers. While this may look like an attempt at fairness, where it is possible to check, bias is noticeable: for example, in select quotation used to imply that Porphyry approved of animal sacrifice.

[103] In the term *homoousios*, 'of the same substance as'.

[104] In Justin Martyr, Plato is assumed to have learnt from Moses, including in his mention in the *Timaeus* of a cross-like structure to support the creation: Justin Martyr, *First Apology*, 59.

[105] Compare Charles Bigg, *The Christian Platonists of Alexandria* (Bampton Lectures for 1886). The traditional account of Origen's Platonism has been challenged by Mark Edwards in *Origen Against Plato* (Aldershot: Ashgate, 2002). Edwards sees him as essentially a biblical theologian, but Maurice Wiles remained unconvinced: *Journal of Theological Studies* 55 (2004), 340–43.

of Christian ethics,[106] while a little later comes a Platonist approach to the doctrine of the Trinity from Augustine.[107] Although some like Tertullian challenged the close linkage,[108] the final result can be seen in the theology of Aquinas where the Bible is read through a distinctly philosophical lens that has no difficulty in detecting major elements of classical metaphysics within scripture itself. To give but two examples, there is his reinterpretation of God's revelation at the Burning Bush as the equation of divine essence and existence,[109] while immutability is found in a prophetic assertion of divine constancy.[110] However, both passages had originally meant no such thing.

From such results it is sometimes argued that the later church betrayed its roots, as in the German church historian, Adolph von Harnack's famous contrast between the simple truths of the original gospel and its dogmatic elaboration under the influence of Greek philosophy.[111] Although this is not the place to argue the issue, it would seem to me one of Christianity's great strengths that it faced the challenge of ancient philosophy and was thus enabled to deepen its vision. What can be done here,

---

[106] Ambrose even gives his work the same title as Cicero's original, *De officiis*.
[107] In the fifteen books of *De Trinitate* c. 417 CE.
[108] As in his famous question, 'What has Athens to do with Jerusalem?' *Prescriptions against Heretics*, 7. For a very different view, Augustine, *Confessions* 7.9.
[109] Ex. 3.14: God said to Moses, 'I AM WHO I AM'. Nowadays usually interpreted as an assertion of consistency or of freedom ('I will be who I will be').
[110] Malachi 3.6: 'I the Lord do not change'.
[111] In his *Dogmengeschichte* (*History of Dogma*) of 1894.

though, is note how what was imported was in fact less alien than has been traditionally depicted. Two recent changes in scholarly understanding have quite transformed the pagan philosophy of the time into a much more sympathetic reality. There was, therefore, good reason why Christian theologians found the move so attractive. The first concerns what was meant by philosophy in the ancient world. It is now contended that it was of its very nature religious. The second is the challenge to the long-standing claim that such philosophy eventually degenerated into magic and irrationality.

The first change of perspective is largely the work of one man, the gifted French academic Pierre Hadot (1922–2010). Basically, his claim is that ancient philosophy should not be understood against the backdrop of modern. Partly because of the role it was assigned in the middle ages as conceptual handmaid to theology and partly because of the modern academy's love in any case of the conceptual model, philosophy is now conducted quite differently.[112] But for Socrates the aim was 'to form people and to transform souls' and that is why dialogue formed such an integral part in his understanding of its role.[113] It then became a pattern to be followed by subsequent thought, as can be seen in the primary aims of the Stoics.[114] A careful study of physics, for example, was included in their proposed curriculum, not primarily

---

[112] Pierre Hadot, *Philosophy as a Way of Life* (Oxford: Blackwell, 1995), 31–32.
[113] Pierre Hadot, 'Preface' in *L'Enseignement oral de Platon* (Paris: Cerf, 2006), 11.
[114] Hadot, *Philosophy as Way of Life*, 265: Peace of mind, inner freedom and a cosmic consciousness.

because of any conceptual issues raised but because such knowledge could contribute towards generating a more universal point of view which they saw as so essential to the good life.[115] Such a pattern of practice was then continued into the Christian era in later forms of Platonism and Stoicism. The result was that their concerns came quite close to those of Christianity.[116]

These general aims also brought with them some further parallel developments. Among them was a form of writing which can easily be misread from a modern perspective, and that is writing which sounds like psychological biography but is really intended to elicit a spiritual response. One example Hadot pursues at length is the *Meditations* of the Stoic emperor Marcus Aurelius. Read by many modern commentators as the work of a depressive with considerable disdain for the world, Hadot argues that the emperor's negative comments should be read only in relation to his more positive comments: as a way of making the workings of providence sound all the more impressive.[117] Likewise, during his inaugural lecture at the College de France Hadot used the research of Pierre Courcelle to suggest that even Augustine's famous conversion story was not intended primarily as a piece of autobiography at all but rather as a means of encouraging readers to reflect on where they themselves stood. Thus,

---

[115] Ibid., 94.
[116] Seen, for example, in later philosophy's concern with providence: George Boys-Stones, 'Providence and Religion in Middle Platonism' in Esther Eidinow, Julia Kindt & Robin Osborne, (eds.) *Theologies of Ancient Greek Religion* (Cambridge: Cambridge University Press, 2016), 317–38.
[117] Ibid., 179–205. He was Emperor 161–80 CE.

the fig tree represented the 'mortal shadow of sin' and the child's voice God's call potentially to any of us, including, of course, Augustine himself.[118] Again, both Christian and pagan philosopher alike were concerned enough to respond to authoritative texts by giving them, if necessary, new and pertinent meanings. Hence the reason why Neo-Platonism could feel itself justified in giving very different interpretations of Plato from what modern scholars might suggest; so too why Augustine does not hesitate to impose a metaphysical meaning on one of the psalms where a more innocent interpretation would once have held sway.[119] In short, both pagan and Christian were engaged in similar strategies in their search for underlying truth, and that is why so much of the philosophy of the time could enter into Christianity's conception of itself, even if not always self-consciously.

The second major change seeks to reverse the conclusions of a famous book by E. R. Dodds, *The Greeks and the Irrational* (1951), in which his argument culminates in suggesting that even that most rational and admired aspect of Greek thought, the philosophy of Plato and Aristotle, ended up in the late Empire being reduced to the justification of superstition and magic. *De Mysteriis*, a work by one of the later Neo-Platonists, Iamblichus (245–325 CE), is described as 'a manifesto of irrationalism, an assertion that the road to salvation is found not in reason but in ritual'.[120] Dodds' general verdict on the

---

[118] Ibid., 49–70, esp. 51–52.
[119] The Latin 'in idipsum' in Psalm 4.9 ('at that very moment') becomes 'the self-same God': *Philosophy*, 3; cf. *Confessions* 9.4.11
[120] E. R. Dodds, *The Greeks and the Irrational* (Berkeley: University of California Press, 1951), 286–87.

practice known as theurgy, his negative judgement was very widely endorsed by an earlier generation of experts on Neo-Platonism.[121] Theurgy is the term used to refer to a wide range of practices including visits to oracles, divinisation, astrology and finding hidden meanings in texts. While literally meaning only 'divine work' or 'action', all of these activities had the potential to be interpreted as the magical manipulation of the divine. However, in more recent years that type of analysis has been challenged as more sympathetic consideration has been given to Iamblicus's work, in part because of the considerable influence it exercised on the Emperor Julian (361–63 CE) and his attempt to revive paganism.

While still accepting a sharp contrast with the thought of Plotinus and his pupil and biographer, Porphyry,[122] Gregory Shaw, for example, argues that Iamblicus in fact clearly distinguished his own position from astrology and sorcery.[123] Perhaps as a result of accepting a deeper immersion in matter than Plotinus had allowed,[124] he argued that, by attending to the language inherent in matter in token, symbol and sign,[125] human beings could ease the process of their ascent even as the gods descended towards them. In effect, one could align oneself with the will of the World Soul by careful attendance to

---

[121] For example, J. Rist, 'Mysticism and transcendence in later Neoplatonism', in *Hermes* 92 (1964), 225: 'trend towards irrationalism' which he sees as beginning with Porphyry.

[122] Gregory Shaw, *Theurgy and the Soul: The Neoplatonism of Iamblichus* (Kettering: Angelico Press, 1995, 2nd ed., 2014), 13–15.

[123] Ibid., 191, 243.

[124] Whereas for Plotinus part of the soul remained unembodied, for Iamblichus the descent was complete: 13, 25.

[125] Ibid., 183–91.

being receptive to the symbolism immanent in such things as numbers, statues and stars.[126] A more recent book by Crystal Addey doubts whether quite so sharp a contrast should be drawn between earlier and later Neo-Platonism, or indeed even with Plato himself. After all, Plato acknowledged a major role for the Delphic oracle in the life of Socrates. Even if the evidence on Plotinus is less clear, his pupil Porphyry carefully gathered material on the effectiveness of various shrines.[127] In that connection, although much modern literature on Delphi remains quite dismissive,[128] at least one contemporary scholar has suggested that, if the focus is allowed to shift away from questions of prophecy, it becomes possible to read many of the exchanges which took place at the shrine in a positive, religious light.[129]

Whether such a proposal is accepted or not, a not dissimilar subtlety in the identification of symbolism in nature is proposed by these ancient authorities. The rich

---

[126] Ibid., 57, 162–72.
[127] Porphyry is seen as not far distant (128–42). Even Plotinus, despite not mentioning theurgy (173), can be given a more sympathetic interpretation (149, 290): Crystal Addey, *Divination and Theurgy in Neoplatonism: Oracles of the Gods* (London: Routledge, 2014).
[128] In Joseph Fontenrose's study of the six hundred surviving questions and answers, only those concerned with ritual are deemed veridical: *The Delphic Oracle: Its Responses and Operations* (Berkeley: University of California Press, 1978).
[129] Roger Lipsey, *Have You Been to Delphi: Tales of the Ancient Oracle for Modern Minds* (Albany: State University of New York Press, 2001). Note his conclusion: 'The Delphic oracle did quite well, after all, in reaching to the extremity of our natures, and then beyond to discover a spoken word full of paradox and truth' (257). For another positive but rather different evaluation of Delphi as a 'sense-making mechanism', see Michael Scott, *Delphi* (Princeton, NJ: Princeton University Press, 2014), esp. 9–30.

allusiveness of the divine ideas discovered through ritual is used to argue against any sharp contrast between theory and practice.[130] Even Plato presents Socrates discovering in a dream a line of Homer with such a hidden code.[131] Again, the fact that we are in effect presented with a form of intellectual purification that is a life-long endeavour makes Iamblichus less distant from Plotinus than might initially have been supposed.[132] Although many of the assumptions about such divine coding in the world will remain inherently strange to the modern mind despite the best efforts of Shaw and Addey, it is intriguing to note that both authors draw parallels with wider religious practice. Addey prefers to look towards eastern transcendental meditation techniques,[133] Shaw finds resonances in a wider Christian sacramentalism.[134] It is the latter comparison which seems the more plausible of the two but, either way, the important point is that what these new insights demonstrate is that it was not a case of pagan philosophy being in flight from reason. Rather, it was a case of seeking an appropriate natural theology, supplemented by a sacramental view of the world. If so, their aims were not too dissimilar after all from the Christian writers of the time.

---

[130] Ibid., 64–71, 181–89.
[131] Ibid., 59–60; Plato, *Crito* 44B; Homer, *Iliad* 9.363. The surprising treatment of Homer as a religious text is well explored in R. Lamberton, *Homer the Theologian: Neoplatonist Allegorical Reading and the Growth of the Epic Tradition* (Berkeley: University of California Press, 1986).
[132] Ibid., 25, 194. Effectively, the aim is to so align one's perspective that divine descent on the individual can become a reality.
[133] Ibid., 187, following John Dillon.
[134] Shaw, *Theurgy and the Soul*, 271.

If both my general contentions are true (as I believe they are), we may see influence from ancient philosophy then as the enrichment of Christianity rather than its perversion. This is not to say that every conclusion drawn was right. Quite a number of modern Christian theologians, for example, argue that it is necessary to jettison immutability in order to defend a more involved God. But the point would be that the general conception of the divine which was advocated, as well as a related, sacramental involvement in the world, can be seen as rather more than just 'philosophical' speculation (in the modern sense of philosophy). The divine reality experienced and reflected upon by those pagans was not hopelessly remote from the Christian view, and as such its thought-forms might legitimately be used. As well as formal arguments, there was also an experiential appeal to the sense of all reality being dependent on a single source that was itself dependent on nothing else.[135] Not that disagreements did not arise. Platonism, like Hinduism, would contend that such experience suggests an ultimate form of divinity beyond the personal, but there is no doubt that key forms of influence did prevail, most notably with a more profound stress on the transcendence and mystery of God, as well as a divinity sacramentally involved in the world. In the end not all were persuaded, not least on such questions as divine personhood and immutability. Full consideration of such issues, though, must be postponed until later chapters.

---

[135] In the notion of divine aseity, the divine 'by itself', that is, not dependent on anything else.

Here, we might conclude with a few tentative remarks that apply to the chapter as a whole, and the transition noted in both the Middle East and classical worlds from polytheism to monotheism. It is easy to think of this move in entirely intellectual terms but another way to think of it is as consequent upon new social perceptions of how the total sum of individual experience of the workings of the divine should be interpreted. Put crudely, polytheism is a natural conclusion to draw from all the various types of experience individuals have of the transcendent Other, in all its variety, with myth one way to order and structure those encounters. But another is to gather together the good among them as the dominating form and so relegate the rest to other causes, either in lesser divinities such as demons or else in the consequences of human behaviour.[136] In short, just as the later Platonists suggested, even to a monotheist the workings of polytheism need not be viewed as necessarily inimical. Postulating plurality in the divine can be seen as genuine religious experience misconstrued rather than as totally false. How far such an analysis can be sustained will be severely tested in Chapter 3, as we explore modern polytheism in Hinduism.

---

[136] Mostly, the negative side has been focused on a number of lesser divinities such as demons but occasionally a single larger figure is postulated as in Zoroastrianism or in some versions of the Devil. The human comes into play when human sin is deemed to have consequences for the world as a whole.

3
Different Eyes
Hinduism

Hinduism could well be the oldest of the major religions still practised in the modern world.[1] However, in the eyes of many, far from this being a merit, it is seen as going a long way to explain its essential primitiveness: all its idols and the caste system, for example. Even so, it is proving surprisingly resilient. As one recent book observes, despite its secular constitution and growing industrialisation, in recent years India has become more religiously observant rather than less, with the trend most marked among the new middle-class.[2] Nor can this by any means be attributed exclusively to a new-found Hindu nationalism, though this is undoubtedly making for a less tolerant

---

[1] In the sense that some of its oldest features (Vedic traditions from the early second millennium BCE) still survive into the present day. By contrast, Jewish stories and attitudes from that time appear to have changed quite radically.

[2] Meera Nanda, *The God Market: How Globalization Is Making India More Hindu* (New York: Random House, 2009). Although written from a determinedly secular perspective, she readily concedes that the conventional secularization thesis does not apply. Despite providing a wealth of documentation proving her point, she does not identify any obvious explanation. However, she does note the role played by the post-colonial government. Ironically, through eliminating inefficiency and corruption among temple authorities, their religious and charitable role has become much more conspicuous (108–44).

society.[3] No doubt there are motives good and bad, including superstition and nostalgia for the past.[4] On the positive side, it may be noted that the history of India is more closely bound up with religion than most other societies.[5] It is also a relationship which continues to develop in the present, with greater uniformity of belief now emerging as village and city become more interconnected.[6]

In our analysis here it will be wise not to confine our discussion too narrowly to the present. Instead, I shall endeavour to enter into the entire development of Hinduism as sympathetically as I can. Inevitably, a wide range of disagreements will remain. But, as noted in Chapter 1, deep contrasts in approach do not necessarily always point to ultimately irreconcilable difference. Indeed, two areas will be identified here where Christianity might profitably learn from Hinduism: the way in which images can best function in our conception of the divine; then, more particularly, how reflection on interaction of image and concept could help with often fraught gender issues. The reason why Hinduism might be able to help with such matters is because it approaches these questions with quite different eyes from Western monotheisms. The latter have allowed themselves to be too easily trapped within one particular perspective.

[3] Even a liberal writer such as Shashi Tharoor in *Why I Am a Hindu* (London: Hurst & Co., 2018) finds it necessary to make several gratuitous side-swipes against Christianity.
[4] Nanda notes a rise of interest in pseudo-science and astrology; for example, *The God Market*, 69–70, 121–22.
[5] Witness, for example, the high percentage of religious figures who appear in Sunil Khilnani, *Incarnations: A History of India in 50 Lives* (London: Penguin, 2016).
[6] Although, note the observation of William Dalrymple in *Nine Lives: In Search of the Sacred in Modern India* (London: Bloomsbury, 2009): 'for all the changes and development that have taken place, an older India endures'. (xvii).

Before tackling these questions, however, as with each new religion discussed, I shall first attempt to set the scene more broadly by sketching some of Hinduism's key features. Lest readers be misled by my choice of issues into supposing that I am trying to bypass more substantial questions, it needs noting that the possibility of experience of the divine through polytheism was defended in Chapter 2. Again, in Chapter 4, Religions of India, some further issues that overlap with other major streams in the subcontinent (Buddhism, Jainism and Sikhism) will be tackled. The choice of topics here is intended to reflect my own 'prejudice' that in the past approaches have been theoretical from the start, with insufficient attention given to how the religion is actually to be observed in practice. However, this has not entailed the neglect of more metaphysical issues, only their postponement to Chapter 8 where some more underlying conflicts will be considered.

Setting the Scene

Despite its age, 'Hinduism' as such is a relatively new concept. All the expression means is the religion practised by those living beyond the River Indus (that is, in the Indian subcontinent), a term initially adopted by the country's successive invaders and only later by the inhabitants themselves. The earliest self-reference could be as late as the early nineteenth century.[7] Even now, Hinduism still lacks any centralising authority and so it

---

[7] What accelerated the development was the way in which all non-Muslims (apart from Christians) were treated under the Raj as belonging to the same category.

remains impossible to identify key universal features shared by all, even with respect to something as basic as the nature of the divine. Instead, one might speak of, at most, overlapping similarities.[8] Indeed, in the face of Hindutva (the modern equation of nation and religion),[9] one distinguished American scholar hesitates to go even that far. For Wendy Doniger its stories are 'an infinitely expansible source of meaning', and it is this feature which makes Hinduism necessarily 'a multivocal masterpiece'.[10] While her book is a valuable corrective to those who refuse to recognise such openness,[11] her postmodern relativity surely goes too far. After all, not all possibilities were (or are) regarded with equal favour.

The authority of the Vedas, the religion's earliest texts, for example, is all but universally acknowledged which explains why reformers have, for the most part, sought to accommodate their new position within a Vedic embrace. With the native script still not deciphered it is not possible to know for certain, but one common theory is that initial shape was given to the religion by interaction between the earliest known Indian civilisation, the Harappan culture and invading Aryan tribes.[12] The latter

---

[8] The problem is well illustrated by mention of ten proposed definitions in various degrees of conflict with one another: see Julius Lipner, *Hindus: Their Religious Beliefs and Practices* (London: Routledge, 2nd ed., 2010), 3–5.

[9] Dating from a 1923 pamphlet by V. S. Savarkar, it is supported by the BJP, the party of the present Indian Prime Minister, Narendra Modi.

[10] Wendy Doniger, *The Hindus: An Alternative History* (New York: Oxford University Press, 2009), 653, 690.

[11] Her alternative history explores in particular subversive approaches to women, caste and animals.

[12] A bronze civilization, which was rediscovered in the nineteenth century, it flourished in the Indus valley from c. 2600 to 1900 BCE.

provided the language (Sanskrit) used to memorise the details of Harappan ritual practice,[13] including some fine hymns.[14] Although the texts were not actually written down until centuries later, there is no reason to suspect radical change in the process (with a few exceptions noted below). Even today, the priestly caste or 'brahmins' show an easy facility in committing to memory the huge detail involved. In any event, it is this fact of oral transmission which explains why, in describing the Vedas as 'revelation', the term applied is *smurti* ('what is heard') rather than the weaker *sruti* ('what is read'). The philosophical analysis of their content found in the Upanishads (c. 800 BCE) is treated as part of the former as the 'Vedanta' (the 'end' or 'culmination' of the Vedas). Anything that came later, however influential, is formally treated as secondary:[15] including major moral codes such as the Institutes of Manu, India's two powerful religious epics, the Mahabharata and Ramayana, and the Puranas, the main

---

Harappa and Mohenjo-Daro were its two principal cities, both of which are now in Pakistan.

[13] Although most ritual details of Harappan culture remain unknown, there is evidence that ritual bathing played a major role.

[14] A translation of some of the more interesting is available in Penguin Classics: *The Rig Veda*, translated by Wendy Doniger (London: Penguin, 1981). A more controversial, wider selection is provided in Raimundo Panikkar, *The Vedic Experience: An Anthology of the Vedas for Modern Man* (Berkeley: University of California Press, 1977). For a collection of essays on Panikkar's leading ideas, Peter C. Phan & Young-chan Ro eds., *Raimon Panikkar: A Companion to His Thought* (Cambridge: James Clarke, 2018).

[15] R. C. Zaehner, in his editing of a book entitled *Hindu Scriptures* (New York: Everyman Library, 1966), felt it necessary to go beyond that corpus of Vedas and Upanishads to include the Bhagavad Gita, so indispensable to so much Hindu piety has this section from the Mahabharata become.

written source for stories of the gods.[16] That presumed supreme authority explains why modern reformers have tended to see reinterpretation of the Vedic inheritance as central,[17] or again why in the India of today, rather than abolishing animal sacrifice altogether, the Vedic tradition often continues in the form of the offering of rice cakes in similar contexts.[18]

Such patterns of development are of course familiar in all major world religions, including Judaism and Christianity. Like those two religions it is also possible to detect changes occasionally within the Vedic texts themselves, most obviously perhaps to accommodate the view of an overall divine unity postulated in the Upanishads. The latter's account of divinity as an all-encompassing Brahman plays only a relatively minor part in the Vedas. It was itself a development which came to be interpreted in a number of competing ways. While the advocacy of Advaita-Vedanta or monism by Shankara (d. 750 CE) might seem the most plausible interpretation, various degrees of distinction from the world and the individual soul (*atman*) were supported by other philosophers, as in the absolute non-dualism of Madhva (d. 1317 CE) and the relative non-dualism associated with the earlier Ramanuja (d. 1137 CE).[19]

---

[16] The first is the most important of the Dharma Sastras and dates c. 200 BCE–200 CE. The second pair develop over a wider period of time, perhaps 400 BCE–400 CE, while the last mentioned (of which there are traditionally eighteen) derives mainly from c. 250–550 CE.

[17] Illustrated by the work of Ram Mohan Roy, Swami Vivekananda, Dayananda Saraswati and Sarvepalli Radhakrishnan in Lipner, *Hindus*, 78–87.

[18] Doniger, *The Hindus*, 655–57.

[19] Madhva is the customary English abbreviation for Madhvacharya. Both his position and that of Ramanuja are described as Dvaita-Vedanta.

Where later change is most marked, though, is in the deities on whom devotion is primarily fixed. Agni, Indra, Soma and Varuna all have major roles in the Vedas, yet the gods of later Hinduism are almost wholly absent.[20] Thanks to the rise of the bhakti or devotional movement, for many Hindus the Vedic tradition has in actual practice become largely marginalised.[21] The two great epics mentioned earlier which offer their own account of the story of the two best-known *avatars* or 'incarnations' of the god Vishnu (as Krishna and as Rama) have in effect become scripture to large numbers, not least because of the exchange between Krishna and the warrior Arjuna in the great spiritual classic, the Bhagavad-Gita, part of the Mahabharata.[22] The huge popularity of the two epics' serial dramatisation on television in the late 1980s and subsequent availability on DVD has also solidified knowledge of the plot of both epics and their underlying theological themes.[23] The other male god with whom bhakti is

Essentially, the difference is that Ramanuja, unlike Madhva, thinks that the difference between Brahman and the human soul can be overcome.

[20] Although Vishnu is mentioned at various points, he only has one hymn dedication: Doniger, *Rig Veda*, 225–27.

[21] Originating towards the end of the first millennium, it produced large amounts of devotional poetry between the twelfth and eighteenth centuries.

[22] Although the number can vary, conventionally Vishnu had ten avatars, with one still to come and several involving animals.

[23] Indeed, the project even insured that Krishna's earlier behaviour as boy and teenager is now firmly locked into the tradition, despite originally appearing in a separate place, in the fifth century CE *Bhagavada Purana*. In the case of the *Ramayana* it was the more devotional version produced in the sixteenth century by the poet Tulsidas which was used. For these sessions the television was often garlanded and given other signs of religious veneration: Joyce Burkhalter Flueckiger, *Everyday Hinduism* (Oxford: Wiley Blackwell, 2015), 70.

especially associated is the more ascetic (but also erotic) Shiva.[24] A third deity needs to be mentioned at this point, with the confusing name of Brahma (that is, neither Brahman nor for that matter a brahmin!)[25] When Hinduism first became generally known in nineteenth-century Europe, just as parallels were often drawn between avatar and incarnation, so talk of a Hindu Trinity became common, in the so-called Trimurti of these three gods (Brahma, Vishnu and Shiva). Portrayed as representing the divine as creator, preserver and destroyer (and renewer), it was suggested that there were some analogies with the Christian Trinity.[26] But the parallels are more artificial than real, inasmuch as Brahma is a god from an earlier generation who plays almost no role in contemporary Hinduism. Indeed, there are almost no temples left that are dedicated to him.[27]

Accordingly, it needs to be acknowledged that contemporary realities are rather different. In many of the

---

[24] Rudra in the Rig Veda is often seen as an early anticipation. For the complex history, see further Gavin Flood, 'The Śaiva Traditions' in Gavin Flood ed., *The Blackwell Companion to Hinduism* (Oxford: Blackwell, 2005), 200–28. For some early lyrical expressions of such devotion, A. K. Ramanujan ed., *Speaking of Śiva* (Harmondsworth: Penguin, 1973).

[25] A reminder might be helpful! 'Brahma' is the name of a specific god, 'Brahman' alludes to an all-encompassing divine reality, 'brahmin', an individual priest belonging to the highest caste.

[26] For Hegel's discussion, see Peter C. Hodgson ed., *Hegel's Lectures on the Philosophy of Religion* (Berkeley: University of California Press, 1988), 270–82.

[27] Jagatpita Brahma Mandir is one of the very few temples in India dedicated to Brahma (at Pushkar in the state of Rajasthan). However, there is a major temple in Bangkok, the Erawan Temple (built in 1956). Unfortunately, it has been subject to various forms of terrorist violence in this predominantly Buddhist land.

villages of India otherwise unknown divinities quite frequently still hold preeminent place,[28] and various other minor deities can at times become quite prominent, as with Ganesh and Hanuman.[29] Considering the nation as a whole, three deities are effectively the principal foci of worship: the already mentioned Shiva and Vishnu along with Devi, the Mother Goddess.[30] Not that these are ever worshipped together. A more common pattern is the adoption of one or other as a primary focus, with the worshipping communities then known as Vaishnavism, Shaivism or Shaktism. The situation is thus rather like what was identified in Chapter 2 as henotheism, though with more tolerance in that all can be seen as aspects of the one overall divinity, Brahman. It is by virtue of this relation that today most well-educated Hindus would describe themselves as monotheists. It is an intellectual position which is commonly buttressed by a metaphysics that calls into question the reality of ordinary, everyday experience.[31] It might also seem supported by the mythic quality of so many of the stories told about the gods, including Vishnu's avatars, for so exaggerated are the themes that they seem almost to invite translation into another medium. Nonetheless, it should be noted that for some contemporary Hindus the stories are to be taken

---

[28] For a discussion of the present situation but also how things are changing, see Flueckiger, *Everyday Hinduism*, 30–34, 224–26.
[29] Hanuman is the monkey god who helped Rama in his campaigns. Ganesh is the son of Shiva with a substitute elephant head who is invoked by most Hindus before any significant new endeavour.
[30] With goddesses such as Durga and Kali commonly identified as the same reality. Devi is the female form of the term for a male god (*deva*).
[31] The notion of *maya* or 'illusion' is particularly associated with Advaita Vedanta, with everything else dissolving into a single divine reality.

quite literally. This became tragically all too clear during the violent arguments which eventually led to the destruction of the Babri Mashid at Ayodhya in 1992.[32]

Some of this rich array of ideas will be considered later in this chapter but, inevitably, due to limitations of space only a small segment. However, another reason is because, just as Western monotheisms overlap in various ways, so do the religions of the east. So it makes sense to consider some aspects of Hinduism's conceptualisation in relation to competitors such as Buddhism (treated in Chapter 4). An obvious issue where this applies is to questions concerning the overall unreality of the world. Another is reincarnation, which needs to be considered less in its own right and more with regard to potential 'solutions' to the problem of evil. Ironically, although now as firmly rooted in Hinduism as in Buddhism, it is doubtful whether the belief was held in Vedic times.

A weaker but not dissimilar claim could also be made about caste.[33] Yet there is no doubt that in due course it became deeply rooted, and indeed embarrassingly so. On the established pattern, there are four main classes: the priests or brahmins, the military and rulers (*ksatriyas*), merchants and farmers (*vaisyas*) and labourers and servants (*sudras*). Then outside are those deemed 'untouchable' because of the pollution caused by their occupation

---

[32] A mosque that had allegedly been built on the site of a former temple marking the birthplace of the god Ram (or Rama). Encouraged by the BJP, there are now quite a number of other such cases working their way through the Indian courts.

[33] One could say that it is implicit in the myth of primal man (*Purusha* – Rig Veda 10.90) and the different functions assigned to different parts of the social body. But, if so, not much use was made of the idea.

(everything from tanners to toilet cleaners). A further separate category is constituted by those belonging to early indigenous tribes. On the positive side, it is sometimes observed that over the centuries the system helped to make India a relatively stable and peaceable society, though how much this was due to the caste system as such and how much to other factors within Hinduism it is hard to say. After all, medieval Europe also operated a kind of caste system with feudalism but the world of the time was scarcely peaceable. Although seldom acknowledged, there are even parallels in the racial and other divides of contemporary American society, which surely no right-thinking person would wish to see continue.[34] Despite modern attempts to abolish the practice within India, it has remained extraordinarily resilient, with most couples still finding a partner within the same caste. Although Mahatma Gandhi (1869–1948) was a great campaigner against its worst aspects (renaming untouchables as *harijans* or 'children of God'), surprisingly he did value its contribution to social stability.[35] More radical was B. R. Ambedkar. Unlike Gandhi, he was himself an untouchable. While he succeeded in securing various favourable changes to the Indian constitution, he still despaired of real progress. So, in the year of his death (1956) he converted to Buddhism, encouraging millions to follow suit.[36]

---

[34] Trenchantly argued in Isabel Wilkerson, *Caste: The Origins of our Discontents* (New York: Random House, 2020).
[35] For his defence of keeping to the same varna or social occupation, see M. K. Gandhi, *My Religion* (Ahmedabad: Navajivan, 1955), 150–56, esp.154.
[36] Probably about five million.

Different Eyes: Hinduism

Nowadays untouchables are described as Dalits (their own favoured word, 'oppressed') and granted government quotas at university and in certain types of job. One even rose to be a past President of India.[37] Whether the slowness of the ideology to disappear is witness to a natural conservatism in religious practice or in Indian society more generally, it is hard to determine. Perhaps pointing against the former as cause is the way in which access to temples has been transformed in modern times. Two centuries ago a ban on untouchables entering temples would have been enforced almost everywhere, whereas now it is very much the exception. So, more radical change continues to be possible. If the conservatism of Hindutva seems to point much of the time in a backward direction, there remain powerful voices on the other side. While arbitrating the worth of still-living authors is beyond my competence, there is no doubt about the continuing relevance of someone such as Rabindranath Tagore (1861–1941). While his novel *The Home and the World* (1916) exposed deep tensions in how change might be achieved, his poetic prayers are ones with which the wider world can still readily identify.[38]

Although now armed with some general sense of context, major metaphysical conflicts such as the nature of divine, human and material identity will be delayed for initial consideration until Chapter 4, with the most comprehensive discussion reserved until nearer the conclusion

---

[37] K. R. Narayanan was President from 1997 to 2002.
[38] He was the first non-European to win the Nobel Prize for Literature (in 1913), primarily for his poetry. See further *Song Offerings* (London: Anvil Press, 2000); *Selected Poems* (London: Penguin, 1985).

of this book. In the meantime, partly in order to induct readers more gently into my general method, I shall focus more narrowly here on two more practical areas where Christianity might have something to learn from Hinduism. I shall consider in turn the predominance of the visual within Hinduism and then its application of gendered imagery to the divine.

Visual Mediation of a Divine Address in Darśan

Elsewhere, I have challenged the long association in the West between visual representation and idolatry.[39] In absolutising something other than God there is no reason to think that the ears are less prone to temptation than the eyes. Indeed, one might argue that, so far from guarding the divine message, fundamentalism is just such a form of idolatry, inasmuch as it requires absolute assent to a text rather than to God as such. Admittedly, the extent of honour shown to some Indian images might suggest a not dissimilar pattern of absolutising. But it is important to note the range of strategies commonly deployed to prevent this from happening. Some images are deliberately made provisional, created but then destroyed by, for example, immersion in the River Ganges.[40] Again, where permanent, a range of representation is

---

[39] See 'In the Beginning was the Image' in my *Divine Generosity and Human Creativity*, eds. Christopher R. Brewer & Robert MacSwain (London: Routledge, 2017), 7–22.

[40] For some examples of the temporary, Ajit Mookerjee, *Ritual Art of India* (London: Thames & Hudson, 1985). Contrast more permanent art created by bhakti devotion, Madhuvanti Ghose, *Gates of the Lord: The Tradition of Krishna Paintings* (Chicago: Art Institute of Chicago, 2015).

deemed appropriate, with imagery on the way to the central shrine often quite different from what greets the worshipper on arrival. Finally, even with respect to that central image, there is not the same cult of reproduction as occurs in the West. So, for example, Eastern Orthodox believers are usually keen to have in their domestic shrine a copy of some well-known icon such as the Theotokos of Vladimir or the Orans of Yaroslavl,[41] whereas Hindus seem quite happy to have only a rough similitude. More important is the repetition of a wide variety of key symbols that are used to identify which divinity is present.[42]

Hitherto I have not as yet mentioned the most important element in the Hindu conception, and that is the notion of *darshan*; that it is a matter of the image viewing the worshipper rather than the other way round, or, more accurately, the divinity mediated through the image.[43] Indeed, so integral is this notion to Hinduism that one book on the subject opens by observing that, when Hindus go to a temple, they do not commonly talk of going to worship but 'to take darśan'.[44] As with practice more generally in the ancient world, an

---

[41] From the twelfth and thirteenth centuries, respectively.
[42] Shiva, for example, can be identified by the phallic *linga* or as the dancer *Nataraja*. In the latter the cosmic symbols of drum and fire are in two of his hands while the two others offer reassuring signs to the worshipper. Vishnu in his cosmic aspect reclines on the waters of creation, whereas in his more usual form he also has four arms, each holding a symbol (club and discus, conch shell and lotus).
[43] For some Hindus the latter more qualified account may seem too weak since the deity is envisaged as embodied in the *murti* or image. But it is important to note that, despite the passage quoted later in the main text, such embodiment does not entail any absolute containment or limitation. For a discussion of the issue, Flueckiger, *Everyday Hinduism*, 77–82.
[44] Diana L. Eck, *Darśan: Seeing the Divine Image in India* (New York: Columbia University Press, 3rd ed., 1988), 4.

image is not deemed to be complete until it is ceremonially given life through, for example, the solemn insertion of its eyes. That could easily be taken to suggest the very depths of superstition. But the action has nothing whatsoever to do with supposing that the image might itself actually be able to see. Rather, the ceremonial indicates that the idol is now available, for the deity to use its eyes as its medium. A notion of divine action or grace mediated to the worshipper is thus seen as integral to what happens. Devotionally, this has had a powerful impact on believers: 'This is the greatest grace of the Lord, that being free he becomes bound, being independent he becomes dependent for all his service on his devotee ... He carries him about, fans him, feeds him, plays with him – yea, the Infinite has become finite, that the child soul may grasp, understand and love him'.[45]

However, the movement is not entirely one way. In the process the individual is assumed to be drawn into what is represented, much as in our ordinary experience another human being looking closely at us can eventually make us aware that we are in fact being observed. But, whereas in that latter case the principal reaction of the person concerned is quite likely to be embarrassment, in the divine case the perception can come with a profound sense of being pulled into awareness of what the image implies about the deity: for example, as an instance of plenitude or fruitfulness, concern for a particular group, or identification with some aspect of the deity's traditional story. Of all such practice, the search for blessing through anointing a *linga*, Shiva's phallic symbol, is perhaps among the more difficult aspects of Hinduism for a Christian to

---

[45] Quoted in Eck, *Darśan*, 46.

comprehend. Yet without any intended offence an analogy could perhaps be drawn with the use of an empty cross, whether on a church altar or round the neck. In marked contrast to a crucifix, its aim is to point beyond any remembrance of the suffering involved to the cross as victory and blessing. Likewise, the original phallic imagery in the *linga* remains firmly subordinate to the grace which it is believed the god can impart through such interconnection.

In trying better to comprehend the notion of *darshan*, it is important to note the ritual context. It is not suggested that the *murti* or image in and of itself will produce such an impact but rather when accompanied by a particular approach to it: so, for example, anointing the *linga* with ghee (clarified butter) and adorning it reverentially with flowers. Of course, to all this it might be objected that the process merely makes the vision self-confirming, the expectation generating the result. But with that response it is surely the objectors who are being naïve. Few today would endorse an account of vision which presupposes no more is involved than rays from the object hitting our retina. Instead, psychologists tell us that any visual perception at all is the result of complex interactions between what is there and what is already stored in our brains. For instance, in his various publications on visual perception, the German psychologist Rudolf Arheim (d. 2007) not only stressed the active contribution that the brain makes but also encouraged readers to become more conscious of this possibility.[46] Certainly,

---

[46] Rudolf Arnheim, *Art and Visual Perception: A Psychology of the Creative Eye* (Berkeley: University of California, 1954, 1974); *Visual Thinking* (London: Faber & Faber, 1970).

depending on where we happen to live or which language we speak, it is true that the same object can be understood to have quite different colours, or again snow be seen either as a vague mass or else carefully differentiated.[47] A further complication is that the brain almost immediately resolves potential sources of conflict, for example identifying something as the same when it may nonetheless be significantly different. It is a problem which Claude Monet brilliantly highlighted in his series on haystacks and on Rouen Cathedral as they appeared at different times of day: any uniform brown or yellow had disappeared.[48] So, similarly then with the murti, it may be argued that ritual has opened up for devotees a quite different kind of impact from any narrowly aesthetic evaluation.[49]

But it is not just a case of some particular sculpture or painting producing such a result, the effect can also come from the wider artistic and architectural context within which the image is set. While treatises were written in Europe on how various architectural styles might evoke divinity, in India the whole process was carried much further.[50] Although a range of different styles

---

[47] Notoriously, the Latin *purpureus* is almost impossible to identify in English with a single colour. In Russian there are two words for blue to the English one. Again, Inuit allows the viewer to distinguish over fifty types of snow.
[48] He painted twenty-five haystacks between 1889 and 1890, and over thirty of the façade of the cathedral between 1892 and 1893.
[49] Some art historians and critics would also argue for a more active role in the perception or appreciation of works of art, for example, James Elkins, *The Object Stares Back* (New York: Simon & Shuster, 1996).
[50] Vastu Shastras prescribe rules for architecture, Shilpa Shastras guidance for the arts and crafts within.

exist,[51] all were expected to conform to certain general principles. These combine careful mathematical aping of the presumed structure of the universe with symbolic forms of representation that speak of both divine transcendence and divine immanence. A central tower evokes the transcendent mountains associated with the gods,[52] while the main cultic image is placed immediately beneath in an area known as the *garba griha* or 'womb', to speak of immanence. Its precise location is determined by applying grids of the mythical cosmic body or *perusha* to each element in the total structure.[53]

Even so, it is not just art and architecture which communicate a particular placement within a sacred reality, also communicated can be the way in which the worshipper is set within a particular landscape and its wider story. Such transformative experience occurs through the medium of the ubiquitous Indian practice of pilgrimage, a custom which has been markedly on the increase in recent years.[54] Pilgrims find themselves set within a larger story not simply because of their own actions but also by

---

[51] The most obvious contrast is between the style adopted in the north and the more elaborate southern or Dravidian style. Not only is the central tower or shikhara more highly decorated in the south (now called the vimana), the temple's wider setting is also commonly provided with more impressive entrances, known as a gopuram.

[52] While Mt Meru, the traditional home of the gods, is mythical, Mt Kailash, the special home of Shiva, is situated in present-day Tibet.

[53] For a brief statement of the principles, Christopher Tadgell, *The History of Architecture in India* (London: Phaidon, 1990), 39–43.

[54] For example, pilgrimage to Sabarimala in Kerala has increased from fifty thousand annually thirty years ago to over ten million today: Diana L. Eck, *India: A Sacred Geography* (New York: Three Rivers Press, 2012), 444.

virtue of what is given to them by the contours of the countryside which they find themselves visiting. The favoured term for pilgrimage is *tirtha* or 'crossing'. Rivers, mountains and caves are perceived as providing points of access to 'cross over' to the divine, or indeed, as with the River Ganges, with the medium itself being seen as divine. Such points of access are by no means few and far between. Because of Hindu tolerance of apparently competing myths, it is quite usual to find the same story told of more than one location. As one scholar observes, 'the critical rule of thumb is this: those things that are deeply important are to be widely repeated. The repetition of places, the creation of clusters and circles of sacred places, the articulation of groups of four, five, seven or twelve sites – all this constitutes a vivid, symbolic landscape characterised not by exclusivity and uniqueness, but by polycentricity, pluralism and duplication'.[55] Sometimes this can be rationalised as in the story of the numerous parts of Shiva's dead partner, Sati, which fell to earth.[56] But more commonly the same story will be told of several places without any sense of embarrassment. In like manner, stories of particular village goddesses are increasingly incorporated into the life of the mother goddess without any sense of potential conflict. Even the Himalayas as 'the abode of the gods' have found alternative locations in the deep south of the country.[57] As one scholar observes, who has herself travelled thousands of miles on such pilgrimages, it is a case

---

[55] Eck, *India*, 5.
[56] According to the myth, the body parts of Shiva's dead partner, Sati, fell to earth as he was carrying her through the air. Numbers vary between 51 and 108.
[57] Eck, *India*, 36–37.

of the infinite, transcendent space of divinity localised in its experiential fullness to a specific place, summed up in the neat phrase 'God is vast, yet God is here'.[58] It is, therefore, perhaps not surprising that even the subcontinent as a whole can be seen in this way. A temple on the edge of Varanasi has Mother India as its primary dedication, its marble map clearly assumed to be the means by which divine grace is mediated.[59]

In my view, so far from being alien, these ideas are something from which Christianity might profitably learn. Irrespective of the extent to which believers view their faith in essentially verbal terms, they are in fact also surrounded by its affirmation in visual form. Even in the most apparently Protestant of churches this can happen, as in the plain buildings of New England and the Deep South where a preference for classical design speaks of belief in an ordered and structured world. Indeed, each of the various architectural styles can be seen to say something about God: Romanesque about embedded presence, Gothic about soaring heavenwards or Baroque about drama and the unexpected.[60] Likewise, paintings and statues found in churches should not just be seen as aesthetically significant; they also make claims to relate believers to God.[61] One way to view this relationship to

---

[58] Eck, *India*, 451–54, esp. 452.
[59] Inaugurated in 1936 by Mahatma Gandhi, the map in Bharat Mata Temple represents major geographical features in what was then undivided India.
[60] For these contrasts developed, see my 'Architecture and Theism' in *Divine Generosity and Human Creativity*, 156–66.
[61] See further my article 'Supplying Theology's Missing Link' in *New Blackfriars* 101 (2020), 153–62.

art and architecture is in terms of something required of us as worshippers: the need to reflect more deeply on such works. But an alternative perspective is appreciation of how, even without any action on our part, they can often say something to us, even if at times only subliminally. For instance, it is surely almost impossible to enter a major Gothic building without experiencing something of its mediated claim to transcendence. That being so, given that each style has usually been chosen by church authorities to say something about God,[62] it is surely not implausible to go a step further and see the choice as enabling the divine to communicate something of itself through these means, in a way not much different from how, as we saw above, Hindu thought regards the role of the architect in temple building. Of course, one might object that God is not at all like what a particular architectural style seems to be suggesting. Under such circumstances surely some supplementation will be required rather than the proposed message be declared inherently wrong in itself. After all, only some particular aspect of divinity is thereby identified, not its total reality. In any event, precisely by being there its message cannot be ignored entirely. A preacher who wants to assert that God is to be found overwhelmingly or even exclusively in other people will find himself implicitly rebuked by the Gothic building in which he delivers such a sermon. So there will be a need either to acknowledge the

---

[62] True even of a modern, secular style where the aim is to suggest commitment to the local community, in a lack of ostentation. Rather different is the following of fashion, as in the nineteenth century preference for Gothic. Even then, its underlying meaning probably remained, if somewhat in the background.

counterweight, or else of necessity launch an attack on the appropriateness of that particular type of church building.[63] In short, there is good reason to encourage Christian worshippers to seek to experience the Christian equivalent of *darshan* in their churches. The building itself functions as one of the ways in which the presence of God is mediated.

That being so, I would suggest that it is not just scripture that should be viewed as demanding attentive listening in order to hear an address from elsewhere, a similar principle applies equally to the general ambience in which a service may be set. There is also an address to our eyes from the divine eye in the sense that we are being seen for better or worse through an embedded presentation of divinity in our church buildings. Of course, that message can be challenged but in this it is surely no different from readings from the Bible. Our attending to the address of scripture requires not only an initial, careful hearing but also subsequent willingness to explore how it should be applied or modified in the light of what else we know about God. So, similarly then, with art and architecture.

It is also into this context that we might fit the particular challenge that stained glass presents. Ubiquitous in our churches, it is often seen by outsiders as the most obviously saccharine aspect of Christianity. Even believers commonly treat the work as no more valuable than colourful wallpaper. The problem here is that any

---

[63] That is no doubt why, balancing the transcendent upward thrust of Gothic, medieval church planners added a strongly immanent dimension in church art with its strong emphasis on the humanity of Christ, for example, in the child Jesus playing with Mary's veil or deep expression of emotion at the crucifixion.

reading usually starts from an assumption that, at most, what we are being offered is an illustration of scripture. Yet even if only taken at this level, one could still ask what might constitute a good or a bad illustration, and so with a more trained eye learn to distinguish degrees of value in the art concerned. Mixed verdicts are likely to be quite common, with different groups of believers responding in radically different kinds of ways. For example, is setting the nativity in the context of the local town legitimate or not? Or introducing coal mines and computers a step too far in the direction of modernity?[64] Is a dramatic sea creature enough to remind us of the Resurrection, or Christ surrounded by rabbits and birds enough of a prompt to encourage a different perspective on Jesus' forty days in the Wilderness?[65] An educated awareness of the themes and general approach of the artists concerned could transform not only appreciation of the work of stained-glass artists but also allow them to function quite otherwise from present indifference. As with the building's architecture, stained glass could become an effective means of mediating divine presence and address. No longer would the congregation see itself as waiting for something to happen when the liturgy begins, their darshan could effectively commence at the point of entry to

---

[64] Both examples are from my own experience: the main chancel window from All Saints' Church, St Andrews, and the Millennium window in Durham Cathedral. Many continental churches go much further. I recall the presence of a model railway at one Nativity in Poland.
[65] Two examples from St Paul's Cathedral, Dundee: an exotic 'whale' used to remind viewers of Matt. 12.39–40 ('just as Jonah was three days and three nights . . .'); the holy's intimacy with the animal creation, as in Mark 1.13 ('he was with the wild beasts').

the building, in an experience of worshippers finding themselves already seen and addressed by God. In other words, the building and its artefacts could conceivably then operate in their totality in support of the liturgy rather than being seen, as so often at present, as at most an indifferent background to it.[66]

Feminine Imagery and the Divine Essence

Arguments in contemporary Christian theology for increased use of feminine imagery in describing the divine constitute a very wide range of proposed revisions. Some would see their proposals as still within the bounds of Christian orthodoxy,[67] while others move to the edge, or even step beyond it.[68] Quite a few feminist theologians choose to rely on conclusions about equality already drawn in secular discourse. To distribute the imagery

---

[66] This theme is further developed in the address I gave to Studia Liturgica at its annual conference in 2021: available in its journal: 'Liturgical Constraints and Openness in Divine Address' in *Studia Liturgica* 52.1 (2022), 65–79. In appreciating stained glass there is a strong need to provide education in the traditions within which particular periods of glass might be operating, such as Art Deco in the work of the well-known Irish artist, Harry Clarke.

[67] For example, Ann Loades, *Feminist Theology: A Reader* (1990); *Feminist Theology: Voices from the Past* (2001); Elizabeth Johnson, *She Who Is: The Mystery of God in Feminist Theological Discourse* (1992).

[68] Grace Jantzen (d. 2002) in *Becoming Divine: Towards a Feminist Philosophy of Religion* (1998) argues for a spirituality that is internally based rather than in the form of help from an external male saviour. The approach of Mary Daly (d. 2010) in *Beyond God the Father: Towards a Philosophy of Women's Liberation* (1973) was initially well received. Subsequent books of hers, however, such as *Gyn/Ecology* (1978) began to move well beyond anything compatible with traditional Christianity. She even refused to have male students in her classes.

equitably is seen as the affirmation of an already acknowledged equality between the human sexes. Not that appeal to scripture is unknown but this is assigned a relatively small place, perhaps not least because reliance must be put on a relatively few, select number of passages.[69] This is perhaps one reason why disagreement on the matter has sometimes been so bad-tempered, because 'father' is sometimes seen as an integral element in preserving the notion of God as a figure of power and authority.[70] Those who take the conservative position tend to view the innovation as a sustained attack on the trustworthiness of divine revelation itself. Of course, those taking that latter position are just as likely to be equally dissatisfied by appeal to practice in another religion. But there is this significant difference: that the appeal turns out now not to be to basically secularist ideas but to how divinity has been experienced within a particular religious tradition. Were that to be combined with good reasons for discounting the patriarchal pull within Christianity, an essentially intra-religious discussion would be the result, and so in some sense a concern with the same ultimate values. So what I want to do here is explore how Hindu imagery and religious experience could be seen to point beyond any absolute distinction between sex or gender, beyond even complementarity, into 'feminine energy' as part of the very essence of the divine.

---

[69] For example, Deut. 32.11–12; Hos. 11.3–4; Isaiah 49.15; Isaiah 66.13; Mt. 23.37. Even with the first two examples, it could be argued that the writer still had a father in mind.
[70] As in Barth's equation of 'Father' and 'Almighty' in the Apostles Creed: *Dogmatics in Outline* (London: SCM Press, 1949), 46.

However, while the formal structure of the argument might be deemed acceptable, critics will no doubt immediately observe how far the Hindu conception of the divine feminine is from anything within Christianity. While that is true, it is, I think, worth persevering, even to the extent of taking with the maximum seriousness the extent of the contrast. As mentioned earlier in the chapter, one of the principal gods of Hinduism is Devi, the 'goddess' identified with Durga or Kali, or one of the various female consorts associated with male deities. Although Brahma is no longer widely worshipped despite being part of the Trimurti, his partner Sarasvati continues to hold a prominent place as goddess of wisdom. Again, mention should be made of Vishnu's consort, Śri Lakshmi, as well as Sita associated with his avatar as Rama in the Ramayana.[71] Shiva's partner is best known under the name Parvati.

While all this detail might seem simply to increase the extent of the distance from Christianity, it is important to note that like is not as yet being compared with like as the Hindu conception still lies in the realm of mythology. Some sort of translation exercise is required before proper comparisons can be made. One recent, impressive such attempt is the work of the American Jesuit scholar, Francis Clooney (b. 1950).[72] Taking expressions of religious experience as central, he compares three hymns in praise of such female deities with comparable hymns in

---

[71] Śri is a confusing term. As honorific it can be applied to both deities and human persons. But it can also be used by itself alone to speak of Lakshmi, when it means 'the lustrous one'.
[72] Francis X. Clooney, *Divine Mother, Blessed Mother: Hindu Goddesses and the Virgin Mary* (New York: Oxford University Press, 2005).

honour of the Virgin Mary.[73] Although concluding that it is best to keep the two traditions distinct and that Catholicism rightly stops short of ascribing divinity to Mary,[74] he does believe that such comparisons can be mutually enriching. The treatment of Mary clearly demonstrates a belief that the feminine can be a way of access to God,[75] while the various Hindu hymns are wrongly interpreted if it is ever assumed that the goddess is a mere matronal figure quite subordinate to the god concerned.[76] On the contrary, both Vishnu and Shiva are seen to be not only fundamentally dependent on the shakti or female energy of their partners,[77] but also made more receptive thereby to the appeals of their devotees. As one commentator observes in respect of the first hymn Clooney discusses: 'She [Lakshmi] makes the Lord subordinate to her, so that he does everything for her sake. Hers is the enjoyment capable of binding him... her accessibility... the fullness of her qualities in her temple presence, her flourishing: all of these are summed up in the mention of her beauty. And none of it is separable from her role as the mediator'.[78]

---

[73] A twelfth century Sanskrit hymn in honour of Śrī Lakshmi is compared with the Greek hymn the Akathistos; a tenth century hymn to the Devi (associated with Shiva and attributed to Shankara), with the Stabat Mater; and two eighteenth-century Tamil hymns, one Hindu and the other Christian.

[74] *Divine Mother*, 227–37.

[75] For example, *Divine Mother*, 17, 185, 217, 222.

[76] This version is seen most obviously in the story of Sita as the ideal wife in the Ramayana.

[77] In the first hymn Vishnu is portrayed as subordinate to her (113, 125). In the second the Devi is declared at once 'female and supreme' (180). In the last (199) Shiva is portrayed as 'incomplete without his Apirami' (Parvati's local name).

[78] Quoted, 113.

However, given what Clooney says of such relationships, I wonder whether the implications for Christian self-understanding may not be pushed further. To see why, it is necessary to consider in more detail why it is that the hymn-writers mentioned above developed their understanding of the key role of the goddess in the way they did. It was not merely idiosyncratic or the result of excessive flights of devotion. Rather, the ideas were rooted in the myths and images of the goddess concerned. That is to say, we can speak of a whole tradition of experience of the divine that runs counter to much of the actual practice of Indian society which was just as patriarchal as in the West.[79] Take the main myth associated with Durga: it states that all the gods failed to prevent the havoc being created by Mahisha (the buffalo demon), and it was only when this virginal goddess intervened that he was stopped – by a mere kick of her feet.[80] Equally, the power of the three gods in the Trimurti is explained by the role exercised by their partners: 'I am Saraswati who bestows on Brahma the knowledge to create the world; I am Lakshmi who gives Vishnu the wherewithal to preserve the cosmic order; I am Parvati who allures the ascetic Shiva into worldly life'.[81]

---

[79] Historically, women were denied property rights and the opportunity of education. There was also the dreadful practice of sati or suttee, according to which widows were expected to immolate themselves on their husband's funeral pyre. The British authorities progressively banned the practice from 1829 onwards. On the complexities of any potential impact from religion, see Jessica Frazier ed., *Bloomsbury Companion to Hindu Studies* (London: Bloomsbury, 2011), 285–302.

[80] Devdutt Pattanaik, *Devi: The Mother Goddess* (Mumbai: Vakils, Feffer & Simons, 2000), 11–15.

[81] Ibid., 16.

How richly imaginative the stories can be is best indicated by what happens in the last case. Shiva's austerities as an ascetic caused so much animated debate that he was transformed into a pillar of fire, whose threatening aspect was only finally and successfully appeased when set in the yoni of the mother goddess. This allowed him to take Sati as wife, only for her to commit suicide when he was insulted by her father.[82] Parvati was her replacement who then persuaded Shiva to patronise the arts, dance and drama. But her union too was not without its problems. Shiva remained too ascetic to agree to a child and so Parvati produced one on her own, only for Shiva to cut off its head when he first encountered it in close proximity to his wife. Repentant, he then gave the child the head of the first creature that came to hand, an elephant, and so was born one of Hinduism's most popular deities, Ganesh. In support of her other son, Scanda, who could not defeat demons opposed to him, Parvati changed herself into the dreaded Kali. But once slaked with blood she could not stop and only Shiva appearing in her path as a corpse was finally able to restrain her. Thereafter, she was transformed into the radiant Gauri.[83] Temple imagery of course ensures that all these stories are very familiar to the average Hindu. But they are rather more than just a good yarn. They indicate not only the interdependence of male and female but also the way in which both genders can take on the other's characteristics. For example, twice we discover Parvati to be a more effective warrior than

---

[82] It is immediately following this incident that the many parts of her body were distributed across India, as described in the previous section.
[83] Pattanaik, *The Mother* Goddess, 33–44.

any of the male deities. This is symptomatic of a gender fluidity in relation to which the male god is seldom found acting on his own or exclusively in the 'male' role. In fact, both on questions of sexuality and of securing justice for one's worshippers, the female gods can often be found exercising the more decisive role.[84] So dependent are male gods on shakti or female energy that one of the subcontinent's most popular images is of Shiva and Parvati conjoined.[85]

It has already been noted as one of our recurring themes that all experience of the divine can be seen to arise from and be conditioned by the details of specific cultural contexts. These details need, therefore, to be taken into account when considering what might actually have been communicated. Some scholars have supposed that any such premise must result in the lowest common denominator, with only some very vague description the necessary result. But this would only follow if all content was treated on a par, and some not seen as more obviously conditioned by circumstance than others. Thus, in the case of the Hindu goddesses it is one thing quite naturally to doubt the historical reality of their various stories; quite another to challenge the possibility that those stories and the experiences resulting from them did not bring real knowledge of the divine nature. In other words, it is

---

[84] A recent British Museum exhibition pursued this issue across religions. For its discussion of Indian religion Belinda Crerar, *Feminine Power: The Divine to the Demonic* (London: British Museum, 2022). 94–104, 191–205.
[85] As Ardhanarishvara ('the Lord who is half-woman'). Note also Shiva demoted to a small figure alongside their two children, compared with a huge Pravati given central place: Crerar, 195.

possible without subscribing to the accompanying mythologies (though this is the means by which such knowledge was mediated) to read the interaction between god and goddess or the goddess where presented as acting in her own right as indicative of something quite fundamental about the ultimate divine nature or Brahman. If so, female divine energy or *shakti* may be seen to be at the heart of that reality but in a way which suggests mutual interdependence between characteristically 'male' and 'female' attributes. In other words, there appears to be something more radical indicated than the mutual complementarity customarily endorsed by Western theology. Instead, a richer strain implies that gender should be seen as more of a transitional concept in which female shakti or energy has become indispensable to the flourishing of any divine reality, whether male or female. As such, it might also give some support at the human level to those currently challenging any absolute distinction between the two sexes or genders.[86]

Admittedly, the original context in which these myths were developed is now lost, and so also their precise relationship to actual human experience of the divine. We only have evidence (but a considerable amount of it) of their implications being taken to heart in subsequent religious experience as reflected, for example, in poetry and other media. But to my mind this seems sufficient to justify the kind of observations made above. Even so,

---

[86] A legitimate question is how far on the human side such dissolving of difference should go. For a well-argued argument for limits, Kathleen Stock, *Material Girl: Why Reality Matters for Feminism* (London: Fleet, 2021).

some readers aware of some of the less pleasant aspects of the goddess cult may be hesitant. So let me tackle that issue head on by exploring the worship of Devi in some of its more extreme forms, in the veneration of Kali in Bengal. There are two famous temples dedicated to her cult in Kolkota. In one, the Kalighat Kali Temple, she is portrayed with three eyes and four arms, two of which have hands raised in sign of blessing. But the other two hold a scimitar and severed head. In addition, in contrast to most pujas that characterise Hindu temple offerings, animal sacrifices continue to be offered there, with goats ceremonially slaughtered, and until quite recently in large numbers. Not far away is another such temple, the Dakshineswar Kali Temple on the banks of the River Hooghly.[87] Here the image is more frightening still. As well as scimitar and severed head and a shiny black face and jutting-out brilliant red tongue, she wears a garland of fifty skulls with Shiva trodden upon beneath her feet.[88]

What makes these two temples fascinating is that, despite the crudity of the imagery (or perhaps because of it), they have in fact become great centres of devotion and spirituality. Kalighat is one of the places where Shiva is reputed to have dropped one of Sita's body-parts but, intriguingly, unlike with what might have been claimed in Christianity, the legend is not used to suggest the presence of a physical relic. Rather, it underlines her spiritual power as effectively located there. Moreover,

---

[87] The Kalighat Kali Temple was originally also on the Hooghly but the course of the river has changed over the centuries.
[88] Elsewhere she is sometimes also found with a girdle of severed arms.

although there is an accompanying myth about destroying demons, the primary message is taken to be the need to destroy the human ego if one is to receive her blessing. The situation in the other temple (Dakshineswar) is more complicated. It only dates from the nineteenth century when a wealthy widow founded it as part of a large complex that also includes twelve smaller temples dedicated to Shiva and one to Vishnu.[89] Its fame largely derives from the mystic Ramakrishna (1836–86) who spent most of his life living as an ascetic in the complex with his wife.[90] He had numerous visions which have been recorded and much discussed.[91] His most influential pupil was the reformer Vivekananda, whom we mentioned at the beginning of this chapter. He went on to found the Ramakrishna order, which has mission posts all over the world.[92] Intriguingly, he was first encouraged to visit the saint by his Principal at the Scottish Church College in Calcutta. He much admired Ramakrishna and thought some of his religious experience similar to Wordsworth's.

---

[89] Rani Rashmoni (1793–1861). Her husband died in 1836 and the temple building was begun in 1855. She participated in numerous other charitable projects, often to the benefit of the poor and in opposition to oppressive British colonial laws.

[90] He married Samada Devi in 1859 but the marriage was never consummated. Instead he treated his bride as the Divine Mother in person.

[91] Recorded in *The Gospel of Sri Ramkrishna* (1942), the text is based on notes taken by others from the last five years of his life. A debt to him was acknowledged by Mahatma Gandhi, Sri Aurobindo and Leo Tolstoy, and among composers by Dvorak and Glass. In *La vie de Ramakrishna* (1929) Romain Rolland interpreted positively his notion of cosmic consciousness. By contrast, in *Kali's Child: the Mystical and the Erotic in the Life and Teachings of Ramakrishna* (1995), Jeffrey J. Kripal reduces the experiences to symptoms of repressed homoeroticism.

[92] Vivekananda turned him into an exclusive advocate of Advaita Vedanta and underplayed the role of Shaktism.

In his own self-description Ramakrishna treated Kali as identical with Brahman. In moving towards such god-consciousness, though, techniques were employed which help explain the popularity that Kali had for him. As random examples of his behaviour one might mention the fact that, despite being of a high caste, he committed himself to cleaning the temple's public toilets, the meditation seat he used was a bench with three skulls beneath and he was often to be found dressed in women's clothes.[93] Apparently, the aim of such strange behaviour was to banish certain kinds of attitudes by starkly facing their opposite, in a pattern known as tantra.[94] Its relevance here is that both Shiva and Kali can be seen also to embrace opposites as a way towards transcendence, Shiva in the combination of asceticism and eroticism, Kali in extreme violence and tenderly motherly care. The danger of course is that any apparent absolutes are relativised. Yet in the case of gender stereotyping (whether of the divine or of human beings) such relativising could be seen as entirely appropriate.

In deciding to opt for that balance over the patriarchal bias found in Jewish and Christian texts, one might then argue that the latter are not so much wrong as one-sided. Cultural reasons can explain why the trajectory was so different in eastern experience and Western. As noted

---

[93] Elizabeth U. Harding, *Kali: The Black Goddess of Dakshinesvar* (Berwick, ME: Nicolas-Hays, 1993), 77, 105–6, 252. In the case of female dress, Ramakrishna argued that seeing oneself as a gopi or cow-maid to Krishna was precisely the kind of attitude that both male and female needed to adopt. Dressing in female clothes specifically addressed the male tendency towards carnal lust by humiliating the desire.

[94] Briefly discussed in Chapter 5, fn. 130.

earlier, the eastern belief in a single ultimate divine reality came early in the Upanishads. So any plurality was developed against the backdrop of a Vedanta that was already regarded as authoritative revelation. By contrast, as Chapter 2 indicated, monotheism arose late in the development of the Hebrew scriptures, probably with Second Isaiah. Before that time henotheism was the first approximation to develop, and in a situation in which goddess figures were still common in the home and, in a somewhat different guise, also in places of worship as well.[95] In other words, even henotheism towards Yahweh did not go unchallenged. So in trying to secure monotheism it was necessary for prophets such as Second Isaiah not only to ridicule the idols of other male deities but also practices associated with female divine figures, both within Israel and beyond. In short, the triumph of monotheism was secured at a significant (though necessary) cultural price. Fortunately, this can now be rectified by taking seriously the way in which the divine spoke of its nature within a different set of historical and cultural assumptions, namely what happened in India. This way of putting matters is by no means meant to discount alternative hints of feminine aspects to deity found in scripture and in later Christian tradition. Rather, it is intended to underline the fact that in countering the cultural conditioning which pulled in a quite different direction, there is no need to place heavy reliance on the

---

[95] Small motherly figures known as *astarte* were common in the home. *Asherim* or female obelisks were the nearest parallel found in temples. For further details, see Chapter 2, fn. 2.

secular world for the right kind of correction.[96] Instead, the divine revelatory address may be seen as already suggesting an alternative perspective on gendered attributes from within a quite different religious tradition.

Even if unwilling to accept instruction from another religion on this matter, most readers are likely to accept my general conclusion that gender is more fluid in Hinduism's treatment of the divine than is the case within Christianity. However, my earlier example of darśan is likely to be contested by some at a more fundamental level: that the practices of Orthodox Christianity could equally well have engendered the same result. Admittedly, it is true that there is an intensity of imagery in the Orthodox East that the Catholic West lacks, with church walls almost entirely covered and icons everywhere. Nonetheless, there are significant differences that suggest that there is still much to learn from Hinduism. To mention one key difference, the fundamental direction in reflection is essentially different. Icon and wall fresco are intended to draw viewers into another world rather than, as in Hinduism, the gods invading our own. The contrast can be seen in a number of ways. Various devices are used to suggest that other world, such as the saints on elevated pedestals rather than touching the earth, or again the use of inverse perspective to draw us into their world. The point is well illustrated by the primary reason why so many Western churches have

[96] This is not to deny that God can also speak through the secular world and indeed in later traditions of the church. Josephine Butler (1828–1906), for instance, was a powerful early advocate of change. But here we are concerned with noting how God also interacted more directly with others beyond Christianity, to push towards change.

introduced icons: they are seen as encouraging a sense of transcendence that is felt to be absent in Western art. Another major contrast is the degree of variety in approaches found in Hinduism as compared with Orthodoxy. In the latter a strong canon of conventions about forms of representation is maintained. By contrast, Hinduism is more open, and so correspondingly less likely to absolutize any particular image. Darśan thus challenges us on the multi-faceted character of divine immanence in a way that Orthodoxy does not.

Important though these conclusions are, in this chapter we have discussed only two of many areas of potential inter-religious exchange between Christianity and Hinduism. In Chapter 4 others will be explored but also in relation to some of the other religions of India where similar issues will be found to arise: within Buddhism, Jainism and Sikhism, each shaped in large part in reaction to what they encountered in Hinduism.

4
The Religions of India

India's Variegated Landscape

Over the course of Chapters 4–6 we will explore in turn the religions of India, China and Japan. There are a number of reasons why I have decided to adopt this approach rather than focus on a different single religion in each chapter. Partly this is because of the unusual history of Buddhism. Unlike Hinduism, it spread significantly throughout Asia but in forms which proved hugely different elsewhere from its earlier characteristics in India. From the perspective of many in the modern West, these transformations constitute a marked decline in value, indeed even a 'corruption' or 'perversion'. The more philosophical, non-theistic system that characterised the Theravada Buddhism of India is seen to give way to Mahayana Buddhism, the more 'superstitious', religious version of Buddhism, found in countries such as China and Japan.[1] Whether such evaluations are fair will need to be considered in due course. In the meantime another major reason for considering each country separately may be noted, which is that in none of the three cases did Buddhism function entirely on its own. The Buddhism that emerges in all three countries, to varying degrees, consciously interacted with the other religions of

---

[1] Each claims to be the correct version, with 'Theravada' meaning 'School of the Elders' and 'Mahayana' the 'Great Vehicle'.

that country – if not always at an intellectual level, then at the very least in terms of religious observance. Worshippers are quite commonly found combining more than one approach.

In the case of India, though, there are rather more religions than can comfortably be considered in the space of a single chapter. On those grounds, I shall largely ignore Christianity, Islam and Zoroastrianism in what follows.[2] Islam will be given its own separate treatment in due course. However, such exclusion here should not be misunderstood as a denial of significant influence in both directions. Although Christianity and Islam largely came as the faiths of invading conquerors, a hostile distance did not always remain. The openness of the Mughal emperor Akbar (r.1556–1605) is well known. In 1575 he established an open forum for religious discussion at his newly founded city of Fatephur Sikri.[3] While that position stood in marked contrast to the fanatical exclusionism of a successor such as Aurangzeb (r.1658–1707),[4] nonetheless signs of fruitful interchange continued to be seen, not least between Muslim mystical Sufism and the Hindu devotional bhakti movement. Both sought a more intimate relationship with divinity than had hitherto

---

[2] Known as Parsis, the 70,000 or so Zoroastrians who now live in India are descendants of the Persians who fled the Muslim conquest of their own country in the seventh century.

[3] A special 'House of Worship' was established where wide-ranging discussions were held. Apparently, they were frequently acrimonious. Akbar was influenced towards a more tolerant position by Sufism.

[4] Akbar's immediate successor, Jahanjir, executed the Sikh leader Arjan. It was the next ruler, Shah Jahan, who built the Taj Mahal. His elder son sought cooperation between Islam and Hinduism but was overthrown by his younger and more intolerant brother, Aurangzeb.

existed within their respective traditions.[5] Again, with regard to Christianity, it would be wrong to assume influence in only one direction, in the elimination of abuses within Hinduism and the latter's move to a more monotheistic position,[6] still less to the worryingly confused blending of cultural and religious difference in the minds of so many members of the Raj.[7] Not only the first Christian community to be established there, the Mar Thoma church of the early centuries introduced some Hindu practices,[8] there was also a lively interchange with both Hinduism and Islam in the visual arts.[9] In addition, by the nineteenth century Hinduism was being taken seriously as a religion by some Western intellectuals. Particularly influential was the movement known as

---

[5] Influence seems to have run in both directions. Sufism emerged under the Delhi sultanate of the tenth and eleventh centuries. While elements of the bhakti movement originated somewhat earlier, it is true that the wide appeal of Sufis beyond caste gave additional impetus to the common devotional style found in both.

[6] Stress on a shared monotheism seems to have become more common under British rule. Although the British did nothing about caste, sati – or the burning of widows on their husband's funeral pyre – was eventually banned in 1829.

[7] Removing shoes before entering a temple or mosque was treated by some of the colonial British as a contentious issue.

[8] This branch of the Christian church, which is found mainly in the state of Kerala, claims to date from a mission of St Thomas the Apostle in AD 52. Before the arrival of the Portuguese there seems to have been much mutual acceptance. Even today their current leader, Geevarghese Mar Theodosius, is a guru scholar. While the cross and the lamp in the church's emblem clearly suggest Christianity, at the centre of the cross is Ashoka's wheel and at its foot a lotus flower.

[9] For a comprehensive analysis of what happened and is happening, Anand Amaladass & Gudrun Löwner, *Christian Themes in Indian Art* (New Delhi: Manohar, 2012).

Theosophy. Several of its advocates spent significant periods of time in India.[10]

Even so, such interchange was relatively minor compared to what happened with the other three religions on which we shall focus here: Buddhism, Jainism and Sikhism. All three were indigenous in inspiration and, as such, in conscious rebellion against the dominant Hindu view. While the first two are roughly contemporary, it is possible that Jainism may have originated a little earlier. By contrast, Sikhism first occurred a full two millennia later. I shall use such putative dating to justify taking them in likely order of origin: Jainism, Buddhism and then Sikhism. Inevitably, in the midst of so much difference, it is possible to consider only one issue at length with respect to each religion. I shall, therefore, use Jainism to explore the question of reincarnation and Buddhism to examine issues of suffering and their cause in craving. Finally, with Sikhism I return to the question of the nature of divinity, to examine the extent to which God must necessarily be viewed as personal.

Jainism and the Issue of Reincarnation

To ease comprehension of my text, in each case I will proceed in two stages: first, by giving some account of the origins and general characterisation of the religion concerned; and second, by homing in on one particular issue

---

[10] During the first period of her life, Annie Besant (1847–1933) was married to an Anglican cleric. After meeting Helena Blavatsky she went to India where she established various educational institutions. She also became President of the Theosophical Society, then based at Madras (Chennai).

of difference for discussion. My argument will be that, although significant divergences remain, these need not be judged as irreconcilable as might once have been supposed.

Origins and Characterisation

Jainism claims a very long history stretching into the mists of the distant past. Twenty-three individuals who achieved *moksha* (liberation from the cycle of samsara or reincarnation) are acknowledged as predecessors to Mahavira,[11] undoubtedly the historical character who launched the religion in its present form. He is mentioned in some early Buddhist texts and probably was a decade or so older than Buddha.[12] Mahavira (fl. sixth or fifth century BC) and his predecessors are all known as Tirthankaras, or 'ford-makers': that is, those who, as with the general aims of pilgrims mentioned in Chapter 3, 'forded' or moved successfully from one type of reality to another. Another popular image for what was achieved has given the religion its name, for they are also seen as 'victors' (from the Sanskrit *Jaina* for a saint who has 'overcome'.) To achieve this result Mahavira embarked on a life of

---

[11] Apart from Mahavira, the penultimate Tirthankara, Parshvanatha, is the most commonly represented (with a snake crown). However, the son of the most distant, Bahubali, has a huge image in Karnataka. For an explanation of why Babubali's legend became so important, see Mary Pat Fisher, *Living Religions* (London: Laurence King, 8th ed., 2011), 124.

[12] For a list of the references, Jagmanderlal Jaini, *Outlines of Jainism* (Cambridge: Cambridge University Press, 1940), xxx–xxxii. The general consensus is now to put both figures a century later than was once thought.

asceticism and preaching when he was about thirty years old and he expected his followers to do likewise. Perhaps in view of that ascetism and other factors mentioned below, the religion is best characterised as a more extreme version of Hinduism, whereas Buddhism, as we shall see, responded by challenging several basic Hindu assumptions.

Nowadays, Jain numbers amount to about five million, the vast majority of whom continue to be resident in India. There are, though, a few teaching institutes elsewhere, such as in southern California. This development is an interesting example of adaptability in the religion, since in the past the only form of transportation allowed was walking. Other forms of conveyance were rejected because of the potential harm that could be caused to microscopic forms of life. Even to this day, monks and nuns may be seen wearing face masks or brushing the air before them in order to avoid such challenges. Indeed, a more extreme order (the 'sky-clad' ones) notoriously refuses to even wear clothes because of such problems.[13] Inevitably, the laity are not expected to go this far. Indeed, the Jains are well known in the business world, pushing well above their weight compared to what might be expected from their relatively small numbers, especially in comparison to India's population as a whole.

Two points of conflict with Christianity (where Jainism is more strident than Hinduism) are in its very strict reverence for all forms of life,[14] and the rejection of

---

[13] The *Digambara* order, which is based mainly in the south of India. The very much larger group is the *Svetambara* order ('white clad').
[14] It is often forgotten that Hinduism was once not consistently vegetarian. There are stories of Shiva eating meat in the Vedas and Puranas.

divinity as having any significant role to play in guiding practice. As we will discover in due course, the two positions are linked but it is appropriate to begin with the better known. The severity of their vegetarian code is undoubtedly the aspect of Jainism that is most widely familiar outside the community. This they connect closely with the law of karma or the moral effect of actions. Somewhat surprisingly, karma is treated more like a physical than metaphysical principle.[15] Good and bad karma are viewed as sticking automatically to the soul, the degree determined by one's conduct. Better by far, then, to free oneself entirely from such accretions. Good karma can at most improve one's situation in a subsequent life, whereas release (*moksha*) secures escape from the process altogether. And this is achievable only by abstaining altogether from any impact on other life.

Bound up with this notion of karma is not just what happens to human beings and animals but to all sentient life, seen as including even the microscopic. So even drinking water or pulling up root vegetables are potentially problematic because of the microbes in them. While resulting attempts to avoid such consequences may sound excessively over-scrupulous, they are based on a principle (*ahimsa* or the intention not to harm) that has proved surprisingly influential in the modern world. The most conspicuous influence proved to be the non-violent campaign of Mahatma Gandhi against the occupying British but the idea also influenced

---

[15] Emphasised several times in Kanti V. Mardia & Aidan D. Rankin, *Living Jainism: An Ethical Science* (Winchester: Mantra, 2013), 58–83; Parveen Jain, *An Introduction to Jain Philosophy* (New Delhi: Printworld, 2019), 99–113.

Martin Luther King's attempt to win basic human rights for black Americans.[16] Even in its early origins the notion can be seen to have had some impressive outworkings. From their inception, Jains were already found opposing the caste system and also supporting women's rights to a far greater degree than might have been envisaged given the surrounding culture.[17] Consequently, even today, although women are not permitted to be sky-clad monks,[18] they are allowed to be part of the main monastic body. Indeed, the great majority of that group is female.

Ahimsa, however, is not based simply on respect for other sentient beings. It has also been seen as a way of helping to eliminate the basic human defects or desires that keep us attached to this world, such as anger, lust and so on, as well as appetite for more than what we strictly need for human sustenance.[19] The world is divided into two fundamental categories, *jiva* and *ajiva* (soul and matter), and it is to *jiva* that we must adhere for our ultimate deliverance. Traditional Christianity can, therefore, be seen to be in conflict with Jainism on this matter at a number of key intersections. Both religions would agree that there is something fundamentally wrong with the

---

[16] Gandhi's guru, Rajacandra Maheta, was influenced by the Jains. He plays a prominent role in Gandhi's autobiography, first published in 1927, *The Story of My Experiments with Truth* (London: Penguin, 2007).

[17] Both were seen as imparting negative karma from the individual to others, through participation in such relationships.

[18] Apart from the difficulty for women of appearing naked in public, the *Digambara* also alleged that menstruation involves the killing of microscopic life.

[19] While the substitution of good emotions would be one solution, the better is what gets rid of attachment altogether: Jaini, *Outlines*, 40; Paul Dundas, *The Jains* (London: Routledge, 2nd ed., 2002), 42–43.

world. But, whereas Christianity allows a positive enjoyment of it (for example in food and even meat-eating), Jainism retains an element of suspicion in one of its major principles, that of non-attachment (*aparagraha*). Yet one need only reflect on the history of Christian monasticism to see that such more restrictive attitudes have not been entirely absent from within Christianity. The more substantial problem is thus the metaphysics, both in the kind of status assigned to all life and in the associated notion of karma operable through reincarnation.

For the Christian the worth of human beings is closely tied to the fact that their existence is a consequence of a theistic creation which sought to make them in the divine image, whatever that might be taken to mean.[20] By contrast, both Jainism and Buddhism deny the reality of a personal God. It is in virtue of this fact that both religions are sometimes described as atheist positions and as more philosophy than religion. But this seems a mistake, given the fundamentally spiritual character of ancient philosophy.[21] In denying applicability of the term 'atheist' there is also another aspect that needs mentioning, and that is the continuation of forms of worship, including temples and accompanying rituals. These temples are sometimes extraordinarily beautiful.[22] The aim, it is said, is only to honour Mahavira or Buddha,

---

[20] Numerous options have been canvassed over the centuries, including authority over creation, rationality and a social existence modelled on the Trinity.
[21] See further the discussion of Pierre Hadot's arguments in Chapter 2.
[22] The fifteenth-century Ranakpur Temple in Rajasthan is world famous for its intricate architectural style. The temple rises from the ground on 1,444 pillars.

not to ask for their aid. Actual practice is more complicated. Jains can even be found on occasion reverencing Hindu gods.[23] A highly complex cosmology of extraterrestrial worlds was also eventually postulated.[24]

Such phenomena are not without significance for what subsequently occurred in the transformation of Theravada into Mahayana Buddhism. But let us leave that issue for the moment to one side. More important to consider are the reasons for the rejection of divinity, or, more accurately, a certain type of divinity.[25] A creator god is deemed unsatisfactory because any god so described is made dependent on a desire to produce and sustain the world, which implies unfulfilled desires and thus a supreme being less than perfect. Mahavira and Buddha are admired and reverenced precisely for the reason that they have escaped such a cycle of want and desire. Any notion of petitionary prayer should also be rejected since that would call into question the heavenly being's escape from desire (in this case, a longing to fulfil others' wishes).

On the other hand, it certainly must be conceded that traditional monotheisms have often presented the alternative in too narrowly anthropomorphic terms. Although contemporary science makes it easier to speak of creation

---

[23] The inclusion of Hindu deities, especially Sarasvati, the goddess of wisdom, has been common for centuries. See further Pratapaditya Pal ed., *Jain Art from India* (London: Thames & Hudson, 1994), 13–37, 168–97. But for an internal Jain critique, 239 (illus. 106).

[24] For details, C. Caillat & R. Kumar, *Jain Cosmology* (Chicago: Art Media, 2004).

[25] Not only are some Hindu divinities accepted but the Tirthankaras are also considered divine, in possessing omniscience.

than was once the case,[26] revelation need not be understood as necessarily committing Christianity to only one particular account of the world and its origins. An eternal universe might equally have been a matter of divine support and concern.[27] Just as orthodox Christianity speaks of the eternal origination of the three persons of the Trinity, so the existence of the world could have been dependent on the divine will from all eternity. The real issue between the religions thus lies elsewhere, in whether in either scenario an active interest in the world may be regarded as compatible with divine bliss. Would not concern for its welfare undermine any such notion, whether such love is presented in traditional terms or in the more radical forms which it often takes today?[28] To begin with, note how more ordinary expressions of concern would be quickly transmogrified by the omniscient perspective that is assumed to be characteristic of divinity, since so much of the negative aspects of desire stem from a lack of knowledge of eventual outcomes. More fundamentally, though, disagreement would remain. For the Christian the world is a place of value in which divine interest and indeed love is natural; for the Jain and Buddhist such attitudes remain at most transient and limited.

[26] 'Big bang' as a scientific explanation for the universe's origins is relatively recent. The theory of steady state, advocated by Sir Fred Hoyle (1915–2001) amongst others, was once much more popular.
[27] Both in the classical world and in ancient India the notion was more common, even if myths of creation were not unknown.
[28] Divine impassibility has dominated traditional approaches, a notion rejected by modern theologians such as Jürgen Moltmann and those inspired by process theology.

There remains an alternative method of possibly effecting a reconciliation, and that is through the Jainist doctrine of *anekantavada*. Not only does the notion undermine the Jains' own absolutist position on this question, in the process it also calls into question everyone else's. It is nicely illustrated by the famous parable of six blind men attempting to describe an elephant. They are brought before a king and asked to describe the creature. One holding the trunk claims that it is like a snake, another clinging to the tail that it is like a rope, the ones nearest to the ear and tusk that it resembled, respectively a fan and a spear, the one with a leg that it is like a tree and, finally, one next to its side that it is like a wall.[29] In other words, no one position contains all truth. Such considerations as these explain why Jains are reluctant to condemn other religious perspectives.[30] Not that the idea is unknown in the West. Among the best known is a tale from the German Enlightenment playwright, Gotthold Ephraim Lessing. In *Nathan the Wise* (1779), Nathan, a wise and wealthy Jewish merchant living in Jerusalem during the Third Crusade, is challenged by the Muslim sultan, Saladin, to declare which of the three religions, Judaism, Christianity and Islam, is true. His response is the parable of the three rings. A father is inspired to make two identikits to an original ring which is reputed to bring blessing so that the three indistinguishable rings may be

---

[29] Although the earliest written version of this tale is to be found in the Theravada Pali canon (*Udana* 6.4: 66–69), Jains claim that it originated with them.

[30] For an extended defence and careful differentiation from relativism, see Jeffrey D. Long, *Jainism* (London: I. B. Tauris, 2009) 117–72.

distributed equally among his three sons.[31] Again, in the following century, Tolstoy ended one of his short stories with a similar conclusion.[32] There is also a fine film from the Far East which nicely illustrates the same point. In *Rashomon* (1950), by the famous Japanese film director Akira Kurosawa, a death is described from four different, almost contradictory perspectives, those of a bandit, the victim's wife, a samurai and a woodcutter, none of which contains the entire truth.

My point here is that neither blissful indifference nor animated concern can quite capture the truth of an overarching deity. What precisely might be entailed is hard to determine, until these alternative conceptions of divinity have been developed in rather more detail. From a Jainist perspective, not only does the Christian notion of incarnation sound altogether too mythological, equally it cannot fail to call into question the aseity or absolute self-containment of any completely fulfilled reality. From a Christian perspective, a major concern would be whether *ahimsa* really goes far enough. Is it not of equal moral importance, if not more, that such concern moves beyond non-harm into an active concern for the other's flourishing? If so, should this not apply as much to the divine as to the human? In other words, *aparagraha*, or

---

[31] Initially, the ruse does not work since they begin to fight among themselves. Eventually, however, they agree to prove their worth instead through their actions.

[32] 'The Coffee House of Surat', first published in the 1885 collection *What Men Live By*. Numerous types of faith are arguing with one another when a Chinese Confucianist asks each to explain the nature of the sun. He then suggests each be allowed to live by their own understanding.

non-attachment, is not quite enough.[33] For the moment we might let a rebuke stand against both types of religion: too much indifference to the world on the one hand and too anthropomorphic an account of divine motivation on the other. It is a debate to which it will be necessary to return, not only at the end of this chapter when considering Sikhism but also in Chapter 8.

The Test Case: Reincarnation and a Moral Universe

Here a more familiar issue may be selected, that of reincarnation. Initially, consideration under Jainism might seem somewhat artificial. After all, nowadays the notion is primarily associated with Hinduism. It is important to note, though, that in Hinduism's earliest revelatory material (the Vedas) there is no mention of the idea. The notion was only introduced in the philosophical Upanishads. Not long after, this was also the means by which it entered Buddhism and Jainism. Even so, that earlier absence could be used to challenge whether it is an indispensable element within any of these three religions. As will emerge in due course, this is a matter of no small moment for the discussion which follows. The issue will be approached in two stages: first, by considering the value apparently thereby assigned to all life; second, through the metaphysics assumed to lie behind any such approach.

Given that erstwhile Christians often opt for a belief in reincarnation because the notion appears to assign greater

---

[33] Implicitly conceded by Jains in the amount of charitable activity which many of them undertake.

value to animals, it can come as something of a shock to learn that not all believers in reincarnation in fact abstain from meat. Some Buddhists do not, while within Hinduism major controversy surrounds the question of whether the cow has always been respected in the way it is now in contemporary India.[34] That said, it is also true that in more recent years Christianity has come under attack for its indifference to other species. An often rehearsed argument is that Genesis 1. 28 ('fill the earth and subdue it; and have dominion over ... every living thing'.) has been responsible not only for the mistreatment of animals in Christian countries across the centuries but also for the environmental crisis more generally.[35] Some biblical scholars have sought to reject the claim entirely.[36] More likely, Christianity must be understood to bear some of the responsibility but with various other Western attitudes also thrown into the equation.[37] Noting that a

---

[34] For the contention that Hindu culture was originally meat-eating, see Dwigendra Narayan Jha, *The Myth of the Holy Cow* (Delhi: Oxford University Press, 2004). For what is now known about the life of cows, Rosamund Young, *The Secret Life of Cows* (London: Faber & Faber, 2017).

[35] The debate was started by Lynn White, 'The Historical Roots of our Ecological Crisis' in *Science* 155 (1967), 1203–7.

[36] See, for example, Richard Bauckham, *Bible and Ecology* (London: Darton, Longman & Todd, 2010), esp. 11–12. I have attempted a more nuanced response in 'The Bible and Wider Culture: Animals as a Test Case' in Daniel M. Gartner, Grant Macaskill & Jonathan T. Pennington eds., *In the Fullness of Time: Essays on Christology, Creation and Eschatology in Honour of Richard Bauckham* (Grand Rapids, MI: Eerdmans, 2016), 65–81.

[37] Descartes maintained that animals were no more than machines and so unable to think. See, for example, the relevant section of his *Discourse on Method* in E. S. Haldane & S. R. T. Ross eds., *Philosophical Works of Descartes* (Cambridge: Cambridge University Press, 1973), I, 115–18.

passing verse ascribes vegetarianism to pre-Fall humanity,[38] and no doubt reflecting in part on its present new-found popularity, some theologians now argue that Christianity should be seen as also demanding a similar abstinence from meat.[39] In fact, despite the centrality of animal symbolism, such as the Paschal Lamb, there have been sustained attempts in recent years to dislodge meat-eating from the central place in Christian tradition that it once enjoyed.[40]

While not necessarily demanding vegetarianism as an absolute requirement, in my view Jainism may nonetheless be seen as legitimately challenging Christianity's very human-centred approach. To Christianity's shame, for instance, it cannot really be claimed that its leaders showed much concern when factory farming of animals was first introduced. Pressure for change from non-religious groups proved far more effective.[41] Again, while it is true that methods of training animals have been transformed in recent years, the new spirit of kindness which has replaced the harsh disciplinary approach of the past was inspired by factors other than the Christian

---

[38] Gen. 9.3-4.
[39] Most impressively in the work of David Clough, *On Animals*, 2 vols. (London: T & T Clark, 2012 and 2018). About 20 per cent of the British population is believed to be vegetarian.
[40] Andrew Linzey, beginning with *Christianity and the Rights of Animals* (London: SPCK Publishing, 1987) is an obvious case in point. Also relevant are some of the articles in the two collections edited by Rachel Muers and David Grumett: *Eating and Believing: Interdisciplinary Perspectives in Vegetarianism* (London: T & T Clark, 2008) and *Theology on the Menu: Asceticism, Meat & Christian Diet* (London: Routledge, 2010).
[41] For example, Compassion in World Farming was founded in 1967 by Peter Roberts, an otherwise quite ordinary dairy farmer.

faith.[42] Even catering for the genuine bereavement that results from loss of a long-standing household pet has met with little progress in attitudes among the clergy, which is why alternative provision has markedly increased, not least in the United States.[43] Even to this day, among Anglicans the church in New Zealand remains unique in providing a liturgy for pet funerals. Of course, the issue is complicated by questions of whether the pet might in any sense be said to survive death. But that surely does not alter the undoubted fact of a profound sense of loss and the need not only to mourn but also express gratitude for the difference the animal may well have made to the quality of the 'owner's' life. Indeed, the pet may well have been instrumental in its human partner's salvation. Meeting its needs may well have moved the individual decisively towards other-regarding concerns.[44] One small sign of more positive attitudes has been the increasingly widespread popularity of the introduction of pet dedication services around St Francis' tide.[45]

In short, there is good reason to accept the precedent set by Jain behaviour towards animals in encouraging Christianity to move to a greater interest in animal welfare. Yet, although both dogs and cats encountered a largely negative response in Christianity's earlier

[42] Dog training was until fairly recently punishment-based. Now encouragement has become the more common pattern. Similarly, horse training was transformed by the so-called horse whisperer, Dan 'Buck' Brannaman. He was the inspiration for the 1998 Robert Redford film of the same name.
[43] In 2016 it was estimated that the pet funeral industry in the USA was making $100 million profit annually.
[44] A dog, for example, needs a walk whether or not the weather is clement.
[45] His feast day is set in the calendar of saints for 4 October.

history,[46] more positive pressures in the opposite direction are also to be found.[47] Change could, therefore, be justified by stressing already existing tendencies within the Christian tradition. Nonetheless, it would be a valuable concession in our increasingly pluralistic world if due note were taken of insights from elsewhere, such as those noted above from the Indian subcontinent.

More problematic is the setting of such attitudes within a wider metaphysics of karma and reincarnation. As already noted, karma is treated as an iron law of the inevitable impact of each and every action in a way that parallels the physical laws of the universe. Indeed, at times it seems viewed as having comparable status. But have we any reason to believe the pattern to be true? Claims to transmigration even within the human species seldom gain much credence in contemporary philosophical reflection. The lack of supporting evidence does not of course prove the hypothesis false. A deeper problem is the way modern science appears to have established that our mental faculties are heavily dependent on the workings of brain and body, and so humans are really a single organism rather than a combination of two distinct substances, mind and body. If correct, this would throw into question whether mind can exist apart from body in order to effect

---

[46] Notoriously, apart from the companion of Tobias in the Apocrypha, dogs meet with a consistently negative response in scripture. Even those excluded from heaven were labelled dogs (Rev. 22.15). Cats are not even mentioned. In much later Christian history they were treated as suspicious, as possible associates of the Devil.

[47] It is not just Francis who associates with animals but many of the saints, all perhaps inspired by Isaiah's image of the lion lying down with the lamb (Isaiah 11.6–9). Intriguingly, Mahavira's sermons were also supposed to be intelligible to animals and birds: Dundas, *The Jains*, 35.

any kind of transition of the soul from one person to another. While it might be tempting for Christians at this stage to gloat over the failure of eastern religions in general to generate adequate metaphysics, such self-congratulation should be short-lived.[48] For much of its history, Christianity also assumed the potential separation of soul and body as a metaphysical principle independent of religious conviction, in the widely held belief in the immortality of the soul. It was one aspect of Platonism that ran deep,[49] and indeed even survived the Reformation.[50]

Nowadays Christian theologians often write as though the psychosomatic unity that is for the most part assumed in scripture is a revelatory truth, and that this is now proved to be justified by the findings of science. But to my mind this is a misjudgement. What was revealed was the divine desire to draw closer to the created order, and thus a willingness to grant human beings eternal life. But the means towards this goal is surely a separate issue. The biblical world assumed that this would come about through a rather literalist version of the doctrine of the resurrection of the body, the Greek through immortality of the soul. The early church somewhat uneasily combined both.[51] To ensure compatibility with science we need to think in less rigourist terms, and adapt accordingly.

---

[48] This is not to deny the possibility of a less literal defence of reincarnation, for instance through the idea that the bad effects of our actions are passed in various ways to subsequent generations.
[49] Plato offers four arguments in the *Phaedo* for the immortality of the soul.
[50] The Westminster Confession of 1648 accepts the soul's immortality (ch. 32).
[51] The soul's survival of death ensured that it would be available to resurrect at the end of time by once more joining with its body.

After all, resurrection is scarcely likely in the very literalist interpretation which commonly prevailed for most of Christian history. It was assumed that mortal remains should be available for such a restoration and so cremation was almost universally opposed until the twentieth century.[52] Yet, as Paul was perhaps already implying with his analogy of the difference between seed and wheat, something quite different from either immortality or a narrowly physical resurrection really needs to be envisaged:[53] a radically different kind of post-resurrection world rather than one very obviously continuous with present reality. In other words, what matters is that the totality of human identity survives, including what has been mediated through the body, not that the form of its mediation has to remain exactly the same. There can thus be no sense of triumph in maintaining that there are good conceptual reasons why reincarnation must go. Indeed, reincarnation might have been the dependent truth implied, if that were indeed how persons are best conceived of as surviving death.

For some, any such suggestion may well be seen as excluding altogether too much from the sphere of revelation. But, just as modern scholarship has required rethinking the role of prophets, moving their primary role away from prediction towards an understanding of them as spokespersons on behalf of God,[54] so equally there is

---

[52] Although the first meeting of the Cremation Society of England took place in 1874, by the end of the century there were still only four crematoria in the whole of the United Kingdom.
[53] 1 Cor. 15. 35–49.
[54] In any case, the prefix in the Greek *prophetes* is more naturally interpreted to mean 'on behalf of' rather than 'before', 'forthtelling' rather than 'foretelling', as it were.

reason to doubt whether scientific information of whatever kind was ever part of what was revealed. Just as the two versions of the creation story in Genesis can both be true without either being in any sense a factual record of what happened, so (as we saw earlier), while the origin of the world must lie entirely in divine hands, whether that origin stood in or outside time remains a matter for scientists to determine, not theologians.[55] Similarly then, here there are various philosophical options which have been advocated to respond to the more fundamental shared religious conviction that the justice inherent in the universe requires human beings to survive death.

For eastern religions, although 'remembered' past lives may have played a small part, the impetus towards reincarnation presumably largely came from an experiential conviction that principles of justice are embedded in the ordering of the world. Within Hinduism one might see the principle as part of the constituting character of Brahman. More difficult for a Westerner to comprehend is what could be meant by the Jain supposition that karma is a physical law of the universe, not dependent on any deity. Perhaps the thought is simply that, given the universe's law-like character, moral laws are as likely to be embedded in its operations as any physical law. At all events, however conceived, in a similar way an experiential conviction arose in late biblical Judaism that God would not fail to secure justice for his saints and it was this conviction which led to its own characteristic doctrine of resurrection. Earlier analyses had found answers either

---

[55] Even with the Big Bang the 'initial singularity' still stands outside of time.

in reward in the here and now or else in the requital of subsequent generations.[56] Now, however, came the conviction not only that God would vindicate his faithful but also that there would be a drawing closer to God through encounter with the more personal aspects of divinity, a longing in love that was then intensified within Christianity.[57]

Not that any one person was responsible for these insights but a pattern of such experience would have led both positions to become deeply embedded within their respective traditions, and from that semi-common base the alternative conceptual possibilities were then developed: that is, towards reincarnation in India, and towards resurrection in Judaism. In seeking to disentangle these various elements, it is important to emphasise that my aim has not been to promote one religion above another but rather to indicate why it is not nonsense to suppose that such widely differing perspectives could nonetheless have common roots in shared assumptions about the nature of ultimate reality. Whether such encounters were personalised or not, they were founded on a common experiential conviction that ultimate reality was not just good but also just.

To conclude, in differentiating carefully between theological claim and scientific or metaphysical support it has proved possible to draw the two religions much closer together in a shared theological vision, the

---

[56] For former, for example, Ps. 37.25-6, Ps.34; for latter, for example, Exod. 20.5.

[57] Second century BCE books like Daniel (esp. 12.1–3) and Maccabees (esp. 7.13–38) seem concerned both with a just ordering of the universe and that God's 'saints' be brought closer to God.

perception of a transcendent world orientated towards justice. While they differ radically in the means that might be used to achieve this objective, their rival merits need to be assessed by addressing scientific and philosophical questions rather than through reference back to the original religious insight which can be allowed to stand. While it would be satisfying if our discussion of the issue could stop here, complications arise as soon as we note further elements in both pictures: release from karma in the eastern and heaven as an additional feature in the Western. So it will be necessary to return to the issue once more in Chapter 8.

Buddhism and the Question of Craving and Suffering

The one thing every reader is likely to know about Buddha is that his teaching was intended, and is still presented, as an answer to 'suffering' or discontent'.[58] This applies whether there is in view the more spartan version, Theravada, or the complex form in Mahayana. As with the previous section, I will first explore origins and development before focusing more narrowly on this central contribution.

Origins and Characterisation

For some, Buddhism should not even be part of this book's discussion since they conceive it to be essentially

---

[58] Although physical suffering is included, Buddha was primarily concerned with dissatisfaction in all its various psychological aspects.

a philosophy and not a religion. Its founder did not take any cognizance whatsoever of help from the supernatural, while argument was substituted for any appeal to the experience of faith. Such assumptions are common in the West and indeed are sometimes reinforced by contemporary exposition from native Buddhist writers. But how much more complicated interpretation can become is well illustrated by a number of factors that pull in the opposite direction.

First, we are faced not just with uncertainty about the date of the Buddha's birth (whether it was in the sixth or fifth century BCE) but also about how reliable the various details of his life and preaching really are.[59] The incipient community chose to rely on oral tradition for several centuries until the Pali canon produced an established corpus of 'early' records about him at the turn of our own present era.[60] Of course, in the past, as already noted with respect to the Hindu Vedic canon, human memories were once more finely tuned in the absence of alternatives. Some elements can also be seen to accord best with periods of social change. Thus, Richard Gombrich makes revolt against the 'social religion' of brahminism central to his analysis, with a more individualistic liberation seen

---

[59] Until relatively recently, 566–486 BCE was the accepted date, but majority opinion now puts his death at c. 400 BCE with his birth therefore in 480 BCE.

[60] The earliest written record is from 29 BCE. Preserved in three baskets, it is therefore sometimes known as the *Tipitika*. Pali was the lingua franca of northern India at the time. Key terms are now sometimes given in Pali and sometimes in the sacred language of Sanskrit. In Penguin Classics a selection which focuses on lay concerns is provided by Edward Conze ed., *Buddhist Scriptures* (Harmondsworth: Penguin, 1959).

as a meaningful alternative for dwellers in the newly-established towns.[61] Even so, legendary material was not unknown, most obviously perhaps in stories surrounding the Buddha's birth and temptation.[62] Nonetheless, the rough outline is clear. Born Gautama Shakyamuni of a wealthy family,[63] he was led by shock at his first sight of various signs of illness and death to pursue an alternative lifestyle. Initial attempts at extreme asceticism were abandoned as a 'middle way' was developed between that approach and his earlier life of pleasure. Enlightenment came when he worked through 'the four noble truths' to the cause of suffering ('craving') and its eventual elimination by means of the 'eightfold path', a combination of right action and correct attitudes.[64] Forty-five years of teaching then followed, ending in his death at eighty, in *parinirvana*, or 'final nibbana' (often beautifully portrayed by a statue of the Buddha lying prostrate in elegant repose).[65] While such principles are sometimes presented as entirely intellectual discoveries, such a perspective

---

[61] Richard Gombrich, *Theravada Buddhism* (London: Routledge & Kegan Paul, 1988), 5–86, esp. 24, 50, 55, 72–73, 78.
[62] The temptation is by a Satan-like figure, Mara. In the case of his birth, Queen Maya dreams that an elephant entered her womb. She then gave birth at Lumbini, standing up and without pain: *Buddhist Scriptures*, 35–36.
[63] 'Shakyamuni' refers to the tribe to which he belonged, located on the present borders between Nepal and India.
[64] The four 'noble truths' are the truth of suffering, its cause in craving, the cessation of suffering through the cessation of craving and, finally, the path to such a result by means of the 'eightfold path' in right actions and attitudes.
[65] In the main text I have added the Pali word for nirvana as a reminder that, because there are the two languages involved, different textbooks will often spell the key terms differently.

probably stems from a later shaping of the tradition in a more abstract direction. Indeed, some scholars argue that the story was originally much more explicitly experiential.[66] Just as the conviction that craving could be eliminated came from personal experiment, so too did the power of meditative experience. This may well have included a visionary element, perhaps involving the recalling of past lives and noting their conditioned character.[67] The modern emphasis on mindfulness can, therefore, be seen as a relic of that earlier point of view.

Secondly, whatever we finally conclude about Buddhism's earliest character, development into the stream that came to call itself the 'greater vehicle' or Mahayana did generate explicit acknowledgement of notions such as grace and supernatural help. Most notable was the notion of the bodhisattva, a figure seen as delaying nirvana in order to help others towards the same goal, of whom the most famous is Avalokiteśvera. In addition, more than one Buddha was acknowledged, which is why within Mahayana the historical figure is usually given his tribal name, Shakyamuni. Parallels with Christian notions of divine compassion also become strikingly close. But, as already indicated, I do not want to discuss these ideals until Chapters 5 and 6 on the place of religion in China

---

[66] This is the central contention of Eviatar Shulman, *Rethinking the Buddha: Early Buddhist Philosophy and Meditative Perception* (Cambridge: Cambridge University Press, 2014). His targets include Gombrich who, in a later book, *What the Buddha Thought* (2009), had compared Buddha with Plato and Aristotle. As Shulman expresses it, Buddha's appeal was 'personal and concrete' rather than universal, with an 'an enhanced role for experience' (28, 47).

[67] Ibid. Compare 24, 50, 61, 70.

and Japan, respectively, where the ideas of Mahayana become dominant.[68].

Thirdly, even in the version that most scholars agree is closer to the religion's origins (Theravada), it is implausible to exclude a religious characterisation once actual practice among ordinary people is taken into consideration, and not just that of an intellectual elite. Although Theravada is now chiefly found in countries other than India,[69] both versions have deep Indian roots, as can be seen from cultural survivals in India where Buddhism remained a major force until its collapse in the twelfth century.[70] That mix of the intellectual and more traditionally religious is surely no accident, since any attempt to speak of Theravada as strictly 'Protestant' in conception and Mahayana as exuberantly 'Catholic' turns out to be an absurd exaggeration. Both were more complex in their initial conception. Even at an early stage, in art and architecture, Theravada was already on the way towards a not dissimilar position from Mahayana. While initial presentations of the Buddha were aniconic (that is, mediated through symbols rather than any physical image),[71] it is implausible to suggest that such symbols were only ever

---

[68] Similar to terms such as 'Catholic' and 'Orthodox' within Christianity which embody claims to truth. Mahayana calls Theravada 'Hinayana' or the 'lesser vehicle'. Theravada is no better since its self-designation means 'the teaching of the elders'.
[69] In Sri Lanka, Myanmar and Thailand. Of the former Indo-China, only Cambodia is overwhelmingly Theravada.
[70] Although Muslim invasions played their part, it appears to have been a gradual decline, seen most spectacularly in the loss of its major seat of learning at Lalanda. The university was revived in 2007.
[71] Symbols included the bodhi tree (where enlightenment occurred), the wheel of rebirth and footprints.

intended as reminders of the Buddha's teaching. Rather, they were already being offered as patterns for incorporation into the founder's inspiration and power. Their dissemination was encouraged by Buddhism's most famous convert, the Gupta emperor, Ashoka (r. 268–232 BCE).[72] As one textbook puts it, 'devotional practices are so widespread and so influential in popular Buddhist practice that scholars have begun to examine them as perhaps being part of the mainstream of Buddhism after all'.[73] Certainly, pilgrimage to the key sites associated with Buddha's life was a common pattern in early centuries and has now been successfully revived.[74]

Accordingly, when (probably under Greek influence) physical images of the Buddha began to appear, this may be interpreted as clarification of the profound calm expected through the imitation of such meditative practices.[75] In addition, despite the degree of agnosticism advocated in respect of any help from beyond the world,

---

[72] The conversion occurred after an extremely violent, expansionist period in his reign. Some of the memorial tablets and stupas he ordered to be built have survived to this day.
[73] Fisher, *Living Religions*, 153.
[74] A book which provides both early records of the life and accounts of visits across the centuries is Molly Emma Aitken ed., *Meeting the Buddha: On Pilgrimage in Buddhist India* (New York: Riverhead Books, 1995). Not only is Lumbini (his birthplace) and Bodh Gaya (place of first enlightenment) covered but also the Deer Park at Sarnath (first sermon), Sravasti (subsequent preaching and miracles), Sankasya (place of return from preaching to the gods) and Kusinagara (place of death).
[75] Art produced in Gandhara was influenced by Alexander's invasion. From thence its influence spread across India. For an excellent account of the history of Buddhist art, see Tom Lowenstein, *Treasures of the Buddha: The Glories of Sacred Asia* (New York: Sterling, 2007). For an illustration of that calm contrasted with the effects of the asceticism which he rejected (both from third century CE Gandhara), 16–17.

the conventional account was soon complemented by stories of Buddha's own relation with the gods and other supernatural divinities.[76] This is not to deny that such elaborations could easily be characterised as superstitious accretions, but it is to note that, if this is how such practices are to be treated, then they run very deep indeed. Think, for instance, of the major annual tooth procession in Sri Lanka (a Theravada land) or the reverential adding of gold leaf to statues of the Buddha in Myanmar (another such country).[77]

Test Case: Responses to Craving and Suffering

Instead of looking further at such practices, let us focus here on where the heart of the original response to Hinduism lay, in the rejection of Vedic sacrifice and ritual as a means of escaping samsara, the continuous cycle of rebirth. Instead of the Hindu notion of liberation (*moksha*) as consisting in identification with, or absorption into Brahman, in its place comes the idea of nirvana. Although sometimes translated as extinction, it is more accurately seen also as a form of liberation, from the entanglements of the present world in samsara and karma. Any direct comparison, though, is complicated by the fact

---

[76] After the Buddha's enlightenment he seems to have seen himself as beyond both human and divine: Peter Harvey, *Introduction to Buddhism* (Cambridge: Cambridge University Press, 1990), 28. In addition to Hindu deities, reference to Nagas, a race of half-snake and half-human supernatural beings, also finds common mention throughout Asia.
[77] The tooth relic is at Kandy. Once seen, never forgotten is the devotion shown in adding gold foil to Buddha's statue in the Swedagon Temple in Yangon.

that not only are a different set of moral recommendations made to secure this end but also, more profoundly, an analysis of the human condition that demotes the central Hindu idea of an eternal soul or atman. That latter difference we shall consider in subsequent chapters. In the meantime, a narrower moral focus will be assumed.

Ritual is eliminated in favour of an ethical basis for conduct which in the process, it is claimed, will dissolve the cravings that generate human unhappiness. Christianity too sees ethics as important to salvation, but by contrast, like Judaism and Islam, finds the 'solution' to suffering in acceptance of the divine will.[78] Nonetheless, what I would like to suggest here is that Shakyamuni's principal suggestion on suffering does provide a useful corrective to some versions of the Christian approach, though neither can be seen to offer a complete answer. Fortunately for our discussion at this point, there exists a useful comparative analysis across three relevant religions of their differing ascetical practices as ways towards salvation. In this illuminating work, Gavin Flood gives Hinduism and Christianity several chapters. Sadly, though, from our present perspective only one chapter is devoted to Buddhism.[79] An additional difficulty is that, to some extent, he seems torn between an analysis based

---

[78] 'Solution' is in inverted commas because this is how the issue is often described in standard approaches to 'the problem of evil'. In my view, it is vital to differentiate clearly between the philosophical and theological issues. See further my 'The Problem of Pain: Why Philosophers and Theologians Need Each Other' in Christopher R. Brewer & Robert MacSwain eds., *God in a Single Vision: Integrating Philosophy and Theology* (London: Routledge, 2016), 28–40.

[79] Gavin Flood, *The Ascetic Self: Subjectivity, Memory and Tradition* (Cambridge: Cambridge University Press, 2004). For the chapter on

on conformity to a particular cosmic view and one drawing upon inculturation into a tradition and its favoured texts.[80]

The book ends with the huge difference stressed between modern self-assertion and the key role played by elimination of the will in ascetic practice across all three religions.[81] However, despite the ascetic's aim being undoubtedly sometimes expressed in this way, I do wonder whether identification of wills is not a more accurate summary of the most common approach, not least because this would better accord with the notion of inhabiting particular texts or their equivalent.[82] Certainly, there would be no shortage of Christian scholars who would wish to challenge his opening chapter in which Simone Weil is taken as a representative figure of the Christian tradition, with her call for self-annihilation.[83] At any rate, if we modify Flood's terminology in this way, a comparison between Buddhism and Christianity along these lines may well prove fruitful. Just as the earlier adaptation of trees, wheels and feet were presumably intended to help followers inhabit a remembered story

---

Buddhism, 119–43. Within Christianity most space is devoted to monasticism, within Hinduism to yoga and tantra.
[80] Ibid. For his cosmic analysis, for example, 10, 76, 102; for tradition, for example, 131, 136, 181; with both together, 212.
[81] Ibid., 235–54, esp. 240.
[82] Two books by Mary Carrithers from Cambridge University Press are especially important in this respect: *The Book of Memory: A Study of Memory in Medieval Culture* (1990); *The Craft of Thought: Meditation, Rhetoric, and the Making of Images 400–1200* (1998).
[83] 37–63, esp. 50. For example, Ann Loades, 'Eucharistic sacrifice: the problem of how to use a liturgical metaphor with special reference to Simone Weil' in S. W. Sykes ed., *Sacrifice and Redemption* (Cambridge: Cambridge University Press, 1991), 247–61.

of the Buddha's life, so crosses and crucifixes were far from ever intended as just a reminder of Christ's atoning role. Rather, they were utilised as devices for encouraging imitation of a particular style of life which could then be embedded in the memory, as the subjective 'I' became more closely identified with how Christ had died. It needs, therefore, to be recalled that the aim was thus rather more than the Buddhist would claim for Buddha. Rightly or wrongly, identification with a suffering figure is part of the aim, however many apparently close parallels may be produced between the two figures in art.[84]

A different pattern of development can also be detected for the iconography of Buddha and Christ across the centuries. Both religions began somewhat suspicious of direct imagery.[85] When first introduced, Buddhism offered what was in effect still a human being, though of perfect calm, who only gradually became the image with which we are most familiar today: of overwhelming size and very obviously immune to any of the storms this world can bring. Christian art effectively began with just such a victorious figure, only for him to become very much more human as the medieval period advanced,

---

[84] Robert Elinor in *Buddha and Christ: Images of Wholeness* (Cambridge: Lutterworth, 2000) is engaged in the commendable aim of attempting to bring the two religions closer together. Nonetheless, he does so at the cost of almost entirely ignoring the suffering side of Christ; for a rare exception, 45.

[85] Although imagery arrived very early in Christianity as at Dura Europus and in the Roman catacombs, suspicions remained. Clement of Rome, Origen and Lactantius thought imagery essentially pagan: compare Clement of Rome, *Letter to the Corinthians* 16.3; Origen, *Contra Celsum* VI, 75; Tertullian, *de carne Christi*, IX. Following Isaiah 53.2 it was also assumed that Jesus' body could not have been beautiful.

indeed more and more fully immersed in the world of suffering.[86]

Where I suggest both religions went wrong was in supposing that their central focus was sufficient in itself to be applicable in all situations. Taking Christian teaching first, in exactly analogous cases such as a call to martyrdom it is not difficult to see the point, or in cases where incurable physical or mental suffering presents itself. But this was often extended to the deliberate cultivation of suffering in other contexts in order to achieve identification with Christ and so absorption into his heavenly identity. The result can be witnessed not only in relatively harmless actions such as a restricted diet but also in more questionable activities such as self-flagellation.[87] Nor were such practices confined to a distant, past world. Examples at random from more recent times would include St Thérèse of Lisieux (d. 1897) offering up her toothaches for the sins of her relatives, the composer Francis Poulenc (d. 1963) believing that the unexpected and painful death of his boyfriend enabled him to live longer, or the rigours of a modern lay order such as Opus Dei, which include corporal punishment as one of its ways of atoning for sin.[88]

---

[86] At the risk of muddying the waters, we might speak of Christianity beginning its artistic story (from Constantine onwards) with a Christus Victor figure and Buddhism concluding its own in the same way with Buddha now seen as speaking triumphantly from another reality altogether.

[87] An egregious example from the Middle Ages is the treatise of St Peter Damian (d. 1072) in praise of flagellation: *De laude flagellorum*.

[88] Opus Dei was founded in Spain in 1928. For the impact of Poulenc's idea on his opera *Dialogue of the Carmelites*, see my *God and Grace of Body: Sacrament in Ordinary* (Oxford: Oxford University Press, 2007), 289–90.

Instead of such a narrow focus on pain what needs to be considered is the alternative models of sacrificial love which the Christian tradition as a whole exhibits. Quite different ways of fulfilling a Christ-like pattern need to be examined: for example, in ordinary jobs or motherhood or indeed in any context where self-suffering has ceased to be the primary focus, as with the lives of saints such as Francis of Assisi or Mother Teresa of Calcutta.[89]

It is at this point that the Buddha's central claims become pertinent. Sometimes demoting the significance of 'suffering' or 'dissatisfaction' could well be the right way to approach matters.[90] It is often forgotten that an approach not entirely dissimilar to Buddhism entered Christian reflection through the influence of Stoicism. A prominent example from the patristic period is Ambrose's *On Duties*. Here it will suffice to note the general strategy. The philosopher slave, Epictetus (d. 135 CE), provides a succinct example from within the classical world: 'You ought to treat your whole body like a poor loaded-down donkey, as long as it is possible, as long as it is allowed; and, if it be commandeered and a soldier lay hold of it, let it go, do not resist nor grumble. If you do, you will get a beating and lose your little donkey just the same. ... Since the body is a little donkey, the other things become little bridles for a little donkey,

---

[89] See further my discussion of how different kinds of precedents, though still recognisably Christian, might be set by saints and novels: 'Pattern and Particular: Saint and Novel' in my *Discipleship and Imagination: Christian Tradition and Truth* (Oxford: Oxford University Press, 2000), 62–101.

[90] It is important to note that 'suffering' is used very widely to include all forms of dissatisfaction with life.

little pack-saddles, little shoes and barley, and fodder. Let them go too, get rid of them'.[91] In similar vein, the Emperor Marcus Aurelius (r. 161–80 CE) recommends: 'What is left to be prized? This methinks: to limit our action or inaction to the needs of our own constitution... This once fairly made thine own, thou wilt not seek to gain for thyself any of the other things as well. Wilt thou not cease prizing many other things also? Then thou wilt neither be free nor sufficient unto thyself nor unmoved by passion'.[92] Some of these sentiments cannot help but recall Jesus' injunction about cloak and coat, or, more generally, about lust for possessions.[93]

It is hardly surprising, therefore, that further variants on these sentiments entered Christian ethics. Clement of Alexandria (d. 215 CE), for example, advises an initial moderation in the passions that will in due course yield place to 'impassibility' or 'passionlessness'.[94] Again, the monk, Evagrius Ponticus (345–99 CE), interprets the symbolism of the monk's various items of habit as pointing in the same direction. The sheep skin, for instance, is 'worn by those who ... muzzle the irrational passions of the body'. So in his summary of the symbolism he observes that faith 'is secured by self-control, and self-control is made unshakeable by endurance and hope, and

---

[91] Epictetus, *Discourses*, IV.1.73; cf. III. 22.13.
[92] Marcus Aurelius, *Meditations*, VI.16.
[93] Matt. 5.40: 'if anyone wants to sue you and take your coat, give your cloak as well'. Cf. also the parable of the new barns: Luke 12.13–21.
[94] Clement, *Stromateis* VI. 13. 105. The Greek *apatheia* came to mean impassibility (the inability to experience suffering) but it is arguable that writers using it as an ethical term intended this weaker sense of an intended absence of passion.

from these is born passionlessness, whose offspring is charity'.[95] Here, in effect, the elimination of craving is seen, as in Buddhism, as the way towards a salvation that is a passionless and no longer a suffering existence.

While it must, therefore, be conceded that there are some deep parallels between the two faiths on such matters, it is still the case that Buddhism in general takes this line of thought in directions where most Christians would not wish to go. As with Stoicism, there is an inherent danger of cultivated indifference to whatever happens. And, just as in Stoicism,[96] this is reinforced by the way in which the whole approach is backed up by various metaphysical postulates such as notions of impermanence and the no-self doctrine. *Anatta*, or the no-self doctrine, is the claim that there is no underlying substance or soul to a human person. Instead, the individual is composed of elements which are constantly changing. Because all existence is like this (*anicca*) it becomes foolish to attach too much value to any particular thing or moment.[97] It will be necessary to pursue these claims further in subsequent chapters.

---

[95] Evagrius Ponticus, *Prologue to the Practicos* (Letter to Anatolius), 6 & 8.
[96] Which explains why physics was so important to the Stoics.
[97] The two terms are quoted in Pali in the main text. Their Sanskrit equivalents are *anatman* and *anitya*. Further undermining any treatment of the proximate as contact with reality itself is the doctrine of 'dependent origination', the view that our perceptions are constructed out of past experience and belief rather than just through direct encounter. One textbook even claims that as a result Buddha may be seen as 'the first person in history to reject, let alone entertain, the notion that the external world apprehended through the senses is a mind-independent reality': Alexander Wynne, *Introduction to Buddhism* (London: I. B. Tauris, 2015), 5.

In the meantime, we may admit the force of such considerations at a more practical level. It is all too easy to exaggerate the importance of some event that has happened. Great offence is taken when a better course might well have been to ignore the incident altogether. Again, in a highly self-assertive culture like our own a recommendation to downplay the self would again seem to make good sense. One approach within Christianity which acknowledges the legitimacy of this approach has already been mentioned, in the attempt either to identify or else replace one's own will with that of God's. But the danger in such attitudes is that not only can they very easily lead to self-deception, it also surely ignores what are sometimes legitimate concerns for a more fully developed sense of self-responsibility.[98] Equally, it is sometimes important that a person's worth be affirmed, not denied, as some of the issues arising out of the contemporary focus on sexual abuse well illustrate. Such treatment sometimes leads to a self-hatred in which abusers are exempted by their victims from all blame.[99] So, complex strategies are often required to re-establish victims' sense of their own self-worth. Even so, qualifications such as these are hardly sufficient in themselves to eliminate the major role Buddhist-type meditation could play in a spiritual path that still remains fundamentally Christian.

---

[98] That a particular course of action is the divine will may well be sincerely believed, yet actually be used as a means of manipulating others in order to get one's own way.
[99] Victims effectively blame themselves for what happened, an attitude often encouraged by the abuser since it makes abuse easier to accomplish and justify.

Finally, something needs to be added on the authoritarian character of some Christian practice. While there is a place for justified outbursts of anger,[100] some of Jesus' confrontational responses to the Pharisees are so extreme that many contemporary scholars suggest an exaggerated record created by the prejudices of the gospel writers rather than a true account of how Jesus acted.[101] Unfortunately, however, that presumed pattern of behaviour may well have influenced subsequent Christian practice for the worse, not least in the behaviour of church authorities.[102] If so, we may conclude that Christianity could again greatly benefit from the more reflective and calm approach enjoined by the Buddha. If by no means entirely eliminating the causes of suffering, such attitudes would at least help prevent the assertiveness and manipulation that is so much a pressing sore in some patterns of Christian counselling.

In short, my suggestion here is that, if we focus on the experiential element in Buddhism (which, as we have seen, could possibly be its original form) and equally on the Stoic inheritance in traditional Christian ethics, then the two religions, while not exactly converging, do in fact

---

[100] In Jesus' case, most obviously perhaps in the expulsion of the money-traders from the Temple.

[101] Modern research suggests that the vitriol against the Pharisees ('whited sepulchre', etc.) was quite unjustified in terms of the sincerity of the Pharisees' own religious convictions: for example, E. P. Sanders, *Judaism: Practice & Belief 63 BCE–66 CE* (London: SCM Press, 1992), 413–51. Accordingly, NT scholars suggest that, as currently framed, the exchanges reflect the bitterness of later exchanges with the incipient church.

[102] A severe, condemnatory Christ can easily be used to justify a church quick to condemn, and indeed may well explain why John 7.53–8.11 was almost lost from the gospel tradition.

come considerably closer on the question of practical attitudes to suffering than might have been anticipated. More importantly, such a limited rapprochement also allows mutual learning. Even so, huge differences remain, not least on the question of supernatural help. Yet, as Chapter 6 on Japan in particular will reveal, Mahayana did move closer in taking seriously the issue of grace. But first, our final Indian religion.

Sikhism and the Divine as Personal or Otherwise

Despite the huge difference in date of origin compared to the other two religions discussed, there are many points of overlap with both Jainism and Buddhism but also, perhaps most significantly, with Hinduism. As usual, I begin by exploring the religion's origins and general characterisation, where some degree of influence from Islam is also evident. However, the topic given special attention is one where Islam and Christianity would both disagree with Sikhism on the personal character of God. While after our analysis some differences will remain, the root disagreement will turn out once more not to be quite as fundamental as is commonly supposed.

Origins and Characterisation

In comparison with Jainism and Buddhism, Sikhism is very young. It first came to prominence in the fifteenth century of the common era.[103] Somewhat surprisingly,

---

[103] There are about twenty million Sikhs in India and almost two million elsewhere.

despite its arrival being almost two millennia later, historical details about the religion's founder, Nanak are not in much better state than proved to be the case with Shakyamuni. Known as *janam-sakhis*,[104] extant biographies were written down seventy-five to a hundred years later.[105] W. H. McLeod, the leading expert on these tomes, created a storm of protest when he first argued that general implausibility and inconsistencies combine to make much of the material unreliable.[106] Most of his claims are almost certainly largely true. Yet, what is ignored in his discussion is the symbolic significance of such legends. It is extremely unlikely that Nanak ever visited Mecca. Nonetheless, there is a ring of truth in the story of how he responded to a reprimand for his discourtesy in allowing his feet to face Mecca's central symbol (the black stone of the Kaaba): 'tell me then where I may not face God?' Even if not historically true, the question asserts something fully concordant with Nanak's own perspective: God is immanent everywhere, and so no more present in one direction than any other.[107]

Fortunately, as with the life of Buddha, there is no difficulty in providing a basic outline of his life.[108] While

---

[104] Literally 'birth-evidences' or 'evidences of his life'.
[105] W. H. McLeod, *Guru Nanak and the Sikh Religion* (New Delhi: Oxford University Press, 1968), 147.
[106] McLeod sets out a strong position at the outset: 5. As example, note his rejection of any extensive travel: Assam (111), Dacca (112), Ceylon (113), Mecca (122), Bagdad (125).
[107] For a popular use of the story, compare Gurbachan Singh, *The Sikhs: Faith, Philosophy & Folk* (New Delhi: Lustre Press, 1998), 18; for an equally powerful non-historical application, Nikky-Guninder Kaur Singh, *Sikhism: an Introduction* (London: I B Tauris, 2011), 6.
[108] On which McLeod is agreed.

the place and date of birth is uncertain, we do know that Guru Nanak worked in an estate office at Sultanpur. It was near there that his search for spiritual truth culminated in what was clearly a defining experience.[109] Whereas for Buddha enlightenment happened under a bodhi or fig tree, in Nanak's case (also at the age of thirty, probably in 1499 CE) the experience occurred in or near a river. The biographies relate his mysterious disappearance for three days. Whatever precisely occurred, the guru emerged with a passionate conviction that he was to spread the true aim of religion: like his own experience, mystical union with God, and available to all without any distinction of caste or requirement for priestly mediation.[110] Instead, people were expected to listen to the divine word mediated through him as their guru or 'teacher'. It was a word in which, although questions of morality were not altogether absent, the central focus was now on how to draw closer to the divine, with most of what survives from Nanak's lips in fact hymns of praise.[111] In addition, the rituals of India's two major religions were attacked as embodying a false piety which did nothing to lead the individual closer to God. After an itinerant ministry, Nanak eventually settled at Kartarpur near Lahore, with a small body of Sikhs or 'disciples' practising a daily cleansing of both mind and body. There he died in 1539.

---

[109] Sultanpur is a city in modern Uttar Pradesh, 135 miles east of Lucknow, the state capital.
[110] That strong sense of equality continues in the offer of free meals without distinction to all who visit Sikh places of worship. The largest temple in Britain at Slough even provides basic skills courses for free, again to anyone who applies.
[111] More than any other guru apart from Guru Arjan at 2,218.

Given that, in the region of the Punjab where most of his followers would be concentrated, the adherents of Hinduism and Islam were roughly equal, it is sometimes suggested that Nanak's aim was either some form of syncretism or else a half-way path between the two. But as an analysis this does not really work as the teaching is not presented in any sense as lying in succession to either tradition. Qur'an and Vedic texts are alike ignored. More plausible, therefore, is the suggestion that he be seen in continuity with not only Muslim Sufi mystics and Hindu bhakti devotees, who had been active since at least the twelfth century, but also the more recent *sants* who bypassed Hindu avatars and directly addressed their love to the supreme God.[112] Of the latter the most famous is Kabir who was a somewhat older contemporary of Nanak, although there is no evidence that they ever met.[113] Looking further back to more long-standing traditions in the two religions, some major changes are evident. Although the idea of reincarnation is retained, the Hindu gods are now seen as either another name for the One or as something less than divine reality itself.[114] Again, although Islam's focus on the divine names is still there, they are given a much more metaphorical interpretation. The Sikh version of meditation on the divine

[112] Although in practice like-minded people might be identified, despite the similar spelling there is no etymological connection with 'saint'. A *sant* is someone who has experienced the truth of ultimate reality.
[113] Although from a Muslim family, Kabir mostly expressed himself in bhakti terminology in poetry that is among India's most famous. Like Nanak, he condemned the sacred thread as a mark of caste among Hindus and the use of circumcision in a similar exclusory role among Muslims.
[114] For some textual examples, see McLeod, *Guru Nanak*, 165–66.

names eventually took the form of a simple recitation of *Waheguru* or 'wondrous Guru'. In the terminology of praise nothing is seen as absolute. So divinity at its most ultimate should be characterised as without any specific attributes or indeed any adequate description at all: as *nirguna* (without form or attributes).[115]

What precisely such limitations on expression might entail is an issue to which we shall return shortly. But first something needs to be said about the fluid subsequent history of the movement until the time when everything becomes more or less fixed, with the death of the last guru in 1708. While all nine of Nanak's successors as leaders of the community are highly regarded, only a couple need concern us here. Although the Mughal emperor Akbar visited the third and fourth gurus, the next one, Guru Arjan, was eventually tortured and put to death under Akbar's successor, Jehangir. Apart from his writings, Arjan (the fifth) is important for two main reasons. Not only did he complete the building of Sikhism's most holy shrine at Amritsar, he also made the first attempt to produce a canon of scripture. This included not only hymns by the first five gurus but also compositions by Sufi and bhakti writers, as well as a large number by Kabir. As such it is enormously long.[116] A second collection of equal length was produced by the tenth guru,

---

[115] The term is borrowed from Hinduism. The contrast term is s*aguna* (with attributes).
[116] It is 1,430 pages long. For a list of its contents, Kaur Singh, *Sikhism*, 33. For a more easily comprehensible selection: Christopher Shackle & Arvind-pal Singh Mandair eds., *Teachings of the Sikh Gurus: Selections from the Sikh Scriptures* (London: Routledge, 2005).

Gobind Singh. Although their quality is more uneven,[117] it includes some memorable poetry, such as the following, describing the soul's longing for its divine Lover:

> Tell the friend whom we love
> The state of His disciples:
> Sickened by their quilts without You,
> Our mansions are like snakes' nests.
> Flasks are torture, cups are knives,
> We're cut by butchers' choppers.
> Longing for His simple bed,
> We curse this rich existence.[118]

It was Gobind Singh who decreed that after him the voice of such books should replace living gurus. It is as such that Arjan's collection reigns as Guru Granth Sahib or the Eternal Guru, with a central and permanent place in all contemporary Sikh places of worship. Indeed, the common name for such places clearly indicates just such a centrality. Called a gurdwara, the term means 'door to the guru', in this case obviously that book. Like all sacred texts some parts are treated as more important than others. The honour in which the book is held may be illustrated in a number of ways, all ceremonial, including admission to the community and weddings or funerals taking place in its presence. The practice of continuous recitation is common and guidance may be sought by opening it at random. Most powerfully of all, at the main Sikh shrine of Amritsar it is treated in the manner of a

---

[117] Its opening, the Jaap, is still used in worship (not to be confused with the Japji which opens the Guru Granth).
[118] *Teaching of the Sikh Gurus*, 116.

Hindu deity, duly honoured during the day and put to bed in a separate room at night.[119]

While this is to note what takes place within the community, it is what is presented externally which is likely to be better known in society more generally, such as the turban and other distinctive items of wear. The group also enjoys a glowing reputation for military service. No less than a hundred thousand Sikhs served in the British army during the First World War. Nanak could hardly have envisaged that focus but it became inevitable once the full might of the Mughal emperors was launched against adherents of this faith.[120] The various symbolic items of dress helped forge a common resistance and ultimately an army, with all men now surnamed Sikh or 'lion' and the women Kaur or 'princess'. The most memorable story from this time is Gobind Singh's request for five volunteers to be sacrificed on behalf of the community. In a manner reminiscent of the biblical story of Abraham and Isaac, it was made to look as though they would die, but they finally returned, found both living and faithful.[121] The incident has proved inspirational in the face of many subsequent challenges. Most notable was the terrible situation in 1922 caused by a British decision not

---

[119] The one day I spent at Amritsar left me surprisingly moved by these rituals. Even Guru Granth Sahib being put to bed was enacted with impressive solemnity, while earlier in the day a delicious meal had been served with efficiency and charm to huge numbers.

[120] The ninth Guru was executed for advocating religious freedom, while the tenth (Govind Singh) was engaged in almost continuous conflict with Emperor Aurangzeb.

[121] Remembered as the day in 1699 when the special order of the Khalsa was inaugurated. Five goats were substituted. For further details, Kaur Singh, Sikhism, 48–52.

to allow a train carrying prisoners to stop for food. Two Sikhs lay on the line in an attempt to compel a different decision. Their resultant deaths were inevitably treated as martyrdom.[122]

In trying to comprehend present attitudes, the past is of course a good guide. Past militancy, for example, continues to resurface. This was perhaps most evident in response to the actions of Mrs Gandhi's government in 1984 in attacking the temple at Amritsar but it can also be seen in continuing demands for a Sikh homeland (two thirds of the former Punjab is now in Pakistan).[123] Or, to take a rather different example, rather than appealing to secular arguments, rectifying unfairness towards women tends to be argued from appeal to the radical equality which was proclaimed in the faith's origins.[124] So far, where attitudes to other religions are concerned, despite the elements of critique of other faiths which we have already noted, Sikhism remains essentially non-missionary in character. This is because other pathways to God, even if imperfect, are treated as also of value, something clearly implied by the inclusion of some non-Sikh texts in their scriptures.[125] In part, such attitudes are

---

[122] A detailed history of Sikh struggles is available in Khushwant Singh, *A History of the Sikhs* 2 vols. (New Delhi: Oxford University Press, 2004).

[123] The attack resulted in much destruction and loss of life. Indira Gandhi was assassinated by her Sikh bodyguard later that year. For further details, Khushwant Singh, *A History*, 351–76.

[124] As in Kaur Singh's book, *Sikhism*, esp. 101–21, where she protests against recent patriarchal attitudes such as only allowing men to read in the gurdwara.

[125] 'It is the same God in different religions': Kawaljit Singh, *Thoughts to Heal: The Shri Guru Granth Sahib Way* (Amazon, n.d.), 33

generated by their strong perception of the transcendence of God. By this is not meant that God is remote or distant. Rather, the point is that no description of the divine could ever adequately capture that reality.

Test Case: Divine as Personal or Not

In accordance with the view of divinity just noted, each morning a Sikh will recite the Jap Ji or opening of the Guru Granth Sahib which stresses a single, impersonal source to the universe: 'My sovereign is One. One It is, yes One only!' 'No idea of him can be conceived through thousands of thoughts. Ultimate silence evades the deepest meditation'.[126] While some Sikh intellectuals want to equate this affirmation to monism,[127] the strong stress on creation throughout their scriptures suggests a rather different view.[128] It is sound and word coming to birth that give specificity but in itself the divine remains ineffable.

It is surely here that the Sikh challenge to Christianity is at its most evident. It shares with Christianity the language and imagery of a personal monotheism and also

---

[126] Unfortunately, translations vary widely. The second element comes from Shackle & Mandair, *Teaching of the Sikh Gurus* (4), the first from Kaur Singh (59). The latter points out that the sign for the number one is followed by the first letter in the Gurmukhi script which is also the sign for Om (the sound that originates the universe), and that this is followed by an arc for 'is', indicating infinity.

[127] For example, Arvind-Pal Singh Mandair, 'Sikh Philosophy' in Pashaura Singh & Louis E. Fenech eds., *Oxford Handbook of Sikh Studies* (Oxford: Oxford University Press, 2014), 298–314.

[128] For example, 'God has no limits, Nanak, nor any boundaries, He causes the creation, then its destruction too': Shackle & Mandair, *Teaching of the Sikh Gurus*, 40.

the desire for union with that divinity, yet insists that the God into whom the worshipper is absorbed is ultimately beyond all such categories. So where stands the common Christian assertion that God is ultimately personal and that it is in this respect that human beings are declared to be in the divine image? While such disagreements are not capable of easy resolution, Christians ought to be hesitant about too readily endorsing the claim that the truth of the matter is entirely on their side. God cannot possibly be personal in precisely the same way that human beings are. So much of human identity and interaction is provided by temporal sequence. Most of our thinking, for instance, is a matter of working through to particular positions. Again, so far from having immediate intuitive knowledge of another person, our relations and understanding need time to develop. Yet for most of its history these characteristic features of personhood have been excluded from the Christian understanding of divinity. Admittedly, given that the Bible's more metaphorical language does not explicitly endorse any such contrast, many contemporary theologians (desirous of greater divine involvement) have described God as not only in time but interactive with the world in numerous ways, including the potential for suffering.[129] But even if this were deemed to be a legitimate move, huge differences would remain. Not only does an omniscient being have no need to engage in sequential reasoning, but also such knowledge excludes so much of the suffering associated with the human condition where it is uncertainty about the outcome that most often brings

---

[129] Jürgen Moltmann (b. 1926) is the best known of numerous other such examples.

the greatest burden: will the pain last a few hours or many years? In addition, the absence of a body not only excludes all physical pain but also much mental as well, since emotions largely express themselves through the body.

It will be said that what I am ignoring is that 'the personal' is, like all other language about God, analogical. Only some of its content as applied to the human is applicable to God. But such a contention is hardly sufficient of itself to imply that truth lies wholly with the conventional Christian image of God as personal. If all knowledge is simultaneously present to the divine, it is not as though anything has to be done to acquire it: it is just there. Indeed, Plotinus (d. 270 CE), the most famous philosopher in the early period of the Christian era, in his adaptation of Plato's philosophy from six centuries earlier insisted that such considerations entailed a level of divine reality beyond discursive thinking, beyond any division between subject and object. That is one reason why he postulated a threefold level to divine existence, the One, Mind and World Soul. While the last represents divine action, the Mind is constituted by divine awareness of the objects in its reflection, whereas the One operates at a blissful, higher level in the fusion of all understanding into a single, undifferentiated reality.[130] His writings are not always easy to understand but perhaps an analogy with human experience might help. Self-awareness is in fact what gets lost when our enjoyment is at its most

---

[130] A Demiurge and World Soul are both present in the *Timaeus*: see further Sarah Broadie, *Nature and Divinity in Plato's Timaeus* (Cambridge: Cambridge University Press, 2012). The One emerges from the *Philebus* and *Parmenides* by a more complex process: compare Harold Tarrant, *Plato's First Interpreters* (London: Duckworth, 2000).

intense. Think, for instance, of reading a novel or watching a film or football match. If our attention is wholly absorbed, not only do we cease to have any sense of time passing, we also have no notion that it is 'me' who is doing the reading or watching; for that sense to be revived, someone needs to interrupt. While it is true that Plotinus thought of such moments of absorption as models of intuitive awareness that could be extended more generally in our imitation of the divine, our interdependence with one another would seem to preclude this as a general pattern. It thus remains entirely appropriate to differentiate the strong sense of personal identity which characterises human beings from any higher form of existence universally characterised by knowledge of this kind.[131] Indeed, so united is the One with the objects of its thoughts, the good and the beautiful, that according to Plotinus such a reality may equally be called by their names. The Good and the One can thus effectively be treated as a single reality.[132]

The early church chose a different path. Although three aspects to the divine were distinguished, all three were declared personal.[133] Yet there remain some obvious unresolved problems in the history of the resultant doctrine of the Trinity. Already with Augustine we find a

---

[131] For a valiant attempt to defend the value of intuitive thinking more broadly, Sara Rappe, *Reading Neoplatonism: non-discursive thinking in the texts of Plotinus, Proclus and Damascius* (Cambridge: Cambridge University Press, 2000).

[132] His inspiration here is Plato, *Republic* Bk. 6, 509.

[133] Although the intention was to have three personal elements, in practice a neuter was commonly used for the Spirit, as is even the case sometimes in Paul.

mixture of personal and less personal images.[134] By the high Middle Ages this was to resolve itself into a version of the doctrine, according to which the 'persons' were equated with relations, and so all sense of real differentiation removed.[135] Divine simplicity was thus effectively defended but with trinitarian doctrine no longer seen as making any real contribution to some sense of the personal within the divine.[136] As such, the position offered a marked contrast to the strong sense of differentiation affirmed in the New Testament where even in John's Gospel the Father and Son are seen as strongly interacting with one another.[137] That said, it ceases to be surprising that at various periods of history a more social analogy for the Trinity has been advocated as a way of preserving personal interaction.[138] To such an approach the objection is often urged that either it creates too much

[134] With Augustine even questioning the use of the word 'person' itself: 'the answer is given three "persons," not that it might be completely spoken but that it might not be left wholly unspoken'. (*De trinitate* 5.9).
[135] The Fourth Lateran Council (1215) asserted that the three 'persons' were solely differentiated by their relations and indeed affirms, somewhat incoherently, that 'we believe ... and confess ...that there is one supreme reality...which is truly Father, Son and Holy Spirit, at once the three persons taken together and each of them singly': H. Denzinger & A. Schönmetzer, *Enchiridion Symbolorum* (Freiburg: Herder, 36th ed., 1976), no.804.
[136] The demand for simplicity is already there in Plotinus, for example, 'There must be something simple before all things. A reality of this kind must be one alone'. (Enneads 4.1.5–16).
[137] John postulates a more intimate relationship than is found in the synoptics but without compromising any sense of distinction and interaction between them.
[138] While boldly tracing such an approach to the Cappadocian Fathers belies somewhat the subtlety of their writings, these did mark the beginning of imagery that can be found across Christian history, in Richard of St Victor in the Middle Ages, F. D. Maurice in the

separation or else it is too anthropomorphic, but the latter is in fact an objection that could equally be urged against most attempts to say anything at all about the life of God. Talk of an internal dance, for example, or even of detailed dynamics in the love between the persons are more naturally interpreted as poetic engagement with the notion rather than serious philosophical explanation.[139]

Perhaps such an acknowledgement of underlying problems provides enough material to feed into greater humility when talking with Sikhs. Although their scriptures are overwhelmingly poetic rather than explicitly doctrinal or systematic, they do make clear that the divine word came out of the One, to address humanity, and by its grace draw us into relationship with that supreme reality.[140] Is it possible, then, to think of the Trinity in the same way? Of course, if we said that it was only in the world that this happened, this would not be what the church affirms, an ontological reality that is constitutive of God and not just a divine way of accommodating to the world. But there is an alternative option for thinking of that emergence and so of how divinity might appear in itself were it to choose to adopt more personal forms of expression. Although the analogy is somewhat remote, the reality of the divine that remains non-personal (or more than personal) and ineffable might be compared with our own unconscious

---

nineteenth century and Leonard Hodgson in the twentieth before its great expansion in more recent times.

[139] Although the language of perichoresis is now widely translated in terms of the image of a dance, in fact the Greek root comes from a quite different verb, from placement rather than dance.

[140] Note that this is not the same idea as the Christian emergence of the Word from the Father, in that the latter is already seen as personal.

(at least in terms of self-awareness) and the Trinity as its more personal self.[141] That latter self is brought to expression not just to benefit what happens in the world or even to human beings after death,[142] it is surely also because divinity's extension into self-expression is part of its more general strategy of choosing to launch into what is other than itself, in creation.

Such questions and comparisons will be pursued in more depth in Chapter 8. For the moment, though, suffice it to say that both religions can now be seen to acknowledge divinity at its most profound as something greater than personhood, even as they differ on what might constitute human appropriation of the divine. For Christianity the stretch of grace is all the greater in that human personality is not allowed to disappear into divinity. Rather, it is invited into a personalised form of interaction where human beings' basic identity as personal can still be retained. Might Christianity, though, have claimed too much in identifying that relationship as also what ultimate divine reality is like? More needs to be said, and so it will be a topic to which we will return in Chapter 8.

It is time now to move further east, and observe how a new version of Buddhism flourished in its new Chinese context, with two native religions, Confucianism and Taoism, not just competitors but all three interacting and helping to shape one another.

---

[141] The human unconscious is obviously different in still involving sequential thinking.
[142] It is after all so much easier to understand how we might relate to the divine as Trinity than to a being bereft of all the more obvious features of personality, as was suggested above.

5
The Religions of China

A Nation in Transition

In moving from India to China and Japan over the course of Chapters 5 and 6, respectively, we enter a rather different world. Whereas in India, as previously noted in Chapter 4, interest in religion seems to be increasing in what is already a religion-soaked country, in modern China and Japan serious religious concerns are confined to a relatively small minority of the population. The situation is thus more like Western Europe but the dominant religions are quite different so they can still provide Christianity with some important options to ponder. One of these is the capacity of religion to adapt to different circumstances. The Mahayana version of Buddhism found in both lands is quite different from the earlier Theravada form. However, as with India, earlier forms of religious belief and practice also survived. Inasmuch as these are significantly different from India's Hinduism, the Shintoism of Japan and the Confucianism and Daoism/Taoism of China will also raise some interesting challenges.[1] In this chapter I begin with China's two native religions before exploring how Buddhism changed as it acclimatised to its new Chinese context, effectively

---

[1] Daoism is the preferred modern transliteration of Taoism, as in the move from 'Peking' to 'Beijing'. The nineteenth-century British system of Wade–Giles was replaced in 1982 by Hanyu Pinyin. In what follows an occasional use of the older form is retained.

making it China's third 'native' religion. While few would doubt that Shintoism is a religion, with both Confucianism and Daoism there are many scholars both within China and beyond who would challenge such an interpretation.[2] So in each case our analysis will begin by considering that issue before we go on to explore a test case for dialogue: in the case of Daoism, in attitudes to the beginning and end of life; with Confucianism, the potential contribution of religion to society.

It would seem appropriate to begin with some more general remarks on the current state of China. It is a vast country which, in the last few decades, has transformed itself not only into the fastest growing economy in the world,[3] but also one which has successfully released the great majority of its citizens from acute poverty.[4] As a result there has been a huge influx of migrant workers into cities, both old and new.[5] Although working conditions remain inferior to those in the west, outside of politics there is a wide range of cultural freedoms which involve both old and new types of media. It is into this context that fresh interest in religious and spiritual issues

---

[2] The stronger form of denial is the claim that any inclusion of a religious element is a perversion. A weaker form acknowledges religious elements but denies their centrality. The former position is more common with Confucianism, the latter with Daoism.

[3] Its GDP has already overtaken that of the United States but of course the result is spread over a much larger population.

[4] The rule of Mao Zedong (1949–76) was a disaster for the country. Tens of millions died in the Great Leap Forward (his attempt to industrialise the country, 1958–62), while much of value was destroyed during the Cultural Revolution (1966–76).

[5] Twelve cities have a population of over 10 million. Three exceed 20 million: Beijing, Shanghai and the largest, Chongqing (in south-west China), at nearly 32 million.

needs to be set, with some clearly feeling that the new economic prosperity is not quite enough to satisfy. As one commentator (concluding his survey of recent trends) observes, 'perhaps because Chinese traditions were so savagely attacked over the past decades, and then replaced with such a naked form of capitalism, China might actually be at the forefront of a worldwide search for values.'[6]

During a visit to China in 2019 I observed people praying in Confucian and Daoist temples, even where these remained fully under state control.[7] Large numbers were also to be seen participating in pilgrimage to traditional mountain sites.[8] Even Muslim and Christian places of worship were packed with the committed, and such people were apparently unhindered by any form of government interference.[9] However, to stop there would be to present altogether too positive a picture. Older readers will recall the way in which maps used to represent Great Britain as the centre of a world over which its empire presided, with more than a third of the world's land mass coloured in red. Historically, Chinese attitudes have not been much different. Even the native name for the country (*Zhongguo*) reflects such a perspective: the word means

---

[6] Ian Johnson, *The Souls of China* (London: Penguin, 2017), 400,
[7] As with the Confucian temple in Qufu, near which the sage is buried. Since 1994 it has been a World Heritage site. I am hugely grateful to the insights of the architectural historian Jon Cannon of Bristol University, who led an extensive tour to 'sacred sites of China' in 2019, in which I participated.
[8] Such as the Buddhist site of Wutaishan in Shanxi province and the Daoist Mt. Tai, north of the city of Tai'an in Shandong province. I found Chinese tourists and pilgrims happily intermingling.
[9] My trip did not include the Uighur state of Xingiang. Elsewhere, though, no obvious forms of surveillance were to be observed. It was thus quite unlike my experience on visits to the former Soviet Union.

literally 'middle land' or 'central state'.[10] Not surprisingly, therefore, Buddhism was really only fully accepted once it adopted a Chinese face.[11] Islam and Christianity continue to be viewed with suspicion as essentially foreign. Some of Islam's buildings at least demonstrate adaptation but this is seldom so with Christianity.[12] The main Catholic cathedral in Beijing, for instance, is uncompromisingly Gothic, and of course the authority of the pope is seen as alien. Ironically, earlier encounters represented more of an interchange, as in the Nestorian mission from the seventh century onwards,[13] or again in the Jesuit encounters in the sixteenth.[14] Sadly, however, the best remembered period is the nineteenth century when the arrival of missionaries is hard to disentangle from the savagery of Western colonialism.[15] That explains why native Catholic

---

[10] The English 'China' is borrowed from Portuguese, probably ultimately deriving from the name of the dynasty that first united the country (the Qin).

[11] It was first brought to China during the Han dynasty (c. 150 CE) but suffered persecution even as it tried to assimilate, for example, under the Tang (845 CE).

[12] The Great Mosque of Xi'an, which was built in 740 CE, is in a thoroughly Chinese style.

[13] Now a shadow of its former self, the Nestorian mission was accelerated from its base in the Middle East by the advance of Islam into its own lands.

[14] The extent of accommodation is explored in Martin Palmer, *The Jesus Sutras: Rediscovering the Lost Scrolls of Taoist Christianity* (New York: Random House, 2001). In the late sixteenth and early seventeenth century Matteo Ricci and the Jesuits made good progress, partly through accepting the legitimacy of ancestor worship. Under counter-attack from Dominicans their approach was eventually condemned by the papacy.

[15] In the nineteenth century evangelisation was unfortunately closely associated with attempts to force trade in opium on China, as in the First and Second Opium Wars (1839–42 and 1856–60, respectively).

and Protestant associations have been founded under government control. Large numbers, though, prefer to go under the radar as it were, and worship in small charismatic or quasi-fundamentalist groups.[16]

Muslim Uighurs and Tibetan Buddhists fall into a rather different category, forming as they do part of the eight per cent of the country that is not Han Chinese. Some other racial groups are treated quite well but only because they have chosen not to offer any form of political challenge to the regime in Beijing.[17] By contrast, Xinjiang and Tibet constitute the Western edge of the country so their nationalist aspirations are seen as a real threat to the country's attempt to push its influence westwards.[18] One strategy has, therefore, been to flood the two provinces with new Han immigrants; another to undermine the ability of their two distinctive religious identities to undergird that nationalism.[19]

> The resulting chaos even made possible the eleven-year rule from Nanjing of someone who believed himself to be the Christian God's own Son. Millions died in the ensuing conflict (known as the Taiping rebellion). See further Jonathan Spence, *God's Chinese Son* (London: Flamingo, 1996).
>
> [16] In 2018 the government set the total number of Christians at 44 million, whereas the Pew Forum had already estimated their number in 2011 at 67 million.
>
> [17] An excellent survey of what is happening among the racial minorities, especially in Xinjiang, Tibet (both in the west), Yunnan (south) and Dongbei (north-east), is provided by David Eimer, *The Emperor Far Away: Travels at the Edge of China* (London: Bloomsbury, 2014).
>
> [18] One way to look at what is happening is to understand it as part of the present government's determination to create a new 'Silk Road'. A new oil pipeline from Kazakhstan has been built and a new port in Pakistan (Gwadar) is almost complete. There is also now a high-speed rail link to Urumqi, the capital of Xinjiang.
>
> [19] For some details about the compulsory detention and 're-education' of Uighurs, see Sean R. Roberts, *The War on the Uyghurs: China's*

Very different are recent attitudes to what has been termed the three 'native' religions of Confucianism, Daoism and Buddhism. In more recent times these have all been seen as potentially useful in helping to create a more cohesive society, as well as one more in touch with its past. It is a strategy particularly associated with the leadership of Xi Jinping, who has been president of the country since 2013, although change began as early as the death of Mao in 1976 when Deng Xiaoping inaugurated both economic and religious toleration.[20] Xi has oscillated somewhat, at times expressing sympathy for traditional religious belief and at other times forcing the destruction of newly-built temples and statues.[21] Nonetheless, some level of toleration has been maintained throughout. Continuing influence on the wider literary culture is also to be observed.[22] An intriguing example is the dissident Ma Jian who, in his book *Red Dust*, describes his own unsuccessful search for a spirituality based in Buddhism.[23] Yet, while religion was undoubtedly in a bad way at the point of collapse of Imperial China in

---

Campaign against Xinjiang's Muslims (Manchester: Manchester University Press, 2020).

[20] Although not always holding an official position, he was effectively in charge until his death in 1997.

[21] For example, in 2019 a new 60-metre-tall statue of the Buddhist Guanyin (in norther Hebei province) was detonated. It had taken the previous five years to build.

[22] See David Jasper, 'Finding theology in contemporary Chinese fiction' in *International Journal for the Study of the Christian Church* 19 (2019), 160–74.

[23] His reports on religious belief and practice are mainly negative, including for Tibet itself: Ma Jian, *Red Dust* (London: Vintage, 2001), 291–324.

1911,[24] that past now seems all but forgotten as all three religions aspire to deeper foundations in the life of the Chinese people. Although strongest in places such as Taiwan and Hong Kong, even in mainland China there is no shortage of signs of growth, including lively debate about how their future might best be realised.

Daoism and the Goodness of Nature

As in Chapter 4, I shall first offer a general sketch of the religion before narrowing to a specific test case for interfaith dialogue.

Origins and Characterisation

Writing about the religions of China is complicated not only by the extent of their interaction but also because the stories once told about their actual history have sometimes proved wildly inaccurate. Thus, in the case of Daoism it used to be thought that its foundation was due to someone called Lao Tzu, an older contemporary of Confucius (551–479 BCE). It is now widely believed that Lao Tzu may well have never existed. His classic work *Tao Te Ching* could itself be even later than the work by the next major figure in the history of the faith, Chuang Tzu.[25] Almost

---

[24] The three Chinese traditions were seen as too closely bound up with the imperial family. The leader of the revolution, Sun Yat-sen, saw himself as a Christian. Both the Ming dynasty (1368–1644) and the Qing (1644–1911) had a policy of compelling 'the unifying of the three teachings'.

[25] In his history of Chinese philosophy, A. C. Graham suggests that Lao Tzu's work may be as late as the third century BCE: *Disputers of the Tao:*

certainly Chuang Tzu is an historical figure from the late fourth century BCE. Even so, both his work and that of Lao Tzu were probably only incorporated much later into the Daoist canon,[26] during the period in which Daoism developed some of the most obvious characteristics of a religion.[27] The two works are in fact quite different. Lao Tzu's is a short, incisive poem, whereas Chuang Tzu's is an extraordinary (mainly prose) mixture of travelogue, teaching incidents that are sometimes amusing and didactic story.[28]

In both, the role of the Dao or Way is absolutely central. Although the term is used mostly to speak of the constant flow of the natural order, occasionally the idea is projected back into the origin of all things where it is then made to antedate both heaven and earth in ultimate mystery:

> The name that can be spoken of
> Is not the constant way;
> The name that can be named
> Is not the constant name.
> The nameless was the beginning of heaven and earth;

Philosophical Arguments in Ancient China (La Salle: Open Court, 1989), 170, 215–34.

[26] Chuang Tzu is also known as Zhuang Zhou or Zhuangzi. The creation of the formal notion of Taoism perhaps dates from the early years of the present era.

[27] Eva Wong identifies two stages in this transformation, the first, that of an organised religion (from 20 BCE onwards) and the second a more mystical version (from c. 300 CE): *Taoism: an Essential Guide* (Boulder, CO: Shambhala, 1997), 31–65.

[28] In his introduction to his translation, Martin Palmer describes it as a 'travelogue of life': *The Book of Chuang Tzu* (London: Penguin, 1996), xx.

> The named was the mother of the myriad creatures.
> ....
> These two are the same
> But diverge in name as they issue forth.
> Being the same they are called mysteries,
> Mystery upon mystery -[29]

Such a position would thus contrast with Confucianism which makes the mandate of heaven central but sees this as endorsing society, rather than something higher in the order of nature itself. Although (as with Confucius) Lao Tzu's poem is presented as offering guidance to a ruler, it clearly develops a quite different message: that it is by a keeping as close to nature as possible that any such person will do well.

In choosing Heaven (*T'ian*) as his preferred term, Confucius was in fact following established precedent. Archaeologists have identified the existence of a pantheon of gods in the second millennium BCE, presided over by a male supreme deity known as Shangdi.[30] For whatever reason, these gave way to the more impersonal notion of T'ian under the Zhou dynasty. While some have attempted to draw parallels between Dao or the 'Way'

---

[29] This is Lao Tzu's opening stanza: *Tao Te Ching*, trans. & ed. D. C. Lau (London: Penguin, 1963), 5. One way to think of the relationship between the two understandings is of two concentric circles: the smaller, central one at the root of the emergence of the world, and the other larger circle as 'the patterned cycle of life and visible nature' within it: see further Livia Kohn, *Daoism and Chinese Culture* (Magdalene, NM: Three Pines Press, 2010), 20.

[30] Popular under the Shang kings of the second half of the second millennium BCE. The Zhou dynasty was at the height of its power from circa the eleventh century to the eight BCE.

and John's developed concept of the Logos,[31] it was not from notions such as these that more personal ideas of divinity were to re-emerge within Daoism. Instead, a heavenly administrator was eventually identified ('the Jade Emperor'),[32] with various subordinates including the 'Queen Mother of the West' and the Eight Immortals, as well as lesser deities such as the kitchen god, a statue of whom is commonly found in the home. Some even identified Lao Tzu as both creator and revealer.[33] It is these personages whose images are to be found in modern-day Daoist temples, including some impressive examples in Ho Chi Minh City, Penang and Taipei.[34]

Daoism has a large, open canon which includes an extraordinary variety of material[35] – significant experiences, alternative forms of medicine, alchemy and also aspects which even the kindest of observers might find hard to regard as anything other than superstitious nonsense.[36] While from a Christian perspective it might be

---

[31] It was in fact the earliest word used in translations of John's Gospel into Chinese.
[32] Sometimes also treated as a creator.
[33] Kohn, *Daoism and Chinese Culture*, 104, explaining why, for some, Lao Tzu's text must be seen as the beginning of the religion's story.
[34] The Vietnamese Jade Emperor Pagoda is also known as Phuoc Hai Tu ('Sea of Blessing'), indicating the presence of Buddhist influence. The main Jade temple in Taiwan is known as the Tiangong temple, that in Penang as the Jade Emperor's Pavilion.
[35] It numbers 1,500 distinct items. Although in theory closed in 1445 CE, the contemporary, persecuted sect known as Falung Gong shows how open it continues to be.
[36] The modern practice of burning real or, more commonly, counterfeit money on behalf of ancestors is an example of what I would find difficult to regard as anything other than superstition.

tempting to treat the divine figures as belonging entirely to this last category, a more sympathetic interpretation would acknowledge partial parallels. After all, some Christian saints have also been discovered in retrospect to have been invented, while the range of types of angels postulated in both Judaism and Christianity reads more like imaginative fiction rather than anything corresponding with reality.[37] As in the Western case, though, such a concession need not entail that genuine religious experience was never mediated through such fictional entities. The divine may be seen to operate through conditioned reality (patterns of tradition) which do not necessarily admit to one-to-one direct comparison with ultimate truth. To give an obvious example from within Christianity, the fact that the composite figure of Mary Magdalene developed by medieval tradition generated a largely fictional character with a rather different life story from the likely historical personage should not be taken to call into question the reality of numerous religiously transformative experiences in the medieval world largely generated by that figure.[38] Again, the cult of angels in Western monotheisms could be seen in many ways as more like symbols of divine interaction from a

[37] The complexity of the full list goes well beyond anything found in scripture. For some of the detail, Stephen Miller, *The Book of Angels: Seen and Unseen* (Cambridge: Cambridge Scholars, 2019); for an exploration of the reasons for their popularity at different stages in Christian history, Dylan David Potter, *Angelology* (Eugene, OR: Wipf & Stock, 2016).

[38] In recent times numerous books have been produced arguing that the legends are simply the result of hostility to women (seen as being forced into a strict dichotomy between either a pure virgin like Jesus' mother or else a whore). That the tradition is much more positive than this, I argue in my *Discipleship and Imagination* (Oxford: Oxford University Press, 2000), 31-61.

transcendent world rather than beings in their own right. Yet they have on occasion generated significant transformative religious experience for the individuals concerned. Thus it does not seem impossible to suggest that the Jade Emperor could conceivably invite comparison sometimes with the Archangel Michael in a way that is derogatory to neither,[39] or even on other occasions with the Christian God, given the considerable fluidity in how many powers are assigned to this Daoist figure. My point is that it would be quite wrong to find value only in the religion's more easily accessible, meditative aspects. Millions continue to pray through the supernatural structures outlined above. So there remains the potential for both the best and the worse within them, as indeed is true of all religion. In short, Daoism found religious meaning embedded both in the flow of nature and in a mythological superstructure, and so both merit our attention.

The Test Case: The Beginning and End of Life

The most important thing to consider further here is the heart of Daoism in its attitude to nature. Although I shall begin by offering a general characterisation, I want to eventually home in on two specific areas for comparison that relate to the beginning and end of life. Not only will that more limited objective make our discussion more manageable, it will also allow me to highlight a couple of ways in which Christianity might learn from the Dao approach.

---

[39] Both are assigned the principal role in the final judgement of individuals.

In the west only a very secularised version of the Daoist attitude to nature tends to be well known, as in Feng Shui and its guidelines for the placing of buildings and even particular rooms,[40] or the various forms of Tai Chi exercise for maintaining a healthy body.[41] Even more familiar is talk of yin and yang and its accompanying symbol (Figure 5.1).

Although the notion is older than Daoism, dating to at least the ninth century BCE,[42] these days it is most commonly associated with what is involved in following the Way. Basically, the idea is that nature consists of two complementary sets of energies: yin, which is characterised as inward, still, dark and negative and yang, outward, masculine, hot, bright and positive. While initially this might sound rather disturbingly similar to conventional prejudices against women, in practice the idea is that both need each other and indeed elements of the one are also to be found in the other, as in the two smaller circles in the diagram below. In addition, they can be seen to flow into one another, with one expanding as the other retreats. The image has been compared to two tadpoles chasing one other. So night and day, sun and moon, and the seasons are all obvious examples.

---

[40] Meaning literally 'wind and water', it assumes that all matter contains energy (*qi*) with the potential to do good or harm: see further Wong, 137–41. In its original Chinese context, of particular importance has been the use of such divination in the selection of grave sites.

[41] The Norwegian Pytt Geddes was responsible for introducing Tai Chi to Britain. For her life story, Frank Woods, *Dancer in the Light* (Portland, OR: PSI, 2008).

[42] The idea is developed in the ninth century BCE classic, *I Ching* or *The Book of Changes*.

The Religions of China

Figure 5.1 The yin-yang symbol (with black representing yin and white yang).

When the Daoist classics were first discovered in the west in the nineteenth century it was common to differentiate strongly between their philosophical or spiritual context and religious practice,[43] and such attitudes remain common today. I have tried to avoid that artificial distinction in what I have said thus far, not least because the more obvious religious practices such as the ritual of

---

[43] Among Christian missionaries for obvious reasons. Hegel was among the first philosophers to take an interest: *Lectures on the History of Philosophy*, ed. E. S. Haldane (New Jersey: Humanities Press, 1983), I, 125.

temples and domestic meditation and prayer are viewed within the tradition as integral to cultivating the types of disposition recommended. It is after all a special inner dynamic which is required where external force is rejected and great stress placed on the initially strange notion of non-action or *wu wei*.[44] A powerful analogy is provided by the indispensable contribution made by empty space through its use in such things as wheels, cups and doors: although the frame is essential, it is the space created that performs the relevant role.[45] By *wu wei*, then, is understood not doing nothing at all but rather realising how often much is achieved by less rather than more: by instead just going with the flow, rather like water.[46] To allude to two of Daoism's own examples, 'not to honour men of worth will keep the people from contention; not to value goods which are hard to come by will keep them from theft.'[47] So a radical cult of simplicity is adopted, which is also reflected in politics by the avoidance of complex structures. The best leader turns out to be one of whom the population seldom hears and small communities are to be preferred.[48]

Such attitudes are found reflected in the arts, especially in poetry, calligraphy and painting. One short poem from the eighth century nicely illustrates the point:

> In Spring I was soundly asleep;
> Hardly did I notice the break of day.
> Everywhere I heard the birds singing.

---

[44] Lao Tzu commends the 'non-action' of the sage, translated as 'desires not to desire' in Lau's edition, *Tao Te Ching*: 71 (ch. 64).
[45] Ibid., 15 (ch. 11).   [46] Ibid., compare 12 (ch. 8).
[47] Ibid., 7 (ch. 3).   [48] Ibid., compare 21 (ch. 17); 87 (ch. 80).

> Last night there was a noise of storm and rain;
> I wonder how many blossoms have blown away.

In other words, the poet is able to find joy in each changing mood.[49] But so too does many a painter. The activity is seen as essentially one in which artists lose themselves in contemplation as the underlying nature of the world is allowed to unfold.[50]

None of these recommendations immediately resonate with Christian teaching. Although Christianity does have a passive side, more commonly interventionist stances are presupposed. One sympathetic translator and commentator who is a Christian rightly warns of deep differences lying just under the surface, even where terminology is remarkably similar. For instance, for the Daoist it is with the aim of achieving tranquillity that harm to others is avoided, not primarily because human beings are valued as such.[51] Nonetheless, there do seem to be lessons that could be learnt from Daoism. Perhaps the most obvious is some application to the present environmental crisis, given the huge contrast between characteristic Western interventions in nature and Daoism's insistence that we think of the world as a whole as our body and thus as

---

[49] The poet is Meng Hao-jan. His words are considered in Chung-yuan Chang, *Creativity and Taoism: A Study of Chinese Philosophy, Art and Poetry* (London: Jessica Kingsley, 2011; first published, 1963), 203–4.

[50] There is an excellent final chapter on painting and calligraphy in Chung-yuan Chang, *Creativity and Taoism*, 227–66, including a number of illustrations with commentary at the beginning of the work.

[51] Contrast Chapter 48 of Lao Tzu with John R. Mabry's comment on its injunction not to harm even evil people as 'purely functional',: *God as Nature Sees God: A Christian Reading of the Tao Te Ching* (Berkeley, CA: Apocrophile Press, 1994), 30. My previous chapter noted similar attitudes among Jains.

sacred.[52] But to pursue that issue further would require examination of quite familiar terrain, so two other aspects will be briefly considered here to do with the beginning and end of life.

Although other options were available during the patristic period,[53] Augustine (d. 430 CE) was to set the pattern for the future in talking of 'original sin', a bias towards sin inherited at birth, ultimately from Adam. Yet, it now appears highly unlikely that there ever was a first man and woman and so anything like an historical fall.[54] Indeed, ranged against a single starting point there is strong archaeological evidence which demonstrates the presence of some spiritual characteristics already, even among Neanderthals: for example, in their care for the dead and some artistic work. Presumably, apart from any supposed truth in the claim, Christian theologians continue to use such language in large part because it is thought to reinforce the need for Christ's redemptive action. Not unsurprisingly, any such historical notion is absent from Daoism. Yet it does recognise the capacity of individuals to go wrong, but with an existentialist, individual account offered, not unlike some nineteenth century reinterpretations of the fall, among them those of Hegel and Kierkegaard. That is to say, the 'fall' becomes the kind of decisive experience which is repeated in each individual's life (the tension between ideal

---

[52] Compare Lau, *Tao Te Ching*, chs. 29 & 34.
[53] Irenaeus (d. c. 202 CE), for example, had a much gentler view of the human situation *Heresies* 4.37.1; 4.38.3.
[54] *Homo sapiens* are now thought to have originated in a common group in Africa. For an attempt to tell a more complicated story, though, see Madelaine Böhme et al., *Ancient Bones: Unearthing the Astonishing New Story of How We Became Human* (Vancouver: Greystone, 2020).

and actuality). The importance of a social dimension, though, is not discounted, most obviously in the kind of societal pressures to which the individual may be subjected.[55] In other words, we are not born with any particularly strong disposition either way. It is repeated right or wrong decisions that will determine our ultimate direction with, for some, the pressures becoming so strong one way as to make any further resistance almost impossible.[56]

In the past, Christian theology also did not hesitate to detect the fall's effects in wider nature, but might not application of the notion of yin and yang make better sense of the more aggressive side of nature, given the way in which the practice of animals killing one another actually helps to maintain an overall ecological balance? This is not to say that Isaiah's vision of the lion lying down with the lamb was wrong but it is perhaps better interpreted as opening up alternative possibilities, rather than necessarily requiring us to consider deviations from that ideal as inherently evil.[57] It is, for instance, surely part of the nature of birds of prey and other such animals to be predatory.[58] In other words, a broader perspective is needed,

---

[55] For my own attempts to reinterpret the notion of original sin, including the incorporation of some ideas borrowed from Kierkegaard, see my *Continental Philosophy and Modern Theology* (Oxford: Blackwell, 1987), 86–100, esp. 98–99.

[56] Addiction can include not just the obvious cases such as alcoholism or pornography, there can also be other psychological scenarios such as delight in the exercise of power over others or malicious pleasure in their suffering.

[57] Isaiah 11.6–9. For example, the special circumstance of being reared together can make a major difference, as with dogs and cats.

[58] The philosopher Mary Midgley (1919–2018) is someone who consistently emphasised the naturalness of the actions of birds of prey: for example, *Beast and Man* (London: Routledge, rev. 1995), 144.

particularly one where human aspirations are not always allowed centre stage or automatically projected onto the rest of creation. As the third great Daoist classic from Lieh Tzu observes, 'one species is not nobler than another; it is simply that the strongest and cleverest rule over the weaker and more stupid.'[59]

Then there is the question of death. Despite Christianity offering a marvellous vision of human life culminating in a closer relationship with God after the present life, Western culture is still dominated by fear of death as something evil.[60] Indeed, in the opening chapters of Genesis death is made part of the consequences of the fall. Yet, if there never was an historical Fall and thus never a loss of immortality, should death not be seen as ineluctably part of the divine gift of life? Daoism might help in coming to terms with this alternative perspective: 'If you are like the cosmos, you are like the Tao. If you are like the Tao, you will have eternal life, and you needn't be afraid of dying.'[61] In other words, it will be seen as simply part of the way things are. Inasmuch as most of us in the West now attain the biblical 'three score years and ten', is simple acceptance not possible of the fact that our mortal remains will be reabsorbed into the resources of the earth, with there being little or no need for further memorial?

---

[59] Words put into the mouth of a twelve-year-old boy in Ch. 8. He is objecting to the idea that animals are there entirely for human benefit. Since other animals sometimes attack human beings, he adds, 'Does this mean Heaven originally created us for the sake of the mosquitoes, gnats, tigers and wolves?' Quoted in Martin Palmer's Introduction to *The Book of Chuang Tzu*, xxiv–v.

[60] Contrast John Donne's sonnet which begins and ends: 'Death be not proud ... death, thou shalt die.'

[61] Mabry's rather free translation of Ch 16 of the *Tao Te Ching*.

In other words, whatever may come next, it is still worth cultivating the Daoist acceptance of death and dissolution as part of the natural cycle of the universe. As one of the masters quoted in Chuang Tzu puts it, 'Yin and yang are the mother and father of humanity ... The cosmos gives me form, brings me to birth, guides me into old age and settles me in death. If I think my life good, then I must think my death good.'[62] Even so, as with Christianity there is a belief in life beyond. Humans are assumed to have two souls, one of which remains attached to the body, the other of which is capable of a complete separation.[63] The important difference, though, is that value is also seen in the mere fact of death in itself. It is not, as in conventional Christian theology, regarded as not part of the original divine intention. That said, Daoism would seem to have the capacity to liberate Christian theology into more positive attitudes towards both the beginning and the end of life.

Confucianism and the Importance of Social Rituals

Once more I shall begin with a general account of origins and characterisation before turning to a test case in social rituals. The latter may seem a surprising choice but many still regard Confucianism as so inherently conservative as to be incapable of offering any new insights.

---

[62] *The Book of Chuang Tzu*, 53–54 (ch. 6). For similar sentiments, compare also 47–48, 107–8.
[63] Kohn, *Daoism and Chinese Culture*, 56–58.

Origins and Characterisation

In marked contrast to Daoism, in the case of Confucianism there is no doubt about the existence of its founder, Confucius or Kong Fuzi (551–479 BCE) or indeed his principal disciple, Mencius or Mengzi (372–289 BCE).[64] Both left behind writings, although in the case of Confucius much has probably been added to his *Analects*, as well as other aspects appearing which he had probably inherited from a more distant past.[65] Arguably, Mencius contributed as much, if not more, in the overall shaping of the movement's perspective.[66] Indeed, from the Song dynasty onwards he joined Confucius as one of the four classics taught to every Chinese schoolboy.[67] One key emphasis which they share is what they identified as the primary problem that needed to be addressed: the disintegration of society. Both Confucius and Mencius were writing in times of social disorder. The small state in which Confucius lived was riven by civil war, while Mencius experienced one of the most turbulent periods in all of Chinese history, known as the Warring States. China split up into rival kingdoms

---

[64] Confucius is the Latinised version adopted by the Jesuit Matteo Ricci for 'Kong Fuzi' (Master or Teacher Kong).
[65] In Chinese there is no exactly equivalent word to Confucianism. Instead, talk is of the school of the 'ru' or 'scholar', which includes elements antedating Confucius' own life. See further the essays by Nicolas Zufferey and Robert Eno in *The Analects*, ed. Michael Nylan (New York: Norton, 2014), 129–52.
[66] Mengzi's main rival was Xunzi or Master Xun (Hsün Tzu is the alternative spelling). More pessimistic, he was also much less of a stylist.
[67] Confucius had proposed one such list. Various modified alternatives were proposed across the centuries.

which often engaged in pointless wars with one another.[68] Confucius suggested looking back to much earlier times, the beginnings of the Zhou dynasty, and bringing back some of the traditions associated with that period.[69] These included *ren* (benevolence or 'humaneness') and *li* (respect for natural law and civil decorum which was seen as including conventional hierarchical structures). The latter was deemed especially important because its two main elements could be used to reinforce common social values and so help generate a more integrated and thus more peaceable society. These included care for children, which was taken to involve a corresponding deferential respect for parents. Similar attitudes were advocated between older and younger siblings, husband and wife, teacher and pupil, and ruler and ruled.[70]

Inevitably, there was considerable adaptation over the centuries. Fortunately, most of that complex story can be ignored here, except to note the important medieval development known as Neo-Confucianism. Although its scholasticism was once upon a time blamed for the demise of Confucianism along with the empire and its famous pattern of civil service examinations, contemporary philosophers and historians have now come to view this collection of thinkers much more positively. For example,

---

[68] Confucius' state of Lu was split between the ruling duke and three aristocratic families. The Warring States period lasted from 474 BCE to 221 BCE. As well as some minor enclaves, there were seven major contenders for control of the country as a whole.

[69] The golden age of the Zhou dynasty was from 1046–771 BCE. It was nominally still in power for most of the Warring States period.

[70] *Li* had originally meant a religious sacrifice before it came to mean ritual and rules of propriety, as well as laws of nature.

the historian Peter Bol argues that, so far from proving an ideological justification for an ever more stagnating state, the movement really offered constructive alternatives in changing times. Effectively, attention was focused away from the centre and towards the transformation of local society.[71] Again, as we shall see in more detail later, the contemporary philosopher Stephen Angle argues that the ideas of two of its principal thinkers, Zhu Xi and Wang Yangming,[72] can be used (in conjunction with Western writers such as Iris Murdoch and Martha Nussbaum) to illuminate questions in contemporary moral and political philosophy more generally.[73]

None of this may initially seem to have much to do with religion. Indeed, there are many scholars who assert that any reference to that dimension is incidental, and really just a reflection of the times during which Confucius lived. While it is true that there is a statement in the *Analects* that he intends to ignore questions about the gods,[74] T'ien or Heaven is referred to no less than fifty-one times. Confucius' programme is presented as a reflection of Heaven's will, although it remains important to note that this is in no sense a personalised deity.[75]

---

[71] Perter K. Bol, *Neo-Confucianism in History* (Cambridge, MA: Harvard University Press, 2008).
[72] Zhu Xi (1130–1200 CE) was the great synthesizer under the Song dynasty; Wang Yangming (1472–1529 CE) was the most influential writer during the Ming dynasty.
[73] Stephen C. Angle, *Sagehood: The Contemporary Significance of Neo-Confucianism* (New York: Oxford University Press, 2009).
[74] *Analects* 7.21.
[75] Although earlier in history China did have a personal supreme deity (*Shangdi*), Heaven was substituted by rulers keen to eliminate a potential rival source of authority: so Xinzhong Yao, *An Introduction to Confucianism* (Cambridge: Cambridge University Press, 2000), 143–44.

Indeed, though admitting change under Neo-Confucianism, some scholars insist that initially at least 'Heaven is not transcendent ...it is a dimension of the same world that we inhabit.'[76] Whether so or not, on the relevance of T'ien, Mencius is, if anything, even more insistent. In his view, human nature is inherently good, with all of us capable of aspiring to the status of a moral 'sage'. So, 'as it is Heaven which is responsible for making morality the unique distinguishing feature of man, his moral nature is that which links him with Heaven... Mencius has absolute faith in the moral purpose of the universe... [and] added to Confucianism a depth that it did not possess before.'[77] Although the lack of priests, monks and initiation ceremony certainly make Confucianism quite unlike China's two other native religions, in this it is of course similar to some versions of Christianity, such as the Society of Friends or Quakers. Again, just as in the past, central to the imperial cult had been the seeking of Heaven's mandate at Beijing's central shrines, so nowadays with the reopening of temples in modern China it turns out that not only are people found actually praying to Confucius but also leaving prayer cards for the attention of some more generalised notion of divinity.[78]

---

[76] Chakravarthi Ram-Prasad, *Eastern Philosophy* (London: Weidenfeld & Nicholson, 1988), 41–45, esp. 42.
[77] D. C. Lau in his introduction to *Mencius* (Harmondsworth: Penguin, 1970), 45, 46.
[78] See further Anna Sun, *Confucianism as a World Religion: Contested Histories and Contemporary Realities* (Princeton, NJ: Princeton University Press, 2013), 162–67. Prayers to Confucius are usually for success in exams. Prayer cards are apparently a modern innovation.

So the two early investigators, James Legge and Max Müller at Oxford, were surely right in their insistence that Confucianism be treated as a religion, an advocacy which led to its appearance at the very first World Parliament of Religions in Chicago in 1893.[79] It is also not without significance that, by encouraging the revival of Confucianism, China's present leader, Xi Jinping, did not neglect its religious dimensions. Quite a number of former temples have now been reopened, with the principal one at Qufu permitted to broadcast (from 2004 onwards) its annual celebration of the founder on state television. This is not to say that Xi necessarily values the religious elements as such, but his support may be taken to imply commitment to the notion that religious rituals help reinforce social values. But there may be more. One way of reading state policy is to deduce in Xi a concern to bring fully to his people's consciousness the possibilities within their own history of an alternative basis for Chinese society in something other than either Marxism–Leninism or Western liberalism.[80]

Angle is therefore, quite wrong to describe Confucian temples as 'now no more than tourist attractions': 223.

[79] James Legge was a Scottish Presbyterian missionary to China for thirty-four years before he became Oxford's first Professor of Chinese in 1876. Max Müller (son of the poet whose words are used in two of Schubert's song cycles) is often regarded as the founder of comparative religion. He worked in Oxford for many years on the translation series *Sacred Books of the East*. For further details about their contribution, Anna Sun, *Confucianism as a World Religion*, 38–42, 45–76. For Legge on the meaning of T'ien, 59–60.

[80] This would also explain the recent founding of numerous Confucian institutes at home and abroad, as well as the prominent place given to Confucius at the inauguration of the Olympics in Beijing in 2008. His

Test Case: Religion and Social Values, the Role of Ritual

I shall first examine more generally the relationship between religion and social values before then homing in more specifically on the contribution that ritual might make.

Daniel Bell is an American political scientist who has taught in Beijing for many years. In a recent book he sought to explore what a modern appropriation might mean. One popular television series watered down considerably some of the relevant principles. However, in the process it did illustrate quite nicely a possible way round some forms of hierarchy that are no longer acceptable in the modern world, such as those between women and men.[81] He outlines an approach that would still take *ren* or humaneness seriously, even as it ignores questions of individual human rights.[82] Certain other features, he suggests, could have wider applicability beyond simply the concerns of the present regime, among them the teacher–pupil relationship and that of employer and home help.

---

birthday is also a public holiday, not only in Taiwan but also in parts of China.

[81] Daniel A. Bell, *China's New Confucianism: Politics and Everyday Life in a Changing Society* (Princeton, NJ: Princeton University Press, 2008), 163–70. A more effective response to the feminist issue is to be found in Sun (who is also reacting to the TV and publishing success of Yu Dan), *Confucianism as a World Religion*, 137–52. Rather than jettisoning the past, Sun argues that male hierarchy ignores the historical reality, that in past and present alike women have played an essential, innovatory role.

[82] He argues for the Chinese government's intervention in North Korea on the basis of humaneness (concern for the people's extreme poverty) rather than out of any commitment to their political rights as such: 19-37, esp. 32–4.

Thus there are, he argues, considerable advantages in deference to teachers at the earlier stages of a student's career, while treating home help as part of the family can totally transform that relationship.[83]

Although these examples are intriguing, there is little on how such attitudes might be inculcated, a major theme of Stephen Angle's book to which reference has already been made. Drawing on the contemporary revival of virtue ethics among Western philosophers, he argues that Western moral education could have much to learn from the incorporation of some Neo-Confucian ideas. Equally, the latter might need to accept some modification from the West, its approach to democracy being one obvious such case. By contrast to Utilitarianism and Kantianism which, in their crudest form, see each moral decision as needing to be rationally determined anew, Angle suggests that drawing on virtue ethics emphasises the importance of training in the acquisition of the right habits or 'virtues' in moral attitudes and practice.[84] Much of Angle's discussion is excellent, for example in identifying the importance of moral education, in spontaneity and ease in action being the final aim, in the key role of imagination, in the difference between 'sage' and saint and in finding an indispensable place for specific as against general commitments.[85]

---

[83] For attitudes to home help, Bell, *China's New Confucianism*, 75–90; for relations between student and teacher, 107–27, esp. 118.

[84] Deriving ultimately from the approach to ethics found in Plato and Aristotle, it has been opularized in recent times by philosophers such as Philippa Foot and Alasdair MacIntyre.

[85] For education, Angle, *Sagehood*, 135–43; for spontaneity, for example 15; for imagination, 95–98, 170–72; for the difference between sage and saint, 22–25; for the importance of particular commitments, 77–83.

However, where the book is less satisfactory is in its underplaying of a more explicitly religious contribution. Reverence for the coherence of the human moral project replaces even the transcendent Good of Iris Murdoch,[86] and various practical recommendations from the Neo-Confucians displace their more searching and reflective type of approach. Spiritual exercises, ritual, reading, attention and quiet sitting are all given somewhat superficial interpretations in which religion ceases to play any part.[87] Even at the practical level the difficulties are somewhat obvious. For example, in his attempt to introduce democracy as part of the Confucian ideal Angle notes the manipulation of voter qualifying rules perpetrated in recent American elections.[88] But can such malpractice really be successfully circumvented without incorporating some kind of ritual perspective on what it is to vote: an inalienable 'sacred' act that recognises the worth of each and every fellow citizen, even if one profoundly disagrees with how they may choose to exercise their vote? More broadly, can the famous passages in the Confucian classics about harmony between heaven and earth and between all humans really be seriously endorsed unless there is a more profound return to the assumptions of Mencius? Angle to some extent agrees. He talks of such ideas being built into the very fabric of reality,[89] but still resists moving any closer to a religious perspective.

[86] Ibid., 86–89.   [87] Ibid., 144–60.
[88] Angle, *Sagehood*, 200–4. Angle does talk about the relevance of reverence and ritual, but the question would be whether his version goes deep enough.
[89] The passage from *The Doctrine of the Mean* (ch.1) about 'heaven and earth in their proper order' is quoted, 65; 'heaven as my father and

It is worth noting that the virtue ethics approach upon which Angle draws was once deeply embedded in Christian ethics, as, for example, in the notion of seven Christian virtues and seven corresponding deadly sins.[90] So it is of considerable interest to note here how a religious side to the Confucian approach is also acknowledged by some commentators. Rodney Taylor does not hesitate to open his book on *The Religious Dimensions of Confucianism* by describing Confucianism as 'profoundly religious.'[91] By way of justification he appeals particularly to Mencius as 'the orthodox interpretation' of Confucius and notes that the sage is in effect defined as someone who listens to Heaven.[92] That being so, Confucian classics can even be seen as a form of scripture or revelation.[93] Nor are traditional questions of religion ignored, such as the meaning of suffering. In a number of passages Mencius displays a real concern for animal suffering, while human suffering is sometimes accorded an educational role.[94] In his own work, Xingzhong Yao adopts a similar approach, noting that the virtuous individual finds the endorsement of heaven in two key aspects, a moral universe and one also infused with laws of nature.[95]

---

earth as my mother', with 'all people brothers and sisters, and all things my companions' from Zhang Zai's *Western Inscription*, 68.

[90] Prominent in both Aquinas and Dante. Three theological virtues (faith, hope and charity) were effectively added to Plato's original four (wisdom, courage, temperance and justice).

[91] Rodney L. Taylor, *The Religious Dimensions of Confucianism* (Albany, NY: State University of New York Press, 1990), 1.

[92] Ibid., 17 ('orthodox' apparently only since the thirteenth century); 24 (the word for 'sage' – *sheng* – is closely related to the word for 'to listen'.)

[93] Ibid., 31–37. [94] Ibid., 115–34, esp. 122, 131.

[95] Yao, *An Introduction to Confucianism*,142–52, 155.

However, a difference to Taylor is in the amount of attention the latter devotes to the Ming thinker, Kao P'an-lung (1562–1626). Although elements in Kao's stress on quiet sitting are derived from Buddhism, Taylor is at pains to emphasise the difference when this process climaxes in eventual enlightenment. Instead of a loss of personal identity, the result is 'a religious experience' of mystical union, 'a fundamental unity or oneness ... felt between self and the universe.'[96] So yet again a religious analysis is seen as fundamental to what is being claimed.

But, while the above suggests parallels between the two religions, the role of social ritual within Confucianism has perhaps the most to offer as a potential contribution to Christian self-reflection, not least in the context of Western societies no longer confident in their foundations. Certainly, its role in cementing and reinforcing social relationships is currently much under-estimated. Take something as simple as the Western handshake. It can make an unobtrusive yet significant contribution to fostering relationships: effectively, a foundation in trust can be offered even prior to either side knowing anything about the other. Although deferential bowing still flourishes in much of south-east Asia,[97] the use of titles of address and even surnames is in the process of disappearing in the West. Not that such change is necessarily a bad thing. More worryingly, however, it is often accompanied by the disappearance of many other marks of respect for the other,

---

[96] Taylor, *Religious Dimensions*, esp. 110.77–114.
[97] It is important to note the influence of Confucianism elsewhere in south-east Asia, particularly in Korea, Japan and Vietnam. For an exploration of the first two, Yao, *An Introduction to Confucianism*, 115–38.

including in those areas where religion once made a contribution. It is unclear, for instance, how successful secular forms of the marriage rite really are at maintaining the solemnity of the occasion, while the transformation of funerals into encomia means that they no longer offer a moment for quiet reflection. Indeed, the need for something different from present practice even within a Christian context is well illustrated by the increasing popularity of special services at All Souls tide when the dead are solemnly recalled in the presence of relatives and friends.[98] Ironically, that Christian observance of the dead is now remarkably similar to the Confucian where there have always been annual rituals at the graveside.[99]

Perhaps the cement that the monarchy gives to British identity provides the best example of a contribution based to a significant degree on religious ritual. The extent to which such ideas will have survived the death of Elizabeth II in 2022 remain to be seen. The supplementary glue proposed by successive British governments in the notion of 'British values' has been a signal failure. They are insufficiently distinctive in indicating something that truly identifies and individuates. In any case, as with the United States, society is just too divided over what really matters. There is no longer any real consensus over how past history should be told for example, whether as the glories of empire or as a series of acts exploitative of native

---

[98] Historically, All Saints Day (1 November) has been more popular but in many churches All Souls (currently set for 2 November but formerly on the last day of October) is now the better attended.

[99] Even closer Christian parallels are provided by the Swedish practice of lighting candles at All Souls by the graveside and in Mexican rituals associated with the Dia de Muertos.

populations. It is here that the Confucian notion of *ren* or 'humaneness' could play a role, with training required in schools and elsewhere to respect real (and perhaps irresolvable) differences in values,[100] and not always simply education in the same values. Where *ren* becomes particularly relevant is in the notion of 'respect' or 'benevolence' towards others, intended as a more basic notion than the Christian ideal of love.[101] It is well known that Confucius enunciated the golden rule but it is important to observe that it was in a negative version ('what you do not wish for yourself, do not do to others').[102] The undoubted advantage this version has is that it offers a more manageable foundation for social and political action in not requiring as much. Respecting the other in their difference is in effect what is demanded. This could then be reflected in appropriate attitudes towards relevant social rituals such as ensuring the casting of each citizen's vote or the requirement that the voice of the opposition should be heard. Current legislative attempts to exclude significant elements of the population from voting in both the United States and Great Britain clearly need something stronger than merely formal arguments against.[103] Similarly, revival of the Roe v Wade abortion debate needs to somehow get

---

[100] Too much emphasis in the contemporary approach is on the sharing of values, whereas sometimes it is fully acknowledging difference that is precisely the most pertinent point at issue.

[101] For the range of differences considered, Xinzhong Yao, *Confucianism and Christianity: A Comparative Study of Jen and Agape* (Brighton: Sussex Academic Press, 1966).

[102] *Analects*, 15.24.

[103] In both the United States and Great Britain the proposed requirement for proof of identity would effectively exclude many poorer citizens from the ballot box.

beyond the depressingly polarised options that fail to acknowledge any worth in opponents' positions.[104] Embedding the sacred value of the other in moral and religious education could be part of the answer.[105]

Equally, though, there would seem a need for a similar change of attitude within Christianity itself if it is ever to make a significant future contribution to social cement in what is now a religiously plural society. Christians can no longer afford to stand apart from those of other faiths as though the truth of their own was all that mattered. Particularly with the near neighbour, there is a need to engage with what others value most profoundly, even if such attention does not necessarily result in the same conclusions. Even in modern secular society a ritual emphasis in education and public conversation on the sacred valuing of the other could still play a significant role in banning suspect means, even where these are aimed towards an allegedly good end. In short, as in Confucianism, ritual acts that are given a religious aura could help secure the maintenance of ultimate values above the intermediate.

Chinese Buddhism and the Need for Change

Buddhism first reached China in the first century of the present era. Although Christianity arrived shortly after

---

[104] In 1973 the American Supreme Court had made abortion a nationwide, legal right during the first trimester. This right was repealed in 2022.
[105] Rather than just a reflection of conservatism, the reluctance of all the world religions to endorse abortion probably reflects that kind of valuing of the other. To say this much, though, is not to imply any position on legislation as distinct from personal commitment.

with Nestorian missionaries it never succeeded in acclimatising to the same degree. A fine illustration of Buddhist accommodation is the classic sixteenth-century novel *Journey to the West*. The tale, combining comedy with great spiritual insight, re-envisages the travels to India of the seventh-century monk Xuanzuang, in search of more Buddhist texts. Although relying mainly on Buddhism, it also demonstrates creative borrowings from both Confucianism and Daoism, which is one reason for its continuing great popularity.[106] Contrasts are often drawn between the presumed simplicity of the New Testament gospel and the elaborate doctrinal superstructure which became the later church.[107] Even if wholly true, that contrast would still pale into insignificance when measured against the development of the earlier Theravada Buddhism into the type that came to be accepted in China, known as Mahayana. It is a type of which most Westerners are unaware, largely because of the extent to which instruction in schools and philosophical popularisation in the community at large naively equates Buddhism with the teaching of the historical Shakyamuni. This is a pity because the version practised in China, as well as in quite a number of other Asian countries, among them Japan, Korea, Nepal, Tibet and Vietnam, is thereby ignored. Both Buddhism's motivation

---

[106] Although I myself read Wu Cheng'en's tale under this title *Journey to the West* (Beijing: Foreign Languages Press, 1993), Arthur Waley's abridged version *Monkey* is perhaps still the best known.

[107] Seen most obviously in the work of the famous German church historian, Adolf von Harnack, popularised in his *Das Wesen des Christentums* (*What is Christianity?*) of 1900, in which he contrasts the simplicity of the synoptic gospels with John and later Hellenism.

for action and its accompanying metaphysics were fundamentally altered. It is also worth studying because of potentially illuminating parallels with transformations within Christianity, but before getting to that point we need to examine its more general character.

Origins and Characterisation

In Theravada a self-interested motivation had been endorsed,[108] the desire to secure for oneself escape from the endless round of suffering with a solution found in the rigours of monastic practice. Thereby, laypersons had been effectively demoted. At most they could gain merit for subsequent lives either through acts of devotion or else in helping monks in their quest. Mahayana, however, was radically egalitarian in insisting that any proposed goal should be available to all. Helping others and the cultivation of wisdom rather than the elimination of desire were seen as the most appropriate means for acquiring the ultimate end.[109] As such, although personal enlightenment remained the ultimate goal, the model set by others was now found not in already completely enlightened figures but rather in a bodhisattva, someone who had delayed the final steps on that course in order to help others.[110] Of the

---

[108] 'Self-interest' is not meant to imply selfishness, only that the primary motivation is concerned with improving one's own lot.

[109] The contrast is sometimes expressed in terms of Theravada's practice of 'mindfulness' and Mahayana's of 'compassion and wisdom'. They can, though, sometimes merge as in Thich Nhat Hanh, *The Miracle of Mindfulness* (London: Rider, 1975).

[110] The contrast is primarily with the arhat, who has achieved nirvana in this life and now sees no further need for relations with others.

many acknowledged to have fulfilled this role, the most popular is the figure known in India as Avalokiteshvara but in China as Guanyin and in Japan as Kannon. While such an assumption could have resulted in the historical Buddha now viewed as the less valued character, the implication was resisted through changes in the way in which the Buddha's mission was understood. Instead of being treated as a mere past example of a nirvana already achieved, he became a cosmic figure, as capable of helping the individual in the here and now as any bodhisattva.[111] Again, while remaining unique in this present world, it was observed that there must be many Buddhas in other worlds who could also help humans on their path, of whom Maitreya (the future Buddha) is perhaps the best known.[112] It was from scenarios such as this that notions of salvation in an alternative world were developed, with Amitabha and the Pure Lands Buddhism of Japan the most familiar instance.

The best-known Mahayana writing is the Lotus Sutra. Its very title well indicates its intended reach. Its message emerges, like a lotus, out of the mud of the human condition into a work of exquisite beauty. Yet, it opens in such an obviously mythological way that it is hard initially not to see the entirety as a corruption of an earlier, much simpler faith. Shakyamuni himself, now a cosmic figure with infinite powers, is presented initially as being in the presence of eighty thousand bodhisattvas. As if not contentious enough, these are then increased to two billion,

---

[111] Even in Theravada, Shakyamuni had supernatural powers (as in his miraculous birth), but these increase hugely.
[112] Maitreya is the only bodhisattva with a celestial destiny also accepted within Theravada. The name derives from *mitra* (friend).

along with 'hundreds of thousands of billions of Buddhas' from different aeons and other worlds.[113] While some contemporary Buddhists take the details of such cosmology quite literally,[114] it is important to penetrate behind the symbolism. It is, in effect, a way of presenting the universality of Buddhism's relevance, not just to the historical period during which Shakyamuni lived but equally to all times both past and future, as well as to all spaces however distant: through, for example, the future Buddha, Maitreya, or, from the opposite end of the temporal perspective, the primordial Buddha Vairocana. Vairocana, who appears in the Flower Garland Sutra, is presumed to possess powers just as extensive as those assigned to the other Buddhas mentioned above.[115]

Such a desire for greater inclusivity can also be taken to explain the transformation of the most popular bodhisattva, the male Avalokitesvara, into the female Guanyin.[116] In Theravada Buddhism, Shakyamuni had been presented as only reluctantly conceding the

---

[113] *Lotus Sutra*, trans. Gene Reeves (Somerville, MA: Wisdom Publications, 2008), Introduction, 53, 66, 67; compare 'two trillion buddhas' (107).

[114] Chan Master Sheng Yen gives a surprisingly literal/mythological answer to the question of the origins of the universe in his otherwise very helpful question and answer approach in his *Orthodox Chinese Buddhism* (Berkeley, CA: North Atlantic Books, 2007), 21–24.

[115] For an example, Paul Williams, *Mahayana Buddhism: The Doctrinal Foundations* (London: Routledge, 2nd ed., 2009), 134. The Flower Garland or Avatamsaka Sutra is much longer even than the bible.

[116] For a very helpful study of the process, Chün-fang Yü, *Kuan-yin: The Chinese Transformation of Avalokitesvara* (New York: Columbia University Press, 2000). The female author identifies a mixture of human need and competition with indigenous religions, combined with support from artistic movements (e.g. 14–21).

legitimacy of a female order of nuns.[117] Indeed, there are passages where we are told that females would have to become male first before they could possibly aspire to the status of Buddhahood.[118] A more clearly universal message effectively explains the transformation.[119] The message of Buddhism is now available to both sexes alike. However, the process can also be seen to go much further, in a willingness to cater for all kinds of sinner, however despised.[120] In a similar way, Maitreya not only became accessible to prayer but also, from the thirteenth century onwards, seen as one incarnated in a life identified with the poor: apparently, the origin of the laughing Buddha with potbelly.[121] Likewise, a Medicine Buddha is provided to address people's physical ills.[122]

Although Mahayana's underlying metaphysics is at times quite hard to understand, it does have a practical

---

[117] For the story and also various limitations applied to nuns but not to monks, see Chün-fang Yü, *Chinese Buddhism: A Thematic History* (Honolulu: University of Hawaii Press, 2020), 138–39. A similar injunction is to be found in the apocryphal Gospel of Thomas.

[118] The Eighth Great Vow of the Medicine Buddha even promises such a transformation: *Chinese Buddhism*, 93.

[119] She became in effect a goddess of mercy and compassion who also ritually offers forgiveness: Yü, *Kuan-yin*, 263–91; Yü, *Chinese Buddhism*, 86, 111–17. Even so, eventual progress towards sexual equality was not without some difficulty, *Chinese Buddhism*, 218–39, 250–60. There is also a female Buddha (Tara) associated with Avalokitesvara in Tibetan Buddhism: Williams, *Mahayana Buddhism*, 225–26.

[120] The message of the *Lotus Sutra*, chapter 25: for commentary, Williams, *Mahayana Buddhism*, 159.

[121] Yü, *Chinese Buddhism*, 79–80.

[122] Also called 'The Master of Healing', his relevance to human concerns should be obvious. For a collection of Chinese texts on the subject and some commentary, Raoul Birnbaum, *The Healing Buddha* (Boston, MA: Shambala, rev. ed., 1989).

dimension in the intention to make pursuit of nirvana easier to comprehend. Indeed, it is worth observing that the term *darshan*, which we encountered in Chapter 3 on the Hindu gods, was once also the term for philosophy, its aim being seen as the acquisition of a certain 'vision' of the world. In general, Mahayana turned out to be even more suspicious of any underlying objectivity. Whereas Theravada had spoken of impermanence (*anicca*) and no eternal self (*anatta*), Mahayana posits an overall emptiness (*sunyata*) with no continuing foundation whatsoever. Even Theravada's momentary phenomena (*dharmas*) are declared to have no real status, amounting to no more than what might be characterised as like flickers of burning gas.[123] The aim, though, was less the metaphysics as such and more to undermine the wrong kind of concern and attachment. This was effectively brought out in two distinctive types of philosophical approach. One influenced by Nararjuna and the 'middle-way' school (Madhyamaka) came to dominate Tibetan thinking and can still be seen at work in the teachings of the present-day Dalai Lama. This distinguishes between relative and ultimate truth, with the latter used to undermine too much concern with what should be seen as the merely transient. The other was Yogachara or the 'Yoga practice' school which was brought to China by the Chinese pilgrim whose name we have already encountered, Hsuan-tsang. Here three types of nature are identified: dependent, imagined and perfected.

---

[123] Williams, though, also notes some pressure the other way: to admit after all the existence of some ultimate reality, even in a philosopher such as Nagarjuna (and in some sutras): *Mahayana Buddhism*, 75, 108–9.

'Imagined' proposes treating the world like a dream, while 'perfected' implied the realisation of the assessment. However, in the process this is held to entail acknowledgement of the reality of the mind that makes this assessment. So, whereas the Tibetan tradition refuses ultimate reality even to emptiness itself, on the Yogachara analysis achieving Buddhahood becomes rather like a perfect awakening from some controlling dream. It was this more positive imagery that particularly appealed to the Chinese.

The changes are so many and so various that any claim to some simple overall explication seems unlikely.[124] Nonetheless, given the larger role accorded mythology, it would be a natural temptation to dismiss the entire development as the corruption of an original ideal. That seems to me a serious mistake. Not only is there a wealth of new ideas here, there are also at least some from which Christianity could learn. Given that Chapter 6 on Japan follows this, various aspects of the new metaphysics, such as the universality of Buddha-nature and the eschatology of another world, can be safely left until then. Instead, a more basic question may be raised here: how might a claim to continuity be justified, and in particular Shakyamuni as the faith's continuing source of inspiration?

Test Case: The Legitimacy of Change

It is commonly suggested nowadays that the Mahayana approach probably originated in India alongside

---

[124] Among possible causal factors, Paul Williams mentions a possible lay revolt, as well as a newly acquired, more central place in society: *Mahayana Buddhism*, 11, 21–27.

Theravada in shared monasteries, with the rebels perhaps eventually retreating to become forest hermits.[125] Anyway, the important point is that its origins may be seen as initially stemming from shared reflections and so as truly embodied in the same type of questions. Indeed, from the surviving literature it is possible to observe various degrees of divergence emerging. Particularly intriguing is how overwhelmingly the critique is put into the mouth of the historical Buddha himself, not, I think, to deceive but in order to argue for real continuity. Yet to express matters thus is to conjure altogether too narrowly argumentative a process. Shakyamuni is given the credit precisely because that is how such perceptions were experienced intuitively, as more like a revelation of an alternative way of seeing things. And from this, important further conclusions were deduced. Among them was the idea that the nirvana into which the Buddha had entered could not possibly be seen as one of 'extinction' or even of exclusion from all contact with this particular world.[126] Not only did he need to be able to communicate the type of programme now proposed, but also such a move was in any case required by what had come to be seen as his now primary attribute of compassion.

With such backward projections also came the question of the need to account for the earlier advocacy of what was now viewed retrospectively as something less than the full truth, yet nonetheless attributable to

---

[125] For the same monastery, Williams, *Mahayana Buddhism*, 5.
[126] 'Nirvana' literally means extinction. It was compared to what happens to a fire when there is no more fuel. But, of course, it could be argued that what was extinguished was all desire, not everything.

Shakyamuni. The answer given was found in appeal to the notion of 'skilful means': of truth always spoken in ways most appropriate to the particular recipients at that time.[127] The Lotus Sutra, for example, offers several powerful analogies for such a practice of expedient means. These include a story of partial truths told to children in order to encourage flight from a burning house and a version of the parable of the prodigal son.[128] The result was that a whole range of means of pursuing enlightenment could now be added, without them being necessarily seen as originally proposed by the historical Buddha. These varied from a number of forms of visual meditation,[129] to what has always puzzled (and intrigued) Western minds, tantric practices (the cultivation of spirituality by the apparent pursuit of its opposite).[130]

---

[127] In the Lotus Sutra the bodhisattva is contrasted both with the *arhat* who relies on another's teaching rather than personal experience and with the *pratyekabuddha* who pursues his path in complete isolation. See further Carl Bielefeldt, 'Expedient Devices, the One Vehicle, and the Life Span of the Buddha' in Stephen F. Teiser & Jacqueline I. Stone eds., *Readings of the Lotus Sutra* (New York: Columbia University Press, 2009), 62–82, esp. 66 (cf. 15).

[128] In chapters 3 and 4: Reeves, *Lotus Sutra*, 103–57. In the latter, the son is left to work on a dung heap until the right attitudes have been inculcated.

[129] See, for example, Alan Sponberg, 'Wonhyo on Maitreya Visualization' in Alan Sponberg & Helen Hardacre eds., *Maitreya, the Future Buddha* (Cambridge: Cambridge University Press, 1988), 94–109.

[130] The basic idea is so easily parodied that it was a relief to discover a recent exhibition (in 2020) at the British Museum taking the approach seriously: 'by engaging with the transgressive and the taboo (either literally or symbolically), the repressed power of traditionally forbidden practices and substances can be harnessed': Imma Ramos, *Tantra: Enlightenment to Revolution* (London: Thames & Hudson, 2020), 9.

Even with these explanations readers might still be tempted to lament the disappearance of the earlier, simple form of the Buddha's message and so in the process summarily dismiss what happened as of any relevance to Christianity. Let me, therefore, end this chapter by noting some interesting Christian parallels. Consider first the way in which the early church had also to wrestle with the wider significance of Jesus of Nazareth. The Resurrected Lord was now seen as available more widely than just in the Holy Land. He not only appears to Paul on the Damascus Road and to John on the island of Patmos but his presence is also promised through the liturgy of bread and wine. Allusion to such parallels is not intended to imply mythological claims. There remains an historical earthing to the way in which the experiences are described. Even so, resort to mythological imagery is by no means entirely absent from Christianity, as can be seen for instance in Jesus' presumed visit to the underworld on Holy Saturday, again motivated by a desire for more inclusive significance, in this case affecting past generations.[131] Secondly, as in these examples Christian theology has also had to wrestle with possible reasons behind such gradualism in revelation and so with notions of accommodation to specific historical contexts, its own 'skilful means', as it were. In order to explain some strong contrasts between Old Testament and New, across the centuries a number of thinkers proposed just such an approach: to mention two quite different examples, Gregory Nazianzen in the fourth century and

---

[131] Based on Matt. 27.51–3 and I Peter 3.18–20 and dramatically developed in the hugely popular, apocryphal Gospel of Nicodemus. For further discussion, see my *Gospel as Work of Art: Imaginative Truth and the Open Text* (Grand Rapids, MI: Eerdmans, 2024), p. 134–47.

Gotthold Lessing in the eighteenth.[132] The former speaks of a divine 'gentleness' in 'gradual changes' to ancestral ideas, since 'nothing that is involuntary is durable'.[133] Given the new understanding of development that biblical criticism has brought, there is now the need for more extensive application of the same principle.

For some, such parallels may speak of nothing more profound than the inventiveness of religion. Alternative interpretations, though, are available. Indeed, Christians might detect the hand of God in such transformations of another religion. Buddhism and Christianity are both now drawn closer together in the common values of compassion and love. This is not to deny continuing major differences, not least on the question of underlying metaphysics. Buddhists may well contend that Christianity has halted its deliberations too soon. With nothing permanent in an ever-fluctuating reality, it makes better sense to speak of the value of attributes rather than any particular 'persons' who happen to bear them. That kind of debate is one to which we will need to return, both in the context of Japanese Buddhism and in Chapter 7. But I end these reflections by observing that, even if it is only in modern times that Christianity has come to recognise the extent to which it too has changed across the centuries, retrospective analysis surely demonstrates that Buddhism and Christianity were alike renewed and strengthened by such processes.[134]

---

[132] Gregory Nazianzen, *The Fifth Theological Oration*; Gotthold Lessing, *The Education of the Human Race*.
[133] Fifth Oration, XIX. A few pages later (XXVI) the Trinity is given similar treatment, with the Son seen as only clearly manifested in the New Testament and the divinity of the Spirit in his own day.
[134] See further my *Gospel as Work of Art*, chs. 3–4.

6

The Religions of Japan

Following the procedure adopted in Chapters 4 and 5, we will begin with a brief survey of the history of Japan and of religion's place within that nation before turning to its two main variants, Shinto and Buddhism. While in the case of Shintoism it will prove relatively easy to identify an appropriate test-case, in the case of Buddhism two contrasting approaches from within that religion will be set against one another. The aim is to demonstrate how radically divergent streams of the same religion can offer surprisingly different pointers for Christian self-reflection.

A Distinctive Island Culture

Japan is an archipelago of five main islands and literally thousands of others.[1] It is often remarked both by outside observers and by the Japanese themselves that this island status continues to make the country significantly different from other industrialised nations,[2] even though its post–war economic miracle thrust it into the first rank. Far more of the earlier attitudes have survived than is so elsewhere, despite the destruction and occupation which

---

[1] There are 6,852 in total. The five main islands are (from north to south) Hokkaido, Honshu (the central and largest), Shikoku, Kyushu and (at a distance from the others) Okinawa.

[2] Arguably, Great Britain is different too but not primarily because of religious differences.

marked the end of the Second Word War and the subsequent expansion of Tokyo into what is by some estimates the largest city in the world.[3] Visitors to the country quickly become aware of quite distinctive perspectives and traditions, yet the islands are not nearly as remote as maps may sometimes suggest.[4] An alternative explanation is, therefore, sometimes canvassed in terms of Japan's relatively recent opening to the wider world. The restoration of the emperor in 1868 followed two centuries under the shoguns when travel abroad had been strictly forbidden.[5] Indeed, despite a brief period during the sixteenth century when traders and missionaries were allowed entry, there was an even longer time before that when isolation had been the norm.[6]

Yet, as historians have again been quick to point out, even though official isolation had proved the best means of preserving independence, various more hidden forms of contact and influence were maintained throughout. For example, Nagasaki and the Ryukyu islands were used as a means of extensive trading with China, even though the terminology deployed sounded as though not much was happening.[7] So it is not altogether surprising that cultural

---

[3] With greater Tokyo roughly 40 million, a third of Japan's total population.
[4] At its two extremities the distance from mainland Asia is only a few miles.
[5] From the 1630s onwards.
[6] Particularly intense between c. 900 and 1300, with some relaxation thereafter.
[7] Although the Chinese traders were confined to a walled compound, during the Tokugawa period (1603–1868) Nagasaki had extensive trading relations with China and Korea. However, in order to disguise the extent of such contact, disputes were not settled at ambassadorial

influence from its two nearest neighbours, China and Korea, extended well beyond religion. A case in point is the language itself. Japanese script consists principally of Chinese ideograms, but the various ways in which their interpretation was modified indicates well how the Japanese gave their language its own distinctive identity.[8] Similarly, then, with religion: elements of Buddhism, Confucianism and Daoism were all imported but again these were adapted and changed in the process.

Some accounts describe modern Japan as essentially secular. While opinion polls identify only a minority of the people as 'religious' and there is much syncretism,[9] some observers suggest a different analysis. Because of the character of its two major religions, a deeper religious identity has after all been preserved through the medium of various aesthetic values. While in a Western context such a presumption might have been taken to entail that only the aesthetic element survived, there is more of a blending present in Japan that refuses any artificial distinction between aesthetics and religion.[10] Accordingly, although there is very little of the religious enthusiasm which is commonly found in India,

---

level. Instead, this took place at an institution rather strangely known as the Nagasaki Chinese Translation Office.

[8] The borrowing produced some odd results. As Japanese is not structurally related to Chinese (it is closer to Mongol and Turkish and even Finnish), each ideogram has two possible pronunciations (one Chinese and the other Japanese). Still further modifications were added through agglutination, the addition of syllables at the end of words.

[9] A common pattern is for individuals to have a Shinto or even a Christian wedding, while funeral rites are reserved for Buddhism.

[10] A point made by Alan Macfarlane, *Japan: Through the Looking Glass* (London: Profile, 2007), 47–48, 175–77.

underlying religious attitudes do appear more pervasive than is the case in China.

Take, for example, the interior of Japanese homes. Not only is there frequently a domestic shrine but also the simplicity of the home's layout evinces underlying religious values.[11] Nor does a different conclusion emerge when we turn more explicitly to the arts. Both classical forms of drama (Noh and Kabuki) display various religious emphases. This is most obvious in the simplicity of Noh plots, suggestive, as they are, of the ephemeral, transient character of the world. Although Kabuki's origins were quite different in bawdy comedy, overlaps with religion are now more obvious, in its purified, modern form of performance.[12] Again, even today the majority of the population apparently still engages in the composition of a form of poetry (the haiku) which traces its origins to Buddhism.[13] Not that this is just a matter of classical precedents; even the cinema shows such a pattern but in a way that nicely illustrates foreign debts, even as the films are given their own distinctive Japanese identity. For example, the plot of Ozu Yasujiro's 1953 *Tokyo Story* was based on the American 1937 film *Make Way for Tomorrow*, while Kurosawa Akira's 1961 *Yojimbo* finds its origins in Dashiell Hammett's novels and in the film

---

[11] Macfarlane, *Japan*, 175. The Japanese novelist, Tanizaki Junichiro, contrasts the Western search for strong light with the subtle play of simplicity and shade in the Japanese home: *In Praise of Shadows* (1933; current English trans., 2017). Tanizaki is best known for his classic story of the lives of four sisters, set before the Second World War, *The Makioka Sisters* (1943–48).
[12] A process at work since even before the Second World War. The desire has been to see the plots as repositories of tradition.
[13] Macfarlane, *Japan*, 121.

director John Ford's classic Western scenes.[14] Yet at the same time the biblical simplicity of the first model is subverted, while in Kurosawa's work the hero loses his characteristic American traits and becomes nameless, dirty and unshaven.[15] Then, if we turn to the environment, while gardens in other cultures sometimes also have a religious dimension, Zen gardens are by far the best-known example of this form and also currently deeply influential on Western garden design.[16] Extending the point more widely, one major surprise to emerge from the slowdown in the Japanese economy and the nuclear disaster at Fukushima in 2011 has been how easily people have adapted to a different sort of ethos, in a simpler lifestyle.[17] It is almost as though such attitudes had been there all the time.

However, this is not at all to claim that every distinctive aspect of Japanese culture is at root religious. Take present-day attitudes to sexuality. It is difficult to find any clear historical precedents in religion as such. Instead, one may speak of a story of fluctuating change. So, while the country's oldest myth speaks of a female sun god (Amaterasu) from whom the imperial family is supposedly

---

[14] Note that in Japanese the surname is usually placed first.
[15] A contrast explored in Mark J. Ravina, *Understanding Japan: A Cultural History* (Smithsonian Lectures/ Great Courses, 2015), lecture 23.
[16] For an excellent survey of the history of Japanese gardens, Günter Nitschke, *Japanese Gardens* (Cologne: Taschen, 1999). For advice on imitating the style in the West, for example, Kiyoshi Seike et al., *A Japanese Touch to Your Garden* (Tokyo: Kodansha, 1980); Philip Cave, *Creating Japanese Gardens* (London: Aurum Press, 1993).
[17] Government appeals in 2011 to conserve energy easily overshot their target. A more frugal society, with life expectancy continuing to grow, has been the result.

ultimately descended,[18] the fact that during the Heian period (794 –1185 CE) women exercised a major role both in culture and government seems to have been influenced not by religious precedents but by political expediency.[19] Even the best-known novel from the period was written by a woman, Murasaki Shibuku's *Tale of Genji* (c. 1000 CE). Yet, more recent history has been firmly a story of female subordination. Although romantic notions of marriage are now more common, the survival of earlier attitudes is well illustrated by the pervasiveness of love hotels and other forms of sexual entertainment.[20] However, in making this acknowledgement, it is important to exclude the famous geishas. In their case, unlike with most prostitution, a strong cultural contribution was also expected.[21]

Again, in reflecting upon the extraordinary brutality shown during the Second World War, it may be noted that there appears to be no obvious connection with native religion, nor indeed sufficient evidence to pronounce such attitudes are deep seated. Apart from the war with Russia at the beginning of the twentieth century (1904–5) and the colonisation of Korea a little later in 1910, the Japanese government was mainly engaged in the pursuit of peace until extremists by their actions in the

---

[18] Still the major Shinto goddess, she is often interpreted as indicative of a matriarchal society at the time of the myth's origin.
[19] Marrying female members of the imperial family was used as a means of gaining decisive influence over the emperor, although nominally he remained in overall control.
[20] Attitudes to sexuality is the dominant theme in Ian Buruma, *A Japanese Mirror* (London: Atlantic Books, 1984).
[21] Finely brought out in Arthur Golden's novel *Memoirs of a Geisha* (London: Vintage, 1988).

1930s pulled the nation off course.[22] Historians often speak of a drift into war rather than any concerted plan and it was indeed the case that on any purely rational consideration Japan went to war with the United States altogether too early. It had not yet built up sufficient military and economic resources to fight such a war.[23] Thus, the army had scarcely enough food to feed its own troops in China, never mind prisoners of war. This is not to exculpate the guilty but it is to flesh out the fact that even the famous samurai had become instruments of peace by the time the new Japan was created in the mid-nineteenth century.[24] At the same time, there was an element of contempt for the foreigner in the army's conduct abroad which survives even to this day in treatment of Koreans living within the country.[25] As one observer puts it, 'Japan is like an oyster'. Just as in a pearl, something beautiful is created at the price of the total elimination of what is foreign (the threatening sand which initiates the process), so in Japan there continues to be considerable resistance to any form of foreign influence.[26] As a final feature, again not necessarily traceable to

---

[22] In 1931 a puppet state was formed in Manchuria by the Kwantung army without any explicit authorization by either Army High Command or the Tokyo civil government.

[23] A 1937 five-year economic plan was still not complete. For a good account of the drift towards militarism, Jonathan Clements, *A Brief History of Japan* (Tokyo: Tuttle, 2017), 207–15.

[24] During the peaceful Tokugawa shogunate (1603–1868 CE; also known as the Edo period) the samurai became courtiers and bureaucrats rather than warriors.

[25] Nicely illustrated by the Korean–American novelist, Kim Lee, in his *Pachinko* (2017). There have been similar difficulties with the native Ainu, living in the northern island of Honshu.

[26] For the analogy, Alex Kerr, *Lost Japan* (London: Penguin, 1993), 203.

religion, there is a marked lack of individuality in what proves to be a rigidly hierarchical society. This is expressed as much in subtleties of language and bowing gestures as in formal relations in the home and the workplace.[27]

While a full study of religion in Japan would need to include some consideration of the roles also played by Christianity, Confucianism and Daoism, it will suffice here to examine only Shinto and Buddhism. The two Chinese religions were in the main mediated through Buddhism, itself also a Chinese phenomenon. While Christianity exercises an influence out of all proportion to the number of its converts,[28] it is still very much a minority faith. Although at one point it did look as though history might have turned out quite differently, in the end its foreign associations proved too difficult to overcome.[29] Nonetheless, its martyrs continue to present the wider world with the challenge of reflecting more deeply on what might be required of faith. Shusaku Endo's famous novel *Silence* (1966) about the suppression and the 2016 film of the same name (directed by Martin Scorcese) both raise the question of whether apostasy is necessarily always the wrong course of action.[30] Some

---

[27] Despite an obvious debt to Confucianism, Kerr suggests that such patterns are stronger in Japan than in China, precisely because of the former's island status: Kerr, *Lost Japan*, 82.
[28] Despite the small number of Christians, since the Second World War no less than seven prime ministers of Japan have been Christian: Robert Ellwood, *Japanese Religion* (London: Routledge, 2nd ed., 2016), 235.
[29] For a recent historical investigation of what happened, Jonathan Clements, *Christ's Samurai* (London: Robinson, 2016).
[30] In order to save his fellow Christians, the Jesuit priest, Fr Rodrigues, eventually tramples on an image of Christ but receives a vision

readers might be tempted to go further and suggest that, in addition to the three foreign imports, not even the native Shinto needs serious consideration since it constituted more of a political foundation for the newly reconstituted nation rather than any serious engagement with religion.[31] In what follows I shall suggest otherwise. At the same time it needs to be conceded that not much can be inferred from placing its consideration first, as though it should necessarily be seen as more 'native' or 'primitive' than Buddhism. Not only is there considerable uncertainty about its earliest forms, these were actually only enshrined in writing a couple of centuries later than the arrival of Buddhism's own key documents.[32]

Shinto and Valuing Divine Immanence

Although the common image of Shinto is of a religion largely unchanged from its early origins, the difference from Buddhism in this respect is less marked than might have been anticipated. While generalisations are difficult for a religion that lacks any obvious central controlling structure,[33] there have been some significant changes of direction across its history. This is no less true today, now that a strong emphasis on the relevance of its leading ideas

> reassuring him that Christ is alongside him in the act (a profoundly moving moment in the film).
> [31] Its presumed political role was most obvious at the time of the nineteenth century Meiji restoration of imperial rule.
> [32] Shinto's two main early religious texts date from the early eighth century CE. Buddhism first arrived in the country with already existing texts two centuries earlier.
> [33] The Association of Shinto Shrines is charged with overseeing the 80,000 or so shrines but it lacks legal powers.

to environmental concerns has recently become so prominent. This is the issue upon which I will focus at the end of this discussion, but first some of the alternative possibilities need to be examined.

In common with other early or 'primitive' religions like Native American or Aboriginal,[34] Shinto is rich in myth. As already noted, these were not committed to any written record until a couple of centuries after the arrival of Buddhism and then in two versions in quick succession. The earlier is livelier and racier, the later more accommodating to Buddhism.[35] Some of these myths which concern numerous *kami* or spirits continue to be well known to this day. Partly this is because of particular shrines dedicated to their memory but also because such stories continue to be retold in contemporary media such as anime and manga,[36] with sometimes appropriate lessons for life also drawn.[37] Intriguingly, in the nearest parallel to the biblical creation myth, it is not human beings that are created. Rather, it is the various islands

---

[34] Appropriate terminology is difficult in this area. 'Primitive' or 'primal' tend to suggest a dismissive attitude, while alternatives such as 'traditional' ignore the fact that all religions are to varying degrees traditional.

[35] Kojiki dates from 712 CE, Nihonshoki from 720 CE. The telling is livelier in the former. The latter shows Chinese influence and also records alternative versions.

[36] Anime refers to computer animated stories, manga refers to comics and graphic novels.

[37] For one recent discussion, see Katharine Buljan & Carole M. Cusack, *Anime, Religion and Spirituality* (Sheffield: Equinox, 2014); more briefly but including some specific examples, Helen Hardacre, *Shinto: A History* (New York: Oxford University Press, 2017), 538–49. The director Hayao Miyozaki is especially important in this connection.

of Japan.[38] Given that the details reflect the social structure of the Japan at that time, it looks as though supernatural endorsement is being offered for such structures, including the already very Japanese practice of seeking consensus in any decision. That kind of background influence also explains why the chief kami to emerge from the primal creative pair is not a first-born son but rather a later daughter, Amaterasu, for in early Japan women often played a leading role. Yet, although identified with the sun, which in most cultures is treated as male, the deity nonetheless remains characteristically female, even to the extent of fleeing her brother by hiding in a cave.[39] From that cave she is only persuaded to re-emerge by a provocative display that includes the use of a mirror; hence its symbolic presence in many a contemporary shrine.[40] Another kami worth mentioning is the god of the ricefields, Inaru. In the largely rural economy of the country's past, this figure was obviously hugely important. A large number of shrine dedications still remain. A statue of Inaru's supporting animal, the fox, is usually displayed at the entrance or some other prominent place.[41]

---

[38] The five original deities play no subsequent role except to give rise to five later pairs, the last of which (Isanagi and Isanami) create the Japanese archipelago. For an outline of the story, Michael Ashkenazi, *Handbook of Japanese Mythology* (New York: Oxford University Press, 2003), 76–94.

[39] Despite treating him well, her older brother (Susano-wo) pollutes her fields in various shocking acts: Ashkenazi, 112–13.

[40] An excellent guide to contemporary shrines, their content and rituals is provided by Joseph Cali & John Dougill, *Shinto Shrines: A Guide to the Sacred Sites of Japan's Ancient Religion* (Honolulu: University of Hawai'i Press, 2013).

[41] Despite compulsory separation in 1868 CE from the Buddhist saint, Kobo Daishi, founder of the Shingo sect, Inari remains very popular.

While it is possible to detect in the origin of such myths merely implicit or even explicit reflection of the political status quo, there is no doubt that elements of religious devotion appeared early and became particularly significant at certain periods of Japanese history. Concern for the proper conceptualisation of divinity, a moral dimension, the expectation of religious experience and even a form of revelation (all originally absent) each emerge in due course, though with some elements more prominent than others. Amaterasu, for example, quickly moves into the position of principal deity, with her shrine at Ise treated with great respect.[42] While the majority of the population continued to be polytheistic, an original animism seems to have transmogrified into a more limited number of deities for some, while for others a pantheistic form of monotheism was the result.[43] Such attitudes are reflected in a common lack of interest in the specific name for the deity attached to a particular shrine. Even in a shrine as well known as Kamigano Jinga (on the Kamo river in north Kyoto), the majority of visitors apparently showed no interest in that question.[44] Again, whereas

---

The association with the fox is probably due mainly to the animal's ability to move easily between wild and domestic locations: Hardacre, *Shinto*, 148–50.

[42] The town of Ise is at the south-east end of the main island of Honshu, on the Shima peninsula. Commonly known as Jingu or Ise Jingu, the complex consists of numerous subordinate shrines. Its fame derives from its alleged possession of the original sacred mirror. Its wooden buildings are without nails and rebuilt every twenty-five years or so.

[43] For a contemporary example of the latter attitude, Motohisa Yamakage, *The Essence of Shinto* (New York: Kodansha, 2000), esp. 31–32, 168–69.

[44] Only 14 per cent knew the deity's name according to one survey: John K. Nelson, *Enduring Identities: The Guise of Shinto in Contemporary Japan* (Honolulu: University of Hawai'i Press, 2000), 30.

water purification rites at the shrines were originally only ever intended to deal with problems of ritual pollution,[45] a more moral dimension was eventually to become marked, especially under Confucian influence during the Edo period (1603–1868 CE).[46]

So in view of so many changes it is perhaps not altogether surprising that a number of figures had revelatory visions of Amaterasu and for a period directed large segments of the population along particular paths. In the nineteenth century two individuals achieved especial fame in this regard. Both experienced mystical visions of Amaterasu which led them to found missionary movements.[47] While no one approach came to dominate, such occurrences did help legitimate the search of other adherents for religious experience at the Shinto shrines. Relevant to note here is the very large numbers who participated, and continue to participate, in pilgrimage to the Ise shrine,[48] or again to the numerous temples on the small island of Shikoku.[49] One way in which the more 'advanced' religions have tried to denigrate the more 'primitive' has

---

[45] Such as from dead bodies, which is one reason why Japanese prefer a Buddhist funeral.
[46] Although difficult to prove, the hierarchical character of Japanese society could be said to be the result of earlier Confucian influence. Clearer is the contention that Neo-Confucianism gave Shinto a stronger moral dimension. For the contemporary transformation of water purification into a moral category, see Motohisa, *Essence*, 88–104.
[47] Kurozumi Munetada (d. 1850 CE) and Ioue Masakane (d. 1849 CE). For further details, Hardacre, *Shinto*, 299–322, esp. 306–20.
[48] There were five million in 1830 CE, nine million in 2013 CE.
[49] For an excellent study of contemporary attitudes to pilgrimage, see Ian Reader, *Making Pilgrimages: Meaning and Practice in Shikoku* (Honolulu: University of Hawai'i Press, 2005). The island as a whole (which also includes many Buddhist temples) is treated as a pilgrimage site.

been by suggesting that the latter are fundamentally manipulative, crudely concerned with extracting material benefits from the greater power that is divinity. In a fascinating study of whether such an analysis can legitimately be applied to Shinto and Japanese Buddhism or not, the two investigators came to an intriguing conclusion: almost invariably, such appeals for benefits are 'backed by a set of ethical constraints and values.'[50]

Nonetheless, pulling against all these qualifications is the political manipulation of religion which has occurred throughout Japanese history. It is an especially prominent feature of the Meiji imperial restoration in the nineteenth century. For centuries there had been extensive collaboration between Shinto and Buddhism, even to the extent of them sometimes sharing buildings. That process was put decisively into reverse in the late nineteenth century. Shinto was now harnessed to the task of buttressing the myth of the emperor as the living, divine descendant of Amaterasu. Unfortunately, even with the Japanese defeat in 1945 the situation did not greatly change. Although the new constitution required the separation of religion and the state, in practice conservative opinion rallied round the pre–war version of Shintoism. This explains the contentious, prominent place given to Yasukuni, the Shinto shrine memorialising those who had given their lives fighting during the war.[51] The position was not helped

---

[50] Ian Reader and George J. Tanabe Jnr., *Practically Religious: Worldly Benefits and the Common Religion of Japan* (Honolulu: University of Hawai'i Press, 1998), 257.
[51] The shrine commemorates all those killed in Japanese wars since 1868 CE, now amounting to roughly two and a half million individuals. The troubling aspect is that this includes 1,068 convicted war criminals.

by the absence of any initiatives in a different direction from the still reigning emperor, Hirohito.

Some changes did occur with his successor, Akihito (1989–2019). Although the mysterious Shinto rites that inaugurate a new reign continued,[52] the new emperor's willingness to apologise publicly for Japan's conduct in the last war did make a huge difference. Change also continued with the effects of the sarim toxic gas attack on the Tokyo underground in 1995 and again with the terrible disaster in 2011 at the Fukushima nuclear power station. If, in view of its religious motivation, the former event effectively challenged Japanese religions to demonstrate positive relevance to modern society,[53] the latter showed a way to do so in social concern for all those devastated by the more than 20,000 dead. Both occurrences encouraged the more reflective side of Shintoism to move radically away from its old political past into concern for the local community and also eventually towards its present involvement with environmental issues.

Given its ambiguous political history and the extent of the doctrinal contrast with Christianity, readers may well be reluctant to concede that anything very much could be learnt from such an exploration. So let me add two comments, one about Christianity's own negative past and the

---

[52] As there is a bed present, its origins were probably in some sort of conjugal celebration. For the details, Ellwood, *Japanese Religion*, 25–28.
[53] Those responsible for the 1995 attack were members of an obscure religious cult called Aum Shinrikyo which had been granted official recognition in 1989. Combining Hindu, Buddhist and Christian ideas, it won thousands of converts. The attack was apparently intended to precipitate the apocalypse.

other on the openness of Shinto experience to a more positive interpretation. It is true that Shinto has often had an embarrassing political past. But not only is that changing, it also does not take long to discover similar problematic periods in the history of Christianity. Indeed, within half a century of acquiring a position of power, under Theodosius I (379–95 CE) it embarked on a policy of persecution, or at any rate that is how early Christian historians interpreted what happened.[54] Equally, in modern times to be balanced against the resistance of the German Confessing Church is the existence of numerous Nazi supporters within the church (the so-called *Deutsche Christen*), just as today the Orthodox hierarchy in Russia is found giving unqualified support to Vladimir Putin.[55]

Again, while many of the features of Shinto will continue to remain strange, on the more positive side there is surely no reason in principle why a Christian might not see God's presence and will mediated through a goddess like Amaterasu, just as we argued could be the case with Hindu polytheism. For too long an absolute model of either/or has held sway but, as we have suggested

---

[54] The Edict of Milan in 313 granted toleration to Christianity. The early Christian interpretation of Theodosius' reign is now widely challenged. The destruction of pagan sites came later and the emperor did not ban paganism. See, for example, Alan Cameron, *The Last Pagans of Rome* (Oxford: Oxford University Press, 2010), 68–73; Mark Hebblewhite, *Theodosius and the Limits of Empire* (London: Routledge, 2020), ch.8.

[55] Notoriously, in Patriarch Kirill of Moscow's support for the war in Ukraine. The same policy has been pursued under successive patriarchs. Under Communism in Leningrad's Kazan Cathedral (then called the Museum of Religion and Atheism) a central position was given to an icon identifying Nicholas II with Christ.

throughout this work, all religious experience is necessarily a mixture of divine address and purely human input. So it is not impossible to think of God using the imagery of Amaterasu to mediate something of the divine purposes. In a similar way, Protestant Christians might now be more willing to concede that the divine has indeed sometimes spoken through visions of the Virgin Mary: not least in the visions' common insistence upon God's identification with the poor. At the same time they might want to continue to resist some more specific claims in these visions such as Bernadette of Soubirous' conviction that Mary addressed her as 'the Immaculate Conception.'[56] Likewise, some discrimination would be required in any adequate analysis of experience of Amaterasu.

Test Case: Valuing Divine Immanence

Both Daoism and Shintoism could have been explored in general terms as religions which appear to offer greater respect for nature and the environment than does Buddhism or Confucianism, or Christianity for that matter.[57] But in some ways that might be to state the obvious. So, just as with Daoism in Chapter 5 I chose a

---

[56] Part of the zeitgeist of contemporary Catholicism and so an obvious way for the speaker to identify herself, just as was the use of imagery drawn from her statue in the local church. The fact that these were time-bound does not entail that everything Mary said was, though of course it might do so.

[57] These remarks are certainly not intended to exclude other options. For a fascinating attempt to apply the practice of Hinduism to such interfaith dialogue, see Corinne G. Dempsy, *Bringing the Sacred Down to Earth: Adventures in Comparative Religion* (New York: Oxford University Press, 2012).

narrower focus,[58] so here too I shall select a more precisely conceived topic, in divine immanence. First, reductionist arguments against such an emphasis will be considered; second, the sources of its present environmental interpretation will be considered as part of an interplay between present wider societal concerns and that religion's own past history. But initially something needs to be said about Shinto attitudes to nature in general.

On the surface it may look as though positive attitudes have always prevailed. Indeed, this does tend to be the type of presentation offered by current adherents wishing to highlight Shinto's relevance but there are good reasons for believing that a more complex story needs to be told. Although Japan is numbered among countries with the highest percentage of land devoted to forestry,[59] this is more a result of the terrain than any conscious decision.[60] Again, the history of Shinto shrines demonstrates more often concern with pursuing profit than anything particularly to do with questions of sustainability.[61] A more mixed attitude is in any case what might have been expected from the religion's early myths in which kami are associated with fear of nature as much as with a more positive conception of them working alongside

---

[58] How Christianity might learn from Daoism in attitudes to the beginning and end of life.
[59] At 68.5 per cent: Aike P. Rots, *Shinto, Nature and Ideology in Contemporary Japan* (London: Bloomsbury, 2017), 111.
[60] Unlike with British history, for most of Japan's history there was no marked need for wooden warships.
[61] Priests are mostly poorly paid and so look with favour on projects to augment the shrine's income. Occasionally, this transcends appropriate bounds and lapses into actual corruption: Nelson, *Enduring Identities*, 123–63, esp. 138 & 156-58.

humanity (as can be seen in the negative origins of the term kamikaze).[62]

One indication of change is in how the shrines now commonly present themselves. Not only is much more attention given to the land around them but, as well as a new focus on the cultivation of trees,[63] the shrines' wider relationship to the landscape has also been developed. Rather than looking exclusively internally for signs of the sacred, the position of the shrine in relation to neighbouring hills or mountains is underlined and sometimes strengthened.[64] Such attitudes have even received official endorsement from the Japanese government. When hosting the G7 meeting in 2016, Prime Minister Abe Shinzo invited other world leaders to visit the Ise shrine with him and hear about both past precedents and what new initiatives were being taken.[65]

As Christian expectations of human attitudes to nature have already been discussed in Chapter 5 and elsewhere, here it will be useful to explore evaluations of the relationship from the divine side, as it were, in treatments of divine immanence. Although historically there was a time when Christian theology contemplated using Christ as

---

[62] Literally meaning 'divine wind', the term's original association was with typhoons. However, the dispersal of an attacking Mongol fleet by such means during the medieval period allowed its extension to the suicide pilots seeking to defend their country in the Second World War.

[63] For two examples, one at a small country shrine and the other at Ise, Rots, *Shinto, Nature and Ideology*, 142–48, 183–89.

[64] For a good example of major changes masquerading as the way things always were, note how Mt. Miwa is now viewed in relation to Omiwa Jinja, Rots, *Shinto, Nature and Identity*, 107–11.

[65] Rots, *Shinto, Nature and Identity*, 1–3.

the principal symbol for divine presence in the world,[66] eventually it was of course the Holy Spirit who came to be seen as acting in this role. As we have already noted, many contemporary Shinto writers interpret the various kami as all variants on a single immanent presence. While there remain numerous other points of difference, it is interesting, therefore, to observe that on this question at least it now looks almost as though there is no longer any insuperable distance between the two religions. Both could be seen as acknowledging an overarching divine immanence. Nonetheless, it might be claimed that a major difference remains, in Christianity's claim to a transcendence beyond that immanence. Caution, though, is necessary in embarking on such a contentious assertion. As we saw in Chapter 2, quite wrong were biblical objections to idols as exhaustive of any claims to divinity. In the ancient world generally it was seen as a focused presence rather than an exclusive one. Similarly here, then, with Shinto. In traditional shrine ritual the relevant kami is actually invited to be present which suggests that their existence is not seen as exhausted by their presence in the idol.[67] So, as with immanence, on transcendence there is surely also a difference of degree and not of kind between the two religions.

While Shinto might still need to be pushed further on the question of transcendence, it could be argued no less insistently that there is also a pressing need on the part of

---

[66] Christ as Logos was seen as universal, the work of the Holy Spirit confined to the church; so, for example, Origen, *Contra Celsum* I.3.
[67] The form of the ritual used implies that kami are not bound to one time or place: so Nelson, *Enduring Identities*, 176–78.

Christianity to move in the opposite direction. Stemming ultimately from its biblical perspective, it has required too distant a withdrawal from things of the world, based on a suspicion of its corrupting power which affected attitudes to everything from sacramentality to sexuality. Obvious examples are the exaltation of celibacy in Catholicism and the fear of sacramentality in Protestant theology. It is also not implausible to claim that such a perspective was also a significant contributing factor in determining very negative attitudes towards adherents of other 'primitive' religions such as Native American and Aboriginal. Great Britain and its white colonials demonstrate a history of relations where 'enlightened improvement' in the name of the 'superior' religion cultivated at best neglect and at its worst sheer wickedness in the elimination of native populations.[68] Here too, therefore, there remains much that Christianity could still learn from what survives of these other native forms.[69] Aboriginal dream painting is an obvious case in point.[70] So at the very least we might talk of an expansion of Christianity's immanent perspective through dialogue with these various groups, including modern Shinto. Of course, there remains the danger that too strong an emphasis on divine immanence may result in too close an identification with the values of this world.

---

[68] The Massacre at Wounded Knee in 1890 CE is only the most conspicuous of numerous failures. For an excellent account of the incident, Lee Brown, *Bury my Heart at Wounded Knee* (1970).

[69] Helpful studies include Lee Irwin ed., *Native American Spirituality* (Lincoln: University of Nebraska Press, 2000); Françoise Dussart, Howard Murphy & Max Charlesworth (eds.). *Aboriginal Religions in Australia: An Anthology of Recent Writing* (London: Routledge, 2005).

[70] For a discussion of its significance, see my *God and Enchantment of Place* (Oxford: Oxford University Press, 2004), 92–98.

But, equally, stress on transcendence, in attempting to secure the otherness and independence of God, can all too easily slip into a worrying unwillingness to engage with the challenges that world throws up. So the solution does not necessarily always lie with Christianity's traditional preference for transcendence.

The second question which I said I would address concerns how the mediation of such a change of approach to environmental issues within Shinto could be presented in more explicitly theological terms. On the surface, it might look as though all that is happening in the modern world is the direct impact of external, secular values on a religion desperate to secure a new role. However, that would be grossly unfair because Shinto is really picking up on already existing elements within its tradition, even if these were somewhat dormant. So a more accurate account might be to speak of secular thought triggering further reflection on that past history and Shinto being thus enabled to make a distinctive contribution of its own. But can any sense be given to detecting the hand of God in all of this? While I would in no way wish to confine divine action to operation within existing religious traditions, it is important to acknowledge the positive role these can play, even where the initial stimulus for change may have come from outside. Awareness of that past history can help generate dynamic interaction between external secular knowledge and awareness of what the history of a particular tradition such as Shinto could possibly contribute. Such a model only seems at a huge distance from religions with a more obvious revelation such as Judaism and Christianity for so long as that revelation is understood (as it once was) as direct and immediate, as in the encounter of the divine with Moses or Jesus. But, as we saw in Chapter 2, much more indirect mediation needs now also to be conceded. So, just as Christianity has been renewed by certain aspects of its somewhat ambiguous past,[71] so might the same be said for Shinto. In other words, the address of the immanent divine from outside the tradition can help re-animate what is already preserved within. Of course, the danger is that secular perspectives are too easily endorsed but that is precisely where the testing against earlier tradition, however latent, can play its appropriate part.

Buddhism and Two Types of Minimalism

Buddhism numbers only about half the individuals to which Shinto lays claim.[72] Among these it is possible to detect three main groupings: Nichiren, Pure Land and Zen. Although the first two both appear to command similar numbers,[73] this is misleading as in the modern world Nichiren has splintered into a number of different factions. Indeed, it is responsible for most of the sects that have arisen in recent years, including the best known, Soka Gakkai.[74] Markedly different, Pure Land has remained relatively uniform and so may safely be described as Japan's largest version of Buddhism. That alone makes it worth considering here. Zen is different

---

[71] So, balanced against the 'dominion' of Gen. 1.26 are features such as provisions for the sabbatical year: Lev. 25.1–7 & 20–22.
[72] 47 million to Shinto's 94: Ellwood, *Japanese Religion*, 256.
[73] About 17 million.
[74] Dating from 1928, it simplified, was exclusive and very much stressed this-world benefits.

again. Although actual adherents of Zen are relatively small,[75] its impact on the West has been huge. That result is usually ascribed to the profundity of its ideas. On either ground (whether influence or content) it would seem appropriate that further analysis be offered here. By contrast, until relatively recently Pure Land has commonly been dismissed from serious consideration. That is surely a mistake. Much can be learnt by comparing and contrasting the two approaches, which is what I shall attempt when we come to the test-case section. But first something more needs to be said about the background history of the two groups.

Buddhism first arrived in Japan during the sixth century.[76] However sincere his adherence may or may not have been, Prince Shotoku saw in it a way of transcending the petty differences between tribes (who identified with particular kami) through the creation of a unified state that was eventually based in the first Japanese capital at Nara.[77] It was here that the largest bronze statue in the world was dedicated in 752 CE. Seventy-two feet in height, even its fingers are six feet in length. The reference, though, was not to the historical Buddha but to the originating Vairocana (Dainichi in Japanese).[78] He is regarded as the supreme Buddha and as such the

---

[75] A total of 3 million to Christianity's 1 million.
[76] Prince Shotoku (573–621 CE) was appointed regent by the Empress Suiko who was herself a devout Buddhist.
[77] Capital only for a short time. Established on the Chinese model in 710 CE, it was superseded by Heian (Kyoto) in 784 CE. Kyoto remained the capital until Edo took over in 1868 CE as the renamed Tokyo ('eastern capital').
[78] Briefly discussed in Chapter 5.

originator of all reality, including the historical Shakyamuni and other Buddhas and bodhisattvas. Because the Japanese name translates as 'Great Sun' it was but a short step to his equation with Amaterasu, one of the earliest instances of the blending of the two faiths. Consolidation followed during the high point of medieval imperial Japan, the Heian period (794–1185 CE), during which two rival schools sought to work out a complete conceptual system for the religion.[79] Subsequently there occurred a period of chaos and uncertainty known as the Kamakura period (1185–1333 CE) when an alternative system of rule under a shogunate and samurai warriors was established at the town of Kamakura, even though the emperor continued nominally in charge at Heian (Kyoto).

It was during this later time that Pure Land Buddhism really first took off, as it were, emerging out of one of those two earlier schools.[80] Its focus lay in a Buddha known as Amitabha or Amitayus (immeasurable light or life) who had already served over numerous generations as a bodhisattva. First appearing in second century Indian thought, his influence quickly spread to China, Vietnam, Korea and Japan.[81] Two sutras about Amitabha (or Amida as he is known in Japanese) were composed in India, while a third was added in Chinese that stressed the importance of visionary practice.[82] The longest of the three spoke of a compassionate decision by Amida to delay nirvana so that he might help all who wished to participate reach the

---

[79] Shingon and Tendai. [80] From the Tendai school.
[81] In Tibetan Buddhism he has been provided with a consort and two main disciples.
[82] Conjuring up the image of Amida and the Pure Land.

special, purified land which he had created. In Japan the demand for visualisation gradually gave way to contemplation and then to simple recitation of the divine name, using the formula *Namu Amida Butsu* ('Hail Amida Buddha'). What essentially such an approach offered amid all the many uncertainties of the time was what appeared to be an uncomplicated path towards salvation. While at this stage the postulated Pure Land was consistently treated as a mysterious, distant 'Western' land, more contentious was the question of the correct balance between merit and faith. Initially at least, entry was still dependent on some good karma but once there a relatively easy path to nirvana was promised.

In determining how contemporary Buddhism would eventually look, three monks who lived in the thirteenth century were to prove definitive. One of them was Nichiren (d. 1282 CE) after whom the presently rather divided group which we mentioned earlier is named. His proposal for a simpler approach was based on appeal to the Lotus Sutra, whose contents were discussed in Chapter 5. The other two offered refinements in the Pure Land approach. Honen (d. 1212 CE) instigated the group known as Jodo-Shu, and Shinran (d. 1263 CE) Jodo-Shinshu. The latter is today twice as popular as Honen's version. Shinran was especially concerned with excluding any notion of self-achievement from the appeal to faith. He worried that Honen's stress on repeated recitation of the formula was itself a sort of justification by works.[83] The result was Shinran's provocative claim that it is the wicked person who is best positioned to make

---

[83] Honen is reputed to have recited 60,000 nembutsu a day.

such an appeal. Thereby, he argued, it was made clear that there was nothing else upon which the relevant individual could rely except the grace of Amida. The name Jodo-Shinshu encapsulates this claim: that he is offering the 'pure essence of Pure Land teaching' rather than merely 'Pure Land teaching' (Jodo-Shu).[84]

Zen is the Japanese version of the less well-known Chinese Chan school from which it is ultimately derived. Although the precise nature of the latter's origins is disputed, it appears to have arisen in the early fifth century as a protest against what was seen as the excessive scholasticism of the two then-dominant schools of thought.[85] Partly under Dao influence, it advocated a return to daily meditational practice and a hope for sudden enlightenment. Although present in Japanese Buddhism from the beginning, Zen only really came to prominence in that same creative thirteenth century in two versions known as Rinzai and Soto. While Soto tends to avoid any aids to mediation, Rinzai is famous for its extensive use of koans, questions with puzzling or paradoxical answers.[86] Soto's most famous exponent was undoubtedly Dogen who extended the Mahayana notion of 'Buddha nature' to all reality. Mahayana writers had introduced this notion in the fifth century CE to indicate the potential or 'seed' in all to become Buddhas. Dogen in effect extended the idea to everything, including grass and trees. At the same time,

---

[84] The former is also sometimes called Shin Buddhism (an abbreviation of Shinran).
[85] Madhyamika and Yogacara.
[86] The figure particularly associated with Soto is Dogen (d. 1253 CE); with Rinzai, Eisai (d. 2115 CE) and then later, especially for the use of koans, Hakuin (d. 1768 CE).

he equated this with 'emptiness' or the lack of any permanent distinctions even between apparently qualifiedly substantial existents. Nothing has permanence, not even the various elements that Shakyamuni had accorded some sort of relative existence as constitutive of the discarded notion of self, the five 'aggregates' or *skandas*. In adopting this position he was heavily influenced by the Heart Sutra, a brief Chinese text to which we will return at the end of our discussion of Zen's influence and relevance.

As in the other cases, Zen's appeal lay in its relative simplicity. Enlightenment lay not at the end of a long, intellectual process. Rather, it was suggested this would come in a sudden, intuitive insight in recognition of the fluidity and transience of all existence. That stress on simplicity of approach, especially when combined with its huge influence on the arts, makes it easy to comprehend why Zen has had no great difficulty in finding numerous recruits in Europe and the United States. By contrast, Pure Land sounded too much like a mythology that had strayed altogether too far from the historical Buddha's intentions. Reasons for a more complex evaluation will be given below, as we investigate each approach in turn.

Test Case One: Zen Minimalism and Impermanence

We shall begin with Zen as the more familiar of the two approaches. It will be appropriate to consider first its appropriation in Europe and in North America with respect to the arts and then within Christian belief and practice itself before turning to a more independent assessment. At this later stage, two aspects will be examined in more detail, both of which relate to its doctrine of impermanence. Whereas with one I shall suggest that Christianity has something to learn, with the other I will introduce a challenge that will then naturally lead into consideration of the Pure Land approach.

Quite a number of familiar names in the arts during the twentieth century were identified with Zen Buddhism. These include composers such as John Cage and Philip Glass, the singer Leonard Cohen and visual artists, including Ad Reinhardt and Robert Rauschenberg, as well as, more recently, Nam June Paik and Bill Viola.[87] But it is in literature that its impact proved most marked. Hermann Hesse (1877–1962) and Aldous Huxley (1894–1963) are European examples.[88] But more prominent has been what happened in the United States. The Japanese American, D. T. Suzuki (1870–1966), wrote about sixty accessible works on the subject, many bestsellers and quite a few of which remain in print. He made sweeping assertions about the extent of Zen influence: 'the principle of Zen discipline pervades all the arts as

---

[87] While Philip Glass's primary influence seems to have been Tibetan Buddhism, John Cage acknowledges a major debt to Zen. His notorious 4.33 minutes of silence is sometimes interpreted as illustrating the Zen doctrine of the equivalence of form and emptiness. Glass' Symphony No 5 and the score for the film *Kundun* can both be seen to have a rather different orientation. For a recent study of Cohen's spirituality, Harry Freedman, *Leonard Cohen: The Mystical Roots of Genius* (London: Bloomsbury, 2021).

[88] Although Hesse's *Siddhartha* dates from 1921 in German, it was only translated into English in 1951, which explains its influence in 1950s and 1960s America. The novel tells the story of Siddhartha's spiritual search during the time of the historical Buddha. As can be seen from his *Perennial Philosophy* (1945), although willing to concede some truth in all religions, Huxley was most sympathetic to Buddhism.

they are studied in Japan.'[89] Most scholars would now agree that he claimed altogether too much, ignoring earlier Shinto influence as well as from other forms of Buddhism.[90] In a similar way the English-born Alan Watts (1915–73) also popularised his own distinctive version. Although pursuit of higher education brought him not only to the United States but also even to ordination within the American Episcopal Church, the opposition to Christian dogmatism that he had first acquired at boarding school soon developed into a permanent critique.[91] Only Zen spirituality, he was eventually to argue, could bring the promise of real freedom.[92]

The result was its adoption by many of the fifties and sixties beat generation. Among the best known was Jack Kerouac (1922–69). An earlier novel, *On the Road* (1955), had focused on the idea of travelling lightly across the country without commitments. This was then taken up in a more explicitly Zen form of reportage in *The Dharma Bums* (1959) which included detailed reflections on a Zen approach to life. Kerouac claimed not to have abandoned the Catholicism in which he had been raised but it was clearly now heavily tempered by a different spirit.[93]

---

[89] D. T. Suzuki, *Zen and Japanese Culture* (Princeton, NJ: Princeton University Press, 1959),153.

[90] For example, Bushido (the values of the samurai) also shows influence from Shinto, Daoism and Confucianism.

[91] See, for example, his harsh words in Alan Watts, *The Way of Zen* (Harmondsworth: Penguin, 1957), 31. He had been educated at King's School, Canterbury.

[92] Including, controversially, the right to experiment with psychedelic drugs.

[93] Jack Kerouac, *The Dharma Bums* (Harmondsworth: Penguin, 1977), xxi, 96–97, 103, 116, 170, 205.

Although some other aspects of Buddhism were also allocated a place,[94] prominently featured was the key element in Zen which underlines the lack of permanence in all things,[95] and the resultant freedom which this is alleged to bring. Yet the novels seldom contain any explicit terminology such as an underlying 'Buddha nature' in all things, or even the term Zen itself.[96]

While less well known, more profound perhaps was the work of the Afro-American Charles Johnson (b. 1948). He uses the idea of transience in 'Buddha nature' effectively to undermine all stereotypes, including (bravely) those perpetuated within his own community. Even slavery was not exempt. For example, in one novel, *Oxherding Tale* (1982), the story opens with the narrator born from the comic, voluntary swapping of wives by slave owner and black slave.[97] The result permits half of the narrative to be told from the perspective of a black underdog and the other half from that of the dominant white culture. However, it is *Middle Passage* (1990) which is his greatest achievement. An unscrupulous former slave working his passage on a slave ship wrestles through to a commitment to integrity thanks to the gradual dissolution of all his existing assumptions. We see how the duality of false oppositions is overcome.[98] 'Stupidly, I had seen their

---

[94] Ibid. Including a reference to Kannon (the Japanese version of Avalokitesvara), 10; the Dipankara Buddha (the Buddha of the very distant past), 124.
[95] Ibid. For example, 28, 114, 125, 200.
[96] Ibid. For two exceptions: Zen, 54; Buddha nature, 125.
[97] The title replicates the title of a series of ten paintings by the twelfth century Zen artist, Kakuan Shien.
[98] See, for example, Charles Johnson, *Middle Passage* (New York: Scribner, 1990), 97, 100–1, 178–79, 192.

lives and culture as timeless product, as finished thing... when the truth was that they were process and Heraclitean change, like any men, not fixed but evolving and vulnerable.'[99] So 'the voyage had irreversibly changed my seeing, made of me a cultural mongrel, and transformed the world into a fleeting shadow play I felt no need to possess or dominate, only appreciate in the ever extended present.'[100] Yet, like Kerouac, Johnson does not see such writing as a rejection of Christianity. Instead, he appears to be working towards a potential integration, as in his later *The Dreamer* (1998), an explicit exploration of Christianity through the life of Martin Luther King.[101]

But how far is such integration really possible? In the contemporary world quite a number of Christian clergy and laity have followed courses which have equipped them as fully-qualified Zen teachers. In such cases Zen was interpreted as one way of deepening Christian spirituality. While there can be no doubt about the usefulness of such practices, the question cannot be avoided of whether, in the process, conflation occurs of what should otherwise be seen as quite distinct ideas. The issue may be tested by exploring two examples, one from the Roman Catholic tradition, the other from the Anglican.

Ruben Habito was a Filipino Jesuit for twenty-five years before leaving the order to get married. While still a practising Catholic, he now runs (with his wife) a Zen meditation centre in Dallas. In *Be Still and Know: Zen and*

---

[99] Ibid., 123.   [100] Ibid., 185.
[101] For an assessment of Johnson's work, see Marc C. Conner & William R. Nash (eds.), *Charles Johnson: The Novelist as Philosopher* (Jackson: University of Mississippi Press, 2007), especially the two essays by Conner, 57–81, 150–70.

the Bible (2017) he draws a number of fruitful parallels with the psalms and central aspects of Jesus' teaching, in particular the search for peace and indifference to material possessions.[102] He is also able to draw on insights from the Cistercian monk, Thomas Merton, and from Fritjof Capra's scientific arguments for a less substantial view of reality.[103] However, his intention is to go much further. The general Buddhist doctrine of no-self and the Christian denial of self are equated.[104] He also contends that a proper understanding of the Christian God, like Buddha nature, must mean placing the deity beyond all oppositions.[105] Perhaps most striking of all is his claim that the Christian doctrine of grace can also be seen to be a central feature of Zen.[106] The Anglican Christopher Collingwood is a fully-qualified Zen master.[107] A distinctive feature of his *Zen Wisdom for Christians* (2019) is his careful exposition of traditional koans as a way of explicating parallels between the two faiths.[108] He too argues that Christianity is concerned with getting

---

[102] Ruben L. F. Habito, *Be Still and Know* (Maryknoll: Orbis Books, 2017). There are thoughtful reflections on Ps. 23 and 46 and Matthew 5.1–9 and 13.44–6. As with a book by Michael Ramsey, the title is borrowed from Psalm 46.10.

[103] Capra's 1975 book *The Tao of Physics: An Exploration of the Parallels Between Modern Physics and Eastern Mysticism* was a bestseller in the United States. Disagreement continues over how deep the parallels really are.

[104] Habito, *Be Still and Know*, 2–3, 15, 31.

[105] Ibid., 44–45, 100–2, although carefully noting that Buddha nature is not as such divine (cf. 90).

[106] Ibid., xiii, 14, 43, 99, although he acknowledges that Zen does not actually use the word (cf. 43).

[107] Until his retirement in 2020, he was Chancellor of York Minster.

[108] Christopher Collingwood, *Zen Wisdom for Christians* (London: Jessica Kingsley, 2019), 70ff. For the originals, K. Yamada ed., *The Gateless*

beyond dualism. The Fall is seen as a lapse into such dualism,[109] while Jesus' cry of dereliction on the cross is treated as the fulfilment of 'no-self', with God now no longer seen as separate in any way.[110] Although some limitations in Zen are acknowledged,[111] there is a strong claim for parallels with the doctrine of the Trinity and again also for a notion of grace.[112]

While sympathetic to such extended attempts at dialogue, what I want to suggest here is that both go too far. Although Zen has much to teach Christianity on the value of the impermanent, something essential will have been lost if the Zen notion of Buddha nature is applied universally, even to include transcendent beings. It is vital that there be something unconditionally external to ourselves, otherwise self will almost inevitably be reasserted. It is a point to which I shall return shortly but first something more must be said about positive value in the Zen approach to impermanence.

In the history of its own art there can be little doubt that Christianity has absorbed secular values to an extraordinarily high degree, for example, in the extensive use of expensive commodities such as gold or lapis lazuli to reflect spiritual values.[113] Again, looking at Christian architecture it would be hard to resist the conclusion that

---

Gate: The Classic Book of Zen Koans (Boston: Wisdom Publications, 2004).

[109] Collingwood, *Zen Wisdom*, 49–50.   [110] Ibid., 173–76.
[111] Ibid. Such as its treatment of women (192) and its lack of stress on compassion (221–23).
[112] Ibid. For the Trinity, 112, 211–14 (strengthened by appeal to the medieval mystic Eckhart, 203–4); for grace, for example, 214.
[113] The spiritual importance of figures in icons and other paintings was commonly indicated by the use of such materials. Blue lapis lazuli

the primary value has been one of scale.[114] Equally, in thinking of human beings as immortal souls, too much credence has been given to the ability to act independently.[115] Altogether, there has been insufficient acknowledgement of the degree to which our characters and achievements are in fact in large part the creation of others. Contrast attitudes in Zen and in Japanese culture more generally. Through the centuries wood has been the main building material, with temple authorities unworried about the need for frequent restoration. Again, a simple floral arrangement of the type known as Ikebana is surely just as effective as any more elaborate and expensive approach.[116] Similarly, simple china or pottery can be no less beautiful than famous names such as Meissen or Wedgewood. In part, the problem has been the tendency of human beings to take themselves and their achievements too seriously which makes it all the more intriguing that Zen has consistently refused to treat anything as unqualifiedly sacred. Instead, everything is regarded with a degree of lightness and humour.[117]

That said, it becomes singularly apposite that many Zen practices had their origin at the court of Yoshimasa

---

(mined only in Afghanistan) was used mainly for the Virgin Mary's robe.
[114] Churches and cathedrals have almost invariably been built larger and taller than was strictly necessary.
[115] Although not a biblical doctrine, immortality was assumed throughout most of Christian history.
[116] Ikebana began during the Heian period with simple floral arrangements at altars. It was then developed in the sixteenth century in connection with the tea ceremony and is now common in homes.
[117] A point stressed by Andrew Juniper, *Wabi Sabi: The Japanese Art of Impermanence* (Tokyo: Tuttle, 2003), 94.

(1436–90 CE) who was perhaps the most incompetent shogun ever. Nonetheless, when he turned from ruling to the practice of Zen at the retreat house of the Silver Pavilion, which he built on the outskirts of Kyoto,[118] the result was the extraordinarily creative symbolism of the ritualised tea ceremony which took place there and the development of various garden designs which the later tradition carefully followed.[119] Occasionally in the modern art world such values continue, as in the temporary art works of Christo and Jeanne Claude or, to quote a younger example, Karla Black.[120] The minimalist structures of the Japanese architect, Tadeo Ando (b. 1941), might also be mentioned.[121] Applied specifically to the Christian church, taking Zen values more seriously could encourage Christians to challenge the common Western contrast between utility and beauty: the simple and useful can surely be just as beautiful as a more costly item. Although disinclined to endorse a universal doctrine of impermanence, Christians might nonetheless also go some way with Zen in challenging the dogma of

---

[118] For his story, Donald Keene, *Yoshimasa and the Silver Pavilion* (New York: Columbia University Press, 2003).

[119] Ginkaku-ji. Although a Zen sand garden still exists there, the best known of early survivors is at another temple, Ryoan-ji: Keene, *Yoshimasa*, 136–37.

[120] The former pair are famous for wrapping buildings (including the Reichstag and the Arc de Triomphe). Although a photographic record was kept, the two artists were content that none of their projects survived permanently. The Scottish artist, Karla Black, uses ordinary household products, finding beauty in their use in an abstract, transitory way: *Karla Black: Sculptures (2001–21), details for a retrospective* (Edinburgh: Fruitmarket, 2021).

[121] These include religious structures such as the Christian Church of Light (1989) and the Buddhist Water Temple Hyogo (1991).

individualism that so permeates Western societies. Is there not considerable value in reaffirming human interdependence as the only proper way in which to evaluate the actions and lives of both ourselves and others? Human nature is as much a construct by others as it is a matter of our own devising. The implications of these two concessions could be quite radical, for it would mean challenging not only the contemporary equation of value and price (as in the art market) but also that between human worth and wage or salary levels (where the interdependence of the efforts of all the various grades in the work force in companies and institutions continues to be largely ignored).

Yet, in making these remarks it should be noted that I am in effect siding with one particular interpretation of the Heart Sutra that pushes it in the general direction of Mahayana's stress on compassion. However, that remains only one option. The Heart Sutra is the very brief treatise that is familiar throughout south-east Asia which equates emptiness (*sunyata*) and 'form', and which may possibly have been first written in China.[122] The five principal aggregates or *skandas* of Shakyamuni's original teaching that help to constitute human identity are all found to dissolve,[123] as nothing is held to be ultimate. Instead, everything is found to exist only through 'dependent origination' in its relation to something else. Appeal to contemporary science by way of support is now quite

---

[122] Although challenged, Jan Nattier has argued that the sutra really had its origin in China as a work of Xuanzang: 'The Heart Sutra: A Chinese Apocryphal Text' in *Journal of the International Association of Buddhist Studies*, 15 (1992), 153–223. 'Form' is the material world known to the senses and so sometimes translated as 'body'.

[123] The five 'heaps' or 'baskets' are, in addition to bodily form, accessed through the senses, feelings, perceptions, impulses and consciousness.

common.[124] While it is possible to give this a profoundly compassionate interpretation,[125] it should be noted that, for most interpreters influenced by Zen, even compassion dissolves into relativity. As one commentator observes, 'the Bodhisattvas have left behind the assumption that beings exist as real things' and so Avalokitesvara 'without losing his grip over emptiness, looks down from on high'.[126] That is why, for me, it is no accident that the Pure Land interpretation pushed in a significantly different direction.

And this is also observable in how it treats a notion which is really quite alien to Zen's basic assumptions, the notion of grace. Is such a notion really sustainable if God and soul are treated as though they were understood to be in no sense whatsoever absolutes? In response, the first thing that needs to be conceded is that religions can develop and so there is at least no objection in principle to either religion moving in the direction concerned. After all, both Buddhism and Christianity have changed hugely over the last two thousand years. Of course, claims to continuity are made but it must be admitted that the proposed connections are often quite tortuous and tenuous. As I have already conceded such complexities in the case of Christianity in Chapter 2, let us turn here to what happened with Zen. Thanks to various manuscript discoveries in the Dunhuang caves in China we now know

---

[124] As in the Edward Lorenz's Butterfly Effect and chaos theory, Alex Kerr, *Finding the Heart Sutra* (London: Penguin, 2020), 69, 150–51.
[125] As in the translation and commentary by Thich Nhat Hanh, *The Other Shore* (Berkeley, CA: Palm Leaves press, 2017), for example, 20, 123.
[126] Edward Conze, *The Diamond Sutra. The Heart Sutra* (New Delhi: Dev Publishers, 2017), 67, 93. For a similar demotion, Kerr, *Finding the Heart Sutra* 149, 230–31.

Learning from Other Religions

that any direct chain of masters going all the way back to Shakyamuni himself is pure invention.[127] Instead, a later Zen tried to answer the problems set by the founder in its own distinctive way.

So the point is not the impossibility of change but rather that this is not where either religion is at present located. In considering the matter, it is salutary to read a recent Japanese bestseller which describes in detail a novice's first year in the country's most prestigious monastery.[128] In this account we read that there was no training in Zen aesthetics nor indeed in empathy. Instead, overwhelmingly the focus was on indifference. This was reinforced by various forms of punishment, administered, for example, whenever attention waivered in meditation.[129] I hasten to add that there was no evil intention in such punitive practices. The aim was to secure a mind that could dissolve all craving, the fundamental Buddhist analysis of the roots of human discontent. Judging by the author's own experience, the method could be deemed a success. However, at what price? Zen dissolves all external impact into a transient, ephemeral process, including even Buddhas and Bodhisatvas. They

---

[127] For the manuscripts and commentary, see Sam Van Schaik, *The Spirit of Zen* (New Haven, CT: Yale University Press, 2018), esp. 31–81. Any role for the legendary founder, Bodhidharma, is rejected. The real founder is seen as Hongren (the so-called fifth patriarch) in the seventh century.
[128] Kaoru Nonomura, *Eat, Sleep, Sit: My Year at Japan's Most Rigorous Zen Temple* (New York: Kodansha, 2008; Japanese original 1996). The Soto temple in question was Eihei-ji, fifteen miles east of the city of Fukui.
[129] Ibid. Punishments were frequent and for a variety of faults: 22, 24, 36, 38, 47, 86, 166, 169, 170, 203, 206.

too are viewed as being as much a part of the fleeting world as is our own supposed identity.

Although such an analysis (in which, as already noted, form is equated to 'emptiness') might sound essentially negative, Dogen, the founder of Soto, viewed the message as truly liberating. Because the buddha nature is everywhere, everything and everyone has the potential to be fully alive. Nothing whatsoever external or internal is viewed as able to exercise complete control. However, if such a result is achieved by a meditation which is turned inwards,[130] is there not a cost even in terms of its own analysis which sees the interpenetration of all things as what causes the impermanence and so can bring release? To be fully alive one must actually downplay not just negative influences from outside but also those features which most help to make us the sort of beings we are: the valuing of our specific identity and character by family, friends and colleagues. The Zen objection to accepting such phenomena as part of the solution is that this would once more introduce potential causes of craving, and so disturb the sage's calm. But, while that is true, on the other side needs to be set the fact that deep calm can also come about through such affirmation, not only by others but also through recognition from some kind of transcendent reality. This is precisely where the notion of grace comes in: the greatest Other affirming that individuals and their personhood are valued, whatever appearances might say to the contrary. Although the Zen challenge to any permanent, transcendent reality is an

---

[130] In such meditation (*zazen*) one remains seated in the lotus position, facing a blank wall.

issue to which it will be necessary to return in Chapter 7, in the meantime these present observations lead naturally into consideration of the very different approach to be found in Pure Land Buddhism.

Test Case Two: Pure Land Minimalism and Grace

In the modern Western world the whole idea of worshipping a being greater than ourselves is commonly parodied as the attempt to gain benefits by offering compliments which should in any case be already known if the deity were truly omniscient. Such an objection ignores the sort of situation that provides the impetus to worship in the first place. Need can certainly play a part but more commonly it is coloured by recognition of previous encounters where such need has already been met. This might have occurred, for example in the rain supply for last year's crops, forgiveness for some wrong done or else as a reassuring presence when the odds seem stacked against the individual. Again, the justification for ritual sacrifice is often misinterpreted as entirely transactional ('give to get', as it were). While no doubt sometimes true, a quite different analysis is suggested by the most common scenario for such a practice, in the context of meals where part of the food was offered and wine poured out as a libation. The motivation here can be seen to be fundamentally one of gratitude, the sense of feeling blessed which survives into the modern practice of saying grace before meals. The compliments in worship are, therefore, not there to win over a reluctant deity. Instead, they are there to celebrate an already established relationship which secures the peace of the individual.

In the case of Pure Land Buddhism such peace is secured, not by retreat (as in Zen) into a vanishing personal core but rather by a movement in the opposite direction, in reaching out in gratitude towards an external reality which has already demonstrated its concern. Brief mention has already been made of the three principal sutras on which such ideas are based (two of Indian origin and one of Chinese). The longest and most important, the Infinite Life Sutra, opens with a description from Shakyamuni's disciple, Ananda, of a gathering on Vulture Peak during which the Bodhisattva Dharmakaya (as Amitabha was first known) establishes the Pure Land as part of forty-eight vows he undertakes in compassion for humankind.[131] Although the transmission of its distinctive teaching is thus firmly set in continuity with the earliest traditions of Buddhism, there is no escaping the fact that its ideas stand in marked contrast to the religion's origins and indeed even to a contemporaneous approach such as Zen. As already noted, instead of the movement being away from the world into a self-focused contemplative wisdom, its dynamic is back into the world and discovering there a reality greater than oneself that now makes compassion the central virtue. Much of this principal sutra is in fact concerned with ethics.[132] It is no doubt this practical orientation which secured its popularity with the Chinese.

The second shorter Indian sutra (known as the Amitabha) contains mainly descriptions of the Pure

---

[131] For these vows, Infinite Life, V. 49–102. Extracts from the most important sections are available through Amazon as *Pure Land Sutra* (2013).
[132] Especially V. 216–79.

Land and as such became popular in morning service chants.[133] Although the third Chinese sutra, which encouraged visual contemplation of Amitabha, was initially also quite popular,[134] gradually visualisation and even contemplation were to give way to simple recitation of the name of Amitabha. In securing that direction, the seventh-entury monk Shandao exercised a decisive role. To his creativity is also due the often-quoted parable of the white path.[135] Faced by a narrow way between a river of fire on one side and turbulent waters on the other and ruffians behind, it is only thanks to the call of a friend ahead that the fugitive is delivered. That friend is of course Amitabha. While Pure Land survives to this day in China, sometimes in combination with Chan (Zen),[136] of much greater importance is how it developed once it had moved to Japan.

That transition was mediated through Korea. Under Ryonin (d. 1132 CE), the first Japanese sage, even the emperor was persuaded to make daily appeal to Amida in the traditional nembutsu formula *Namu Amida Butsu*: the finite or lost appealing to *Amida Butsu* (immeasurable Buddha).[137] But it was to Honen (d. 1185 CE) and Shinran (d. 1262 CE) that the greatest debt was owed.[138]

---

[133] The Infinite Life Sutra only provides a brief description: V.114–138.
[134] Usually known in English as the Contemplation Sutra, unlike the other two it has no Sanskrit original. This explains why the deduction is commonly drawn that it was probably first composed in China.
[135] For Shandao's significance, Charles B. Jones, *Pure Land: History, Tradition, and Practice* (Boulder: Shambhala, 2021), 56–68.
[136] Jones, *Pure Land*, 96–106.   [137] Ibid., 122.
[138] Honen is regarded as the founder of contemporary Jodo Shu, Shinran of Jodo Shinsu.

While Honen found merit in repeated appeals,[139] Shinran argued that the admission of sincere dependence was enough. Indeed, as already noted, the worse the light in which one saw oneself the more one would prove open to the effect of Amida on one's own self-understanding. Although integral to Shinran reaching such a position was the inability of Honen's approach to work for him,[140] also apparently involved was some creative re-reading of the original texts. Whereas the eighteenth vow in its Chinese version originally implied the transfer of merit from the individual to the desired goal, Shinran argued from various Japanese principles of translation that the text really entailed the exact opposite, the transference of Amida's merit to the worshipper.[141] A religion based on merit was thus effectively transformed into one entirely of grace. Again, whereas the Infinite Life Sutra had excluded any guilty of the so-called 'five great offences', Shinran simplified these down to speaking ill of teachers or parents. He also added the significant qualification: 'by revealing the gravity of these two transgressions, these words make us realise that beings in all quarters of the universe will be born in the Pure Land without exception.'[142] The nembutsu had thus been

---

[139] There are some obvious parallels within Orthodoxy in its treatment of the Jesus Prayer ('Lord Jesus Christ, have mercy on me'), where frequent repetition is also encouraged.

[140] Apparently, Honen advised at least 10,000 nembutsu a day: Satya Robyn, *Coming Home: Refuge in Pureland Buddhism* (Malvern: Woodsmoke Press, 2019), 31.

[141] For the details, Alfred Bloom, *Shinran's Gospel of Pure Grace* (Ann Arbor: Association of Asian Studies, 1965), 48–49.

[142] Presumably because we are all sometimes guilty of such offences: compare Taitetsu Unno, *River of Fire, River of Water: An Introduction*

transformed from being still part of a system of merit to the expression of an appropriate attitude. Even faith in its effectiveness had itself become a gift of grace from Amida.[143] Given that there was now nothing further to be proved, a further consequence was the abolition of the traditional graded hierarchies of Buddhism, monastic overlay and men over women. Shinran himself married and modern Jodo-Shinju has female clergy.[144]

While some still continue to follow earlier assumptions that Pure Land refers to a specific place,[145] modern interpreters, especially in the English-speaking world,[146] incline more commonly to a metaphorical interpretation.[147] Sometimes even Amida himself is treated to a degree of demythologisation, either in being placed beyond gender,[148] or even identified with the Buddha nature which we all share.[149] The problem with the latter approach is that it then becomes more difficult to sustain the sense of gaining help from a distinct, powerful Other

---

    to the Pure Land Tradition of Shin Buddhism (New York: Doubleday, 1998), 24–25.

[143] Jones, *Pure Land*, 184.

[144] Although the thirty-fifth vow did appear to denigrate women, the wider implications of Shinran's approach eventually led to a different view: Jones, 210–16.

[145] Contemplative visualization and paintings tended to reinforce such a view.

[146] Taitetsu Unno is based in Northampton, Massachusetts; Satya Robyn in Malvern, Worcestershire.

[147] Unno, 179–80 (contrasting his views with Genshin in the tenth century); Robyn, *Coming Home*, 84.

[148] Robyn, *Coming Home*, 1, 105. 'He' and 'she' used interchangeable in what follows. In her defence, note the Chinese transformation of Avalokiteśvara into Guanyin, or the Japanese identification of the male Buddhist Dainishi (or Vairocana) with the Shinto female Amaterasu.

[149] Unno, *River of Fire*, 196.

that is so integral to Shinran's approach. More plausible is the acknowledgement of additional forms of otherness that might also help.[150]

Not unsurprisingly, many have seen in Pure Land's emphasis on grace strong parallels with the theology of Protestant Christianity.[151] It is admittedly tempting to present such developments within Buddhism as legitimately culminating in a position much closer to Christianity, but caution is necessary in ensuring that its own distinctive insights are not lost. In a fascinating passage in his *Church Dogmatics*, Karl Barth, perhaps rather unexpectedly, acknowledges a similar structure and message.[152] Yet he is quick to deny anything beyond a purely formal analogy, not only in Pure Land ideas but also with respect to the parallel Hindu bhakti devotional movement. Indeed, the latter is portrayed as much inferior to Pure Land given its 'substitution of surrender and love for faith'. In response to this latter objection one might observe that the use of different categories does not necessarily exclude something similar being proposed. A more adequate response would require more extensive and careful analysis of how bhakti devotees do in fact express themselves.

Against what he clearly sees as the greater threat of Pure Land, Barth launches a series of counterpoints: (1) its 'starting-point ...is obviously the popular demand for an easier and simpler path to salvation but no one can say

---

[150] Robyn talks of 'the five jewels': Amitabha, the Buddha, the Dharma, the Sangha and the Pure Land (*Pure Land*, 143).
[151] For comparisons with Calvin, for example Bloom, *Shinran's Gospel*, 45; Jones, *Pure Land*, 142–43.
[152] *Church Dogmatics* (Edinburgh: T & T Clark, 1975), 1.2, 342–45. The quotations are from 344.

of either Luther or Calvin that they began at this point.' (2) 'we miss any doctrine of the law and also of the holiness, or wrath of Amida.' (3) 'there is lacking that accent of a struggle for the glory of God against the arbitrariness and boasting of man which is given its proper stress in Paul.' (4) 'it is not Amida or faith in him, but this human goal of desire (sc. for Nirvana) which is the really controlling and determinative power.' Yet to each of these objections Pure Land can offer a plausible response. On the first, one might observe that the early church presented the gospel message as itself a simpler path than the complex demands of the Jewish law. On the second, the extensive discussion of morality in the Infinite Life Sutra has already been noted, as has the original, rigorous exclusion clauses. Third, one only needs to read Shinran's admission of total personal inadequacy to see that boasting could scarcely be further from his aims. While Barth is correct in his final point that the ultimate aim is different, this hardly justified what follows, with him speaking of a simple contrast between truth (in Jesus Christ) and error (in Pure Land). Indeed, one might favourably contrast the simplicity of the Pure Land's message of a divine compassion that transforms with the elaborate transactional structure that characterises later Christianity. Not least is this true of its various theories of the atonement, including those versions found in Calvin and Barth himself. I remain, therefore, of the view that aspects of this approach could help clarify and indeed improve more traditional Christian presentations of grace. So I end by assessing Pure Land more positively than was the case with Zen (apart from the latter's often profound insights into aesthetics).

Nonetheless, there remain in both instances complex metaphysical issues to which it will be necessary to return in Chapter 8. In the meantime, after four chapters in the Far East it is now time to return to the Middle East and to the world's most popular religion after Christianity. Islam presents some strong challenges against the very possibility of dialogue. These lie not only in the fact that it is of later origin but also because it sees itself as a corrective to what had gone before.

7

Islam

Warning or Hope

~

Introduction

Of all the religions discussed in this book, Islam is the most capable of being viewed in radically different, if not incompatible, ways. On the one hand, it can be seen to have exercised one of the great civilising influences on the world, not just in the Middle East but also in the Indian subcontinent. While its contributions in philosophy and science are widely acknowledged, no less important is what was achieved in poetry and architecture. On the other, although at the present time sometimes rightly criticised and even condemned,[1] of all the major religions it is probably the one most commonly misunderstood and maligned. Among the general public it has become strongly associated with terrorism and fundamentalism, although neither position has been particularly prominent in its past. During the Crusades, Muslim troops were on the whole better behaved than Christian,[2] and it was in

---

[1] Most notoriously, of course, in the attack on New York's Twin Towers on 11 September 2001.
[2] In the Fourth Crusade in 1204 the Crusader army sacked the Christian city of Constantinople. But even on the First Crusade there were massacres of Jews in the Rhineland (1096). Despite promising protection, in the process of capturing Jerusalem Tancred slaughtered many prisoners, including women and children (1099).

fact the Ottoman Empire which gave sanctuary to Jews when fleeing mass expulsions from medieval Europe.[3]

While some scholars object to the fundamentalist designation (and, of course, Christian fundamentalism exhibits little or none of the violence characteristic of the Islamic version),[4] there are parallels that suggest some value in noting comparisons. It is really only since the nineteenth century that, in either religion, such an approach has come to dominate so many minds, ironically in large part because of concomitant advances in civilisation.[5] Most obviously, like the Christian version, it is plausibly seen as a relatively recent response to changes in wider society, in particular the challenge presented by Western scientific understanding and rationalism and a rise in literacy and education that makes personal judgements easier. The rise of literacy meant that individual believers, rather than defer to the scholarship or inspired judgements of others, now felt that they could interpret the text for themselves. At the same time, the appeal of representatives of the colonial powers to Enlightenment values in science and history helped generate a defensive counter-attack. Moreover, as in Christian fundamentalism, there has been fast and loose playing with 'proof'

---

[3] Spanish (Sephardic) Jews arrived in the late fifteenth century in large numbers on the heels of smaller, earlier groups of German (Ashkenazi) Jews.
[4] 'Little' rather than none since the contemporary sexual abuse scandals mainly affected such conservative groups: see my *Gospel as Work of Art: Imaginative Truth and Open Text* (Grand Rapids, MI: Eerdmans, 2023), 10–12.
[5] Christian fundamentalism is usually defined by the so-called Princeton 'fundamentals' of 1910. Although the Wahabi movement began much earlier, it only achieved major influence about the same time.

texts, a deliberate attempt to read certain Qur'anic texts in quite different ways from their historical interpretation.[6]

Important though the issue is, the challenge of fundamentalism must not be allowed to dominate our discussion. To illustrate how varied attitudes and practice can be, let me contrast two Muslim countries which I recently visited, Morocco and Uzbekistan. The former Soviet Republic of Uzbekistan is not yet a democracy but, whereas the first post-soviet dictator continued very strict controls on religion, the current leader is more sympathetic.[7] A massive complex known as the Centre of Islamic Civilisation is currently being built in the capital, Tashkent, where one of the oldest manuscripts of the Qur'an is now on display. Many historic mosques throughout the country have also been restored to their original purpose, most notably in Samarkand. Yet he clearly wants to present the land as a model of moderate Sunni orthodoxy as deep hostility remains towards Sufism, the more mystical and emotional version of the faith that had once led to the country's evangelisation and which still predominates in the countryside. In the main cities injunctions against Sufi practice are to be found recorded not only in Uzbek but even in English. The irony is that all three forms of behaviour are quite common in Western Christianity. Signs are everywhere forbidding the kissing of tombs, carrying of

---

[6] Both the Ayatollah's fatwa and suicide bombing violate basic principles in Islamic law: Bernard Lewis, *The Crisis of Islam: Holy War and Unholy Terror*, (London: Weidenfeld & Nicholson, 2003), 117–40, esp. 118–20, 130–32. For a Christian parallel, consider the literal application of 1 Thess. 4.17 as reflected in the *Left Behind* series of novels (1995–2007).

[7] Shavkat Mirziyoyev. President Islam Karimov continued in power until 2016.

candles or hanging prayer requests on trees.[8] There is thus still a long way to go before the land can be seen once more to reverberate with ideas as different as those of Avicenna and Omar Khayyam.[9]

The contrast with Morocco is quite marked. It has enjoyed a long history of good Muslim–Jewish relations. Most of the major cities had Jewish districts and there was even an occasional predominantly Jewish town, as at Chefchaouen. All that changed with the Arab–Israeli Six-Day War when most of the Jewish population fled. The atmosphere, though, is changing once more, as Israeli tourists return and the government subsidises restoration of ancient synagogues, as well as the surrounding areas.[10] There is also a quite different attitude to the visual arts and to music from countries such as Afghanistan and Saudi Arabia, where both are banned. The capital Rabat has a fine national art gallery centrally situated, while in the religious capital of Fez there is an excellent museum of musical instruments with recorded and live performances also available. Perhaps my biggest surprise was visiting a museum and garden dedicated to the French fashion designer, Yves Saint Laurent (in Marrakech). No attempt was made to conceal his gay identity.[11]

---

[8] Admittedly, because of the climate in Western Europe prayer trees are more likely to be artificial and accommodated within churches.
[9] There is, though, already at least one women-only mosque, a tradition that was once not unusual in China.
[10] Even today at Essaouira one silversmith company continues a long-standing tradition of joint manufacture of Jewish and Muslim holy items alongside one another (such as Fatima's hand of blessing and *mezuzot* for Jewish doors).
[11] While homosexuality remains illegal, little action is taken provided gay clubs do not engage in extensive advertising.

Architectural styles also contain some interesting lessons. From the outside smaller mosques look surprisingly like Christian churches, with accompanying towers rather than minarets. So horrified were Saudis by this aspect that, in all new mosques which they have paid for, minarets are required to be included in the plans, as though this was some basic requirement of Islamic faith! Occasionally, Christian churches have also adapted to the local style. A good instance is the Anglican church in Tangier, where 'God is great' is written in Arabic above the altar and the Lord's Prayer similarly reproduced on the horseshoe entrance to the chancel. But perhaps the most inspiring example of good relations was the welcome given to a survivor of the Algerian 1996 massacre of Trappist monks. At his crossing of the border into Morocco and his subsequent death in 2021, the local Muslim population insisted on describing him by the Muslim term for saint.[12]

To cater for that range of interpretation under which Islam can be seen as either a warning to other religions about what can go wrong or as a potential subject for hope, I shall divide the discussion that follows into three parts. First, I want to explore a little further the history of Islam in its wider cultural setting. Thereafter, I shall turn to more specifically religious issues. While first to be examined will be various historical ways in which the Muslim world sought to furnish itself with pathways out of fundamentalism, thereafter the concluding discussion will focus on the present context, to see what additional possibilities might now be available.

---

[12] Fr Jean Pierre Schumacher. The story of the massacre is told in the film *Of Gods and Men*.

Religion and Culture: Past and Present

In this first part of the chapter I want to begin by reminding readers of the richness of the Muslim inheritance before then going on to set that richness against the more complicated dynamic of the present situation. Not only did Western reflections project a 'corrupt' other, its 'colonial' interventions also helped ensure the frustration of Muslim hopes for change.

A Rich Inheritance

Given that Islam is the second biggest world religion after Christianity, it is worth expanding upon some of the more positive sides to its history before considering some specific difficulties. In particular, three features may be noted, the peace and order it created, its philosophical and scientific learning and artistic flourishing.

To speak of Islam bringing peace and order may initially sound somewhat paradoxical, given its reputation for conquering warfare. Admittedly, Islam soon degenerated into major internal conflict between rival actions over the appropriate bearers of leadership in succession to Mohammad.[13] Nor is the resultant division into majority Sunni and minority Shi'a just a feature of some distant past.[14] On the contrary, it can help explain the

---

[13] Over whether leadership should be confined to members of the Prophet's own family. Ali was his cousin and son-in-law but assassinated at Kufa in 661 CE.

[14] Shi'a is short for Shiat Ali ('partisan of Ali'). The term 'Sunni' alludes to tradition or convention and so to the majority who accepted that only a political leader was now required. The alternative choice in Abu Bakr was seen as entirely appropriate.

background to some of the major sites of internecine dispute in the contemporary Middle East. Sunni Saudi Arabia opposes Shi'a Iran not only in a bloody civil war in Yemen but also in quite a number of other contemporary hotspots. Again, one major factor in the problems of Iraq and Syria has been that in Iraq a Sunni dictatorship ruled over a Shi'a majority, while in contemporary Syria the position is reversed.[15] Yet, while it is true that some of the smaller variants on Shi'a represent major deviations from orthodoxy Sunni,[16] the principal variant is not all that different. Most noticeable is the addition of a mention of Ali, the first leader of the minority, to the common declaration of faith and the annual celebrations which mark his martyrdom.[17] On the whole, other differences proved less decisive than is commonly claimed.[18] So, despite the strength of current animosities, for much, if

---

[15] Saddam was a Sunni in a land with some major Shi'a shrines in Baghdad, Karbala and Samarra. Assad in Syria belongs to a Shi'a sect, the Alawites.

[16] Alawites and Druze are minority groups in Lebanon and Syria which split off from Shi'a. Both would now be regarded as separate religions by most Shi'a. Alawites partake in a eucharistic act which unites them with Ali; Druze believe in reincarnation.

[17] The Shahadah (one of the pillars of Islam) with its reference to the uniqueness of God and Mohammad as his messenger is often expanded to include talk of Ali as a 'friend of God'.

[18] Although some Sunnis complain of the prominence given to saints in Shi'a, prayer at Sufi tombs among many Sunnis complicates that alleged contrast. Again, although Shia believe that the caliphate came to an end after twelve imams, and a smaller group (the Ismaeli) after seven, this is hardly a topic of everyday conversation. The same is true of the strong conviction among some Shi'a that a final madhi (perhaps at present in hiding) has yet to return.

not most, of past history both groups succeeded in living peaceably together.[19]

Once the earlier aggressive campaigns were concluded, in general peaceful, ordered and relatively integrated societies were the result. Certainly, this was true of Mohammad's own imposition of order on the warring factions in Arabia. Again, while it is true that the Umayyad (based on Damascus) and the more long-lasting Abbasid empires (based on Baghdad) displaced Christian Byzantine rule in the Middle East,[20] it was not the case that more brutal regimes were the result. Admittedly, Christians and Jews were reduced to second-class citizens. However, unlike other religions under Christian rule, they were allowed to be largely self-governing.[21] Much the same might be said of the Fatimids in their conquest of Egypt,[22] some aspects of medieval Morocco and the eventual assumption of power by the Ottomans at the heart of the former Byzantine empire.[23] Copts have survived as a large Christian minority in Egypt to his day,[24] while the Christian population of Anatolia was to last in significant numbers until the exchange of populations

---

[19] The point is stressed in John McHugo, *A Concise History of Sunnis and Shi'is* (London: Saqi, 2017).

[20] The Umayyad caliphate lasted under a century from 661 to 750. Abbasid rule lasted from 750 until when Bagdad was overthrown by the Mongol invasion of 1258.

[21] A special tax known as jizya had to be paid. It was seen as a charge for protection and exemption from military service. At the same time there was no compulsion to convert.

[22] The Fatimids were an Ismaili Shi'a caliphate that ruled much of north Africa from the tenth to the twelfth century,

[23] Both the Almoravids and Almohads began as fanatical zealots but became more moderate in their later years.

[24] There remain about six million Copts in Egypt.

with Greece after the First World War.[25] Smyrna (now Izmir) remained a predominantly Christian town until then, while, less well known, Salonica even had a Jewish majority.

Again, for the most part the Mughal conquest of northern India did not in general result in persecution of the native Hindus but something more like creative interaction between the two. Indeed, the Emperor Akbar (1556–1605) even officially encouraged interfaith dialogue, as in the discussions he organised at his new capital, Fatehpur Sikri.[26] Not that the story was all positive. Although Shah Jahan, the builder of the Taj Mahal, behaved in a similar manner to Akbar, his own father Jahangir executed one important Sikh leader (Guru Arjan). Yet, whereas Shah Jahan's own son Aurangzeb (1658–1707) was once commonly portrayed as a notorious Muslim bigot responsible for the breakup of the empire, historians now advocate a more complex picture.[27] In short, although important qualifications are necessary, a positive story can in general still be told. Equally, it would be quite wrong to think of conversions to Islam as only ever being accomplished at the point of a sword. Sufi missionaries adopted a gentler approach that produced significant results not only in parts

---

[25] After the defeat of the Ottoman Empire in the First World War, there was war between Greece and the new Turkey under Kemal Ataturk (1919–22). The Treaty of Lausanne agreed the exchange of a million and a half Orthodox Greeks and Turks to Greece and half a million Turkish and Greek Muslims to Turkey.
[26] West of Acra, the place acquired its name ('city of victory') after Akbar's successful Gujurat campaign.
[27] Opinion seems sharply divided on the matter. See Audrey Truschke, *Aurangzeb: The Life and Legacy of India's Most Controversial King* (Stanford, CA: Stanford University Press, 2017).

of Africa but also in what is now Islam's largest nation, Indonesia.[28] It is also central to the story of many central Asian states such as Uzbekistan.

That sense of order and peace throughout Muslim territories did much to encourage the growth of science and the pursuit of philosophy. It is perhaps Western use of 'Arabic' numerals which is best known. The fact that these were originally adapted from Indian mathematicians nicely illustrates how initial debts to others were applied creatively in other areas as well. This is particularly true of its preservation of Aristotle's works and their eventual communication to Christian Europe. The result in the West was a more empirically-based approach to thinking that characterises the thirteenth-century writings of scholars such as Albert the Great (d. 1280) and Thomas Aquinas (d. 1274).[29] While Islam did pursue mathematics and astronomy in its own right,[30] I want here to note instead the continuing relevance of its philosophical investigations. Later in the chapter I shall have occasion to mention Al-Ghazali's Sufi attack on the limitations of philosophy and what came to be known as kalam rationalism.[31] It is important, therefore, to note the other side of that coin

---

[28] Sufism was active from the thirteenth century. Merchant traders also played their part. Indonesia has currently a population of 230 million, with 99 per cent professing themselves Muslim.
[29] With Albert representative of empirically minded science and Aquinas of the new approach in theology.
[30] For a description, A. I. Sabra, 'The Scientific Enterprise' in Bernard Lewis ed., *The World of Islam* (London: Thames & Hudson, 1992), 181–200.
[31] Although *kalam Allah* literally translates as 'word of God', it came to acquire the significance of a defence of that word against philosophical objections.

as it were, in the way in which 'rationalists' such as Avicenna (d. 1037) and Averroes (d. 1198) raised questions about religious thought which had a major impact on medieval Christian reflection. Averroes is often wrongly treated as though he was merely the most significant Arab commentator on Aristotle, whereas Aquinas in fact debated extensively with his ideas.[32] Indeed, the inheritance of these two thinkers continues to raise profound questions of relevance well beyond Islam.[33]

Finally, some attention should be given to the artistic sphere. Although as with the Protestant Reformation in Europe suspicion of instrumental music inhibited growth of new ideas in this area,[34] and fear of idolatry threatened representational art,[35] architecture was an unqualified success. While in theory all that is required for a mosque

---

[32] Averroes or Ibn Rushd worked in Andalusian Spain. He is buried at Cordova, which was also his birthplace. Avicenna or Ibn Sina was born a Persian but thereafter operated in what is today Uzbekistan. Although he was primarily interested in medicine, he wrote extensively also on philosophy.

[33] For some helpful discussion, the section on Islamic philosophy in Arthur Hyman & James J. Walsh eds., *Philosophy in the Middle Ages* (Indianapolis, IN: Hackett, 1977), 203–325; Oliver Leaman, *Averroes and his Philosophy* (Richmond, IN: Curzon, 1988).

[34] Both Calvin and Zwingli objected to the use of instrumental music in church. For a discussion of Islam's contribution to music, A. Shiloah, 'The Dimension of Sound' in Lewis, *The World of Islam*, 161–80. At Samarkand in 2022 I was presented with an extraordinary rich array of possibilities by one Uzbekistani musician.

[35] Severity of application outside mosques varied. One mosque, the eighth-century Umayyad mosque at Damascus, even had extensive representational art inside and out. For a survey, including this mosque, Eva Schubert ed., *Discover Islamic Art* (London: Art Books International, 2007), esp. 28, 29, 37–50. For the more varied character of contemporary art, see Saeb Eigner, *Art of the Middle East: Modern and Contemporary Art of the Arab World and Iran* (London: Merrell, 2015).

is a bounded space,[36] rivalry with the existing Christian churches guaranteed a different direction in the creation of some of the world's most beautiful buildings, among them the Dome of the Rock in Jerusalem and the Great Mosque in Damascus. Even the words of the Qur'an were adapted to this more abstract form of art.[37] Obviously, this is not the place to advance any particular aesthetic theory but it is hard not to see the style employed in its use of formal beauty and abstraction as intended to pull the worshipper into an overwhelming sense of divine transcendence. It is an approach which, in my view, reached its culmination in places such as Isfahan and Samarkand and in the works of architects such as Sinan in Ottoman Turkey.[38] Even as a non-Muslim tourist it proves hard to resist the sense of address by something or someone immeasurably greater than oneself.[39]

Edward Said and Orientalism

Turning now to modern times, we need to consider the claim that Western appreciation of the Muslim world and its culture have been distorted by the false prism through

---

[36] Muhammad's own house was so adapted. Muslim armies in transit marked out a space in the sand. For a short discussion of the architecture of mosques, see my *God and Enchantment of Place* (Oxford: Oxford University Press, 2004), 359–71.

[37] A purely decorative function is clearly indicated by placement in some mosques outside the reach of human legibility.

[38] Probably the best known of the seventy or so mosques of Mimar Sinan (d. 1588) is the Suleiman in Istanbul. The famous Blue Mosque by Sedefkar Mehmed Agha dates to the following century.

[39] In such mosques I have quite often observed apparently secular tourists reduced to silent awe.

which Western eyes have long been encouraged to look. Although still regarded by some as a contentious thesis, there would seem little doubt about its underlying plausibility. Edward Said (1935–2003) was an American academic who was radicalised by the 1967 seven-day war in the Middle East. From that point on he began self-consciously to identify with his roots as a Palestinian. As a consequence, he began to produce a series of books on how Western perceptions of the colonial or third world, far from being based on objective fact, presuppose its primitiveness and decadence.[40] The result has been not only an easy assumption of superiority but also a sense of legitimacy in acting for such peoples' 'betterment', particularly through colonial or related actions. Later books spread the net more widely, in Said's determination to establish how such values remain largely hidden, even in their authors' own eyes. This he nicely illustrates from Jane Austen's *Mansfield Park*. The lawlessness and frivolity round which the earlier part of the story revolves are resolved by the return of Sir Thomas Bertram from his plantations in Antigua, in effect to exercise a new form of colonial control at home.[41]

Said's first major work on *Orientalism* (1978) has had the most lasting impact. Dealing mainly with the Arab world, it opens with some perverse quotations from Arthur Balfour, the British Prime Minister, in which he defends British occupation of Egypt on the grounds of the Egyptians' own

---

[40] For a general survey of such works, Bill Ashcroft & Pal Ahluwalia, *Edward Said* (London: Routledge, 1999).
[41] Analysed in Edward W. Said, *Culture and Imperialism* (London: Chatto & Windus, 1993), 104–14.

self-interest. Also included are appeals to the authority of Lord Cromer, Great Britain's principal representative in the country, who is found observing: 'want of accuracy, which easily degenerates into untruthfulness, is in fact the main characteristic of the oriental mind.'[42] Numerous similar generalisations are noted. While perversions in literary characterisation and political pronouncements occupy much of the book, more interesting in the present context is the extent of the claimed seepage of similar attitudes into some of the writings of acknowledged Western experts on Islam, among them H. A. R. Gibb and Bernard Lewis, and, though to a much lesser degree, Louis Massignon. While much of the response to the book was initially hostile (especially from Bernard Lewis), there seems little doubt that Said was in the main right.[43]

Quite a number of other scholars have followed in his footsteps. Among them, one of the most persuasive is his pupil and friend, Joseph Massad. While I find his work devoted exclusively to Arab sexuality less convincing,[44] his general survey on *Islam in Liberalism* is quite a triumph, not least in its extensive use of examples. As he observes, child brides and female castration are picked out for condemnation as though there were no comparable problems in the West, such as domestic abuse and rape.[45]

---

[42] Edward W. Said, *Orientalism* (London: Penguin, 2003 ed.), 31–49, esp. 38.
[43] For one quite subtle attack on Lewis, *Orientalism*, 314–15; for his later reply (in a 1995 *Afterword*) to Lewis's counterattacks, 342–47.
[44] Joseph A. Massad, *Desiring Arabs* (Chicago: University of Chicago Press, 2007).
[45] Joseph A. Massad, *Islam in Liberalism* (Chicago: University of Chicago Press, 2015), esp. 110–212, 135–37.

Again, looking more widely, the United States constantly employs a rhetoric which sees its mission as the gift or preservation of democracy and human rights in other lands. Yet, in that narrative it fails to acknowledge that for most of its own history the reality was quite different, with rights often better secured in the Arab world, even if nominally there was no democracy. As Massad observes, 'what does it mean for a country whose two-century history is divided between a century of racialised slavery and another century of racial apartheid to broadcast itself internally and externally as the oldest democracy?'[46] Were such faults only on the surface they could perhaps be easily rectified but the point for Said and his supporters is that they run very deep in the West's treatment of the Muslim world. Thus, not uncommonly, inadequacies in the judicial system are blamed on sharia law when they were in fact generated through modifications demanded by the imperial power.[47] Again, modern, self-imposed changes, though presented as 'liberal' reforms, often work to the detriment of the local population.[48] It is also possible to see the effect of such attitudes worked through in the novels of one of the more recent recipients of the Nobel Prize for Literature (2021), Abdulrazak Gurnah, a British citizen.[49]

Two paragraphs can scarcely provide enough detail to convince but I would suggest that such observations do

---

[46] Ibid., 20. [47] For example, Massad, *Islam in Liberalism*, 153–7.
[48] Ibid. For example, 167.
[49] Novels such as *Paradise* (1994) and *Afterlives* (2020) are set in East Africa from which he originally came. For further discussion, Emad Mirmotahari, *Islam in the Eastern African Novel* (London: Palgrave Macmillan, 2011).

need to be taken with maximum seriousness. From a religious perspective, it simply will not do to treat Islam as though it were just a more primitive version of Christianity or like Judaism only to be valued because it can be seen to be in some sense on its way to something better. Admittedly, as with Christianity, negative features must be acknowledged but this definitely should not be turned into a general thesis about the relationship between the two religions. As with Christianity, its insights have developed and changed over the course of time, sometimes for the better and sometimes for the worse. It is that more complex reality that needs to be recognised.

Western Restraints on Change

The previous mention of Western ideological perspectives on Islam helps to provide a context for the religion's own movements towards change in the modern period. In particular, due note needs to be taken of how often it was Western intervention which prevented or delayed change when much of the local population were already well disposed to such possibilities. The most relevant contemporary examples are Afghanistan and Iraq. The terrorist organisations, the Taliban and Al-Qaeda, were in fact relatively ineffective until the American government decided upon financing their armaments in response to the Russian invasion of Afghanistan.[50] Much the same

---

[50] The Soviet–Afghan war lasted from 1979 to 1989. The Taliban ('student'), though not a single group, are best characterised as a mixture of Sunni Islam (Deobandi) and Pashtun tribal practices. Al-Qaeda

can be said of the extremist Salafist group which eventually became known as Islamic State (only founded in 1999).[51] As a result of the allied invasion of Iraq in 2003–4, it was able to exploit Sunni-Shia tensions which eventually led to the creation of the pseudo-state of the same name a decade later.[52] Again, the support of ignorant clerics in Saudi Arabia is often blamed for what resulted but even here a more complex reality needs to be acknowledged. Without doubt, the Wahhabi in Saudi Arabia present an intensively conservative version of Islam. Thanks to the generosity of the Saudi monarchy, it has successfully broadcast its narrow interpretation of the faith throughout the world.[53] Yet, on the other side needs to be set their occasional, if limited, openness to new ideas, as also their more recent policy of reining in some more radical groups.[54]

The conventional defence of Western policy in Iraq often speaks of deliverance from something much worse. Yet, however bad Saddam was, the huge number of

('foundation') was established in 1988 in Pakistan by the Saudi Arabian, Osama bin Laden, as a version of Wahhabi Islam.

[51] Salafist is the generic name for a conservative reform movement found in Sunni Islam. The Wahhabis are its Saudi variant.

[52] It was founded as a fighting group in 2014. For a history and general characterisation, Abdel Bari Atwan, *Islamic State: The Digital Caliphate* (London: Saqi, 2015).

[53] It began in the eighteenth century as a conservative, reformist group within the Hanbali school. Allied with the Saudi family, it helped to unite the Arabian Peninsula.

[54] For a study, Nabil Mouline, *The Clerics of Islam: Religious Authority and Political Power in Saudi Arabia* (New Haven, CT: Yale University Press, 2014). For educational reforms, 133–42; 185–97. For attempts to control more extreme versions of the Wahhabi movement and even dialogue with other groups, 235–56.

casualties subsequently makes any easy assertion of superiority a difficult claim to substantiate.[55] In any case, going back a generation, even the creation of Iraq and Syria was in effect a decision made by Western colonial powers, in essence no more than an arbitrary line drawn in the sand with all its attendant consequences.[56] Equally, the Balfour declaration of 1917 may have been a laudable attempt to solve the lack of a Jewish homeland but a century later positive hopes of a fair and impartial democracy in that part of the world still remain to be addressed.[57] Again, the history of Iran might have turned out very differently, had not oil generated decisions in the West towards intervention, including the toppling of a democratically-elected government. Mohammad Mosaddegh was Iran's great reforming prime minister of the twentieth century. Yet because he proposed the nationalisation of the oil industry MI6 and the CIA combined to oust him.[58]

These are large issues which cannot be pursued here. Instead, let me mention in conclusion one situation which is still developing and that is what is happening in Turkey. In the West Recep Erdoğan (prime minister 2003–14, president since 2014) is often presented as what is only to be expected of Muslims: manipulation of politics for

---

[55] Estimates vary greatly but about half a million civilians appear to have died as a result of the allied war against Iraq. There were a further 350,000 casualties in the later battles with Isis.
[56] The famous Sykes-Picot agreement between Britain and France after the collapse of the Ottoman Empire.
[57] An observation that applies to both the Palestinian territories and to Israel itself.
[58] The United States formally acknowledged its role in 2013.

the religion's own ends.[59] But the history of his interventions surely suggests a more complex reality. Brought up in a poor but devout home,[60] initially he seems to have envisaged the social betterment of the great mass of Turkey's citizens but also in a way that recognised the importance of religion to them.[61] This included acceptance of a secularised democracy, though not quite on the model advocated in Kemal Atatürk's founding charter of the republic, in its emphasis on laïcité.[62] Erdoğan thought that this was enough to appeal to the negotiators at the EU but he soon realised that deep suspicions remained in the West.[63] Consequently, perhaps not unnaturally, he moved to a more explicitly pro-Islamic position. It is against this background that his response to the coup attempt against his regime needs to be understood. Western commentators usually interpret his actions in

[59] Hannah Lucinda Smith was the *Times* correspondent in Turkey for over a decade. Yet in her book about Erdoğan not only does she assume no deeper motives than desire for power, she makes no attempt at all to investigate the nature of his religious beliefs beyond simply labelling him 'pious'. See further her *Erdoğan Rising: The Battle for the Soul of Turkey* (London: Collins, 2019).

[60] His father was a coastguard. The family lived in one of the tougher districts of Istanbul. Erdoğan's earliest ambition was to become a professional footballer: Mehmet Karahan, *President Erdogan's Biography* (Milton Keynes: Lighting Source, 2019), 4–5. The book usefully provides all the statistics for his various elections.

[61] As mayor of Istanbul he initiated a major house improvement programme: Soner Cagaptay, *The New Sultan: Erdoğan and the Crisis of Modern Turkey* (London: I. B. Tauris, 2017), 74–76. Later, he secured the building of a large number of new mosques, as well as a few churches, 128–31.

[62] He accepted freedom of religious observance but not Atatürk's stronger 'French' version in the notion of the exclusion of religion from public life, freedom *from* religion as one commentator puts it: Ibid., 95–96.

[63] Cagaptay, *The New Sultan*, 97–99.

subsequently arresting such large numbers of opponents as indicative of the fact that he never believed in democracy in the first place. But might the explanation not be panic about how far supporters of the Atatürk past were apparently capable of still controlling what happened in the present?

One argument on the other side is how he treated the supporters of his one-time ally, Fethullah Gülen, who were also either arrested or ejected from their posts.[64] Western commentators frequently suggest that Gülen was in any case up to no good,[65] but the evidence remains indecisive and indeed there is much that points the other way.[66] Could it be that both Gülen and Erdoğan had similar aims in a more inclusive Islam but that Erdoğan, embittered by experience, has become a rather frightened despot?[67] Certainly, the degree to which he has imposed Islam on Turkey remains even now much less nasty than some commentators suggest.[68]

---

[64] In 2016, amounting to at least 70,000.
[65] Hannah Smith is unremittingly hostile in *Erdogan Rising: The Battle for the Soul of Turkey* (London: William Collins, 2019): for example, 13, 81, 89, 217.
[66] For an excellent book by a Christian scholar which points the other way, Jon Pahl, *Fethullah Gülen* (New Jersey: Blue Dome Press, 2019). He describes how a poor background and Sufi training inspired a programme of schools and social networks known as Hismet.
[67] Although he later moved to repression of the Kurdish minority, his initial tactic was one of tolerance and integration: Cagaptay, 137, 143–56.
[68] The teaching of Islam has been introduced into schools but there remains no compulsion on veiling, for example.

Historical Resources for Escaping Fundamentalism

Although, as mentioned earlier, of all contemporary religions Islam is most associated with fundamentalism, this is far from being the universal position, either historically or even today. I want, therefore, to examine here first the more complex approaches adopted historically and then in the final part of the chapter explore some contemporary alternatives. In this part, therefore, our attention will focus on two rather different types of strategy: a more corporate approach developed by various schools and endorsed by the community as a whole and a more personal approach in appeal to individual, mystical experience as found in Sufism. With its influence extending well beyond Islam, Sufism is such an important historical phenomenon that it deserves separate consideration. I shall begin, though, with the approach with the larger influence, the various schools and the rules of interpretation which they adopted. While I label both approaches historical, their influence very much continues into the present.

Social Consensus through Analogy, Abrogation, and Chains of Transmission

After the death of Mohammad there was considerable debate about the precise nature of the Qur'an. Eventually, the party (the Asharites) which declared the text uncreated won and so it came to be seen, in some sense, as part of divine reality.[69] But this high doctrine

---

[69] The Asharites (named after their founder) finally defeated the Mutazilites in the tenth century, though the latter's strong assertion of human freedom continues within the Shi'a tradition.

was combined with very practical considerations, the need to give guidance on the application of its own distinctive type of law (shari'a) to the newly arising political systems. Four main schools of interpretation were to develop.[70] Although there are some significant differences between them, from our perspective here two other aspects are of greater importance. The first is that the average believer was thereby set at a certain distance from the text. Its guidance was now mediated through the authoritative pronouncements of others, the representatives of the community. Second, the latter's procedures did at least admit a degree of latitude in how the text might be interpreted. Significantly, although the eternal decrees of the Qur'an had been explicitly contrasted with the time-bound customs of the Meccans,[71] various devices were deployed to admit some degree of interpretative latitude.

One such approach was the appeal to analogy. Two rather different examples may be offered. When Tunisia decided to ban polygamy in 1957, the justification given was the impossibility in a modern context of treating all wives equally, as the Qur'an had required.[72] Again, going back earlier in history to the seventeenth century when coffee was first introduced, it was initially argued that as a drug it should be treated like alcohol and so banned. However, in this instance, consensus in favour of use

---

[70] Hanbali, Hanafi, Maliki, Shafei. One school tends to dominate in any one place, for example, Maliki in Egypt, Hanbali in Saudi Arabia.
[71] For the contrast between two types of *sunna*, H. A. R. Gibb, *Muhammadism* (Oxford: Oxford University Press, 1954), 73.
[72] See further, N. J. Coulson, *A History of Islamic Law* (Edinburgh: Edinburgh University Press, 1964), 207–15, esp. 210

succeeded in eventually overturning the analogy argument.[73] A more common type of argument was abrogation, the view that latter passages in the Qur'an could be used to override earlier. Shorter suras were believed to derive from Mohammad's earlier Meccan residence, whereas the longer ones are dated after his flight to Medina in 622 CE. A particularly good example of such progressive abrogation is the Qur'an's attitude to wine.[74] It seems to move from viewing it as a mixed blessing, to forbidding the intoxicated from prayer, to, finally, calling drink 'an abomination', as bad as idol worship. Unqualified praise for *sakar* at 16.67 is, therefore, treated as more problematic. One Muslim translator of the Qur'an suggests that the allusion should be taken to refer to a wholesome, non-alcoholic drink made from grapes. However, he then adds that, if fermented wine must be accepted as the intended meaning, 'it refers to the time before intoxicants were prohibited: this is a Meccan sura and the prohibition came in Medina.'[75]

However, an obvious difficulty for this concept of abrogation (*naskh*) is that it appears to make the revelation to Muhammad at times just as partial as the earlier revelations which the Prophet criticised for having been corrupted by their followers. Take, for instance, the so-called Satanic verses which endorse asking for the intercession of three local female gods.[76] Made famous (or perhaps

---

[73] Gibb, *Muhammadism*, 11. Analogy (qiyas) yielded to consensus (ijma).
[74] Contrast 2.219; 4.43; 5.90.
[75] A. Y. Ali (trans & comm.), *The Holy Qur'an* (Leicester: Islamic Foundation, 1975), 673, esp. n.2096.
[76] The early Islamic historians, al-Waqidi and al-Tabari, tell us the sentiment once occurred at 53.19.

better 'notorious') by Salman Rushdie's novel of the same name,[77] a possible explanation is to say that they were abrogated by a later text.[78] But the problem with such an account is that it appears to concede that Muhammad at one time accepted the worship of other deities. A charitable interpretation might be to propose that, as with monotheism in the Hebrew Bible, it was a belief into which Mohammad grew.[79] But, in large part because of the implied imperfection in reception of divine revelation, the more common Muslim approach has been to deny that these verses were ever part of the original text. This is a position which has also been endorsed by some non-Muslim scholars.[80] Another problematic example is the so-called sword verse which is seen as abrogating between one hundred and twenty-four and a hundred and forty other earlier verses. The verse sanctions a more aggressive Islam: 'fight and slay the pagans wherever you find them ... and lie in wait for them in every stratagem of war.' Yet not only is the text immediately qualified by the verse that follows,[81] accepting its controlling function again acutely raises the intentions behind all those 'earlier' verses.

---

[77] Salman Rushdie, *The Satanic Verses* (Harmondsworth: Penguin, 1988).
[78] Called 'Satanic' in virtue of that later verse, 22.52: 'God will cancel anything vain that Satan throws in.'
[79] For an early acceptance of other gods, for example, Ex.15.11 (part of Song of Miriam); Ps 138.1. Kenneth Cragg prefers the idea of Muhammad gently satirizing such beliefs: *The Event of the Qur'an* (Oxford: Oneworld Publications, 1994), 139–46.
[80] 'Later forgeries' according to I. R. Netton, *A Popular Dictionary of Islam* (London: Curzon Press, 1992), 226.
[81] 9.6 which offers asylum to pagans. The second half of verse 5 also suggests a different attitude if the pagans repent.

Another traditional approach has been to appeal for clarification to the hadith or oral tradition of Muhammad's teaching.[82] While modern fundamentalists such as President Gaddafi of Libya have entirely rejected any help from beyond the Qur'an itself, in the past the status of such sayings was often extraordinarily high. One ninth century commentator actually declared that 'the Hadith of the Prophet prevails over the Book and constitutes a commentary on it.'[83] Even today, it is to the hadith that one must appeal to justify prayer five times a day rather than three,[84] or for an intensification of the sword verse. However, their line of thought has not always moved in a more rigorous direction. This is true of attitudes towards women: for instance, their right to education and a proper place in the mosque. There is also no shortage of verses discouraging the use of the veil.[85] Yet, given the existence of so many putative hadith, questions inevitably arise about their historical reliability. It is at this stage that chains of transmission (*isnad*) become pertinent: the ability to trace the relevant saying through reliable authorities stretching back, if not to the Prophet himself, then at least to those close to him. To achieve satisfactory results, considerable efforts are in fact made.[86] Even so, it

---

[82] Of the six available collections, the two best known were arranged by Al-Bukhari (d. 870) and Muslim (d. 875).
[83] Ibn Qutayba (d. 889); quoted in A. K. S. Lambton, *State and Government in Medieval Islam* (Oxford: Oxford University Press, 1981), 7.
[84] The Qur'an only mentions three: 24.58; 11.116.
[85] M. M. Ali ed., *A Manual of Hadith* (London: Curzon press, 1944), for former, for example, 33–34, 81, 106–7, 160; for latter, 391–92.
[86] For illustration, see the detailed analysis of the hadith preserved by Sunan Ibn Maja (only three are pronounced veridical); S. H. A.

is hard to resist the conclusion that there is heavy dependence on rather subjective assessments. That is no doubt why modern approaches have moved in other directions, as indeed did Sufism.

Nonetheless, the important point to note here is the attempt to get beyond the rather wooden approach to the text which fundamentalism envisages. Quite a degree of subtlety in how it should be interpreted was already being allowed.[87] A negative feature, though, is that such an approach did place the text in the hands of experts rather than making its meaning and potential implications directly accessible to each individual. While within Christianity the danger of leaving such judgements to the individual had already been demonstrated by some of the extremes of the European Reformation, and would be seen anew in some contemporary developments within Islam, on the other side there needs to be set in both cases potentially liberating qualities in a heightened sense of personal experience of the divine.

Sufism as an Alternative Approach

The willingness of Sufi mystics and the brotherhoods they founded to encourage a greater range of interpretation as well as their stress on personal experience explains the markedly contrasting reception of Sufism across Muslim history. On the negative side may be set

Ghaffer, *Criticism of Hadith among Muslims* (London: Ta-Ha Publishers, 1986), 137–247.
[87] For an earlier attempt of mine to pursue these questions, see my *Tradition and Imagination: Revelation and Change* (Oxford: Oxford University Press, 1999), 151–67.

the crucifixion of the mystic Al Hallaj in the tenth century and the current banning of the movement in contemporary Saudi Arabia.[88] At the same time such phenomena may be contrasted with its central position in Ottoman history and in some present-day African countries.[89] Indeed, its missionary zeal was, as already noted, a prime factor in Islam's spread through south Asia. Its significance for Islam cannot, therefore, be discounted.[90]

One way in which such marginalisation was attempted in the past was to characterise the movement as a foreign import, as a mixture of influences from Christian Syrian monasticism and late pagan Neo-Platonism. While it is possible that its very name derives from the adoption of monastic woollen garments,[91] there is really no need to look beyond the Qur'an itself for its origins. Although outside Islam the Qur'an's references to asceticism and divine transcendence are more familiar, closer examination reveals no shortage of passages that appear to speak of mystical encounters.[92] Indeed, at one point the Qur'an talks of God being nearer to his servant than his 'jugular vein'.[93] Sufism may, therefore, be seen as in some ways an

---

[88] For detailed consideration and some parallels with Jesus, Louis Massignon, *The Passion of Al-Hallaj: Mystic and Martyr of Islam* (Princeton, NJ: Princeton University Press, 1994).

[89] The Ottomans favoured Sufis until a change of policy in 1826. In Senegal 92 per cent of Muslims belong to a Sufi brotherhood.

[90] Contrast the mere half-page devoted to the topic (out of 73 on Islam) in Winifried Corduan, *Neighboring Faiths: A Christian Introduction to World Religions* (Downers Grove, IL: IVP Academic, 2nd ed., 2012), 150.

[91] *Suf* is the Arabic for 'wool'.

[92] Alexander Knysh, *Sufism: A New History of Islamic Mysticism* (Princeton, NJ: Princeton University Press, 2017), 64–84.

[93] 50.16.

attempt to enter into Mohammad's own mystical experience of the divine, though of course without any claim to parity. Either a more immediate holy figure (living or dead) is held up for emulation and discipleship is learnt at their feet,[94] or else the need to draw closer to the divine is seen as incumbent on all alike.[95] At the same time divine transcendence is preserved by speaking of perceiving the divine through Allah's creation,[96] or, if more directly, in essentially negative terms.[97]

Irrespective of loyalty or otherwise to the sharia, there are at least three respects in which Sufism could be seen to help in generating a less fundamentalist approach. The first concerns the movement's generous attitude to other religions. For example, even if now regarded with more suspicion, there has been a clear tradition of various borrowings in both directions on the Indian subcontinent.[98] The Hindu gods, Ram and Krishna, have sometimes even been treated as prophets.[99] While this might seem

---

[94] The leader is seen as 'a friend of God'. In north Africa such saints are known as marabouts. There are also some female saints, the best known being perhaps the eighth century Rabi'a al-Basri.
[95] This was the view of the principal Sufi philosopher, Al-Ghazali (d.1111).
[96] Al-Arabi (d.1240), for instance, interprets the famous light verse to mean that all phenomena reflect the one reality which is God.
[97] Stressed in Toby Mayer, 'Theology and Sufism' in Tim Winter ed., *Classical Islamic Theology* (Cambridge: Cambridge University Press, 2008), 258–87.
[98] Sufis borrowed extensively from Indian religious music, while its message of love and charity was especially attractive to lower-caste Hindus. Sufi shrines were also visited by those of other faiths, as is still the case today for Hindus with the Delhi shrine of the thirteenth century Sufi, Nizam al-Din Awliya.
[99] Ziauddin Sardar, *Reading the Qur'an* (London: Hurst & Company, 2015), 235–40, esp.237.

initially to run completely counter to Islam's customary exclusivism, it is possible to identify some precedents from within the Qur'an itself. Muhammad had declared that each nation has had its own prophets, whilst on one occasion non-biblical prophets are explicitly acknowledged.[100] Although historical pride was undoubtedly a key element, this can perhaps explain in part why pre-revolutionary Iran adopted a positive attitude to Zoroastrianism as a legitimate predecessor, as also why such perceptions did not entirely disappear immediately thereafter.[101] An interesting example specifically related to Sufi practice is what is currently happening in post-communist Albania and its neighbour Kosovo. In 1967 Albania had been declared the first religion-free state in the world and to that end all places of worship had been destroyed. Despite the way in which Saudi Arabia has spent large sums in promoting more conservative versions of the faith, Albania's native Bektashi order is experiencing something of a revival.[102] Not only is its earlier openness towards Christianity reflected in the position adopted at its newly built centre in Tirana but also at the historical pilgrimage site of Mount Tomorr. Due

---

[100] One intriguing such case is the prophet Salih sent to the Thamud tribe to reprimand them for mistreating a camel dedicated to God: 26.142; 91.11–15; Nicolai Sinai, *The Qur'an: A Historical-Critical Introduction* (Edinburgh: Edinburgh University Press, 2017), 170–71.

[101] Openly cultivated by the Pavlavi dynasty because of their claim to continuity with Cyrus' empire (sixth century BCE). After the Islamic revolution Zoroastrian symbols continued for a while on buses. Protest gatherings have continued at Cyrus' tomb.

[102] For a detailed survey, Robert Elsie, *The Albanian Bektashi: History and Culture of a Dervish Order in the Balkans* (London: I. B. Tauris, 2019). This particular order originated among the Janissaries (a military order) serving the Sultan.

honour is given at the latter to no less than three contrasting figures: to the ancient spirit of the mountain, to Ali and to the Virgin Mary.[103]

Second, even where most or many of the details of traditional sharia continue to be observed, differences of emphasis are to found, in what is essentially a more tolerant creed. This is in part a consequence of the type of worship that is enjoined. One feature is the collective remembrance of God (dhikr) which is likely to encourage a more insistent central focus, just as does constant repetition of the Jesus prayer within Christianity.[104] Another is the use of music and dance to induce a mystical state. While the revival of dervish dance in Turkey is still most commonly associated with cultural tourism,[105] its aims have always been much deeper in seeking identity not only with the oneness of God but also the divine presence in everything. That mystic sense of shared identities is finely characterised by the Indian Sufi master, Hazrat Inayat Khan (1882–1927).[106] More recently, another well-known Sufi Iranian scholar, Seyyed Hossein Nasr (b. 1933), has sought to mediate over continuing suspicions of music, observing that even Ayatollah Khomeini

---

[103] Mother Teresa of Calcutta was present at the reopening of the Tirana Kryegjyshata in 1991 (234). For worship on Mount Tomorr: 48–49; 234–37.
[104] There are several versions, all of which involve continuous repetition. For dhikr in the Qur'an: 2.152; 29.45; 73.8
[105] The term is actually derived from the Persian for 'poor' and so almost certainly originally referred to the group's ascetical practices.
[106] Hazrat Inayat Khan, *The Music of Life* (New Lebanon, NY: Omega, 1983); *The Mysticism of Sound and Music* (Boulder, CO: Shambhala, 1996). For a biography, Elisabeth de Jong Keesing, *Inayat Khan: a Biography* (London: Luzac & Co, 1974).

eventually issued a fatwa in its support.[107] Also indicative of Sufi influence is the annual June festival at Fes in Morocco of world sacred music.[108] Given such a wider focus, the centrality of love to Sufi self-understanding will come as no surprise. At the same time it is important to acknowledge that similar positions are also sometimes developed within more 'orthodox' approaches. There is, for example, a fine book on love in the Qur'an by Prince Ghazi of Jordan.[109]

Finally, drawing readers away from a more literal approach is the strong embedding of the Sufi approach within Muslim poetry where, as in the West, extensive use of metaphor helps to encourage less literal attitudes. An obvious example is the use of the imagery of wine and drunkenness to speak of religious enthusiasm despite the traditional abstinence which is enjoined upon Muslims. *The Divan* of Hafez (d. 1390), often regarded as Iran's favourite poet, is replete with such imagery.[110] In a similar way the earlier *Conference of Birds* by Attar (d. 1221) expands upon a brief Qur'anic allusion to the language of birds. The result is a beautiful moral tale which contains imagery both expected and unexpected.[111]

---

[107] Seyyed Hossein Nasr, 'Islam and Music: The legal and spiritual dimensions' in Lawrence E. Sullivan ed., *Enchanting Powers: Music in the World's Religions* (Cambridge: Harvard University Press, 1997), 219–36, esp. 229–30. Music is banned by the Wahhabi sect in Saudi Arabia.

[108] Participants have included Patti Smith and Bjork.

[109] *Love in the Holy Qur'an* (Cambridge: Kazi Publications, 7th ed., 2010).

[110] A large collection of short poems. A dual language version is available in Ismail Salam, *The Divan of Hafiz* (Tehran: Gooya Art House, 2003).

[111] At 27.16 it is said that David and Solomon learnt the language of birds. One of the more unusual images is of distant China as a symbol for

The pervasive extent of such startling imagery means that the real intentions behind the famous Rubaiyat of Omar Khayyam continues to be debated. For some it is an extraordinary work of scepticism, even of atheism, while for others it is a Sufi masterpiece in the same tradition.[112]

Such transformations are undoubtedly seen most clearly in the extraordinary range of images and parables that emerged from Sufism's greatest poet, Rumi (d.1273).[113] Although born Persian, he is now principally associated with the Mevlevi order and their continuing base at Konya in Turkey (where he is also buried). His poetic output was vast.[114] The most profound, his *Masnavi* or 'Spiritual Couplets', consists of allegories and parables illustrative of mystical knowledge and experience.[115] Perhaps easier to access, though, is the imagery deployed in the shorter poems gathered in a collection in honour of his friend, and now commonly called *The Shams*.[116] There is in both a huge openness in the range of his allusion which includes not just Islamic tradition but also classical and Indian. While a present-day successor at Konya is probably right that this did not include subscription to reincarnation as is sometimes

    mystical knowledge. For a translation, Farid Ud-Din Attar, *The Conference of Birds* (London: Continuum, 2000).
[112] For an evocative exploration of the poet's own times and the subsequent history of the poem's influence, note *Samarkand* (London: Quarter, 1992) by the French Lebanese novelist, Amin Maalouf.
[113] 'Rumi' is a nickname borrowed from the title of the 'Roman' or Byzantine kingdom that had held Konya until not long before.
[114] The *Masnavi* alone consist of six books amounting to 50,000 lines.
[115] The first book is available in Penguin classics: trans. Alan Williams, *Rumi Spiritual Verses* (London: Penguin, 2006).
[116] Available in Coleman Barks trans., *Rumi's The Big Red Book* (New York: HarperCollins, 2011).

claimed,[117] there is a willingness to learn widely from a perspective which finds divine love reflected everywhere. The theme is finely explored in an account of his relationship with his friend Shams of Tabriz by the contemporary British–Turkish novelist, Elif Shafak (b. 1971).[118] Indeed, Rumi's poetry could be described as among Islam's best ambassadors, not least if the common contention is true that he is currently the United States' favourite poet.

However, despite the continuing presence of both approaches discussed here, there are powerful sociological reasons why they are now under threat. Because of its stress on individual experience, Sufism can all too easily appear rebellious, and 'liberal', even anarchic.[119] By contrast, the careful reasoning of the four schools can come across as cold and hierarchical, with in effect individual believers made subservient to their rulings. So in an age like the present one, it is perhaps not altogether surprising that both are exposed to extensive critique. Individual believers want to find the truth for themselves in the Qur'an. At the same time many want to feel themselves under divine authority, not merely engaged in the pursuit of more personal goals (as Sufism can sometimes appear from the outside). So fundamentalism has enjoyed a ready breeding ground. The question, therefore, arises of whether there

---

[117] Sefik Can, *Fundamentals of Rumi's Thought* (Clifton, NJ: Tughra, 2015), 225–44. For his willingness to include those of a different faith, 150–51,165–68, 203–4.

[118] In *The Forty Rules of Love* (London: Penguin, 2015). Religious themes are also explored in some of her other novels such as *Three Daughters of Eve* (London: Penguin, 2016).

[119] As a matter of fact, Sufis are for the most part under the direction of spiritual masters. But, given that they do not always agree, it can appear from the outside that chaos is instead the result.

are any new resources in contemporary Islam on which to draw in engaging with such problems.

Contemporary Engagement with the Possibility of Change

In this final part of the present chapter, I want to achieve two objectives. The first is to note where contemporary Muslim scholars are already engaging with a different way of coming to terms with change. Second, some suggestions of my own will be offered about how dialogue with Christianity might be pursued through adopting a less literal approach to the Qur'an but without in any way challenging its revelatory status.

Modern Contextualism

Despite current impressions, some historians strongly contend that the Muslim world went through its own version of the Enlightenment, if somewhat later.[120] Some significant figures would include Muhammad Abduh (1849–1905) in Egypt, the Iranians Jamal al-Din al-Aghani (1839–97) and Abdul Karim Soroush (b. 1945) and colonial India figures such as Sir Muhammad Iqbal (1877–1938) and Sir Syed Ahmed Khan (1817–98).[121]

---

[120] For one such analysis, Christopher de Bellaigue, *The Islamic Enlightenment: The Modern Struggle Between Faith and Reason* (London: Bodley Head, 2017).

[121] Both Iqbal and Khan initially envisaged strong cooperation between Muslims and Hindus, but the latter eventually changed his mind. He is now regarded as the father of the 'two nations' solution (the subcontinent dividing along religious lines into India and Pakistan).

The main difference from the West is that acceptance proved a much slower process, though not always. While the destruction of the Ottoman Empire proved necessary to make possible a more progressive Turkey, in Indonesia and Morocco smoother transitions were accomplished, despite colonialism. Both countries currently have constitutions based on religious toleration.[122] Again, Benazir Bhutto is by no means the only woman to have become head of state in a Muslim country. The hijab has also in recent years developed some more positive associations.[123] Even so, for the most part today progressive Muslims proceed piecemeal and somewhat cautiously.[124] From our perspective here, though, more interesting are some general strategies proposed to deal with change, not least because these, as with change within Christianity, raise the issue of the extent to which revelation may be seen as culture specific. In neither religion should such a view be interpreted to entail relativism. Rather, the point is that apparently universal statements in the Qur'an might now be better understood as intended for particular situations which need then be translated into more

---

[122] The continuing influence of Sufism may be relevant. Fes in Morocco was the place from which the major Sufi order, the Tijaniyya, drew its origins.
[123] For a helpful discussion, Carole Hillenbrand, *Islam: A New Historical Introduction* (London: Thames & Hudson, 2015), 265–73. The hijab is the common headscarf. Contrast this with the niqab which covers the mouth and nose as well or the most extreme burqa where the entire body is concealed, leaving only a visor for the eyes.
[124] For reasons why 'liberal' has come under suspicion, see Carool Kersten, *Contemporary Thought in the Muslim World* (London: Routledge, 2019), 17. For a good example of the progressive range, Omid Safi ed., *Progressive Muslims: On Justice, Gender and Pluralism* (Oxford: OneWorld, 2003).

general principles before they may be once more applied in the present context.

The founding father of such an approach was Iqbal. Although his reputation (and knighthood) stems from the quality of his Rumi-inspired poetry in both Urdu and Persian, he also wrote an important book that includes this idea, *The Reconstruction of Religious Thought in Islam*. The Sudanese activist, Mahmud Muhammad Taha (d. 1985) proposed that the practice was best exemplified in the contrast between Meccan and Medinan suras.[125] The latter should be interpreted as situation-specific legislation, whereas the earlier suras from Mecca offer general principles. More widely influential, however, has been the approach of Fazlur Rahman (1919–88) who suggested a two-stage movement: discovering the specific factors that help determine the original pronouncement and then a further movement back to the present to ascertain what its different application in the context of today might mean.[126] The aim of such approaches is to get beyond the various types of appeal for authorisation whose advocacy we noted earlier: partly because of the difficulty in securing fully justified priorities within them and partly because the results do not always move in a direction that would readily meet with modern approval (for example, in the Medinan period Muhammad was more likely to endorse the use of force). This is not the

---

[125] Summarised in Kersten, *Contemporary Thought*, 67–69.
[126] Probably his most important work is *Islam & Modernity: Transformation of an Intellectual Tradition* (Chicago: University of Chicago Press, 1982). He taught in Pakistan until 1968 when he was expelled and then settled in the United States.

place to pursue such applications in any detail. Suffice it here to note a few interesting examples.

A good number can be found in one of Rahman's more interesting followers, the Australian academic, Abdullah Saeed. In one of his books he considers how a case for democracy might be argued. At one point in the Qur'an Mohammad is ordered to 'consult' (*shura*) with his Companions before embarking on further war with the Meccans. It may seem a small precedent but an underlying implicit principle is thereby offered which could be applied more generally, should adequate opportunity ever arise (which of course was seldom the case in the ancient world).[127] To give a rather different example, take the Qur'an's prohibition of the taking of interest (*riba*). Subsequent sharia law became strictly legalistic on the matter. The result was a failure ever to penetrate behind the deeper reasons for Mohammad's prohibition: seeking to avoid the hardships which frequently result from the amassing of debts.[128]

In contemplating this rather different sort of approach, some potentially illuminating parallels with debates within Christianity may be drawn. Defenders of women's and gay rights often resort to the implausible subterfuge that their ultimate endorsement was already present, or at least implicit within, the biblical text. Apparently opposed positions were, it was alleged, really concerned with something else.[129] An alternative, more

---

[127] Qur'an 3.159. Abdullah Saeed, *Reading the Qur'an in the Twenty-First Century: A Contextualist Approach* (London: Routledge, 2014), 148–59.
[128] Qur'an 2.275. Saeed, *Reading the Qur'an*, 160–75.
[129] Such as hospitality in the familiar passage about Sodom: Gen. 19.1–25, esp. 5–8.

historical approach might pursue contextual reasons to explain why at one stage in history Christianity is found adopting one position and now would like to adopt another. Different social factors might explain the difference, while some overarching principle could still legitimate the contrast.[130] However, standing in the way of acceptance of contextualism among Muslims is the traditional Asherah doctrine of the eternity of the Qur'an. Supporters of innovation suggest reverting to the earlier defeated Mutazilite position that spoke of the creation of the Quran. But while such a stance allows for a greater contribution from active reflection on the part of the prophet, at the same time it might seem to demote the full involvement of Allah in what happened. Might some parallel with modern kenotic understandings of the incarnation prove helpful here? Could Muslims not continue to speak of the Qur'an's eternity (in its overarching principles) even as it adapts to the specifics of being communicated in one particular culture rather than another?

Intriguingly, while Christians and Muslims are not ever likely to agree on the divinity of Christ, such a method could help with resolving what is perhaps the most obvious source of tension between them, the common Muslim claim that Jesus did not die on the cross. Islamic tradition asserts that God saved Jesus from crucifixion (a death too dreadful for one of his prophets). But

---

[130] In an earlier work I suggested that the New Testament applied equality of regard between male and female but not equality of status because of psychological assumptions about disparity which were well-nigh universal at the time. See further my *Discipleship and Imagination: Christian Tradition and Truth* (Oxford: Oxford University Press, 2000), 11–31.

the verse which asserts this is actually quite obscure in its expression: 'They said (in boast), "We killed Christ Jesus the son of Mary, the Apostle of God" – But they killed him not, nor crucified him. But so it was made to appear to them.'[131] While quite a number of other options are possible (including influence from Christian Gnostic sects), close attention to the form of language used, in particular its talk of boasting, has led a number of scholars, both contextualist and otherwise, to propose a different interpretation. The aim of the verse was not to deny what happened to Jesus on the cross. Rather, it was intended as a direct challenge to Jews of the time who were seen as arrogantly claiming that they had defeated one of God's own prophets.[132] It would thus be less a claim that Jesus did not die, as one which asserted that even in dying Jews failed to secure the triumph that they wanted.[133] However, now outside that context, the assertion ceases to be required.

The Qur'an in Dialogue with Earlier Revelation

I want to conclude this chapter by considering whether the Qur'an could in any way be integrated into a Christian view of revelation. Initially, this might seem an absurd idea given Christianity's traditional claim to a story of divine revelation which ended six hundred years earlier.

---

[131] Sura 4.157. A.Yusuf Ali trans., *The Holy Qur'an*
[132] For an historian's comments, G. S. Reynolds ed., *The Qur'an in its Historical Context* (London: Routledge, 2008), 124 (on 3.55) and 180–81 (on 4.157).
[133] For contextualist arguments, including other possibilities, Saeed, 129–47.

But the Prophet's willingness to engage in a sympathetic critique of those earlier stories may possibly offer a way forward. 'Sympathetic' may seem an odd term to use but in the Qur'an the basic outlines of earlier tradition are in fact affirmed, it is only specific details which are challenged. Of course, as long as these alterations were viewed as 'corrections' to the historical record (the way commentators and scholars generally continue to view them), no way forward is possible. But, as we observed in Chapter 1, contemporary research suggests a different evaluation of both Bible and (by implication) Qur'an as a mixture of historical record and imaginative insight. What, then, if the Qur'anic versions are re-examined, to see if they might sometimes contain non-historical, imaginative insights which Christians could now also endorse?

First, however, it might be helpful to provide some updating of approaches to the Qur'an. Apart from its initial, short introductory sura or 'chapter' which is recited on each occasion of prayer,[134] the Quran is, like Paul's corpus, arranged in order of length rather than chronologically. The text itself informs readers of when the first revelation occurred on the Night of Power in 610.[135] Because the Arabic text is apparently beautifully structured with a poetic use of rhyme and assonance,[136] it

---

[134] For a fine selection of prayers in common use across the Muslim word, Constance E. Padwick, *Muslim Devotions* (Oxford: Oneworld, 1961).

[135] Sura 97: 'The Night of Power.' The auditions were apparently received in a trancelike state.

[136] Though not strictly poetry as such. For a brilliant study of the language and its impact, Navid Kermani, *God is Beautiful: The Aesthetic Experience of the Quran* (Cambridge; Polity Press, 2015). For some extraordinary physical effects, 303–19.

quickly came to be seen as derived from an 'uncreated' original.[137] Nonetheless, as with the Bible, continuing acceptance of a divine origin should not be taken to preclude acknowledgement of more human sources. Some Western scholars are convinced that the book is a composite work from a number of different hands, perhaps spanning a century or more.[138] Others argue that the text as present constituted failures to reflect an advance of Islam into Palestine during Mohammad's own day.[139] Yet other scholars propose an early but as complex a manuscript tradition as early Christianity.[140] Which approach is the most plausible we may leave undecided here, except to observe that a wider openness to alternative possibilities may have been lost as a result. At the very least later emendations resulting from the prophet's own response to a complex environment seems likely, or expressed more

[137] The Ash'arite or 'uncreated' view eventually came to dominate.
[138] The best-known advocate so far of this position was the American John E. Wansbrough (1928–2002). He suggested developments over a span of two hundred years. Two important books were *Quranic Studies: Sources and Methods of Scriptural Interpretation* (Oxford: Oxford University Press, 1977); *The Sectarian Milieu: Content and Composition of Islamic Salvation History* (Oxford: Oxford University Press, 1978).
[139] Advocated on the basis of other non-Islamic sources by Patricia Crone and Michael A. Cook, *Hagarism: The Making of the Islamic World* (Cambridge: Cambridge University Press, 1977). Supporting them is the claim of Stephen J. Schoemaker that the traditions of the church of the Kathisma (or 'seat' of 'God-bearing' Mary) near Jerusalem were a decisive influence on Mohammad: 'Christmas in the Qur'an: the Qur'anic account of Jesus' Nativity and Palestinian local tradition' in *Jerusalem Studies in Arabic and Islam* 28 (2003), 11–39.
[140] François Déroche, *The One and the Many: The Early History of the Qur'an* (New Haven, CT: Yale University Press, 2021), esp. 230–31, 234.

carefully from a Muslim perspective, modified by the divine address as the oral tradition continued to develop. Not that this was a long process as much of the Qur'an probably received something like its final form not long after Mohammad's death.[141] Even so, it is not difficult to detect some changes of emphasis between the earlier, shorter suras that were received in Mecca and the later which occurred subsequent to the Prophet's flight to Medina in 622 CE.[142] As well as a stronger commitment to military action, these also included more suspicious attitudes to those of other faiths, especially Jews.[143]

Nonetheless, in all of this Mohammad never wavers from his belief that he is the latest in a long line of prophets, called to summon humanity to repentance. So Jewish and Christian claims about their own revelations are seen as defectively recorded rather than totally wrong.[144] Within the Jewish dispensation Adam, Abel, Noah, Abraham, Joseph and Moses are all deemed to have made legitimate contributions, just as Jesus did in the Christian dispensation. Muhammad's modifications to the more storied elements obviously need careful

---

[141] A committee under Uthman (or Osman), the third caliph, produced the first definite version in 652, only twenty years after the prophet's death.

[142] So significant is this date taken to be that Muslim calendars begin at this point (AH – anno Hegirae). Known at the time as Yathrib, Medina's mixture of Arab and Jewish tribes combined to fight the Meccans. It acquired its new name because of its role in Muhammad's story: Madinat an-Nabi ('city of the prophet').

[143] The major differences are pursued in Sinai, *The Qur'an: A Historical-Critical Introduction*, 161–214.

[144] For example, 2.75; 4.46; 5.13, 41–43; 6.91.

consideration, but something should be said first about his attitude to Christian doctrine.

From one long sura (called Mary) we learn of Mohammad's acceptance of the Virgin Birth and of the Resurrection. As noted above, although it remains disputed whether he accepted there the crucifixion or not, contextualisation could possibly offer a way out, with Christ's death not denied but his enemies' power over him. Where, however, Mohammad did definitely differ from orthodox Christianity was in total rejection of the divinity of Christ as well as the doctrine of the Trinity. Both were seen as challenges to one of his central claims, the oneness of God. It is worth adding, though, that almost certainly the version of the Trinity to which he took exception was significantly different from that entertained by mainstream Christianity. It appears to have identified Christ and Mary as the other two members of the Trinity.[145] In appreciating how such misunderstandings could have arisen, it is important to note that Mohammad was illiterate and based in a part of the world that was then on the fringes of civilisation.[146] So, although he may also have heard accounts nearer to the standard version of such doctrines, his critique is best understood historically as providing good grounds for supposing that there were indeed Christian groups who espoused some

---

[145] See Reynolds, *The Qur'an*, 208 (on 5.73); 217–18 (on 5.116–18). Jews are criticised for treating Ezra as Son of God (9.30). It is possible that the familiar threefold character of the *Basmalah* ('In the name of God, the Merciful, the Compassionate') was intended as a deliberate contrast to any Trinitarian notion.

[146] Mecca was not on a major trade route, though nearby Yemen flourished thanks to its production of frankincense and myrrh.

such belief in the divinity of Mary, just as there were Jews who were to be found engaging in the worship of angels.[147] This is not to contend that he might well have accepted a more orthodox version of the doctrine, had it been presented more clearly to him. But it is to claim that the degree of his hostility was affected by major misunderstandings of what was in fact at stake.

Equally, then, in considering the often quite different way in which Mohammad tells biblical stories, factors beyond the merely historical need to be taken into account. Undoubtedly, there is a very large number of cases where parallels with the Bible are evident, some more obviously borrowings than others. In addition, note needs to be taken of evidence of connections with the thought of some early Christian writers, such as Ephrem the Syrian (d. 373) and Jacob of Serugh (d. 521).[148] Many more historically minded scholars record such differences without further comment, as though no better explanation were required than lapses of memory in terms of what then appears in the Qur'an. But to my mind there is a more interesting possibility to consider. For Muhammad there is no doubt that such stories were indeed revelation. But precisely for that reason he thinks them imperfectly recorded, inasmuch as in his view they failed adequately to reflect divine reality. Some changes to

---

[147] There were Christian communities in southern Arabia. Najran even had its own bishop and martyrs' pilgrimage centre. Although not mentioned by name, there could be allusions to the town at 34.18 and 85.10.
[148] Both were poets as well as theologians. Ephrem was made a Doctor of the Roman Catholic church in 1920. Serugh or Sarug is now in the Kurdish part of Syria. Many parallels are noted in Reynolds.

the content and structure of the story were, therefore, in his view deemed necessary if a truthful account of divine interaction with humanity was to be preserved.

Indeed, such a dialogue with the past seemed almost required, given the fact that the text of the Qur'an is very far from being self-contained. Instead, it alludes to Jewish and Christian stories as though already known. What happens, therefore, is that they are implicitly given a new focus in the retelling, one that accords better with Muhammad's own view of the divine. How far the prophet saw himself as engaging in a carefully planned, deliberate critique is a moot point. What, though, is beyond contention is the fact that the various alterations he makes have theological force. While it is conceivable that at times he was indeed relying on false memories of the details either in his own mind or in that of others who had transmitted the story to him, surely more likely is that the argument in his imagination went from the character of the God he had encountered in his own mystical experience to the most appropriate way to tell the story of other such encounters. In effect, he is thus implicitly challenging those of us who are Jews or Christians to a similar change of perspective. Under such an assumption Mohammad could sometimes be right, given that in a non-exclusively historical interpretation 'later' does not necessarily imply less astute.

A theological commentary on some of the changes made will help clarify Mohammad's theological intentions. Take first the Qur'an's account of creation. Gone now is not only God 'resting' on the seventh day but also any suggestion that Eve was the primary mover in the Fall. Instead, both Adam and Eve must bear equal responsibility.[149] Although the Qur'an can scarcely be described as according equal rights to the two sexes, there is no doubt that Mohammad's views did represent an advance on assumptions of the time.[150] Both men and women are to bear full, individual responsibility for their own actions. Again, while in the context of that same story Muhammad follows a Jewish (and Christian) tradition which asserted that Satan was reprimanded for not doing obeisance to Adam, he will have nothing to do with the idea that such a call to action was because human beings are seen as bearing within themselves a reflection of the divine image. Satan (Iblis) is even demoted to the status of a mere spirit or jinn. Both alterations are clearly intended to safeguard the overwhelming mystery and uniqueness of Allah's divine majesty.[151] Again, whereas the biblical version of the Cain–Abel conflict is conspicuously without any accompanying explanations regarding motivation on the part of the two brothers, the Qur'an specifically seeks to make appropriate sense of what occurred. Both brothers are allowed to emerge with some merit.[152] Abel pleads with Cain, while Cain repents after the deed. With the story of Noah, the tale is again quite transformed. Whereas the Hebrew scriptures focus almost entirely on what happens after the flood is announced, Mohammad

---

[149] 2.34–6; 7.20–2; 20.120–3. Although it is perhaps relevant to add that Eve is not mentioned by name, nor indeed is any other woman in the Qur'an except Mary.

[150] For example, their dowry can remain their own property: 4.4.

[151] For a fascinating contrast with the Syriac Christian *Cave of Treasures*, see Sinai, *The Qur'an*, 145–8. Jinn is commonly anglicised as genie.

[152] 5.30–5. Neither brother is actually named in the story. The story was to become a major interpretive tool in the writings of the famous medieval historian, Ibn Khaldun (d. 1406).

insists that it is precisely because Noah has preached so strongly a message of repentance, and the people not listened to him, that he has been chosen to survive.[153]

Just as such alterations in earlier history provide an increased emphasis on both the absolute character of divine transcendence and the necessity for a strong sense of individual human responsibility, so a similar pattern is to be found in subsequent developments of the later Jewish story. This can be seen, for example, in how Muhammad treats Abraham. He derives from later Jewish expansions Abraham's hostility to his father's acceptance of idolatry. But he gives that rejection his own characteristic qualifications. While Abraham initially prays for his father's forgiveness, when he fails to repent, Abraham is shown dissociating himself entirely from him, despite his natural disposition being 'tender-hearted, forbearing'.[154] So, in a similar manner to the teaching of Jesus, the need to put commitment to God above family loyalties is emphasised.[155] Then in the subsequent story of the sacrifice of Abraham's son, the development in later Islam which speaks explicitly of the older illegitimate son, Ishmael, as fulfiller of this role emerges as an entirely natural trajectory. This is because for Muhammad it is the one who makes the primary or greater commitment who should be emulated (the son) rather than the father who must necessarily remain a secondary figure because it is not his life that is on the line.[156]

---

[153] Noah is one of Mohammad's favourite exemplars: 7.59–64; 11.24–49; 23.23–30; 37.75–82; 54.9–15; 71.1–28 (the last entitled Noah).
[154] 9.114.   [155] Compare Luke 14.26.
[156] There is a dialogue between Abraham and the unnamed son (in subsequent tradition identified with Ishmael) which results in them both submitting their wills to God: 37.102–3. Some commentators

Likewise, in the case of Joseph, a Jewish legend is accepted which makes it evident that the innocent party in the affair of Potiphar's wife was Joseph himself.[157] Not that the aim was merely to exonerate a prophet, the tale has also been commonly read as an allegory for the true nature of love, not lust.[158] In a similar way, in the story of Moses, Allah shows more concern for the cares and responsibilities of other individuals in the narrative than is true of the biblical account. This is especially true of Moses' mother where a rather moving interchange is described, with Allah clearly concerned for the mother in her anxieties for her child.[159] Even Pharaoh becomes a less wooden figure: he is offered the choice of repentance, though he rejects it.[160]

In this all too brief survey of some of the main stories in the Qur'an, the most obvious conclusion to draw is that they are being retold in a way that is presumed to be most compatible with the identity of who God really is: not, for example, partial towards the Jews, nor someone who grants special privileges to his favourites. In short, my suggestion is that we think of the Qur'an as a challenge to re-think what is really implied by the biblical scriptural witness. Of course, in the past it was assumed that the biblical account was unadorned history (as well as theological truth) which imposes severe limits on what can be

---

suggest that the mention of Isaac at 112–13 is a later addition intended to make explicit that the promise made to him had no connection with this earlier act.
[157] 12.22–34.
[158] For a detailed exposition in this direction see A. Yusuf Ali trans., *The Holy Quran*, App. VI, 592–600.
[159] 27. 3–13.
[160] The change of emphasis is noted in Sinai, *The Qur'an*, 170.

changed. But, if we accept, as I think we must, that there is a stronger imaginative element than merely factual history, then the further question arises of what is really the best way of telling such stories. Within such a perspective, it is surely not impossible to concede that sometimes this is to be found in how the Qur'an chooses to tell the story. That is to say, not only does the Quranic text consciously seek through Muhammad to generate a more adequate theological account,[161] even from a Christian perspective it must be concluded that it does actually sometimes succeed in that task.

Less it be objected that only examples from the Hebrew scriptures have been provided, let me mention one small detail from the gospels where I think the Qur'an has the edge. According to the opening narrative in Luke, Zechariah is struck dumb as a punishment for not believing the angel's promise that his wife would bear a son. By contrast, in Mohammad's version a three-day dumbness is requested by Zechariah as an immediate sign that God would indeed accomplish what was being promised. Surely it is the Qur'an which offers a more sympathetic and less petty conception of divinity.[162] Zechariah is no longer punished for not believing what he might reasonably doubt. Instead, some reassuring sign is requested. Of course, if all the biblical details were historical, no other option would have been available than to accept the Christian version. But, as most New Testament

---

[161] Apart from the features mentioned in the main text, the importance of repentance is another major theme. So, unlike with the Bible, Cain repents (5.31), as does Moses when he asks to see God's face (7.143). Two other examples are David (38.24) and Solomon (38.35).
[162] The story of John the Baptist: Luke 1.20; Qur'an 19.10.

scholars would now concede, the infancy narratives are Luke's imaginative expansion of what were most likely only bare historical outlines, created in order to clarify the significance of how his own gospel narrative would subsequently develop.

Accordingly, from this perspective upon the examples quoted above, the emergence of the Qur'an centuries after the Christian revelation should not be seen in itself as sufficient to require a Christian jettisoning of such Qur'anic readjustments. Even its critique of central Christian doctrines such as incarnation and Trinity deserve respect because they raise legitimate points of concern in thinking about divine unity, even if for the Christian these challenges cannot be allowed to have final sway. It is too early to determine whether Islam as a whole will move in such more hopeful directions or instead will turn its face backwards into a rigid fundamentalism.[163] All I can do here is commend to my fellow Christians the more sympathetic understanding of the religion that has just been offered. With these comments our survey of the world's religions is complete. It now remains in Chapter 8 to draw the various threads in our discussion together into a more coherent whole.

---

[163] And so only see one 'history' replacing another, whether Jewish or Christian.

8

Revelation's Enrichment

~

Over the course of Chapters 3, 4, 5 and 6, in attempting to survey the differing natures and contexts of the world's major religions, I have also deliberately sought out one or more features from which I suggested Christianity could learn. In doing so, my aim was not merely one of facilitating improved relations and understanding, I have also had in mind a deeper objective: that through these means a narrative could be told of divine revelation occurring not just within the Christian story but also across the entire spectrum of other continuing religious traditions.[1] On the surface, given the apparent extent of the difference between them, such a claim must have seemed scarcely credible. Indeed, that divergence explains why inter-religious discussion has tended to one or other extreme. Either the validity of all other religions is denied (exclusivism) or else a very much reduced version of revelation postulated in which all might then plausibly be seen to share (pluralism). The obvious disadvantage of the latter option is a very much weakened account of religious experience and insight; of the former a claim that has become increasingly implausible with the discovery of some clear parallels between Christianity and these other religions. However, as I suggested in Chapter 1, a more complex but ultimately more plausible story can be told. While no religion

---

[1] While in theory one tradition might have gone entirely wrong, in practice I would suggest such failures are partial rather than total.

possesses the totality of what may be known, aspects of the beautiful pattern which reflects ultimate reality can be discerned. It is constituted by a jigsaw of broken potsherds, as it were, with no single religion always in possession of the best perspective on the whole: sometimes patterns overlap; sometimes they are more clearly detectable in one religion rather than another; and sometimes there seems to be a fuzziness that precludes any immediate decision about which perceptible 'pattern' is the most accurate guide.

In advocating such an approach, it was no part of my expectation that a single common mind could easily emerge. Inevitably, each faith will consider certain commitments too fundamental to be readily relinquished (such as the doctrine of the incarnation within Christianity). Nonetheless, such beliefs can now be moderated by humble recognition that, sometimes at least, the divine address has been more adequately grasped in some other faith community. To hostile critics this may seem like an attempt to have it both ways, inclusivist yet also pluralist, but my hope is that something rather more is now in play, an enriched rather than reduced account of revelation. To indicate why this might be so, I want to use this final chapter to explore three issues which have arisen in previous chapters. First, the notion of revelation needs itself to be re-examined, in order to identify a more appropriate model than what has usually held sway. However, so far from this resulting in a diminution of past understandings of what has been communicated, I shall contend that it offers their enlargement.[2] Second, we

---

[2] In everything from better understanding the development of the doctrine of the Trinity to why resurrection and reincarnation might have been advanced as alternative answers in different cultural contexts.

need to focus on a dilemma that has run through much of our discussion, the fact that the more fundamental the questions get, the more it appears that it is not even the same reality that is being explored: neither with respect to this world nor ultimate reality. Even so, appearances notwithstanding, I shall suggest that there is sufficient overlap to talk of significant common ground. Finally, I want to end by maintaining that religion at its best has always been involved in questions of changing perceptions, whether one looks to its past history or what may yet lie before us. Consonant with this chapter's general theme, I would suggest that this is part of the dynamic of what is really involved in revelatory processes which work across the religions rather than in only one.

Revelation: Transcendent Engagement within Liberating Constraints

Despite the dominance within Christianity of the theology of Karl Barth for most of the twentieth century with his strong stress on the otherness of revelation, Christian theologians (whether conservative or liberal) have for the most part retreated from any formal analysis of what is supposed to have taken place, or is currently doing so. Instead, focus has moved to its human reception in the canon of scripture or the Christian community more widely. But the root meaning in Latin of the term as 'unveiling' surely suggests that the initiative lies with God. So in any adequate account divine activity needs to be treated as primary, though not of course sole focus. That, therefore, will be our concern here but in a way that takes constraints seriously on its operation as well as its potential for movement towards deeper insights.

A Suitable Model for Encountering Transcendence

This is not the place to argue in detail for any one particular definition of revelation but it may be helpful for what follows if I offer a brief summary of how I understand the term: 'an awareness or encounter with divine or transcendent reality which communicates non-coercively within specific contexts something significant both for the understanding of ultimate reality as well as humanity's relationship with it.' Earlier chapters have already endorsed the need to accept a looser relationship between contingent present text and apparently immutable divine truth that once held sway. There are just too many individual elements that are misleading or even erroneous to adopt any other view. A promising alternative analogy has been proposed by the American philosopher, Nicholas Wolterstorff. The text should be seen as more mediated, like that of a spokesperson or ambassador.[3] But the trouble with such a proposal is that the relationship is often much more remote than this, in the apparent endorsement of many ideas no longer acceptable at all within the modern community, or indeed sometimes almost never within that same tradition.[4] One element that clearly must go, therefore, is any claim that what is ascribed to God in scripture is necessarily always true. Rather, the text can only be guaranteed to record how the divine will

---

[3] Nicholas Wolterstorff, *Divine Discourse: Philosophical Reflections on the Claim That God Speaks* (Cambridge: Cambridge University Press, 1995). The idea is developed in relation to J. L. Austin's speech acts theory.

[4] So, for example, throughout Christian history the horrendous conclusion to Psalm 137 has only quite occasionally been interpreted literally, despite that being the text's obvious meaning.

was understood at some particular point in history. A possible alternative model then is to think of individuals encountering the divine presence and responding (to the best of their ability) in the light of their community's antecedent assumptions, sometimes admitting the need for change, sometimes not. However, if that account is accepted, it raises acutely the question of why God was not concerned at any particular moment to secure the overall truth: that is, why partial answers were allowed, only to be overthrown in subsequent generations or centuries. The answer I proposed in Chapter 1 (and elsewhere) is that God valued something more: the fullest internalisation of the particular values being proposed compatible with an entirely free response.[5]

Put thus briefly, it may sound as though all I am envisaging is an endorsement of the assumptions of one particular thought-world, those of the Enlightenment.[6] While the kind of respect for freedom that movement advocated was hardly in itself wrong, it is just not penetrating enough for the interaction we are considering here. After all, there remains a huge difference between merely acknowledging something to be the case and that same truth entering imaginatively into the individual's consciousness as a cherished impetus towards further reflection and action. Only then does it become truly the recipient's own. For example, it is one thing formally to acknowledge racism to be wrong; quite another to

---

[5] For a defence and reasons for rejecting alternatives, see my two essays on revelation in David Brown, *God in a Single Vision: Integrating Philosophy and Theology*, eds. Christopher R. Brewer & Robert MacSwain (London: Routledge, 2016), 61–85.

[6] And in particular Kant.

engage actively with the advancement of those of another race. Indeed, where one's own interests are threatened it is all too easy to misrepresent to oneself what is in fact wrong conduct as actually legitimate under certain circumstances, a claim as true about how ancient Israel behaved towards native peoples as proved to be the case with twentieth-century 'German Christian' antisemitism, or indeed the attitude and conduct of some present-day Israelis towards their neighbouring Palestinians.[7]

But how, then, is that encounter to be envisaged? The appropriate answer is likely to be heavily dependent on other conclusions in science and philosophy. One possible approach (the one I prefer) is to think of such encounters as like other experiences of transcendence in the area of ethics and aesthetics.[8] Here the work of three analytic philosophers may possibly be of some help, that of the Australian John McDowell, the American Thomas Nagel and the Englishman Roger Scruton. All three oppose materialist reductionism and suggest an analysis of moral value and, in the case of Scruton especially, aesthetic value as ways of appropriating elements of transcendence that are inherent in the aspirations of the human mind. Although only Scruton offers in the process a tentative acceptance of divine reality, the kind of transcendence

---

[7] *Deutsche Christen* refers to a specific group. Similarly, contemporary Israelis differ widely on the extent of their sympathy for the Palestinian situation. For one Israeli critique, Sylvain Cypel, *The State of Israel vs. the Jews* (New York: Other Press, 2021).

[8] The model in the main text assumes the capacity of human beings to reach beyond any determination by their evolutionary origins. Should scientific evidence eventually require a more materialist account, this would seem to me to argue for a different model rather than for the total rejection of any notion of revelation.

canvassed by all three is of such a kind to allow Christian belief once more to re-engage with the potential implications of such thought, whether associated with atheism or not. Thus, in marked contrast to reductionist materialists such as Daniel Dennett, in 2013 Nagel produced a remarkable book entitled *Mind and Cosmos: Why the Materialist Conception of Nature is Almost Certainly False*. What is significant for our discussion here is that central to his argument against conventional science ever being able to explain everything is his contention that there is a teleological orientation not only to consciousness as such but even to its emergence. So, although he rejects God with as emphatic a dismissal as he had rejected evolution as an explanation for such values, his own proposal proved scarcely less contentious, that there is an inherent direction to the universe: what he is even prepared to call 'a natural teleology'.[9]

While McDowell and Scruton would be more cautious in following him that far, they too both insist on the irreducibility of moral and aesthetic value. In *Mind and World* (1994) McDowell rejects 'bald naturalism' in favour of his own 'naturalistic' perspective, according to which the distinctive capacities of mind are a cultural achievement of what he calls our 'second nature'.[10] Again,

---

[9] Although the book was much criticised on publication, it does raise important issues, even though Nagel frankly admits that he does not at present know how adequately to answer all of them: *Mind and Cosmos* (Oxford: Oxford University Press, 2012).

[10] He sees human beings as passive in our perceptual experience of the world but as active in conceptualisation of it. His notion of a second nature is borrowed from Gadamer: *Mind and the World* (Boston, MA: Harvard University Press, 1994).

rejecting ontological dualism, Scruton advocates what he calls epistemic dualism. A particular feature of mental realities is experience of them as essentially other. Contrast, for example, the very different ways in which the other is approached in lust and in love. In love the value of the other is fully acknowledged, whereas in lust the object remains a mere means. So notions of gift and grace (from a rather different sort of Other) become central, which is where he connects with a possible inference to God, as in his Gifford Lectures at St Andrews on *The Face of God* (2012).[11] Revelatory experience could then be seen as part of the general ability of human beings to be challenged beyond their purely physical setting by other-directing values, with that experience in effect constituting the supreme challenge from what is Other.[12]

Such a model for understanding would then also allow some explanation of why the arts and religion have conventionally been so closely allied. Dance, music and art have all been commonly seen in the past as dislocating customary human perceptions and so as a means of giving access to an alternative reality, one which enables participants to reach beyond the purely empirical. It would also accord well with the element in revelation of the mysterious and unexpected.[13] It is that imaginative element

---

[11] Roger Scruton, *The Face of God* (2012) and its companion volume *The Soul of the World* (2014) were both published by Bloomsbury.

[12] Such talk makes the parallel with ethics clear. Whereas in ethics 'others' are given a value not derivable from the empirical world, in religion one encounters an Other of whom this is quintessentially so.

[13] For an analysis of this aspect of revelation, see William Desmond, 'Godsends: On the Surprise of Revelation' in B. M. Metzei, F. A. Murphy & K. Oakes eds., *The Oxford Handbook of Divine Revelation*, (Oxford: Oxford University Press, 2021), 239–57.

which I suggest helps us to make better sense of religious texts. In their engagement with an alternative reality, there is a need to stretch images and metaphors in order to help their readers and auditors to grasp deeper truths. A conversion that is no less imaginative than moral is thus required. If I may put it this way, the recipient of revelation believes that their mind has been unblocked ('unveiled') such that they can now see, if still only partially, what they formerly did not see at all.

Admittedly, drawing parallels with morality and art could have disadvantages in perhaps suggesting the reduction of religious experience to one or the other, but the positive benefit lies in the notion that religion would not stand alone, in its unusual non-empirical appropriation of truth. There is a similar beckoning from beyond that is acknowledged even by those without explicit religious faith. To take the case of morality, it is of course true that certain ethical analyses never transcend the ordinary perceptual world, as in the common appeal to utilitarian calculations for happiness. But matters are quite otherwise when human beings are led to talk about the infinite value of the other, as there seems nothing in this world as such that could justify the claim. While non-believers will want to claim that such transcendent values exist in their own right, for the believer they are more naturally credited to a pattern which is characteristic of reality as a whole and this yields belief in God as the infinite Other no less than the preciousness of each and every human life.

Constraints in the Encounter as Enriching

In acknowledging the conditioned character of revelation, it is all too easy to suppose that this entails the diminution of its significance. But I would contend that this is true neither of circumstances where human prejudice is in play nor, more importantly, where the limitation is some wider cultural constraint. Regarding the former, exaggerated claims for preferential treatment, as in presuming that harsh punishment or worse needs to be visited on those with whom recipients disagree or who stand in their way, was unfortunately all too common.[14] Nonetheless, as I have already indicated, in choosing not to override such prejudices God cherished something more: that such communities and individuals themselves should work toward a freely endorsed different set of values. Conditioning contexts of time and place may initially seem more problematic but what in fact they usually make possible is a more rounded picture. Let me illustrate this with some general examples before focusing more narrowly on one particular issue which has emerged more than once across the book: how life after death should be conceived.

Consider first a doctrinal example, the development of the doctrine of the Trinity. Within the Hebrew canon it is possible to detect a gradual move from an earlier acceptance of the existence of other gods to full-blooded monotheism in Second Isaiah,[15] just as something less than the full divinity of Christ or a doctrine of the Trinity seems to

---

[14] As in the *herem* or sacred ban in Deut. 20.15–20, or the author of Revelation's condemnation not only of all pagans but even of some fellow Christians (2.20 effectively condemns St Paul). Again, the author of Hebrews excludes some of his fellow Christians from ever receiving forgiveness, Heb. 6.4–6.

[15] For acceptance of other gods, for example, Ps. 82.1; for Isaiah, for example, 40.12–31; 43.8–13; 46.5–13.

be on offer in the earliest strands of the New Testament before this developed into a full-blooded model of both in John and especially during the patristic period. One way of understanding such processes is surely to observe that certain insights are only easily acquired once others have already been established: for example, complexity in the divine nature only once monotheism has been firmly secured. In a similar way, then, it makes sense to think of the 'science' of the day being initially assumed in order to ground something far more fundamental, a particular way of seeing the world. To give a contemporary scientific example, just as to appeal to the butterfly effect would have made no sense in the context of nineteenth-century acceptance of iron laws of causality,[16] so with the opening chapters of Genesis the writers were encouraged to ground their exposition in the 'science' of the day, precisely because that was not the central point at issue. Rather, it was a matter of underlying theological insights into such principles as the fundamental goodness of creation and God's general concern for the flourishing of humanity.[17]

But the same surely is no less true of theories such as reincarnation and resurrection. They are often treated as though they are exclusively theological notions. They are not. What makes intellectual sense in any particular time

---

[16] The term derives from the work of the mathematician and meteorologist, Edward Norton Lorenz, on chaos theory. A small change in one area can have large ramifications elsewhere. A butterfly fluttering its wings several weeks earlier can contribute towards the manufacture of a later tornado elsewhere.

[17] The principal content of P and J respectively in the first three chapters of Genesis.

or context is heavily dependent on what is seen as scientifically and conceptually possible. So, just as it may be assumed that God communicates within the context of what is taken as scientifically plausible within any particular culture, so the same should be seen to be the case with respect to such complex metaphysical theories about human identity. So long as the huge differences that exist between East and West are all assumed to be a direct part of revelation, irreconcilable conflict will be the expected result, whereas more careful analysis can suggest a different evaluation. It will do so in two ways. First, it allows believers to appreciate the deeper common motivation behind the two contrasting types of metaphysics, in an overarching concern for justice for the world and its inhabitants but seen as realised in different ways. Second, and perhaps more importantly here, it also alerts both types of approach to a proper appreciation of the imaginative element involved in such constructions.[18] Such conceptual schemes are essentially about the transformation of the individual rather than necessarily one particular way of going about it. So, as we saw in the relevant chapter (Chapter 4), in the eastern case it was less about the continuation of the ego and more about the working through of the consequences of that life on subsequent generations. Meanwhile, on the Christian side the fact that Christ's resurrection body is said to continue to exist in heaven demonstrates nicely that such a body must be of a very different kind from the one he had on

---

[18] That there might be parallels is noted by Thich Nhat Hanh, *Living Buddha, Living Christ* (London: Rider, 1996), 132: 'Elements of reincarnation are certainly present in the teachings of Christianity.'

earth.[19] So by implication all other resurrected bodies will similarly be very different, as indeed was already being acknowledged by Paul.[20]

Perhaps my underlying point can be made clearest by observing that on this issue in both east and west there are really two elements in the total conception, and that provided the nearest equivalent is considered there is not as much difference as might initially be thought. On the one hand one might compare the role of reincarnation in securing justice with that allotted within Christianity to a physical resurrection in an apocalyptic fulfilment at the end of time. On the other hand, escape into nirvana or its nearer Hindu equivalent of *moksha* is most naturally evaluated in relation to the Christian conception of souls being taken up at death into life with God in heaven. Indeed, evident in the latter are Christian attitudes which draw much nearer to the east in accepting immortality or continuity of the soul or ego,[21] as central in a way that physical resurrection does not.[22] I hasten to add that I am not for a moment suggesting that the various elements in western and eastern thought amount ultimately to the same thing, only that there are sufficient similarities to

---

[19] Even the gospel resurrection encounters suggest recognition only after acknowledgment of strangeness and difference.

[20] I Cor. 15. 35-42. For further discussion of this point, see my 'Christ's Resurrection and Our Own' in *Modern Believing*, 64.2 (2023), 142–51.

[21] Whereas in the Hindu case what survives is the atman or soul, the various schools of Buddhism give more complex answers, varying from an inner core to floating spiritual subjectivities.

[22] From at least Augustine onwards, for most of Christian history immortality of the soul has been just as central to Christian belief as resurrection of the body. For some reflections on what this might entail for what is meant by heaven, see the relevant essay in my *God in a Single Vision: Integrating Philosophy and Theology*, 181-90.

suggest that the approach of both east and west might have had their origins in similar questions: a similar motivating religious experience of the transcendent (or overarching) realm as ultimately just (whether experienced in personal terms or not).[23] Indeed, it is possible to detect both East and West across their history experimenting with the same two principal types of metaphysics. The difference is that, whereas in the Vedas Hinduism experimented with a heavenly solution that in due course gave place to the more physical model of reincarnation, Judaism and Christianity began with resurrection only for immortality to assume equal importance in their subsequent history. In other words, although their defining metaphysics has turned out quite differently, the explanation for the difference is provided not by their most fundamental concerns but by where their greater metaphysical focus lay – either on the body (as in the Judaeo-Christian tradition) or the spirit (as in the east). This is not of course to suggest that both positions are equally true, only that determining which is true will be dependent on further complex questions in science and metaphysics. As a matter of fact, few intellectuals in the West now accept that the soul or self is capable of existing apart from the body but that is surely a scientific and philosophical question, not a theological one.[24] Equally, though, as the modern rise in the practice of cremation

---

[23] The words in brackets are intended to cater for the issues being rather differently expressed depending on which religion is in view.

[24] For a defence of the minority view, Richard Swinburne, *The Evolution of the Soul* (Oxford: Oxford University Press, rev. ed., 1997); for a debate about what is at stake, Sidney Schumacher & Richard Swinburne, *Personal Identity* (Oxford: Oxford University Press, 1987).

makes clear, any narrowly literal view of resurrection has also proved increasingly problematic. Both conceptions, therefore, require considerable re-thinking.

In short, stopping the exchange too soon results in too narrow a focus in alleged disagreement about the 'facts' about any future life, whereas the aim of such talk in the first place was less concerned with the mechanics of how the ultimate objective could be achieved and more with the nature of that ultimate goal. Whether one looks to the liberation offered on eastern models or the salvation on Western, for both it is the transformation of the individual that is primary and so the mechanics of how precisely this might be achieved secondary. Of course, as a Christian I naturally tend towards resurrection but this does not mean that I do not acknowledge difficulties, with these increasing the more literally the notion is interpreted.[25]

Enlarging Conceptions of Divinity and the World: That Mysterious Extra

As mentioned in the chapter's introduction, there are at least two aspects to the content of revelation where East and West appear fundamentally to collide: in the question of whether ultimate reality should be conceived in personal terms or not and in what turns out to be the related question of whether this world should be seen as 'real' or not. We shall now consider each question in turn.

---

[25] I take it that resurrection need not necessarily entail any physical continuity. Rather, what matters is that the totality of what constitutes the individual survives, including those aspects that were once best expressed through the physical body.

The Divine as Personal or Impersonal

However plausible our proposed analysis of revelation may seem, human experience of the divine, it will be said, under such an account no longer offers what was once thought to be its principal merit: a strongly interactionist, personal dimension. There has, for instance, long existed, particularly within the three Western monotheisms, a strong presupposition of interaction, as in the various conversation stories told in scripture. While in principle a possibility, such evidence as we have suggests a more indirect route, in a lively awareness that is significantly modified by antecedent beliefs. The experience of Moses on Mount Sinai, for instance, reflects beliefs at the time on how divine presence is mediated, just as Isaiah's vision draws on material from contemporary worship in the Temple.[26] Similarly, in modern times we see this happening in Marian visions and auditions where the recipients' account of the experience is typically coloured by their antecedent expectations and assumptions. The vision of Bernadette Soubirous at Lourdes, for instance, not only reflected the statue of Mary in her local church but also current doctrinal disputes when she introduced herself as Mary of the Immaculate Conception.[27] Admitting this much, though, does not of itself entail that nothing at all of significance could come from the divine

---

[26] Ex.19.16–20; Isaiah 6.1–6. In the former case its location on a mountain reflects a recurring theme in early culture of the divine being found in nature where it reaches closest to the heavens, and so in trees and standing stones no less than in mountains: cf. Gen. 18.1–3; Gen. 28.10–19.

[27] The visions took place in 1858. Pius IX had declared the doctrine of the Immaculate Conception in 1854.

side. Nonetheless, what is most firmly grounded is most likely to lie in continuity with that general theme of otherness. Modern Marian visions are thus probably best interpreted as affirming the deep value of the apparently marginalised and despised rather than as providing support for the details of any particular Marian doctrines.[28]

Mystical experience was once thought to be an exception to such conditioning, with individuals seen as caught up, in whatever tradition, into a recognisable common experience of the Absolute. It is that assumption which not only dominates William James' classic account in his *Varieties of Religious Experience* (1902) but also in many other more explicitly Christian writers.[29] But subsequent decades of research have now disclosed a much more complex reality.[30] As with Marian visions, antecedent beliefs have shaped the character of the experience. Indeed, although it would be an illegitimate exaggeration to say that patristic and medieval writers were solely involved in an exercise in theology rather than in descriptive reflection on what they had encountered,[31] there is much more of the former than was commonly

---

[28] For an excellent consideration of the issues, Chris Maunder, 'Apparitions of Mary as Revelation' in *The Oxford Handbook of Divine Revelation*, 203–18.

[29] For an example of the latter, Evelyn Underhill, *Mysticism* (1901, Oxford: OneWorld, 1999), 86–7.

[30] The preeminent scholar in the field is the American Bernard McGinn (b.1937) who has so far produced seven volumes on the history of mysticism, from its origins up to the seventeenth century (1991 to 2021).

[31] The denial of any interest in experiential issues in Christian medieval writers is most prominent in Denys Turner, *The Darkness of God: Negativity in Christian Mysticism* (Cambridge: Cambridge University Press, 1995).

acknowledged in the past.³² So, although it might be tempting in the face of such complexity to suggest an analysis which necessarily culminates in explicitly personal or even trinitarian experience,³³ taking the traditions of other religions seriously precludes such a simple option. The truth is that, whether one considers the issue experientially or theologically, a plausible case can be made for both the primary Western stress on personal encounter and the east's more impersonal mode. While the former provides reasons for shared communication with humanity, the latter rightly acknowledges the vast differences which continue to exist between finite beings like ourselves and the infinite nature which is the divine source of all.

Most commentators feel compelled to choose between one or the other. But, given that the alternative option is in each case well represented in the other tradition,³⁴ it does look as though experience is pointing to a claim that in some sense both types of experience are true. But how can this be so? The usual objection from the Christian side is that any such position will inevitably lead to something less than a full-blooded doctrine of the Trinity, with, for example, its imagery now seen as only applicable to divine action in the world (an 'economic' Trinity) and

---

[32] For a balanced approach that includes two non-Christian examples (Rumi and Dogen), William Harmless, *Mystics* (New York: Oxford University Press, 2008).

[33] For a hierarchical argument in favour of personal experience of the divine, see R. C. Zaehner, *Mysticism Sacred and Profane* (Oxford: Oxford University Press, 1957).

[34] For example, within Hinduism both Ramanuja (d. 1137) and Madhva (d. 1317) challenged the absolute non-dualism of Shankara (d. 750).

not descriptive of divine reality in itself (the 'immanent' Trinity); or, even if the latter is acknowledged, then the more impersonal reality that lies beyond is seen as necessarily more profound. To see why neither conclusion follows, I want to explore first the ideas of two medieval Christian theologians, Meister Eckhart (1260–1328) from Western Christendom and St Gregory Palamas (1296–1359) from the east.

In the past it was once quite common to dismiss (or commend) Eckhart as profoundly unorthodox.[35] But his condemnation for heresy needs to be set in the context of the fact that not only was he one of the leading Dominican theologians of his day but also that the condemnation in question was part of a wider pattern of other major heresy trials at the time, as well as his admittedly quite frequently incautious (or daring) use of language.[36] He writes from within a scholastic tradition which sometimes challenged the very notion of speaking positively of God.[37] Eckhart does not go quite that far but he does suggest that lying beyond trinitarian language is the essence of divinity as 'Godhead' or 'Ground,' a 'unity' or

---

[35] Schopenhauer equated his own philosophy with that of Buddha and Eckhart, while Rudolph Otto wrote a full-length comparative study on Eckhart and Shankara: Oliver Davies, *Meister Eckhart: Mystical Theologian* (London: SPCK Publishers, 1991), 16–19.

[36] The Beguine, Marguerite Porete, was executed in 1310 and four Spiritual Franciscans burnt at the stake in 1318. Pope John XXII (1316–34) was especially severe.

[37] Both Gilbert of Poitiers and Thierry of Chartres questioned what language might be used of so transcendent a being. William of Auvergne found it necessary in 1241 as Bishop of Paris to condemn the view that the divine essence will never be seen in itself by any human being.

'being' that refuses further predication.[38] Accordingly, Eckhart too is prepared to write: 'God is without name … You must love him as he is; neither God nor spirit, nor person, nor image; rather the One without mixture, pure and luminous.'[39] Yet, while also declaring that 'God and the Godhead are as different from each other as heaven is from earth,'[40] he is also careful to insist that the trinitarian movement from the Ground is not only eternal but also an 'overflowing' (*ebullitio*) in which divinity creates in each one of us a birth that makes us fellow children of God and so capable of union with itself. Equally, however, the soul must strive to get beyond that state of union into 'the silent desert' where divinity at its deepest level can be discovered as it really is.[41] While such claims may seem to lower the value attached to the trinitarian experience and doctrine, there is no doubt that Eckhart's intention is to declare personal and impersonal equally part of divinity in itself. Yet the question remains of whether the imagery adopted does not in the end give too much priority to the impersonal.

At roughly the same time a parallel but unrelated movement was afoot in Eastern Orthodox writings in the work of Gregory Palamas, a monk of Mt Athos and later Archbishop of Thessalonica. Central to his account

---

[38] Eckhart is not consistent in his preferred terminology. For a helpful discussion of the issues, see McGinn's introduction in Edmund Colledge & Bernard McGinn eds., *Meister Eckhart: Classics of Western Spirituality* (London: SPCK Publishers, 1981), 30–39.
[39] From the sermon 'Renovamini spiritu mentis vestrae': trans. In Jeanne Angelet-Hustache. *Master Eckhart* (New York: Harper, 1957), 55.
[40] From the sermon 'Nolite timere eos': Angelet-Hustache, *Master Eckhart*, 54–55.
[41] For a good attempt to re-create the positive side of this imagery, see Harmless, *Mystics*, 127: for example, 'its vast beautiful sameness'.

of divine action was a distinction that, though mediated through the Cappadocian Fathers, came ultimately from Aristotle: that between the divine essence and its energies.[42] On this scheme the absolute transcendence of God is identified with the divine essence, while the human capacity to know and be related to God is mediated through the divine energies as expressed in the life of the Trinity. It is an approach which has been defended by a number of leading twentieth-century Orthodox theologians,[43] but in the main critiqued in Western thought as not only denying full participation in the divine nature but even introducing two gods.[44] One recent form of defence has been to insist that 'the essence is nothing without the energies' and so 'when the deified know God in energy, they know God as God in se (as the divine being is in its own essential reality).'[45] Another, more

---

[42] The debate between Eunomius and Basil seems to have played a key role in shaping Palamas's ideas. For the essence/energies distinction as such in the Cappadocians, see V. Lossky, *The Vision of God* (London: Faith Press, 1963), 64-69.

[43] It is strongly defended by Vladimir Lossky in his *Mystical Theology of the Eastern Church* (New York: St Vladimir's Press, 1956), for example, 73, 77; *In the Image and Likeness of God* (New York: St Vladimir's Press, 1985), 14. Compare also John Meyendorff, *A Study of Gregory Palamas* (New York: St Vladimir's Press, 1998).

[44] This accusation is made by Catherine LaCugna, *God for Us: The Trinity and Christian Life* (San Francisco, CA: Harper, 1991), 189. For a long bibliography of contemporary Western critics, see D. Glenn Butner, 'Communion with God: An Energetic Defence of Gregory Palamas' in *Modern Theology* 32 (2016), 20–45, ft.1. For an Orthodox theologian who is critical, David Bentley Hart, *The Beauty of the Infinite* (Grand Rapids, MI: Eerdmans, 2004), 204.

[45] The conclusion of Butner's article: 40, 43. While no doubt acceptable to traditional Western approaches, it is hard not to see this as the collapse of the very distinction Palamas was trying to make.

promising approach is the suggestion that the distinction between the two forms of God be seen as neither ontological nor epistemological but modal.[46] This is not the place to pursue such subtle distinctions.[47]

More important to note is the sort of implications which can be drawn on the basis of Palamas' distinction. Rather than opening the way to treating the incarnation as an afterthought, the immanent life of the Trinity can now itself be seen as *part* of that same reaching out to the created order which is to be found in the incarnation. Not that this was the sole reason for the existence of the divine in this form, but equally it would be absurd to suppose such an analysis the only way in which to capture the full richness of the divine life. As noted in Chapter 4, though beyond our conception it must be possible for such a reality to go well beyond any of the ways of being with which we are familiar in this world, including personality. Indeed, even within the Trinity thinking becomes instantaneous rather than sequential; emotions occur without any accompanying bodily expression and personal interchange becomes redundant because omniscience already knows.

Attentive readers will have observed that Eckhart and Palamas do not quite agree. For Palamas the individual's experience cannot go beyond being caught up into the life of the Trinity, whereas for Eckhart one should strive to have at least some awareness of the desert landscape

---

[46] Norman Russell, *Gregory Palamas and the Making of Palamism in the Modern Age* (Oxford: Oxford University Press, 2019).

[47] It is worth observing that a major reason why some forms of trinitarian exposition are so minimalist is precisely to avoid making any such distinction.

beyond. However, it was not experiential reasons that primarily motivated Eckhart towards making that further move. It was fear that the too narrow human might be exalted to the detriment of any full appreciation of the vast difference which exists between finite human beings and divine transcendence. Even so, that is scarcely enough reason to exclude one or other type of experience. Perhaps we should say that, while for the Christian scheme of salvation the more personal encounter should take precedence, the other version can stand as a reminder that the divine reality remains infinitely richer than we can ever possibly conceive.

Thus, so far from rejecting accounts in other religions that stress a more impersonal experience, we need to see them as rightly offering support for the minority tradition within Christianity which we have just discussed. While taking the Far East as a whole, insofar as there is some belief in a transcendent deity, it is clearly the impersonal view which predominates. Within India, however, there is a strong competing tradition in the bhakti or devotional tradition which finds support in the particular conceptualisation offered by Ramanuja (d. 1137 CE). Both he and the earlier Shankara (d. 750 CE) were inspired by the same text, the story of Arjuna's encounter with Krishna in the Bhagavata Gita but with quite different results.[48] For Shankara, *moksha* or liberation comes through discovering the unreality of the world and one's core identity (in atman or soul) with Brahman as the divine source

---

[48] For a comparative study, Chakravarthi Ram-Prasad, *Divine Self, Human Self: The Philosophy of Being in Two Gita Commentaries* (London: Bloomsbury, 2013).

beyond all description. By contrast, although his version of *moksha* involves a similar stripping down to essentials, for Ramanuja the atman is not required so much to deny the reality of the world and its mediated experience (indeed in some ways it is rather like God's body),[49] as to retreat to a core where a mutual personal relationship of love for the divine may be developed. Quite different approaches to the same acknowledged ultimate reality are thus being encouraged. Ramanuja offers an enriched understanding of one's past in which karma is clearly seen as part of the Lord's justice,[50] whereas for Shankara the focus is on ultimate mystery in a way that perhaps closely parallels Eckhart.[51]

In short, then, rather than seeking artificial parallels to the Trinity in other religions,[52] we need to see Christianity's own dominant personal approach as complementary to a more balanced approach there also, with personal and impersonal alike acknowledged. Not that this will remove all conflicts,[53] but it will at least open

---

[49] Julius Lipner, *The Face of Truth* (Albany: State University of New York Press, 1986), 37, 121.
[50] Ibid., 79, 101.
[51] Ram-Prasad, *Divine Self*, 22–277, though with Nicholas of Cusa eventually seen as the better parallel.
[52] Such as the traditional version of the Trimurti (Brahma, Vishnu and Shiva) or some more plausible, modern variant (Shiva, Vishnu and Shakti). Or the three internal aspects of Brahman (existence/truth, consciousness, bliss).
[53] Relating Hindu avatar and Christian incarnation, for example, remains a complex issue. The gods are presumed to retain their full powers in such avatars in a way that is not true for Christianity. Nor will it do to treat avatars as simply mythical by comparison since, for many Hindus, the stories are seen as historical (as in the reasons for the protests at Ayodhya in 1992 or objections to the building of a bridge over to Sri Lanka in 2007).

the possibility for a wider debate that takes both positions seriously. For the Christian, I would suggest, the impersonal beyond should be seen not as a higher form of reality but as different. So there remains no justification for any form of radical agnosticism about the divine nature. Instead, precisely because it sallies forth into more personal expression, it can be assumed that some equivalent mode lies behind such action. In other words, the same commitments may be presumed to be there, however radically different in expression. So, as we shall see with the nature of the world, a more mysterious dimension must now be presupposed.

The Reality or Otherwise of the World

Although a gross over-simplification, one way of thinking of the difference between Indian and Christian conceptions of the relation between this world and ultimate reality is to envisage the eastern view of the divine as constituted by a movement away from the world in *moksha* and *nirvana*, whereas within Christianity the movement is towards it, as in the doctrines of incarnation and resurrection. Yet, just as there turns out to be considerable ambiguity in the degree to which eastern philosophy in fact denies the reality of perception, so Christianity's own history forces on us recognition of the challenge towards a more open-ended concept of material reality. Realist schools of thought have in fact found a place in Hinduism,[54] just as Shakyamuni's

---

[54] The Nyaya–Vaisesika school and those influenced by it take reality to be basically as we experience it.

critique of perception proved much less severe than what was to follow in some of Buddhism's later traditions. Equally, as we shall see, within Christianity there have been challenges to the reality of the world which also affected its account of salvation. Not least, one might recall the powerful impact of such ideas in Christian Gnosticism.[55]

That there might again be shared roots in a common experience seems confirmed by the extent to which so much of the history of Christianity has also been world-denying. Just think, for instance, of the whole monastic tradition and its world-denying character. Although the notion is rightly much criticised in modern theology, there remains a sense in which it is true, in its basic premise that too much value has been assigned to this world whenever an exclusive focus is given to this-worldly goals such as marriage, career and so on. Equally, Christians would be wrong to commit themselves to the beauty of their worship spaces to a degree that freezes their worth in material terms rather than situating such value in its ability to evoke a transcendent reality, in other words the ability of the architecture to point beyond itself.

Again, although admittedly isolated examples, there have been at least two cases within the later Christian philosophical tradition where the unreality of the world has been used to bolster belief in God. In an attempt to reconcile the approaches of Augustine and Descartes, the French Oratorian priest, Nicholas Malebranche (1638–1715), in a system known as occasionalism argued

---

[55] With what was rejected, though, usually treated as misunderstood rather than non-existent.

that all our perceptions are mediated through ideas in the mind of God and not via a physical universe. Whereas he delighted in such paradoxes, very different was the philosophy of the Anglican Irish bishop, George Berkeley (1685–1753), writing in the following century. Despite familiar limericks about the tree continuing to be in the quad only because it is observed by God, there was not at all the same love of flouting the conventional. Instead, he saw himself defending common sense, especially against John Locke's unknown substantial reality behind the images we see.[56] Where he did move beyond was in his account of causation. Instead of just observing the regular concurrence of events in nature without any deeper reason, he insists on them being observed as a sign or effect of the power of God. In other words, his account of the physical world was concerned not so much to deny its reality as to draw perceivers into a more sustained impression of its constant source.[57]

More nuanced introductions of the idea have also occurred. One of the most intriguing is how the story of Buddha's own life almost entered the Christian canon through his redescription as a Christian saint. The story of Barlaam and Josaphat was hugely popular in the Middle Ages, entering both the Eastern Orthodox calendar of saints of the Greek and Slavic traditions and appearing in the West in the earlier Roman martyrology, as well as in the *Golden Legend*. While the linguistic steps whereby

---

[56] For Locke 'external bodies' (real physical things), unlike impressions and ideas were supposed to be imperceptible.
[57] One of the most balanced introductions to this aspect of Berkeley remains, G. J. Warnock, *Berkeley* (Harmondsworth: Penguin, 1953), 110–25.

Buddha became Barlaam are difficult to disentangle, the corruption of bodhisattva into Josaphat is more easily recognisable.[58] The story (and thus the name) is thought to have come ultimately from Mahayana Buddhism via Manichaeism. In accordance with that world-denying character, the story goes that Josaphat's father decided to imprison his son in response to a prophecy which he had received (that the son would renounce his princely inheritance as soon as he grew up). But Josaphat encounters the hermit Barlaam, and so does just that, with both father and son eventually alike renouncing earthy riches. The theme was eventually taken up in two seventeenth century plays, one by Lope de Vega (1611) under the same name *Barlaan at Josaphat* and a more famous one from Pedro Calderón called *La vida es sueño* or 'Life is a Dream' (1635).[59] Labelled 'the supreme example of Spanish Golden Age drama',[60] it undoubtedly gains much of its strength from the fact that there are quite a number of other conflicts within the drama, such as illusion versus reality (as in the title), free will versus fate and the proper limits to authority and duty. Nonetheless, at the play's heart lies the conclusion of the imprisoned Segismundo that everything he longs for is actually contained within his cell's walls and indeed within himself.[61] The result is that, when he is given a second

---

[58] From Bodhisat to Josaphat via the Arabic Yudasatf.
[59] Although still frequently performed in Spain, it is seldom to be seen in Great Britain. However, I was lucky to witness a version in 2020 at the Lyceum in Edinburgh, and a Spanish version in 2023.
[60] Gregory Racz ed., *Pedro Calderón de la Barca: Life is a Dream* (London: Penguin, 2006), viii.
[61] See especially Segismundo's magnificent speech at the end of Act III where he begins by parodying the pretensions of kingship but ends by concluding, 'What is life? A thing that seems. / A mirage that falsely

chance at freedom, he now approaches external reality with a new sense of its limitations. For the Catholic Calderón religion is attractive precisely because the secular world is unable to fulfil whatever false promises of happiness it may offer. The dream imagery is, therefore, by no means marginal, in the way that is largely true of Shakespeare's usage.[62] Yet, even if that was not the playwright's intention (as it was not), one can see in Calderón the insights of two very different religions actually drawing quite close to one another. There is a mystery behind the world that makes it wrong to take it at face-value. My point, I hasten to add, is not any superficial equation between the two religions' values. Rather, it has been to identify some grounds for Christians not rejecting out of the hand the alternative perspective. Instead, there is some real potential for dialogue.

Revelation and the Transforming Vision Offered by Religion

I want to end the final section of this chapter on an upbeat note. So much press coverage of religion is so thoroughly negative (from sex scandals to terrorist acts) that it is easy to believe that no alternative account is worthy of credence. But in fact, looking both to religion's past and to its

---

gleams. / Phantom joy, delusive rest / Since is life a dream at best. / And even dreams themselves are dreams': D. F. MacCarthy trans., *Calderon's Dramas* (London: King & Co, 1873), 79.

[62] 'We are such stuff / as dreams are made on, and our little life / is rounded with a sleep': *Tempest* IV, 1, 157–9. There are similar sentiments in Hamlet and Midsummer Night's Dream.

future, a quite different analysis becomes possible. This is what I shall suggest in considering past and future in turn.

A Dynamic Past History

One argument sometimes used against the very idea of revelation is the claim that religious ideas merely reflect the values of the society of which they form part. No doubt this sometimes happens but I doubt if that was ever at the heart of the content of religion, and never more so than in the modern world. So many of our contemporaries presuppose the existence of only one reality (material existence), which inevitably makes religion countercultural in suggesting a reality beyond. But there have also been more specific challenges to its wider cultural setting that, as previous chapters noted,[63] varied as the religion under analysis not only drew on its past but also continued to change, often in direct opposition to society of the time. Such transformations can sometimes be seen to have an impact on more than one religion. There is space to offer only one such example here. My choice focuses on the move to greater emphasis on social interdependence that contrasts so markedly not only with modern individualism and its assertion of the supreme worth of the self-focused ego but also with most earlier versions of how religion understood the social.

---

[63] For example in Chapter 3 with the power of the divine feminine set against a male dominated, hierarchical society, or in Chapter 4 Buddha developing his own more personal teaching against the background of a strictly ordered and ritualistic culture.

I shall illustrate this from the history of two rather different religions (Buddhism and Christianity).

As Seen in Buddhism: From No-Self to Interdependence

Gautama Buddha's denial of the self was partly in response to the Hindu Vedic teaching of his day which asserted the existence of an eternal self or atman and a hierarchical ordering of society in the caste system. Instead of focusing on the liberation of that underlying self, Shakyamuni argued for a more radical solution to the problem of dukka or suffering, in the recognition that there is no such existent, only a no-self (anatman or anatta in the original Pali). All we are is a bundle of constantly changing constituents making for *anicca* or impermanence. Make that thought central and all the concern for the advancement of the ego will disappear. Although the earlier Theravada branch of Buddhism experimented with alternative formulations, including that the question of the nature of the self is simply unanswerable, the focus remained primarily on the individual, with any social concerns seen as strictly subordinate.

All that was to change with Mahayana Buddhism. Its new stress on the work of Bodhisatvas and even the introduction of notions of grace was noted in Chapters 5 and 6. But here we may observe how such a social dimension was considerably enhanced by new understandings of why there is no-self. *Sunyata* or 'emptiness' became the key concept, thanks largely to the work of Nagarjuna and the second-century philosophical school he founded, called Madyamika ('the school of the middle way'). Alleged entities including the self are really empty, having in and from themselves no independent self-existence.

Instead, phenomena only exist insofar as they related to other things; so, strictly speaking, we can neither affirm nor deny their existence, except in so far as we take into account such relationships.

Unfortunately, alongside this development there emerged another doctrine that does not fit quite so easily with emptiness and impermanence. This is the notion of 'Buddha nature', usually explicated as the seed or potential in all things for enlightenment. That notion of potential is certainly inherent in the most common term used.[64] Where complications come is in some of the tradition asserting that such a nature is after all an inner core. Perhaps, though, the more consistent position would be to say that such a nature exists (it is what we are) rather than that any particular individual possesses it. Pursuit of the Buddha nature is, therefore, the wrong point at which to place the emphasis. Emptiness remains more central. This is where, as we saw in Chapter 6, Zen Buddhism for the most part ended up.

But interaction with other contemporary schools of Buddhism has also significantly modified where such emptiness is seen to point. As other Japanese and East Asian traditions have not been slow to observe, the cultivation of emptiness helps disclose the dependence of ourselves on other human beings, both present and past. The point becomes central to the way in which the contemporary Vietnamese monk, Thick Nhat Hanh, translated and commented on the Heart Sutra. Interdependence is noted everywhere. Our bodily limits

---

[64] *Tagathatagarba* or, literally, 'the womb of the thus gone' or 'enlightened one'.

are seen as quite artificial in a scenario in which we have already been shaped by the lives of our parents and grandparents and where even mutual enemies are found to help in the self-definition of their opponents.[65] Escape from the ego is thus secured less by turning inwards and more by discovering the numerous ways in which we are who we are only in virtue of how others have impacted on us. So, while Buddhism began as a retreat from what was seen as an excessively narrow emphasis on the social side in Hinduism, it has in the end returned to such an emphasis but now modified by a scenario in which hierarchy no longer plays any part.

The point of these reflections is to suggest that it was not just in Bodhisatvas and grace that Mahayana Buddhism moved in a more outward-looking direction but also in contemplating what was involved in the notion of self as emptiness. While it is possible to interpret that judgement in largely negative terms, a positive assessment is also possible. Contemporary Buddhism may be seen to be working towards emptiness through positive commitment to others: the interdependency of us all. In short, Buddhism has travelled very far from the rather narrow focus on individual salvation with which the religion began.

As Seen in Christianity: From Hierarchy to Kenosis

Christianity too has travelled far from where understanding of its texts once stood. In the Hebrew Bible so strong was its social emphasis that even corporate notions of

---

[65] Thich Nhat Hanh, *The Other Shore* (Berkeley: Parallax Press, 2017). For familiar relations, 47, 53, 77; for enemies, 60–65.

responsibility and punishment were once entertained. Although eventually rejected,[66] the notion of the people of Israel retained a strongly social conception, as did Jesus' preaching of the kingdom of God. While Paul's analogy of the body stressed mutual interdependence, it was not long before more hierarchical notions began to prevail in the Catholic epistles and some other early Christian writings.[67] Such stress on social hierarchy continued into the medieval period. Only during the Reformation period did a much more personal emphasis develop, on the Catholic side almost as much as on the Protestant. Whereas the patristic period had asserted the indispensability of the church to salvation (*extra ecclesiam nulla salus*), at least since the time of the Counter-Reformation onwards the expectation in the confessional was quite different, in the itemisation of particular acts.[68] Catholics too were now seeking a more personalised salvation. The result has been in modern times a view of salvation just as much individualised as the search for self-fulfilment in secular society at large. Even so, most churches remained strongly hierarchical, Protestant no less than Catholic. Despite apparently democratic institutions such as elders, the minister continued to dominate church worship.

---

[66] For example, Ex.20.5; Joshua 7. 24–6 (the whole family of Achan is punished for a crime he alone committed). Contrast Ezek.18.19–20.

[67] Contrast I Cor. 12.12–30 with the Catholic epistles and still more Ignatius of Antioch's 'one God, one bishop'.

[68] Note how confession became part of the individual's spiritual training whereas previously it had functioned much more formally (required once a year by the Fourth Lateran Council in 1215).

It is this perspective which has now been effectively challenged by new ways of approaching the incarnation, forced on the church by developments in biblical scholarship. On the traditional understanding the human nature of Jesus was presumed always to act under the control and direction of his divine nature. A hierarchical model was thus maintained throughout. Now, however, modern biblical scholarship has compelled a rethink. Kenotic reinterpretations in effect envisage the human Jesus as subject to precisely the same sort of constraints as any other human being. We now know that Jesus was very much affected by the culture of his time, even as in dialogue with his Father he sought to transcend it in various ways.[69] Indeed, one might argue that the approach taken in this book increases the plausibility of a kenotic approach to the incarnation precisely because such a notion can now be seen as entirely consonant with the general pattern of divine action that is to be found elsewhere.

More pertinent here, the model of the divine direction of the human has been replaced by one in which the divine speaks through a human very much dependent on the culture in which he is set. This applies not only to the forms in which Jesus' ministry is expressed but also even to the discovery of his full significance. Thus, it appears that it was only in the light of the resurrection that his disciples appreciated who he really was. While sceptics might use this fact to call into question the evidence for Jesus'

---

[69] For detailed consideration of issues arising from kenosis, see my *Divine Humanity: Kenosis and the Construction of a Christian Theology* (Waco, TX: Baylor University Press, 2011).

divinity, what it suggests to me instead is a thoroughly interdependent view of Jesus' significance, of Jesus setting the pattern of how God operates in the world: through acceptance of the need to be willing to be dependent on the imagery and thought forms of whatever cultural context within which the divine message is addressed.

Looking to the Future

And so, finally, to what the future might bring. One possibility is of course that fear of the modern world will lead the religious to retreat into reactionary perspectives that, in order to condemn present secular society, make their own religion's past appear more uniform and uncompromising than it really was. Currently, this is a phenomenon affecting all religions to some degree but especially Islam and, more recently, Hinduism also. But some aspects of past history give grounds for hope. It is not so long in the past that Christians felt in conscience unable to attend worship led by those of other denominations,[70] whereas for at least a century there have been increasing signs of willingness to learn, for example on questions of liturgical reform among Protestants from Roman Catholic practice or on questions of biblical scholarship the other way round. So it is not impossible to envisage similar progress in interfaith relationships, not least given sufficient sympathetic and imaginative openness to the other.

---

[70] As with Newman and Keble when Newman converted to Rome in 1845. Melvyn Bragg reports how even in the 1990s Roman Catholic mourners remained outside the parish church at his father's funeral in Wigton in northern England: *Back in the Day: A Memoir* (London: Hodder & Stoughton, 2022).

Sympathetic Openness

Throughout this book I have sought to emphasise how Christians might learn from other religions, precisely by not reducing them to a uniform sameness: Confucianism, for instance, offering new perspectives on the value of ritual attitudes within society, Daoism help with attitudes to the beginning and end of life or Shintoism a more immanent conception of the divine's relationship with nature and thus the importance of the environment. But we should not delude ourselves into thinking that such dialogue will ever be easy. Even where strong parallels exist, the results might not turn out as Christians would hope. For example, even if some Hindus were to concede that Krishna is not an historical avatar whereas Jesus was historical, that would not of itself induce them to see Jesus as a more rounded completion of the same idea. Indeed, a comparable situation already exists with respect to Buddhism. Although Gautama's historicity is almost universally acknowledged, the tendency within Hinduism has been to include him among other acknowledged but 'unhistorical' avatars, with Buddhism seen as only one possible approach among several.[71] Likewise, even if Muslim scholars were generally to concede that Muhammad's objection to the Trinity was to a form which Christians would also admit was a perversion,[72]

---

[71] Article 25 of the Indian constitution does not recognise Buddhism as a separate religion. In 2018 a group was formed to pressurize the state to make such an acknowledgement.

[72] See the discussion in Chapter 7, 302–3.

this would not of itself lead them to dismiss entirely their underlying objection to its perceived undermining of the unity of God, although recognition of a common concern for a deeper unitary reality behind such an expression might be of some limited help. More surprising is the fact that it will not necessarily be the most fundamental principles that will prove the most intractable in securing agreement. A case in point is Hinduism's caste system. Despite Mahatma Gandhi's sustained attempt at a defence, it remains a moral outrage, the only appropriate response to which is to act towards elimination of the system. Yet over eighty per cent of Indians continue to marry within caste. Even so, Christians should hesitate to adopt an attitude of absolute superiority since Christian medieval society was for the most part just as hierarchical and class has continued to affect church structures until comparatively recently.[73]

That said, situations of potential conflict will often be greatly eased if the initial approach is one of sympathetic identification with what the other religion has been trying to achieve. I recall a non-believing colleague once telling me that he had decided to give 'Christianity a fair chance' and so proposed reading the Bible from its opening cover to its last page. On that scenario he was unlikely to get beyond Leviticus with all its technical, ritual legislation! In the same way, the Qur'an would need to be read selectively in order to appreciate its full worth, and indeed with some prior knowledge of the stories upon which it

---

[73] Although during the medieval period the church did make possible the elevation of poor children to major posts, one might contrast the impact of pew rents in the post-Reformation church.

builds, since so often the work assumes readers' awareness of various details which are not explicitly repeated.[74] Equally, without some awareness of the role served by Buddhist mythological exaggerations, readers are unlikely to get to the moral heart of texts such as the Lotus Sutra.[75] The same point applies equally to the great religious classics of other traditions which, though not classed as revelatory, nonetheless have been used to deepen faith, such as the two great Hindu epics of the *Mahabharata* and the *Ramayana*, the Chinese Buddhist classic *The Journey to the West* or Islam's greatest poet, Rumi.

There continue to be some churches which ban practices such as yoga from their church halls on the grounds of potential contamination by another religion. That is a very short-sighted attitude, as is the general rejection of others' meditative practices. Sometimes at least there are close parallels as between Pure Land Buddhist mantras and the Orthodox Jesus prayer,[76] while at other times one can see more wisdom elsewhere in accommodating body and mind to a common purpose. Contrast, for instance, the rather inadequate medieval misericord with the great attention to posture for mediation in the East.[77] Of course, Christian growth is only possible through deep immersion in one's own tradition. Even so, supplementing it in such ways can indeed help produce a richer vision of the divine address to humanity, together with a deeper comprehension of the overall purposes of that divine reality for this world.

[74] See Chapter 7.   [75] See further Chapter 5.
[76] See further Chapter 6.
[77] Misericords were intended as rests for monks during services while still giving the impression of them standing. But they provided relief rather than actual comfort.

No one can deny that this is likely to prove a challenging task. Taking the other with maximum seriousness will continue to be a difficult task. But, if the various religions can acknowledge their many similarities in foundation and in goal, there is no reason why they cannot shake off the accusation of pure subjectivism and so contribute successfully (under God) to the shaping of a glorious future for humanity and its wider setting in the natural world.

Imaginative Openness

In facilitating such change, a key role should be accorded to the imagination, for it is precisely through thinking through the implications of certain storied versions of doctrine that various corrections and possible improvements can be envisaged. That proved to be one way in which to understand Muhammad's comments about the corruptions present in Jewish and Christian scriptures. A similar influence can also be seen to be at work in the various changes made to classical and Hindu myths. It was for this reason that I began our examination of other contemporary religions in what must have seemed to many readers a surprising place, in the Hindu notion of darshan.[78] It is so easy for advocates of Western monotheism to find in India's plethora of imagery only indications of the idolatry that their own scriptures already so fiercely condemn. But a more complicated analysis was found to be required, according to which it is the dogmatic interpretation of biblical words and texts which itself sometimes more nearly approximates to idolatry: whenever, that is,

---

[78] See Chapter 3.

they are manipulated to confine the divine within certain precisely defined limits. By contrast, visual imagery is more easily able to move in the opposite direction in opening up a range of possibilities. One way Hindu temples do this is by offering a barrage of different stories as the worshipper approaches the central shrine (rather than just one single narrative). But another is that even within the narrative of a single god the story is not always developed or interpreted in precisely the same way.[79] Looking at matters from the perspective of darshan, the address of the gods can thus be seen to be adapted to speak to specific times and places in new ways, as for example in the rise or fall of various cults in the modern age or again in the current huge popularity of pilgrimage.

A major reason for thinking this an important insight is because for too long the three Western monotheisms have conceived of themselves as essentially verbal religions, whereas their presentation could become more dynamic, more creative, indeed more open, if they recognised the pressure towards the visual as well as the verbal, in both their past as well as in the present day. It is, for example, not just the modern world that has produced numerous Jewish artists, there is now a wealth of evidence for the existence of Jewish visual art in earlier times.[80]

---

[79] For numerous examples, see Wendy Doniger, *The Hindus: An Alternative History* (Oxford: Oxford University Press, 2010). However, it should be noted that she uses 'the infinite inventiveness of this great civilization' (689) simply to argue against intolerance, not to suggest myth as a way of accessing truth.

[80] Two relevant monographs are Steven Fine, *Art and Judaism in the Greco-Roman World* (2005); Uzi Leibner & Catherine Hezser eds., *Jewish Art in its Late Antique Context* (2016).

Equally, in Christianity, although the Reformation pronounced itself suspicious, more careful examination of what actually happened reveals a more complex story. For example, illustrated bibles were the norm in nineteenth-century Britain, while in the twentieth century one particular image of Jesus dominated Protestant reflection in the United States.[81]

However, the biggest surprise is perhaps what happened (and continues to happen) within Islam. In Chapter 7 I adopted the conventional judgement that architecture is the pre-eminent Muslim visual art. It would be easy to deem this a consequence of the rejection of more obvious forms of visual imagery, but even in mosques the line has not always been clear. Surviving in the famous Great (Umayyad) Mosque in Damascus (c. 715 CE) are some very fine landscape mosaics. Many other famous mosques are found with texts from the Qur'an used to conjure images of beauty rather than functioning primarily as injunctions towards a particular form of conduct.[82] Indeed, right at the centre of many mosques in front of the mihrab is often a lit lamp with the famous Light verse from the Qur'an inscribed on it.[83] It is a text which has offered rich veins of imagery, not just as a description of Allah or the Qur'an but also even of Mohammad or of his

---

[81] *The Head of Christ* by Werner Sallman (1892–1968), reproduced over half a billion times worldwide by the end of the twentieth century. For a discussion of this and other popular images, David Morgan, *A History and Theory of Popular Religious Images* (Berkeley: University of California Press, 1998).

[82] Not least because the text is often illegible either due to its positioning or because an old-fashioned form of script is used.

[83] Sura 24.35.

daughter Fatima.[84] It also provides the title for one of the primary sources of Sufi mysticism, Al-Ghazali's *The Niche of Lights*.[85] In a recent study by students at a Protestant seminary in California of Buddhist and Muslim practice, it is encouraging to note how a starting point in comparing beliefs or even texts is seen as not necessarily the best way forward.[86] Instead, the members of the various communities needed to be engaged on questions relating to the actual ritual context of their practices. Although with Islam architecture continued to be given primary emphasis, there was also the recognition of something more; for example, in the way Arabic as a foreign language provides expressions of the faith with greater aesthetic lustre or Islam's wide use of arabesque conjures up a strong sense of a dynamic, creative God.[87]

These are comments that provide a fitting prelude to another scholar's call for a more extensive revision of our understanding of Islam's attitude to images. Here I refer to Jamal J. Elias in his work, *Aisha's Cushion* (2012). It is so easy to think of Islam exercising an absolute prohibition on any imagery whatsoever and to find this reflected in the strict rules followed by the 1976 film *Muhammad* or, still more so,

---

[84] See William A. Graham, 'Light in the Qur'an and early Islamic exegesis' in Jonathan Bloom & Sheila Blair (eds.), *God Is the Light of the Heavens and the Earth: Light in Islamic Art and Culture* (New Haven, CT: Yale University Press, 2015), 43–59.

[85] From late in al-Ghazali's career, it is a short work which elaborates how imagery from the seen world can in general be used as a means of drawing closer to the unseen.

[86] William A. Dyrness, *Senses of Devotion: Interfaith Aesthetics in Buddhist and Muslim Communities* (Eugene, OR: Cascade, 2013), esp. 125–26.

[87] For the importance of architecture, for example, 93, 115–21; for arabesque, 26; for those without Arabic as a first language, 69–70.

in the destruction of the impressive Bamiyan statues of the Buddha in 2001 in Afghanistan.[88] But the fact that the latter survived for so long opens up the possibility of a more complex account. Indeed, Elias' choice of book title is based on a hadith which speaks of Muhammad's wife, Aisha, preserving a condemned image as a cushion.[89] The value of Christian and even Hindu art could be acknowledged, even as it was criticised for wasting resources in the deployment of what was fundamentally intended as a means of exchange.[90] Again, if copying is rejected, analogical representation is not, and this is identified both in imagist dreams and in the way that calligraphy functions more than just as a representation of the text.[91] Even in Samarkand's famous central square (Ragistan), one is confronted by analogical imagery, with partially mythical creatures prominently displayed above the entrance to the Sher Dor madrassah. While in theory justified on the basis of the imagery's non-realist format,[92] it is hard not to detect Sufism pleading for just such a more imaginative approach to the visual.

---

[88] In deference to Muslim susceptibilities the film excluded any visual representation of the Prophet. Created between the second and fifth century, no attempt was made to destroy the 175 ft high Bamiyan structures until under the Taliban.

[89] J. J. Elias, *Aisha's Cushion: Religious Art, Perception and Practice in Islam* (Cambridge, MA.: Harvard University Press, 2012), esp. 1–2, 9–10.

[90] Ibid. For positive evaluations, 87–91, 113–29, 137; for criticism of the misuse of gold and other resources, 131–32.

[91] Ibid. For dreams, 220–5; for calligraphy and text, 268-83.

[92] Two lions that are in some ways like tigers or snow leopards pursue deer, while suns with a human face emerge on their backs. While sometimes interpreted as the glorification of its builder, more commonly the images are seen as indicating the need of those attending the madrassah to pursue knowledge but always subject to acknowledgement of greater realities.

The result is the contemporary paradox of truck drivers in conservative Pakistan who, so far from rejecting all forms of art, adorn their trucks with images of the Ka'ba and the Prophet's Mosque in Medina, accompanied by invocations of Allah and Muhammad.[93] In short, it is a mistake to judge Islam's attitudes by its extremes. Not only does a far greater range of attitudes need to be acknowledged, there is a more basic issue that needs to be faced. What matters for Muslims is not the image as such but how it is used. Even Islam can admit that, when appropriately applied, imagery may sometimes draw the believer closer to God. So even the religion most suspicious of the visual can be seen as also imaginatively using non-verbal means to relate to the different or alternative form of reality which is the divine.

In short, whether we consider openness to change in the past or change in response to contemporary options (as here), the frequent portrayal in the wider secular world of religion as hostile to change clearly belies a more complex reality. On the contrary, in pursuit of transformative potential religion can find itself not only modifying its past but also potentially amenable to further changes in the future. The only condition for this to happen is that full sway is allowed to the sympathetic and imaginative openness which is its natural response to the call of the Other in revelation. A final topic remains, to set my own position here in relation to some of the major past writings on the subject.

[93] Elias, *Aisha's Cushion*, 279–81. The text is integrated with the images so as to be appropriately read by viewers, giving preference to the Ka'ba as Allah's sacred place in Mecca.

9
Beyond Inclusivism and Pluralism

This last chapter might in some ways be described as an Appendix. My own investigations concluded with Chapter 8. Some have suggested, though, that it would be useful to see my own particular approach set within the more recent history of such dialogue. To that end I first reflect on the work of some distinguished writers in the field before concluding by noting other alternative ways of advancing dialogue.

Reflecting on Earlier Interfaith Works

From my own perspective I would see myself going well beyond both inclusivist and pluralist perspectives. In respect of the former, I do not believe it adequate merely to concede that other religions also constitute an address from the divine and can thus help lead towards the more perfect vision which Christianity offers. Also required is acknowledgement of the likelihood that, in some respects at least, the adherents of other faiths may well have perceived the overall nature of divine reality rather better than is true of one's own native religion. This is because all revelation takes place against the background of prior conditioning of perceptions by the historical shaping of the traditions in which believers stand. Balanced, though, against those inevitable limitations, sometimes real insights can be generated that are not yet fully available in other traditions. Accordingly, it is not just the common humanity of others that demands respect for their religious views but also the expectation that there will be things to learn from the positions and practice to which they adhere. In the preceding chapters various examples of precisely this point were provided for each of the major faiths.

In making such suggestions I was certainly not intending to imply that the examples cited were the only benefits on offer, nor that the encounter would necessarily always be positive. Other religions, like Christianity itself, have their negative features that need to be frankly acknowledged, not simply circumvented in polite silence. Examples would include the caste system in Hinduism and fundamentalist violence in Islam, as well as more specific problems such as the part played by Buddhist monks in driving the Muslim Rohingya out of Myanmar. Again, while the abandonment of conventional Christian supersessionist claims in relating Judaism and Christianity is often rightly promoted as a model for relations with other religions, such an admission should not of course lead to the automatic endorsement of every presumed expression of that continuing covenant with Judaism. Even within the Hebrew scriptures there is sometimes displayed a regrettable, rather overweening sense of superiority over other peoples.[1] A dangerous contemporary equivalent is to be found in some present-day Israeli presumptions about what has been labelled

---

[1] Isaiah 60 is typical. While initially talk is in terms of how 'nations shall come to your light' (v.3), the image is quickly transformed into one of subjugation: 'the wealth of the nations shall come to you' (v. 5).

'exceptionalism'.[2] Yet, drawing attention to such failures in others does nothing of course to exempt one's own religion from similar strictures. An obvious case in point has been the manipulation of sexuality within Christianity to produce not only excesses of guilt but also to keep women in subjugation.[3] So it is as a religion also at fault that one must speak of failures and indeed corruptions on the part of other faiths.

The pluralist approach believes that it has a better answer in insisting on a level playing field between all religions: that none should be seen as better or worse than any other.[4] Some qualification in respect of the more distant religions of the past is quite commonly proposed.[5] However, no comparative judgement appears to be canvassed for present-day major religions. Instead, a common

---

[2] Although the claim has been made by numerous peoples in the past, the Israeli version is particularly dangerous since it argues that the dangers to which Jews have been subject in the past exempts them from common moral constraints in defending themselves in the present.

[3] For centuries strict demands for feminine purity ran alongside a relaxed toleration of masculine promiscuity.

[4] Not that this is intended to exclude all learning from one another. Particularly at the practical level, Christian pluralists are often keen to borrow from other religions, for example Buddhist and Hindu meditation techniques. However, at the more theoretical level, the push toward parity seems almost always to underestimate and indeed undervalue difference: for example Jesus and Muhammad both seen as prophets, rather than an exploration of their distinctive contributions and major differences.

[5] Care, though, is needed here also. Even something as horrendous as human sacrifice was not always solely motivated by manipulation of other humans or the divine. For an attempt at an alternative view on one contentious case, see my 'Human Sacrifice and Two Imaginative Worlds: Aztec and Christian: Finding God in Evil' in Julia Meszaros & Johannes Zachhuber eds., *Sacrifice and Modern Thought* (Oxford: Oxford University Press, 2013), 180–96.

pattern is evident in most of the leading figures in comparative theology. For instance, although the Canadian Presbyterian, Wilfred Cantwell Smith (1916–2000), began his academic career as very much the Christian minister and theologian looking at Islam from the outside,[6] his later position, especially in his classic and highly influential *The Meaning and End of Religion* (1962), was to insist that it was only in modern times that a reification of 'religion' as distinct belief systems has occurred. Particularly in the past but even today one could detect two common elements shared across all religions in a personally orientated faith and belief in a transcendent, divine reality.[7] Again, John Hick (1922–2012) moved from an explicitly Christian philosophy of religion to one in which all religions were seen as placed at an equal distance from what he called the Real.[8] Or, to take a third example, prior to his appointment as Regius Professor of Divinity at Oxford in 1991 Keith Ward (b. 1938) was often proclaimed as a defender of Christian 'orthodoxy'. Whereas *Divine Action* (1990) could be seen as marking

---

[6] For an early example, W. C. Smith, *Modern Islam in India* (Lahore: Muhammad Ashraf, 1946 rev. ed.). Intriguingly, prior to what actually happened at Partition, he declared exchange of populations 'utterly impractical' (323).

[7] While he is right to critique the sharp distinctions often made in the modern world, too much attention is given to the actual use of the term 'religion' and not enough to the often quite different perceptions which have accompanied such personal faith.

[8] John Hick, *An Interpretation of Religion: Human Responses to the Transcendent* (Basingstoke: Macmillan, 1989), 10–11. An equality of access is asserted with differences explained phenomenally. The Real in itself is treated as equidistant from all: 233–51. See also John Hick, *Disputed Questions in Theology and Philosophy of Religion* (London: Macmillan, 1993).

the culmination of that trend, *A Vision to Pursue* (1991) suggested a new direction,[9] which was worked out subsequently in five volumes in comparative theology of impressive range where something very much closer to parity was promulgated.[10]

There are two reasons why I believe it inadvisable to follow such precedents. The first concerns the question of what it really means to respect another's position. Although this may be something of a parody, the pluralist's position can come across as presupposing that the only way to honour the religious other is by placing them on a par with oneself, to assume that they are really affirming fundamentally the same thing, even if rather differently expressed. But is this not patronising to say the least, especially if the other continues to insist on fundamental oppositions? Is the expression of such difference no longer to be respected? This is by no means a minor issue. In actual fact, it is indicative of a problem that is endemic to modern liberalism: the extent to which significant difference is actually tolerated. In this book the question was first raised in our discussion of Confucian values, where we suggested that its emphasis on *ren* or 'benevolence' might be used to bolster a demand to respect others' right to vote and express an opinion,

---

[9] Jesus is 'God's definitive self-disclosure' in *Divine Action* (London: Collins, 1990), 196, whereas in *A Vision to Pursue* incarnation is reinterpreted as 'acting in and through Jesus' and so seen as parallel to 'God acting in and through *Torah*, *Sharia*, and Guru Nanak as well' (London: SCM Press, 1991), 123–24.

[10] *Religion and Revelation* (1994); *Religion and Creation* (1996); *Religion and Human Nature* (1998); *Religion and Community* (2000); *Religion and Human Fulfilment* (2008).

even where it is certain that such voting will have contrary aims to one's own. The present situation in the United States in the light of culture wars and the recent reversal of the 1973 Roe v Wade judgement on abortion provides another good example. Typically, American media presents only one side of the issue, with either emphasis placed on the violation of women's absolute right over their own bodies or else the unborn child's unqualified right to life.[11] But seldom are these conflicting positions discussed together or with an acknowledgement of any underlying moral tension that might pull in two competing directions. Indeed, the conflicts over such widely diverging perspectives have become so serious that several analyses now suggest that the United States is on the verge of civil war or else the breakup of the union.[12]

No doubt these suppositions are exaggerated. Nonetheless, they do demonstrate where lack of respect for difference might lead. The two aspects to such debates need to be properly weighed and given an equal hearing. Equally, in religion it is surely rather patronising to suggest that it is always the case that either one or the other has misunderstood their own religion (the usual strategy of the pluralist), with the one in error always taken to be whoever makes the more substantial claim. Of course, that could be true but it is surely significant that such an

---

[11] As, for example, in the contrasting presentations from CNN and Fox News.
[12] See, for example, Stephen Marche, *The Next Civil War: Dispatches from the American Future* (2022); Barbara F. Walter, *How Civil Wars Start: And How to Stop Them* (2022); Steven Simon & Jonathan Stevenson, 'These Disunited States' in *New York Review of Books*, Sept. 22, 2022, 51–53.

analysis usually flies in the face of what most adherents actually believe (in the case of Christianity, the divinity of Christ; in the case of Islam the finality of Mohammad).

But there is another reason more directly and immediately connected with what has gone before. This is the extent to which cultural conditioning within different traditions not only makes such surface comparisons and reinterpretations difficult, it also results in a flattened landscape in the context of which original discoveries are less likely to be detected. The other's teaching becomes reinterpreted as simply a shared perspective rather than one that offers genuine new insights. Take Ward on the pantheism of the Hindu medieval theologian Ramanuja and his identification of soul (*atman*) and the ultimate reality of Brahman. Ward informs us that Christianity in effect takes a similar view, inasmuch as it asserts that God was in Christ and that Christians are part of the body of Christ, and so in effect part of God.[13] Apart from this rather dubious syllogism,[14] the history of the Christian tradition would in any case caution against total equation of its beliefs with pantheism precisely because there is a clear sense in which, however much one may turn to find God within, it is also important that an alternative aspect be also identified: an otherness that enables human beings to acknowledge dependence as a way of making progress in

---

[13] Bentall Lectures at the University of Calgary on 'Christianity and the Indian Religious Traditions', available on YouTube.
[14] With metaphorical language different rules of discourse apply. Even where it is the same theologian offering the different images as in this case (Paul), it does not follow that the same implications hold as would apply if the terms were being used more literally. In making such comparisons metaphor always carries with it a 'yes' and a 'no'.

the spiritual life. In other words, divine transcendence or otherness is no less important than divine immanence. Again, in reconciling Islam, Ward insists on a modalist view of the Trinity and a non-incarnational account of the life and significance of Jesus.[15] But might not the doctrine of the incarnation, particularly in its more recent kenotic form, be precisely the new element in revelation that can offer to world religions in general an expression of something radically new about how service is meant to apply? Again, Ward has a tendency to parody social accounts of the Trinity.[16] But could not such an account tell us something instead about the richness of the divine life, as Chapter 8 suggested?

This is not to suggest that such dialogue could never result in major revision of some of the central positions of Christianity. Some have already been noted. But if a still more central example is desired, although not discussed in this book, I would have no hesitation in including traditional approaches to the atonement.[17] So my point is not the avoidance of major revision. Rather, it is that a pluralist approach is basically reductive and so is unable to deliver genuine new insights. At most, terminology is re-described to fit more than one religion, rather than anything radically new seen to be disclosed. In part, this may be because theology is viewed as human construction rather than reception of a divine address in revelation.

---

[15] Interview with Paul Williams on YouTube: 2 May 2021.
[16] For example, 'an everlasting committee meeting – a man, a boy and a mysterious bird, locked forever in mutual flattery': *The Turn of the Tide* (London: BBC, 1986), 127.
[17] For a partial explanation, see my *Gospel as Work of Art: Imaginative Truth and the Open Text* (Grand Rapids, MI: Eerdmans, 2024), ch. 12.

In part, it may also be due to an inadequate view of what it is to respect the other where real difference is valued rather than elided. But, however generated, what is thereby ignored is the real creativity that can come about when alternative approaches are fully acknowledged and their distinctive insights duly appropriated. Take the mutual exclusivism which currently plagues relations between Hinduism and Islam in the Indian subcontinent. Instead of an implausible parity, it is possible to encourage exploration of the subcontinent's religious history in which each faith has in the past been enriched by the other. Hinduism learned of the need to attach greater importance to the issue of monotheism, Islam to questions of religious experience.[18]

This different approach can be nicely illustrated by the work of two Roman Catholic theologians. Although Peter Phan (b. 1943) was earlier criticised by the Vatican for apparently calling into question certain Catholic beliefs,[19] a later volume makes it quite clear that he would wish to stand firm with the doctrines of the Trinity and incarnation, even as at the same time he makes significant moves towards Asian religions.[20] By contrast, Paul Knitter (b. 1939) so redefines Christianity in order to make it comparable with Buddhism that it is no longer clear whether he remains a follower of Christianity at all. This may sound unkind but major elements such as divine

---

[18] Particularly through the mediation of Sufism.
[19] For the content of *Being Religious Interreligiously: Asian Perspectives on Interfaith Dialogue* (Maryknoll, NY: Orbis, 2004).
[20] Peter C. Phan, *The Joy of Religious Pluralism: A Personal Journey* (Maryknoll, NY: Orbis, 2017). For his approach to Trinity and incarnation, 51–98.

transcendence or human sin simply disappear.[21] His fellow Catholic, Roger Haight (b.1936), tries hard to be sympathetic but an implicit critique runs through their common discussion, that Knitter is so concerned with establishing a common view that real differences are simply circumvented rather than faced.[22] Yet, given that Knitter opts for a version of Mahayana Buddhism, it is not clear why he felt he had to go quite so far along the path he does. As he himself admits, some versions of Mahayana actually come quite close to Christian stress on transcendence,[23] while there is much to learn from its emphasis on interdependence and forms of meditation, both of which Phan succeeds in bringing to prominence. Again, rather than Cantwell Smith's proposals for absolute parity, one might consider how the English inclusivist Kenneth Cragg (1913–2012), scholar of Islam, missionary and bishop, pursued the question of Christian relations with Islam. For most of his life, while showing great respect for Muhammad as a prophet of God, he insisted that elements of Islam paralleled Christianity but were never equal to it, as in Muhammad's Christ-like pacifist suffering during his ministry at Mecca. While for most of Cragg's career that assessment entailed a negative judgement on Muhammad's later activity in Medina, intriguingly

---

[21] Paul F. Knitter, *Without Buddha I Could Not be a Christian* (London: Oneworld, 2009). The first chapter attacks the notion of God as transcendent Other, the second, God as personal: 1–52.

[22] Paul Knitter & Roger Haight, *Jesus and Buddha: Friends in Conversation* (Maryknoll, NY: Orbis, 2015). For Haight the aim is not agreement (32). Indeed, distinctions may be made more apparent (24), such as the centrality of the personal to Christianity (44, 88) or its strongly directional understanding of personal and social history (51–52).

[23] For example, *Without Buddha*, 109–10.

towards the end of life Cragg's studies led him to a rather different conclusion, with this period now treated as a progressive insight into how the exploited were to be defended and from which Christianity too might learn: 'Perhaps it is the vocation of Islam among the religions to represent the indispensability of the power dimension in human affairs and in the will, however precarious, to subdue those affairs to the authority which is God's alone?'[24] His inclusivism had been modified in the direction advocated here.

Methods of Dialogue

Such factors suggest to me that three different types of dialogue need to be differentiated. First, there are the practical sides of cooperation and the willingness of some to live as though part of the other's practices. There are some familiar learned and holy examples of this phenomenon, such as Bede Griffiths, Raimon Pannikar, Aloysius Pieris and Thomas Merton. It would, however, be unreasonable to expect such a degree of commitment from the great mass of any religious group. In any case, merging of identities should not be the aim but a better understanding, one of the other. Far from being a minor objective, it requires real effort to think oneself into the other's position and in the process take their concerns seriously. This could be facilitated by occasional attendance at each other's

[24] For a detailed comparison between Cragg and Smith, including this change of mind (pursued particularly in a 1998 essay and, more briefly in his 1999 book *The Weight in the Word*), see Bård Maeland, *Rewarding Encounters: Islam and the Comparative Theologies of Kenneth Cragg and Wilfred Cantwell Smith* (London: Melisende, 2003), esp. 260–76.

worship or even the inclusion of readings or prayers from the other religion as part of one's own worship. This need not necessarily be syncretistic. Sometimes much the same sentiments can be found, and in any case there is of course the precedent set by having the Hebrew scriptures adapted to a Christian interpretation. Perhaps an analogy could be drawn with attendance at the worship of another Christian denomination whose practices and thought-world are quite different from one's own, for example a conservative Evangelical at a Catholic mass. There may well be aspects of the service to which exception is taken (such as invocation of the saints or prayers for the dead) but that hardly deflects from the overall sense of a common identity and bond. With other religions there may not necessarily be a huge difference as in the case of Judaism or Islam. But even where major issues exist, such as the conspicuous presence of idols in a Hindu temple, it is possible to make some sense of this from a Christian perspective. The Hindu practice of bowing the head before the statues of the gods could be used to demonstrate not only respect for the other's faith but also reverence for a mediated transcendence that even within Christianity does not always meet with the believer's full approval.[25]

Second, there is the element of theological discussion and awareness. Some theologians today now argue that comparative theology should always be part, and perhaps even the major part, of the normal syllabus of Christian

---

[25] Bibles, statues, flowers and works of art can all produce mixed reaction among some. One notes too how bowing the head at the name of Jesus was once common in a way that it is no longer so.

theology. Such a requirement surely demands too much, especially when knowledge of one's own traditions is likely to be at a relatively low starting point among those beginning the study of theology. It would inevitably encourage superficiality. Much more pertinent is the need to know the history of one's own tradition better and the way in which, as we saw in earlier chapters, its form and content has been partly shaped by other religions and its continuing need, therefore, now to be open if it is to learn in the present.

Third, one very underdeveloped form of dialogue is better imaginative appreciation of how another religion's visual symbols in art and architecture are intended to function. One reason for such underdevelopment is a lack of interest within Christianity itself of its own history of art and architecture. While this is changing, there still remains a long way to go. Sometimes the symbols are very much the same across the religions, as, for example, in the use of light, water or pilgrimage. More often they differ substantially. Even so, a common pattern of intentions is evident in evoking transcendence, immanence, mystery or presence and in encouraging the worshipper's sense of engagement with an external reality.[26] Simply through becoming more aware of those underlying parallels, adherents of different faiths could draw closer to one another in shared aspirations. Indeed, it is precisely by asking such deeper questions that the most apparently

[26] For some explorations on this theme in architecture, see my *Divine Generosity and Human Creativity: Theology, through Symbol, Painting and Architecture*, eds. Christopher R. Brewer & Robert MacSwain, (London: Routledge, 2017), 151–203.

suspect or even repulsive aspects of other faiths might acquire a new sensibility, as in the case of Shiva's lingam or the skulls of Kali.[27]

I end this book as I began, by insisting that comparative theology should not be seen primarily as a task of human construction at all but rather as a response to the outreach of the divine to humanity, or in other words a listening to revelation. Whereas in the past revelation was conceived of as a single, uncomplicated stream, now we can appreciate how it flows in many channels, its various addresses adapted to the way in which human beings are necessarily conditioned by the particular tradition in which they find themselves. This inevitably makes comparisons more difficult, with the various shards or imperfect realities not always neatly or easily fitting together. Nonetheless, to change the metaphor, there is a common music to them, in the kenotic adaptation of the divine to the human condition in its gradual elicitation of a truth to which all those of faith can aspire.

---

[27] See further Chapter 3, 106–11.

SUGGESTIONS FOR FURTHER READING

Buddhism (General and Indian)

Aitken, Molly Emma. *Meeting the Buddha: On Pilgrimage in Buddhist India* (New York: Riverhead Books, 1995)
  Buddhist Scriptures ed. Donald S Lopez (London: Penguin, 2004) *Thematic selection*
Gombrich, Richard. *Theravada Buddhism* (London: Routledge & Kegan Paul, 1988)
  What the Buddha Thought (London: Equinox, 2009)
Harvey, Peter. *Introduction to Buddhism* (Cambridge: Cambridge University Press, 1990)
Lowenstein, Tom. *Treasures of the Buddha: The Glories of Sacred Asia* (New York: Sterling, 2007)
Shulman, Eviatar. *Rethinking the Buddha: Earliest Buddhist Philosophy and Meditative Perception* (Cambridge: Cambridge University Press, 2014)
Wynne, Alexander. *Introduction to Buddhism* (London: I. B. Tauris, 2015)

Buddhism (Chinese and Japanese)

The Diamond Sutra, The Heart Sutra trans. Edward Conze (New Delhi: Dev Publishers, 2017)
Lotus Sutra (Somerville, MA: Wisdom Publications, 2008)
Conner, Mark C & Nash, William R eds. *Charles Johnson: The Novelist as Philosopher* (Jackson: University of Mississippi Press, 2007) *Discussion of Afro-American novelist much influenced by Zen.*
Jones, Charles B. *Pure Land: History, Tradition and Practice* (Boulder: Shambhala, 2021)

Juniper, Andrew. *Wabi Sabi: The Japanese Art of Impermanence* (Tokyo: Tuttle, 2003)
Kerr, Alex. *Finding the Heart Sutra* (London: Penguin, 2020)
Lee, Min Jin. *Pachinko* (London: Fourth Estate, 2017) *Brilliant novel about Koreans living in Japan.*
Macfarlane, Alan. *Japan through the Looking Glass* (London: Profile, 2007)
Nazianzen, Gregory. Fifth Theological Oration in A. J. Mason trans, *Five Theological Orations of Gregory of Nazianzus* (Hanse Books reprint of Cambridge Patristic Texts, 1899)
Nhat Hanh, Thich. *The Other Shore* (Berkeley: Palm Leaves Press, 2017) *Vietnamese monk's controversial translation and commentary on Heart Sutra.*
Nitschke, Günter. *Japanese Gardens* (Cologne: Taschen , 1999)
Nonomura, Kaoru. *Eat, Sleep, Sit: My Year at Japan's Most Rigorous Zen Temple* (New York: Kodansha, 2008)
Robyn, Satya. *Coming Home: Refuge in Pureland Buddhism* (Malvern: Woodsmoke Press, 2019)
Suzuki, D. T. *Zen and Japanese Culture* (Princeton: Princeton University Press, 1959)
Tanizaki, Junichiro. *In Praise of Shadows* (London: Penguin, 2017) *Aesthetics in Japan.*
Teiser, Stephen F & Stone, Jacqueline I eds. *Readings of the Lotus Sutra* (New York: Columbia University Press, 2009)
Unno, Taitetsu. *River of Fire, River of Water: An Introduction to the Pure Land Tradition of Shin Buddhism* (New York: Doubleday, 1998)
Van Schaik, Sam. *The Spirit of Zen* (New Haven: Yale University Press, 2018) *Includes discussion of Chinese contribution from Dunhuang caves.*
Williams, Paul. *Mahayana Buddhism: The Doctrinal Foundations* (London: Routledge 2nd ed., 2009)
Yamada, K ed. *The Gateless Gate: The Classic Book of Zen Koans* (Boston: Wisdom Publications, 2004)
Yen, Sheng. *Orthodox Chinese Buddhism* (Berkeley, CA: North Atlantic Books, 2007)

Yü, Chün-fang. *Chinese Buddhism: A Thematic History* (Honolulu: University of Hawaii Press, 2020)
Kuan-yin: The Chinese Transformation of Avalokitesvara (New York: Columbia University Press, 2000)

Christianity (Specific Issues)

Amaladass, Anand & Löwner, Gudrun. *Christian Themes in Indian Art* (New Delhi: Manohar, 2012)

Bauckham, Richard. *Bible and Ecology* (London: DLT, 2010)

Brown, David. *Divine Humanity: Kenosis and the Construction of a Christian Theology* (Waco, TX: Baylor University Press, 2011)
God in a Single Vision: Integrating Philosophy and Theology ed. Christopher R Brewer & Robert MacSwain (London: Rouledge, 2016) *Part II on revelation.*
Gospel as Work of Art: Imaginative Truth and the Open Text (Grand Rapids: Eerdmans, 2024), ch. 12.

Calderón, Pedro. *Life is a Dream* (London: Penguin, 2006)

Cameron, Alan. *The Last Pagans of Rome* (Oxford: Oxford University Press, 2010)

Carrithers, Mary. *The Book of Memory: A Study of Memory in Medieval Culture* (Cambridge: Cambridge University Press, 1990)

Clough, David. *On Animals* 2 vols. (London: T & T Clark, 2012 & 2018)

Davies, Oliver. *Meister Eckhart* ed. Edmund Colledge & Colin McGinn (London: SPCK, 1981 *Classics of western spirituality.*
Meister Eckhart: Mystical Theologian (London: SPCK, 1991)

Edwards, Mark. *Origen against Plato* (Aldershot: Ashgate, 2002) *Rejects traditional view of strong Platonic influence on Origen.*

Ferguson, Everett. *Baptism in the Early Church: History, Theology and Liturgy in the First Five Centuries* (Grand Rapids: Eerdmans, 2009)

Harmless, William. *Mystics* (New York: Oxford University Press, 2008)

Hart, David Bentley. *The Beauty of the Infinite* (Grand Rapids: Eerdmans, 2004)
Hebblewhite, Mark. *Theodosius and the Limits of Empire* (London: Routledge, 2020)
Loades, Ann. *Feminist Theology: Voices from the Past* (Oxford: Wiley Blackwell, 2001) *Argues that feminist insights are best developed through creative interaction with female writers of the past.*
McGinn, Bernard. *History of Christian Mysticism* (in 9 Volumes) (New York: Crossroad, 1991 to 2019)
Metzei, B M, Murphy F A & Oakes, K eds. *The Oxford Handbook of Divine Revelation* (Oxford: Oxford University Press, 2021)
Meyendorf, John. *A Study of Gregory Palamas* (New York: St Vladimir's Press, 1998)
Midgley, Mary. *Beast and Man* (London: Routledge rev. ed., 1995)
Morgan, David. *A History and Theory of Popular Images* (Berkeley: University of California Press, 1998)
Potter, Dylan David. *Angelology* (Eugene: Wipf & Stock, 2016)
Russell, Norman. *Gregory Palamas and the Making of Palamas in the Modern Age* (Oxford: Oxford University Press, 2019)
Scruton, Roger. *The Face of God* (London: Bloomsbury, 2012)
The Soul of the World (London: Bloomsbury, 2014)
Swinburne, Richard. *The Evolution of the Soul* (Oxford: Oxford University Press, 1997)
Wolterstorff, Nicholas. *Divine Discourse: Philosophical Reflections on the Claim that God Speaks* (Cambridge: Cambridge University Press, 1995)
Yarnold, Edward. *The Awe-Inspiring Rites of Initiation* (Edinburgh: T & T Clark, 1994) *Christian sacraments as mysteries.*

Comparative Studies

Collingwood, Christopher. *Zen Wisdom for Christians* (London: Jessica Kingsley, 2019)
Corduan, Winifried. *Neighboring Faiths: A Christian Introduction to World Religions* (Downers Grove: IVP Academic, 2nd ed. 2012) *Well-presented example of conservative approach.*

Dalai Lama. *The Good Heart: A Buddhist Perspective on the Teaching of Jesus* (Boston: Wisdom Publication, 1996). *Major differences recognized.*

Dempsy, Corinne G. *Bringing the Sacred Down to Earth: Adventures in Comparative Religion* (New York: Oxford University Press, 2012)

Dunbar, Robin. *How Religion Evolved and Why It Endures* (London: Pelican, 2022)

Dyrness, William. *A Sense of Devotion: Interfaith Aesthetics in Buddhist and Muslim Communities* (Eugene: Cascade, 2013)

Elinor, Robert. *Buddha and Christ: Images of Wholeness* (Cambridge: Lutterworth Press, 2000)

Fisher, Mary Pat. *Living Religions* (London: Lawrence King, 8th ed., 2011) *Lively, sympathetic introduction.*

Flood, Gavin. *The Ascetic Self: Subjectivity, Memory and Tradition* (Cambridge: Cambridge University Press, 2004) *Buddhist, Hindu and Christian approaches compared.*

Gottschalk, Peter. *Beyond Hindu and Muslim: Multiple Identity in Narratives from Village India* (Oxford: Oxford University Press, 2000)

Habito, Ruben L. F. *Be Still and Know* (Maryknoll: Orbis Books, 2017) *Christianity and Zen.*

Heo, Angie. *The Political Lives of Saints: Christian–Muslim Mediation in Egypt* (Berkeley: University of California Press, 2018)

Hick, John. *An Interpretation of Religion: Human Responses to the Transcendent* (Basingstoke: Macmillan, 1989) *Classic pluralist account.*

Howard, T. A. *The Faith of Others: A History of Interreligious Dialogue* (New Haven: Yale University Press, 2021) *Focuses on modern period.*

Knitter, Paul F. *Without Buddha I Could Not Be a Christian* (London: Oneworld, 2009)

Knitter, Paul F. & Haight, Roger. *Jesus and Buddha: Friends in Conversation* (Maryknoll: Orbis, 2015) *Haight defends a more distinctively Christian position.*

MacGregor, Neil. *Living with the Gods* (London: Allen Lane, 2018) *Artistic comparisons.*

Maeland, Bärd. *Rewarding Encounters: Islam and the Comparative Theologies of Kenneth Cragg and Wilfred Cantwell Smith* (London: Melisende, 2003) *Two quite different approaches compared and evaluated.*

Nhat Hahn, Thich. *Living Buddha, Living Christ* (New York: Rider, 1996) *Differences minimised.*

Palmer Martin. *The Jesus Scrolls: Rediscovering the Lost Scrolls of Taoist Christianity* (New York: Random House, 2001)

Phan, Peter C. *Being Religious Interreligiously: Asian Perspectives on Interfaith Dialogue* (Marynoll: Orbis, 2004)

The Joy of Religious Pluralism: A Personal Journey (Maryknoll: Orbis, 2017)

Despite the book's title pulls back from earlier position to endorse some distinctively Christian doctrines.

Race, Alan. *My Journey as a Religious Pluralist: A Christian Theology of Religion Reclaimed* (Eugene, OR: Wipf & Stock, 2021)

Schmidt-Leukel, Perry. *Religious Pluralism and Interreligious Dialogue* (Maryknoll: Orbis Books, 2017). *Uses image of fractals to support pluralism.*

Thomas, David. *Christian–Muslim Relations* (Leiden: Brill, 2009–13) *Impressive survey across history, with already forty-seven volumes published.*

Ward, Keith. Five volumes beginning with *Religion and Revelation* (1994) and concluding with *Religion and Human Fulfilment* (Oxford: Oxford University Press, 2008)

Yong, Amos. *Beyond the Impasse: Towards a Pneumatological Theology of Religions* (Carlisle: Paternoster Press, 2003). *Pentecostal approach.*

Confucianism

Angle, Stephen C. *Sagehood: The Contemporary Significance of Neo-Confucianism* (New York: Oxford University Press, 2009)

Bell, Daniel A. *China's New Confucianism: Politics and Everyday Life in a Changing Society* (Princeton: Princeton University Press, 2008)

Bol, Peter K. *Neo-Confucianism in History* (Cambridge, MA: Harvard University Press, 2008)

Confucius, *The Analects*, ed. Michael Nylan (New York: Norton, 2014)

Sun, Anna. *Confucianism as a World Religion: Contested* (Princeton: Princeton University Press, 2013)

Taylor, Rodney L. *The Religious Dimensions of Confucianism* (Albany, NY: State University of New York Press, 1990)

Yao, Xingzhong. *An Introduction to Confucianism* (Cambridge: Cambridge University Press, 2000)

Daoism

Chuang Tzu, Book of (London: Penguin, 1996)

Chang, Chung-yuan. *Creativity and Daoism: A Study of Chinese Philosophy, Art and Poetry* (London: Jessica Kingsley, 2011)

Graham, A. C. *Disputers of the Tao: Philosophical Arguments in Ancient China* (L Salle: Open Court, 1989)

Kohn, Livia. *Daoism and Chinese Culture* (Magdalene, NM: Three Pines Press, 2010)

Lao Tzu. *Tao Te Ching* (Indianapolis: Hackett, 1993)

Wong, Eva. *Taoism: an Essential Guide* (Boulder: Shambhala, 1997)

Hinduism

Bhagavad Gita trans. Juan Mascaro (London: Penguin, 2003)

Bharne, Vinayak & Krusche, Krupali. *Rediscovering the Hindu Temple* (Newcastle: Cambridge Scholars, 2012)

Clooney, Francis X. *Divine Mother, Blessed Mother: Hindu Goddesses and the Virgin Mary* (New York: Oxford University Press, 2005)

Dalrymple, William. *Nine Lives: In Search of the Sacred in Modern India* (London: Bloomsbury, 2009)

Doniger, Wendy. *The Hindus: An Alternative History* (New York: Oxford University Press, 2009) *Lively challenge to accepted views.*

Eck, Diana. *Darśan: Seeing the Divine Image in India* (New York: Columbia University Press, 3rd ed., 1988)

India: A Sacred Geography (New York: Three Rivers Press, 2012)

Flood, Gavin ed. *Blackwell Companion to Hinduism* (Oxford: Blackwell, 2005)

Flueckiger, J. B. *Everyday Hinduism* (Oxford: Wiley Blackwell, 2015)

Frazier, Jessica. *Bloomsbury Companion to Hindu Studies* (London: Bloomsbury, 2011)

Gandhi, M. K. *My Religion* (Ahmedabad: Navajivan, 1955)

Ghose, Madhuvant. *Gates of the Lord: The Tradition of Krishna Paintings* (Chicago: Art Institute of Chicago, 2015)

Harding, Elizabeth U. *Kali: The Black Goddess of Dakshinesvar* (Berwick, ME: Nicolas-Hays, 1993)

Jantzen, Grace. *Becoming Divine* (Manchester: Manchester University Press, 1998)

Jha, Dwigendra Narayan. *The Myth of the Holy Cow* (Delhi: Oxford University Press, 2004) *Sacred cow absent from earlier Hindu belief.*

Johnson, Elizabeth. *She Who Is* (New York: Crossroad, 1992)

Kripal, Jeffrey J. *Kali's Child: The Mystical and the Erotic in the Life and Teachings of Ramakrishna* (Chicago: University of Chicago Press, 1995)

Lipner, Julius. *Hindus: Their Religious Beliefs and Practices* (London: Routledge 2nd ed, 2010) *Definitive account.*

Loades, Anne. *Feminist Theology: A Reader* (London: SPCK, 1990)

Nanda, Meera. *The God Market: How Globalization Is Making India More Hindu* (New York: Random House, 2009)

Panikkar, Raimondo. *The Vedic Experience: An Anthology of the Vedas for Modern Man* (Berkeley: University of California

Press, 1977) *Large selection but interpretation at times controversial.*
Ramanujan, A. K. *Speaking Shiva* (Harmondsworth: Penguin, 1973) *Lyrics praising this god.*
Ramos, Imma. *Tantra: Enlightenment to Revolution* (London: Thames & Hudson, 2020)
Ram-Prasad, Chakravarthi. *Divine Self, Human Self: The Philosophy of Being in Two Gita Commentaries* (London: Bloomsbury, 2013)
Ramakrishna. *Gospel of Sri* annotated by Mahendranath Gupta (Hollywood: Vedanta Press, 1942)
Rig Veda (London: Penguin, 1981, trans. Wendy Doniger)
Tagore, Rabindranath. *Song Offerings* (London: Anvil Pres, 2000)
Tharoor, Shashi. *Why I am a Hindu* (London: Hurt & Co., 2018)
Wilkerson, Isabel. *Caste: The Origins of our Discontents* (New York: Random House, 2022) *Parallels detected in other societies.*

Islam

Attar, Farid Ud-Din. *The Conference of Birds* (London: Continuum, 2000)
Atwan, Abdel Bari. *Islamic State: The Digital Caliphate* (London: Saqi, 2015)
Bloom, Jonathan & Blair, Sheila eds *God is the Light of the Heavens and the Earth: Light in Islamic Art and Culture* (New Haven: Yale University Press, 2015)
Can, Sefik. *Fundamentals of Rumi's Thought* (Clifton, NJ: Tughra, 2015)
Cagaptay, Soner. *The New Sultan: Erdogan and the Crisis of Modern Turkey* (London: I. B. Tauris, 2017)
De Bellaigue, Christopher. *The Islamic Enlightenment: The Modern Struggle Between Faith and Reason* (London: Bodley

Head, 2017) *Discusses some major figures in nineteenth and twentieth centuries.*

Eigner, Saeb. *Art of the Middle East: Modern and Contemporary Art of the Arab World and Iran* (London: Merrell, 2015)

Elias, J. J. *Aisha's Cushion: Religious Art, Perception and Practice in Islam* (Cambridge, Mass.: Harvard University Press, 2012)

Elsie, Robert. *The Albanian Bektashi: History and Culture of a Dervish Order in the Balkans* (London: I. B. Tauris, 2019)

Ghaffer, S. H. A. *Criticism of Hadith among Muslims* (London: Ta-Ha Publishers, 1986)

Ghazi, Prince. *Love in the Holy Qur'an* (Cambridge: Kazi Publications, 7th ed., 2010)

Gurnah, Abdulrazak. *Afterlives* (London: Bloomsbury, 2020) *British East African novelist and Nobel Prize winner in 2021.*

Hillenbrand, Carole. *Islam: A New Historical Introduction* (London: Thames & Hudson, 2015)

Kermani, Navid. *God Is Beautiful: The Aesthetic Experience of the Qur'an* (Cambridge: Polity Press, 2015)

Kersten, Carool. *Contemporary Thought in the Muslim World* (London: Routledge, 2019)

Khan, Hazrat Inayat. *The Mysticism of Sound and Music* (Boulder: Shambhala, 1996)

Kynsh, Alexander. *Sufism A New History of Islamic Mysticism* (Princeton: Princeton University Press, 2017)

Lewis, Bernard. *The Crisis of Islam: Holy War and Unholy Terror* (London: Weidenfeld & Nicholson, 2003)

Massad, Joseph A. *Islam in Liberalism* (Chicago: University of Chicago Press, 2015) *Successor in Said tradition.*

Massignon, Louis. *The Passion of Al-Hallaj: Mystic and Martyr of Islam* (Princeton: Princeton University Press, 1994)

McHugo, John. *A Concise History of Sunnis and Shi'is* (London: Saqi, 2017)

Mouline, Nabil. *The Clerics of Islam: Religious Authority and Political Power in Saudi Arabia* (New Haven: Yale University Press, 2014)

Netton, I. R. *A Popular Dictionary of Islam* (London: Curzon Press, 1992)

The Holy Qur'an trans. A. Y Ali (Leicester: Islamic Foundation, 1975) *With helpful commentary.*

Reynolds, G. S. ed. *The Qur'an in Its Historical Context* (London: Routledge, 2008)

Roberts, Sean R. *The War on the Uyghurs: China's Campaign against Xinjiang's Muslims* (Manchester: Manchester University Press, 2020)

Rumi's The Big Red Book trans Coleman Barks (New York: Harper Collins, 2011)

Rumi Spiritual Verses trans Alan Williams (London: Penguin, 2006)

Saeed, Abdullah. *Reading the Qur'an in the Twenty First Century: A Contextualist Approach* (London: Routledge, 2014)

Safi, Omid ed. *Progressive Muslims: On Justice, Gender and Pluralism* (Oxford: OneWorld, 2003)

Said, Edward W. *Orientalism* (London: Penguin, 2003 ed.)

Sardar, Ziauddin. *Reading the Qur'an* (London: Hurst & Company, 2015) *Includes attitudes to other religions.*

Schubert, Eva ed. *Discover Islamic Art* (London: Art Books International, 2007)

Shafak, Elir. *Forty Rules of Love* (London: Penguin, 2007) *British–Turk writing in this novel about Rumi and Shams. Sympathetic engagement in all her novels with Islam.*

Sinai, Nicolai. *The Qur'an: An Historical–Critical Introduction* (Edinburgh: Edinburgh University Press, 2017)

Smith, Hannah Lucinda. *Erdoğan Rising: The Battle for the Soul of Turkey* (London: Collins, 2019)

Truschke, Audrey. *Aurangzeb: The Life and Legacy of India's Most Controversial King* (Stanford: Stanford University Press, 2017)

Winter, Tim ed. *Classical Islamic Theology* (Cambridge; Cambridge University Press, 2008)

Jainism

Caillat, C & Kumar R. *Jain Cosmology* (Chicago: Art Media, 2004)

Suggestions for Further Reading

Dundas, Paul. *The Jains* (London: Routledge, 2002)
Granoff, Phyllis. *Forest of Thieves and the Magic Garden: An Anthology of Medieval Jain Stories* (London: Penguin, 1998)
Jain, Parveen. *An Introduction to Jain Philosophy* (New Delhi: Printworld, 2019), 99–113.
Long, Jeffrey D. *Jainism* (London: I. B. Tauris, 2009)
Mardia, Kanti V. & Rankin, Aidan D., *Living Jainism: An Ethical Science* (Winchester: Mantra, 2013), 58–83.
Pal, Pratapaditya ed. *Jain Art from India* (London: Thames & Hudson, 1994)

Judaism (Ancient)

Fine, Steven. *Art and Judaism in the Greco-Roman World* (Cambridge: Cambridge University Press, 2005)
Goodman, Martin. *A History of Judaism* (London: Penguin, 2017)
Leibner, Uzi & Hezser, Catherine eds. *Jewish Art in Its Late Antique Context* (Tübingen: Mohr Siebeck, 2016)
Römer, Thomas. *The Invention of God* (Cambridge, Mass.: Harvard University Press, 2015). *Despite title, more about origins than demolition of the very idea.*
Sanders, E. P. *Judaism: Practice & Belief 63BCE – 66CE* (London: SCM, 1992)
Smith, Mark S. *God in Translation: Deities in Cross Cultural Discourse in the Biblical World* (Grand Rapids: Eerdmans, 2008)
Somner, Benjamin J. *Revelation and Authority: Sinai in Jewish Scripture and Tradition* (New Haven: Yale University Press, 2015) *Orthodox scholar taking complexities of development seriously.*

Paganism (Classical)

Addey, Crystal. *Divination and Theurgy in Neoplatonism: Oracles of the Gods* (London: Routledge, 2014) *Reorientation towards religious experience.*

Suggestions for Further Reading

Apuleius, *The Golden Ass* (Oxford: Oxford University Press, 1994) *Novel with account of author's own religious experience.*

Beard, Mary, North, John & Price, Simon. *Religions of Rome* (Cambridge: Cambridge University Press, 1998)

Bowden, Hugh. *Mystery Cults in the Ancient World* (London: Thames & Hudson, 2010)

Broadie, Sarah. *Nature and Divinity in Plato's Timaeus* (Cambridge: Cambridge University Press, 2012)

Burkert, Walter. *Greek Religion* (Boston: Harvard University Press, 1985) *Strong emphasis on social context.*

Eidinow, Esther & Kindt, Julia eds., *The Oxford Handbook of Ancient Greek Religion* (Oxford: Oxford University Press, 2015)

Eidinow, Eesther, Kindt, Julia & Osborne, Robin, eds. *Theologies of Ancient Greek Religion* (Cambridge: Cambridge University Press, 2016)

Foley, Helene P., ed. *Homeric Hymn to Demeter* (Princeton: Princeton University Press, 1993)

Hadot, Pierre. *Philosophy as a Way of Life* (Oxford: Blackwell, 1995) *Argues for essentially religious character of ancient philosophy.*

Kearns, Emily. *Ancient Greek Religion: A Sourcebook* (Oxford: Wiley–Blackwell, 2010)

Kiley, Mark ed. *Prayer from Alexander to Constantine: A Critical Anthology* (London: Routledge, 1997)

Lamberton, R. *Homer the Theologian: Neoplatonist Allegorical Readings* (Berkeley: University of California Press, 1986)

Leibeshuetz, J. H. W. G. *Continuity and Change in Roman Religion* (Oxford: Clarendon Press, 1979)

Lipsey, Roger. *Have You Been to Delphi: Tales of the Ancient Oracle for Modern Minds* (Albany: State University of New York Press, 2001) *Positive evaluation.*

Parker, Robert. *Polytheism and Society at Athens* (Oxford: Oxford University Press, 2015)

Rappe, Sara. *Reading Neoplatonism: Non-Discursive Thinking in Texts* (Cambridge: Cambridge University Press, 2000)

Rüpke, Jörg. *Religion of the Romans* (Cambridge: Polity, 2007) *Takes issue of religious experience seriously.*
Scott, Michael. *Delphi* (Princeton: Princeton University Press, 2014) *Positive evaluation.*
Shaw, Gregory. *Theurgy and the Soul: The Neoplatonism of Iamblichus* (Kettering: Angelico Press, 1995) *Stress on religious experience rather than magical character.*
Tarrant, Harold. *Plato's First Interpreters* (London: Duckworth, 2000)

Paganism (Middle East)

Assmann, Jan. *From Akhenaten to Moses: Ancient Egypt and Religious Change* (Cairo: American University in Cairo, 2016). *Controversial argument for debt of Judaism to thought of this ancient pharaoh.*
Coogan, Michael D. & Smith, Mark S. eds. *Stories from Ancient Canaan* (Louisville: Westminster John Knox, 2nd ed., 2012)
Dalley, Stephanie ed. *Myths from Mesopotamia* (Oxford: Oxford University Press, 1989)
George, Andrew R ed.*Gilgamesh, Epic of* (London: Penguin, 1999)
Hayes, B. ed. *Hidden Riches: A Sourcebook for the Comparative Study of the Hebrew Bible and the Ancient Near East* (Louisville: Westminster John Knox, 2014)
Hoffmeier, James K. *Akhenaten and the Origin of Monotheism* (Oxford: Oxford University Press, 2015) *Akhenaten considered in his own context.*
Leeming, David. *Jealous Gods, Chosen People: The Mythology of the Middle East* (Oxford: Oxford University Press, 2004). *Over-simple attempt at reductionism.*
Prichard, James B. ed. *The Ancient Near East: An Anthology of Texts and Pictures* (Princeton: Princeton University Press, 2nd ed., 2011)

Saggs, H. W. F. *The Encounter with the Divine in Mesopotamia and Israel* (London: Athlone Press, 1978) *Takes both types of encounter seriously.*

Shaw, Gary J. The Egyptian Myths (London: Thames & Hudson, 2014) *Sympathetic approach.*

Teeter, Emily. *Religion and Ritual in Ancient Egypt* (Cambridge: Cambridge University Press, 2011) *Another sympathetic approach.*

Shinto

Buljan, Katharine & Cusack, Carole M. *Anime, Religion and Spirituality* (Sheffield: Equinox, 2014)

Cali, Joseph & Dougill, John. *A Guide to the Sacred Sites of Japan's Ancient Religion* (Honolulu: University of Hawaii Press, 2013)

Ellwood, Robert. *Japanese Religion* (London: Routledge 2nd ed, 2016)

Hardacre, Helen. *Shinto: A History* (New York: Oxford University Press, 2017)

Nelson, John K. *Enduring Identities: The Guise of Shinto in Contemporary Japan* (Honolulu: University of Hawaii Press, 2000)

Reader, Ian & Tanabe, George J. *Practically Religious: Worldly Benefits and the Common Religion of Japan* (Honolulu: University of Hawaii Press, 1998)

Reader, Ian. *Making Pilgrimages: Meaning and Practice in Shikoku* (Honolulu: University of Hawaii Pres, 2005)

Rots, Aike P. *Shinto, Nature and Ideology in Contemporary Japan* (London: Bloomsbury, 2017)

Yamakage, Motohisa. *The Essence of Shinto* (New York: Kodansha, 2000)

Sikhism

Kaur-Sigh, Nikky-Guninder. *Sikhism: an Introduction* (London: I B Tauris, 2011)

McLeod, W. H. *Guru Nanak and the Sikh Religion* (New Delhi: Oxford University Press, 1968)

Shackle, Christopher & Singh-Mandair, Arvind-pal eds. *Teachings of the Sikh Gurus: Selections from the Sikh Scriptures* (London: Routledge, 2005)

Singh, Gurbachan. *The Sikhs: Faith, Philosophy & Folk* (New Delhi: Lustre Press, 1998)

Singh, Khushwant. *A History of the Sikhs* 2 vols. (New Delhi: Oxford University Press, 2004)

Singh, Pashaura & Fenech, Louis E eds. *Oxford Handbook of Sikh Studies* (Oxford: Oxford University Press, 2014)

INDEX

Aboriginal 232
abrogation, *see naskh*
Addey, C 74–75
aesthetics, Japanese 214–16
Afghanistan 353
ahimsa (non-injury) 121–22
Aisha 352–53
Akbar 116, 268
Akhenaten 33
Akihito 226
Alawites 266
Albania 288
Al-Ghazali 352
Ali 265, 266
Amarna 33
Amaterasu 216–17, 222
Ambedkar, B R 88
Ambrose 68–69, 148
American, Native 232
Amitabha (Amida) 236, 238, 254–56
Amritsar 160
Amun 53
analogy 280–82
Anatta (no-self) 150, 206, 240
anekantavada (many-sidedness) 126–27
angels 178–79
Angle, S C 190, 194–95
Anicca (impermanence) 150, 206
Apuleius 64–65
architecture, Christian 97–99
  Hindu 94–96
  Muslim 264, 270–71
Arnheim, R 93–94
art, 349–52
  Christian, 97–101

Hindu, 90–101
  Islamic 351–54
Asharite 280, 297
Asherim 32
Assmann, J 33
Astarte 31–32
Augustine 68–69, 71–72
Avaita-Vedanta 86, 110
Avalokiteśvara 203, 243
avatar 9–10, 84, 333
Averroes 270
Ayodhya 87
Aztec 45

Babel, Tower of 38
Babylon 34–35
Bhakti 117
baptism 65–66
Barlaam & Josaphat 336–37
Barret, J L 13–14
Barth, K 257–58
Bektashi 288–89
Bell, D A 193–94
Berkeley, G 336
Bhagavad-Gita 84
Boddhisattva 202–3, 236, 340
Bowden, H 61
Bragg, M 345
Brahma 85, 103, 105, 333
Brahman 9, 83–86, 108, 111, 135, 143, 331–33, 361
Buddha nature 238, 245, 251, 256, 341
Buddhism, Mahayana 115, 200–11, 214, 234–59
Buddhism, Theravada 115, 137–53

Index

Calderón, P 337–38
Cambridge Ritualists 58–59
Cantwell Smith, W 358, 364
Capra, F 244
Caste 87–88, 347
change, religious 207–11, 339–45
Chefchaouen 213
China 168–211
Christianity 171–72, 210–11, 219, 226–27, 232, 342–45
Chuang Tzu 175, 187
Claude, C 247
Cleanthes 63–64
Clooney, F X 103–5
Clough, D 130
cognitive, science 13–14
Collingwood, C 244–45
compassion (Buddhism) 202, 253
conditioning 318–21, 325
Confucianism 168, 170, 187–200
Confucius 188–89
contextualism 293–98
Cragg, K 364–65
craving 141, 143–53
creation 37–38
crucifixion 297–98
Crusades 260
Cybele 62
Cyrus 36

Dalai Lama 23, 206
Daoism 168, 170, 174–87
Darśan 90–101
Davies, O 328
death 186–87
Delphi 74
Demeter 60–61, 63
democracy 193, 195–200
Desmond, W 317
Devi 88
Dhikr (recitation) 289

divine, gender, 101–14
  immanence, 228–34
  justice 128–37
  personal/impersonal 161–67, 325–34
  transcendence, 287, 315–18
Dodds, E R 72–73
Dogen 238, 251
Doniger, W 81, 83, 350
Donne, J 186
Dunbar, R 16
Dunhuang 249
Durkheim, E 12–13
Dyrness, W N 352

Eck, D L 91–92, 94, 96
Eckhart 328–29
ecology 129, 228–34
Egypt 50–52
elephant, parable of 126
Elias, J J 352, 353
Elkins, J 94
Enlightenment 314
Enuma Elish 37–38
Epictetus 148–49
Erdoğan, R 277–79
Eusebius 68
experience, religious 46–47, 54, 326–27; *see also* revelation

feminist theology 101–2, 204–5
Feng Shui 180
Flood, G 144–46
Fluechiger, L 85–86
free will 314, 318–24
Fukushima 216, 226
fundamentalism 11–12, 261–62, 280–92

Gandhi, M K 88, 121–22
Ganesh 86
garba griha 95
Gobind Singh 157–58, 159

Index

God, *see* divine
grace 244, 249–50, 252–59
Greek religion 58–59
Gregory Palamas 329–30
Guanyin 203
Gülen, F 270
Gurnah, A 274
Guru Granth Sahib 158–59, 161

Habito, R 243–44
Hadith 284
Hadot, P 70–72
Hafez 290
Harappan 81–82
Harnack, von A 69, 201
Heart sutra 82–83, 239, 248–49, 341–42
Heaven *see* Ti'an
Henotheism 33
Herem 319
Hesse, H 240
Hick, J 11, 21, 358
hierarchy 342–43
hijab 294
Hinduism 78–114, 224–37
Hindutva 81
Honen 237
horns 40–41
House of One 27

icons 91, 113
immanence, *see* divine
immortality 321–23
Inaru 222
Incarnation 9–10, 297, 309, 311, 331, 333, 334, 342–45
Inclusivism 17, 311–12, 355–57
India 115–67, 268, 287
indifference 251
Infinite Life sutra 253
interdependence 340–45
Iqbal, M 293, 195
Isaac, sacrifice of Isaac 8–9, 306

Isaiah, Second 36
Ise 223
Ishmael 306
Isis 50–51
Islam 116, 171, 260–309
Islamic State 276–77

Jacob's Ladder 39
Jade Emperor 177
Jahangir 268
Jainism 117–37
Japan 212–59
Jesus prayer 348
Jizya (tax) 267
Jodo-Shinshu 237–38
Johnson, C 242–43
Journey to the West 207
Judaism, ancient 31=46. 52–57
justice, *see* divine

Kabir 156, 157
Kali 109–13, 368
Kamakura 236
Kami 221, 231
Kao, P'an-lung 197
Karma (consequences) 121–22
Kenosis 342–45
Kerouac, J 241–42, 243
Khayyam, O 291
Knitter, P 363–64
Koans 238
Korea 217–18
Kraemer, H 17
Krishna 9
Kurasawa, A 127, 216
Kyoto (Heian) 235–36

LaGugna, C 330
Lao Tzu 174–75, 177
Lessing, G 126, 211
Lewis, B 262, 275
Linga 91–93, 368
Lion Man 16

387

Linzy, A 130
Loades, A vii, 145
Locke, J 336
Lossky, V 330
Lotus sutra 203–4, 209, 237

Maalouf, A 291
McDowell, J 315–17
McGregor, N 16
McLeod, W H 154–55
Madhva 83
Mahavira 119
Mahayana, *see* Buddhism
Maitreya 204–5
Malebranche, N 335–36
marabout 287
Marcus Aurelius 71, 148–49
Mar Thoma 117
Massad J A 273–74
Massignon, L 286
Maya (illusion) 81
Meiji restoration 225
Mencius 188, 191, 196
Michelangelo 40
mindfulness 202
Mithras 62
Moksha (liberation) 121, 334
Monet, C 94
Morgan, D 351
Morocco 263–64
Moses 39–42
Müller, M 192
Murasaki, S 217
Music, Islamic 270, 289–90
Mutazilite 280, 297
Myanmar 356
mystery religions 57, 60–66
mystical experience 63–65, 326–27

Nabonidus 54–55
Nagel, T 315–16
Nanak 184–86
Nanda, M 78–79

Nara 235
Narajuna 206
Naskh (abrogation) 6, 282–83
Nataraja 91
nature 179–87, 228–34
Neanderthals 14
near neighbour 2–6
Nembutsu 254–56
Neo-Confucianism 189–90, 224
Neo-Platonism 67–74, 286
Newman, J H 19–20, 345
Nhat Hahn, T 22–23, 202, 341–42
Nineveh 35
Nichiren 234, 237
Nirvana 321–24, 334
no-self, *see anatta*

openness 346–55
Orientalism 271–74
original sin 184–85
Orphic 61

paganism, ancient 30–77
Pagels, E 23
Pakistan 354
Palmer, M 175
Panikkar, R 82
Parker, R 59
Parvati 106
Phan, P 363–64
philosophy, classical 67–77
Pilgrimage 170, 224
Pliny, the Younger 65–66
Plotinus 163–64
pluralism 310–11, 355–68
polytheism 47–50, 77
Pure Land 234–36, 252–59

Qur'an, interpretation, 280–85
   and earlier revelation, 298–304, 347–48
   contextualism, 293–98
   theology of, 304–9

Index

Race, A 22
Rahner, K 18
Ramakrishna 110–11
Raman, F 295
Ramanuja 83, 332–33
Ram-Prasad, C 332, 333
Ras Shamra 35–36
reality of world 334–38
reincarnation 128–37, 321–24
religion, origin of 11–17
resurrection 133–37, 321–24
revelation xi–xii, 6, 10, 19–20, 24, 28, 55, 69, 124, 134, 312–24, 338–45
   in Hinduism, 82, 102, 112
   in Islam, 282–83, 298–304
   in Shinto 223–24, 227–28
   in Sikhism 196, 208, 210.
ritual 187, 193–200
Roman religion 60–61
Römer, T 55
Rumi 291–92
Rüpke, J 64
Russell, N 331

sacramentality 67, 75–76
sacrifice 14–15, 43–45
Saeed A 296
Saggs, HWF 54, 56
Said, E 271–74
Saint-Laurent, Y 263
saints 3, 113, 132, 135–36, 178, 286–87
Salafist 276
Sallman, W 351
Samarkand 353
Sarasvati 103
Satanic verses 282–83
Sati 96, 103
Saudi Arabia 276
Schmidt-Leukel, P 21
schools, Islamic 281
scriptural reasoning 18
Scruton, R 315–17

Shafak, E 292
Shakespeare, W 338
Shakyamuni 139, 203; see Buddha
Skanda (aggregate) 239, 248
Shankara 83, 332–33
Shards, complementary 17–25, 311
Shaw, GJ 50
Shaw, G 73
Shi'a/Sunni 265–67
Shinran 237, 255, 258
Shinto 214, 220–34
Shiva 85, 96
Sikhism 153–67
Sinai, N 288, 301, 103
skilful means 209
Smith, H L 278–79
stained glass 99–101
Stock, K 108
Stoicism 67. 71, 148–53
suffering 141, 143–53
Sufism 117, 268–69, 285
Sunyata (emptiness) 206, 248, 340
Suzuki, DT 240
symbolism 367–68

Tagore, R 89
Tai Chi 180
Taliban 275
Tanizaki, J 215
Tantra 209
Taoism *see* Daoism
Taylor, R L 196–97
Teeter, E 51, 51
Tharoor, S 8, 79
Theosophy 118–19
theurgy 73–74
Thomas, D 3
Ti'an (Heaven) 176, 190
Tibet 172, 206
Tirthankara 119–20
Tokyo (Edo) 235
transcendence, *see* divine

Index

transience 239–40, 246–47, 250
Trimurti 85, 103, 105, 333
Trinity 165–66, 302–3, 319–20, 327–28, 333
Turkey 277–79

Uighur 172
Ur 34
Uruk 34
Uzbekistan 262–63

Vairocana 204, 235
Vedas 78–84
vegetarianism 129–30
Vivekananda 110
Vishnu 103

Wahhabi 276
Wansbrough J E 300
Ward, K 20–21, 358–59, 361–62
Watts, A 241
Williams P 204, 206, 208
Wolterstorff, N 313–14
Woolley, E 34
Wu Cheng'en 201

Xi, Jinping 173
Xoana 59

Yasukuni 225
yin/yang 180–81
Yogacara 206–7, 238
Yong, A 18

Zaehner, RC 82
Zechariah 308–9
Zen 238, 239–52
Ziggurat 38–39
Zoroastrianism 36, 77, 116, 288